Language Learning and Teaching as Social Inter-Action

Other recent books by these editors

Zhu Hua

PHONOLOGICAL DEVELOPMENT AND DISORDERS IN CHILDREN: A Multilingual Perspective (*with Barbara Dodd*)

PHONOLOGICAL DEVELOPMENT IN SPECIFIC CONTEXTS: Studies of Chinese-Speaking Children

Paul Seedhouse

THE INTERACTIONAL ARCHITECTURE OF THE LANGUAGE CLASSROOM: A Conversational Analysis Perspective

APPLYING CONVERSATION ANALYSIS (*co-editor with Keith Richards*)

Li Wei

BILINGUALISM: Beyond Basic Principles (*co-editor with Jean-Marc Dewaele and Alex Housen*)

THE BILINGUALISM READER (*editor*)

HANDBOOK OF MULTILINGUALISM AND MULTILINGUAL COMMUNICATION (*co-editor with Peter Auer*)

Vivian Cook

THE ENGLISH WRITING SYSTEM

ACCOMODATING BROCOLLI IN THE CEMETARY: Or Why Can't Anyone Spell?

SECOND LANGUAGE WRITING SYSTEMS (*co-editor with Benedetta Bassetti*)

Language Learning and Teaching as Social Inter-Action

Edited by

Zhu Hua
Birkbeck, University of London, UK

Paul Seedhouse
Newcastle University, UK

Li Wei
Birkbeck, University of London, UK

Vivian Cook
Newcastle University, UK

Selection and editorial matter © Zhu Hua, Paul Seedhouse, Li Wei, Vivian Cook, 2007
Chapters © their authors 2007

All rights reserved. No reproduction, copy or transmission of this publication may be made without written permission.

No paragraph of this publication may be reproduced, copied or transmitted save with written permission or in accordance with the provisions of the Copyright, Designs and Patents Act 1988, or under the terms of any licence permitting limited copying issued by the Copyright Licensing Agency, 90 Tottenham Court Road, London W1T 4LP.

Any person who does any unauthorised act in relation to this publication may be liable to criminal prosecution and civil claims for damages.

The authors have asserted their rights to be identified as the authors of this work in accordance with the Copyright, Designs and Patents Act 1988.

First published 2007 by
PALGRAVE MACMILLAN
Houndmills, Basingstoke, Hampshire RG21 6XS and
175 Fifth Avenue, New York, N.Y. 10010
Companies and representatives throughout the world

PALGRAVE MACMILLAN is the global academic imprint of the Palgrave Macmillan division of St. Martin's Press, LLC and of Palgrave Macmillan Ltd. Macmillan® is a registered trademark in the United States, United Kingdom and other countries. Palgrave is a registered trademark in the European Union and other countries.

ISBN-13: 978–0–230–51700–4 hardback
ISBN-10: 0–230–51700–5 hardback

This book is printed on paper suitable for recycling and made from fully managed and sustained forest sources. Logging, pulping and manufacturing processes are expected to conform to the environmental regulations of the country of origin.

A catalogue record for this book is available from the British Library.

A catalog record for this book is available from the Library of Congress.

10 9 8 7 6 5 4 3 2 1
16 15 14 13 12 11 10 09 08 07

Printed and bound in Great Britain by
Antony Rowe Ltd, Chippenham and Eastbourne

Contents

List of Illustrations   vii

List of Tables   viii

Notes on the Contributors   ix

Transcription Conventions   xiii

1   An Introduction   1
    Zhu Hua, Paul Seedhouse, Li Wei and Vivian Cook

Part 1   Interactional Foundations

2   Interaction and Constructs   9
    Paul Seedhouse

3   Handling Sequentially Inapposite Responses   22
    Gabriele Kasper and Younhee Kim

4   Invitation Talk   42
    Numa Markee

5   'Broken' Starts: Bricolage in Turn Starts in Second Language Talk   58
    Rod Gardner

6   Doing Language, Doing Science and the Sequential Organization of the Immersion Classroom   72
    Simona Pekarek Doehler and Gudrun Ziegler

Part 2   Identity and Social Action

7   Socializing Second Language Acquisition   89
    David Block

8   Identity Repertoires in the Narratives of Advanced American Learners of Russian   103
    Viktoria Driagina and Aneta Pavlenko

9   Presentation of 'Self' in Application Letters   126
    Zhu Hua

10	Identity Construction in Teacher Education *Jennifer Miller*	148
11	Context and L2 Users' Pragmatic Development *Jean-Marc Dewaele*	163

Part 3 Multilingual and Multicultural Classrooms

12	Bilingualism in Mainstream Primary Classrooms *Jean Conteh*	185
13	Social Interaction in Multilingual Classrooms *Nikhat Shameem*	199
14	Untutored Acquisition in Content Classrooms *Juliet Langman and Robert Bayley*	218
15	Learning Styles in Multicultural Classrooms *Tony Young and Itesh Sachdev*	235

Coda

16	Language Learning and Teaching as Discursive Practice *Richard F. Young*	251

Bibliography	272
Index	296

Illustrations

4.1	Framegrab 1	47
4.2	Framegrab 2	48
4.3	Framegrab 3	48
4.4	Framegrab 4	49
4.5	Framegrab 5	53
9.1	Percentage of participants using each category	134
11.1	Mean self-perceived proficiency scores for L1 and L2	175
11.2	Mean communicative anxiety scores for L1 and L2	175
11.3	Mean language perception scores for L1 and L2	176
11.4	Mean self-perceived proficiency scores for instructed, mixed and naturalistic learners in L2	177
11.5	Mean communicative anxiety scores for instructed, mixed and naturalistic learners in L2	178
11.6	Mean language perception scores for instructed, mixed and naturalistic learners in L2	179
13.1	Proficiency scale: multilingual ability of young Indo-Fijians	207
13.2	Class 1 self-report language proficiency.	209
13.3	Observation chart for languages of classroom instruction	210
13.4	Medium of instruction in English, Maths and SH/Urdu classes	210
13.5	Observation schedule: patterns of classroom language use with various interlocutors	212
13.6	Student language choice for classroom interaction in Class 1	213
13.7	Class 1 teacher languages of classroom interaction	214
15.1	Learning style preferences of British teachers	243
15.2	Learning style preferences of Brazilian learners	244

Tables

8.1	Size and lexical richness in the life story corpora	106
9.1	Participants' distribution and cultural orientations	132
9.2	One-way ANOVA on Culture X Category	135
9.3	Comparison of Chinese and British groups	137
10.1	The ESL cohort	153
11.1	Distribution of participants according to context of acquisition of the L2	170
11.2	Distribution of participants according to self-perceived proficiency in the L1 and L2	171
11.3	Distribution of participants according to communicative anxiety in the L1 and L2	172
11.4	Distribution of participants according to perception of the L1 and L2	173
11.5	Comparison of self-perceived proficiency scores in L1 and L2 (Wilcoxon Signed Ranks Test)	174
11.6	Comparison of communicative anxiety scores in L1 and L2 (Wilcoxon Signed Ranks Test)	174
11.7	Comparison of language perception scores in L1 and L2 (Wilcoxon Signed Ranks Test)	174
11.8	Effect of the context of acquisition on self-perceived proficiency in speaking, comprehending, reading and writing in the L2	176
11.9	Effect of the context of acquisition on communicative anxiety in the L2	176
11.10	Effect of the context of acquisition on language perception scores in the L2	177
14.1	Little Manuel's English language vocabulary	224
14.2	Little Manuel's academic vocabulary	224
14.3	Little Manuel's participant frameworks	225
15.1	Oxford's Style Analysis Survey	240
15.2	A comparison of teachers' attributions with actual learning style preferences	245
15.3	Perceived utility of the SAS	246

Notes on the Contributors

Robert Bayley is Professor of Linguistics at the University of California, Davis, USA. His publications include *Sociolinguistic Variation in American Sign Language* (2001) and *What's Your Sign for PIZZA? An Introduction to Variation in ASL* (2003), both with Ceil Lucas and Clayton Valli, and *Language as Cultural Practice: Mexicanos en el norte* (2002, with Sandra Schecter).

David Block is Reader in Education at the Institute of Education, University of London, UK. His books include *Second Language Identities* (2007), *Multilingual Identities in a Global City: London Stories* (2006) and *The Social Turn in Second Language Acquisition* (2003).

Vivian Cook is a Professor of Applied Linguistics in the School of Education, Communication and Language Sciences, Newcastle University, UK. He is mostly known for his work developing the idea of multi-competence and for his books on Chomsky and on the applications of second language acquisition research to language teaching. Recently he has also written on writing systems and on English spelling. He was a founder and first President of the European Second Language Association.

Jean Conteh is Senior Lecturer in Primary Education at the University of Leeds, UK, and has published: *Promoting Learning for Bilingual Pupils 3–11: Opening Doors to Success* (2006), *Writing Educational Ethnographies: The Art of Collusion* (with E. Gregory, C. Kearney and A. Mor-Sommerfeld, 2005), and *Succeeding in Diversity: Culture, Language and Learning in Primary Classrooms* (2003).

Jean-Marc Dewaele is Reader in French and Applied Linguistics at Birkbeck, University of London, UK. He has published on psycholinguistic, sociolinguistic, pragmatic and psychological aspects of second language production and edited *Opportunities and Challenges of Bilingualism* (2002, with Li Wei and Alex Housen) and *Bilingualism: Basic Principles and Beyond* (2003).

Simona Pekarek Doehler is Professor of Applied Linguistics and Director of the Centre for Applied Linguistics, University of Neuchâtel, Switzerland. Her publications include *Leçons de conversation: dynamiques de l'interaction et acquisition de compétences discursives en classe de langue seconde* (1999), and *Französischlernen in der Deutschschweiz? Zur Entwicklung der diskursiven*

Fähigkeiten innerhalb und ausserhalb der Schule (with Georges Lüdi and Victor Saudan, 2001).

Viktoria Driagina is a doctoral student in Applied Linguistics at the Pennsylvania State University, USA, and a research associate at the Centre for Applied Language Proficiency Education and Research. Her research agenda addresses issues in second language learning and teaching pedagogy. She is a co-author of the manual *Narrative and Conceptual Proficiency in Russian* (2006) and an article 'Russian Emotion Vocabulary in American Learners' Narratives', in *The Modern Language Journal* (both with A. Pavlenko).

Rod Gardner is Associate Professor in Applied Linguistics at Griffith University, Brisbane, Australia. He is author of *When Listeners Talk: Response Tokens and Recipient Stance* (2001), and co-editor with J. Wagner of *Second Language Conversations* (2004).

Zhu Hua, PhD, is a Senior Lecturer in Applied Linguistics at Birkbeck, University of London. She has published extensively on child language development and cross-cultural pragmatics. She is the author of *Phonological Development in Specific Contexts* (2002), joint author of *DEAP: Differential Evaluation of Articulation and Phonology* (2002), co-editor of *Phonological Development and Disorders in Children: A Multilingual Perspective* (2006).

Gabriele Kasper is Professor of Second Language Studies at the University of Hawai'i and currently the North American editor of *Applied Linguistics*. Her books include *Misunderstanding in Social Life* (2003, co-edited with J. House and S. Ross) *Pragmatic Development in a Second Language* (2002, with K. Rose); and *Pragmatics in Language Teaching* (2001, co-edited with K. Rose). Her recent work applies conversation analysis to second language interaction.

Younhee Kim is a PhD candidate at the Department. of Second Language Studies at the University of Hawai'i at Manoa, Hawai'i. She has published the chapter 'The Use of the Korean Connective – *nuntey* in L2 Korean Speakers' Conversation', in G. Kasper and H. Nguyen (eds), *Conversation Analysis: Multilingual Perspectives*.

Juliet Langman is Associate Professor of Applied Linguistics at the University of Texas, San Antonio, USA. Her publications include *Urban Sanctuaries: Neighborhood Organizations in the Lives and Futures of Inner-City Youth* (2001, with Milbrey W. McLaughlin and Merita A. Irby) and *Beyond Borders: Remaking Cultural Identities in the New East and Central Europe* (1997, co-edited with László Kürti).

Numa Markee is Associate Professor of English as an International Language at the University of Illinois at Urbana-Champaign, USA. His publications include *Managing Curricular Innovations* (1997) and *Conversation Analysis* (2000). He has also edited a special issue of *TESOL Quarterly* (2002) on Language in Development, and a special issue of the *Modern Language Journal* (2004) on Classroom Talks.

Jennifer Miller is a Senior Lecturer in the Faculty of Education at Monash University, Australia, where she teaches graduate courses in the TESOL area. Her research and publications are in the areas of refugee learners, language acquisition and identity, second language pedagogy and non-native ESL teachers. Her book, *Audible Difference: ESL and Social Identity* (2003) explores the politics of speaking and identity for immigrant students in high schools.

Aneta Pavlenko is Associate Professor at the College of Education, Temple University, Philadelphia, USA. She is the author of *Emotions and Multilingualism* (2005, which was a winner of the BAAL Book Prize, 2006), editor of *Bilingual Minds: Emotional Experience, Expression, and Representation* (2006), and co-editor of *Multilingualism, Second Language Learning, and Gender* (2001, with A. Blackledge, I. Piller and M. Teutsch Dwyer), *Gender and English Language Learners* (2004, with B. Norton, TESOL) and *Negotiation of Identities in Multilingual Contexts* (2004, with A. Blackledge).

Itesh Sachdev is Professor and Head of the School of Languages, School of Oriental and African Studies (SOAS), University of London. He is the Head of School of Languages and Director of the SOAS-UCL Centre for Excellence in 'Languages of the Wider World'. He has published widely in the social psychology of inter-group relations, language learning and teaching, multilingualism and multiculturalism. He has worked with diverse ethno-linguistic groups from several parts of the world including Bolivia, Canada, France, Hong Kong, India, Taiwan, Thailand, Tunisia and the UK.

Paul Seedhouse is Professor of Educational and Applied Linguistics in the School of Education, Communication and Language Sciences, Newcastle University, UK. His monograph *The Interactional Architecture of the Language Classroom: A Conversation Analysis Perspective* was published by Blackwell in 2004 and won the 2005 Kenneth Mildenberger Prize of the Modern Language Society of the USA. He has also co-edited the collection *Applying Conversation Analysis* with Keith Richards (2004).

Nikhat Shameem is Lecturer in Applied Linguistics, Newcastle University, UK. She has lived and worked in Fiji, Aotearoa/New Zealand, Samoa and the UK. Her interests are in multilingualism, language maintenance and shift, curriculum design and language acquisition among young multilingual learners. She has published in the *International Journal of Educational Development; Language, Culture and Curriculum; Journal of Multilingual and Multicultural Development*; and the *Journal of Intercultural Studies*.

Li Wei, PhD, is Professor of Applied Linguistics at Birkbeck, University of London. He is author of *Three Generations Two Languages, One Family* (1994), and editor of *The Bilingualism Reader: Opportunities and Challenges of Bilingualism* (2000, with Jean-Marc Dewaele and Alex Housen), *Bilingualism: Beyond Basic Principles* (2002, with Jean-Marc Dewaele and Alex Housen), *The Blackwell Guide to Research Methods in Bilingualism and Multilingualism* (2007, with Melissa Moyer) and *Multilingualism and Multilingual Communication*, Vol. 5 *Handbook of Applied Linguistics* (2007, with Peter Auer). He is also the Editor-in-Chief of the *International Journal of Bilingualism*.

Richard F. Young is Professor of English Linguistics at the University of Wisconsin-Madison, USA, where he teaches courses in second language acquisition and interactional sociolinguistics. His books include *Talking and Testing: Discourse Approaches to the Assessment of Oral Proficiency* (1998, co-edited with A. W. He) and *Variation in Interlanguage Morphology* (1991). He has served as president of the American Association for Applied Linguistics and general editor of the Language Learning Monograph Series.

Tony Young teaches and directs postgraduate programmes in Cross-Cultural Communication at Newcastle University, UK. He has been involved in language teaching and teacher education in Europe, South East and East Asia and in North America. His most recent research investigates personality, culture and intercultural communication in teaching and learning languages.

Gudrun Ziegler is Assistant Professor in Applied Linguistics and Plurilingualism, Faculty of Language and Literature, Humanities, Arts and Education at the Université du Luxembourg. Her recent publications are *Beobachtungen zum Früherwerb Französisch. Ein Arbeitsbuch für Studierende und Lehrkräfte* (2006, co-edited with Rita Franceschini) and 'Langue voisine, langue étrangère précoce – le français langue étrangère en région transfrontalière', *Babylonia*, 1: 11–16 (2006).

Transcription Conventions

A full discussion of CA transcription notation is available in Atkinson and Heritage (1984). Punctuation marks are used to capture characteristics of speech delivery, **not** to mark grammatical units.

[	indicates the point of overlap onset
]	indicates the point of overlap termination
=	(a) turn continues below, at the next identical symbol
	(b) if inserted at the end of one speaker's turn and at the beginning of the next speaker's adjacent turn, it indicates that there is no gap at all between the two turns
(3.2)	an interval between utterances (3 seconds and 2 tenths in this case)
(.)	a very short untimed pause
word	underlining indicates speaker emphasis
e:r the:::	indicates lengthening of the preceding sound
-	a single dash indicates an abrupt cut-off
?	rising intonation, not necessarily a question
!	an animated or emphatic tone
,	a comma indicates low-rising intonation, suggesting continuation
.	a full stop (period) indicates falling (final) intonation
CAPITALS	especially loud sounds relative to surrounding talk
° °	utterances between degree signs are noticeably quieter than surrounding talk
°° °°	considerably quieter than surrounding talk
↑ ↓	indicate marked shifts into higher or lower pitch in the utterance following the arrow
⟩ ⟨	indicate that the talk they surround is produced more quickly than neighbouring talk
( )	a stretch of unclear or unintelligible speech.
(guess)	indicates transcriber doubt about a word
.hh	speaker in-breath
hh	speaker out-breath
→	arrows in the left margin pick out features of especial interest

Additional symbols

((T shows picture))	non-verbal actions or editor's comments
ja	translations into English are italicized and located on the line below the original utterance
yes	
[gibee]	in the case of inaccurate pronunciation of an English word, an approximation of the sound is given in square brackets
[æ]	phonetic transcriptions of sounds are given in square brackets
〈 〉	indicate that the talk they surround is produced slowly and deliberately (typical of teachers modelling forms)
☺	smiley voice
☹	serious tone (contrasts with smiley voice)
#	creaky voice
X_____	the gaze of the speaker is marked above an utterance and that of the addressee below it. An unbroken line (—) indicates that the party marked is gazing towards the other; absence indicates lack of gaze. Dots (...) mark the transition from nongaze to gaze and the point where the gaze reaches the other is marked by X. Commas (,,,) indicate the moment when gaze is shifted
¿	a stronger rise than a comma but weaker than a question mark

1
An Introduction

Zhu Hua and Li Wei Paul Seedhouse and Vivian Cook
Birkbeck, University of London Newcastle University

Ideas of social interaction are increasingly having an impact upon research into the learning and teaching of second languages. The aims of this book are to:

- demonstrate the importance of investigating second language learning and teaching from a social-interactional and sociocultural perspective;
- describe the implications of the social-interaction perspective for the practice of language teaching and learning including teacher education;
- outline some interdisciplinary links between the social-interactional and sociocultural approaches to language learning and teaching and other approaches such as the social constructionist approach.

The book brings together contributions by some of the crucial people involved in developing this approach. It provides not only an introduction to this important growth point but also an overview of current cutting-edge research.

The central pillar of the social interactional perspective is the belief that language learning and teaching are social acts – the roles and relationships of the learner and the teacher are socially constructed; their social identities are formed and transformed by the very process of learning and teaching; the knowledge of language that is being acquired and taught is social knowledge that is affected by the roles, relationships, attitudes and ideologies of the learner and the teacher. The actual process of language learning and teaching is furthermore seen as social interaction, and consequently relates to other kinds of social interaction in institutional and non-institutional contexts. The social interactional perspective thus contrasts with other long-standing and dominant research approaches that regard language learning and teaching as essentially an individual activity in which the learner passively receives large sets of examples and performs some sort of induction to arrive at abstract concepts and skills, or as a genetically pre-programmed organism in which the role of the environment is restricted to setting some parameters.

From the sociolinguistic and sociocultural perspectives, language learning and teaching are closely linked with, and affected by, the societal structures, cultural values, individual motivations, identities, policies and ideologies, and teacher–learner relationships. While most contributors to the present volume would agree with such views, the emphasis here is on language learning and teaching as a social *process* rather than a social *product*. The key argument is that language learning and teaching is a process of social reproduction. That is to say, the process is not just affected by factors such as ideology, identity and attitude, but itself brings them into being and transforms them.

Taking language learning and teaching to be a social act requires a major shift of analytic focus, shifting from the cognitive process of the individual learner to the interactions that take place between the learner and the teacher, between learners, between the learner and the environment, and between the learner and the wider society.

Contents and themes

The 14 main chapters in this volume cover a wide range of second language learning and teaching contexts and a number of themes.

Part 1 Interactional foundations

The five chapters in Part 1 focus on the fine interactional detail involved in the processes of language learning and teaching. All the writers employ Conversation Analysis (CA) methodology to portray the complex connections between the interactional, social and pedagogical levels in their data: see Hutchby and Wooffitt (1998); Seedhouse (2004); ten Have (1999) for introductions to the methodology. The extracts cover a wide range of language learning and teaching contexts around the world (from seven countries); there is variety in terms of languages taught (German and English), learner characteristics such as nationality, age and level (from young learners to university level) as well as variety in teaching approaches and classroom configurations (immersion, tasks, conversation classes). Taken as a whole, this section shows language learning to be inextricably entwined with complex social and interactional processes:

- Paul Seedhouse analyses classroom data from 5 different countries (New Zealand, the USA, UK, Turkey and Morocco) to determine the extent to which learning constructs such as the Zone of Proximal Development (ZPD) and scaffolding derived from Vygotskyan theories are manifested in the interaction. He concludes that they require further development to cope with the unique nature of second language (L2) classroom interaction.
- Gabriele Kasper and Younhee Kim focus on the organization of repair in an out-of-classroom conversation class in the United States involving a German first language (L1) speaker and a group of learners. While the L2

speakers in this setting often produce answers which are misaligned with questions, the authors show that the L1 speaker conducts repair in a covert manner which enables the interaction to flow. Crucially, this specific interactional repair mechanism is reflexively related both to the L2 learners' need (as social beings) to preserve face and to the pedagogical goals of this particular setting.
- Numa Markee's chapter examines off-task talk in the second language by two students in a classroom setting in the United States. His analysis shows the sophisticated communication skills the students employ to issue and decline social invitations and highlights the L2 classroom as a social setting. Markee argues that such analyses constitute assessments of learners' competence in L2 conversation and discusses the implications for the design and implementation of language teaching materials.
- Rod Gardner examines the phenomenon of broken-turn starts or bricolage in L2 talk involving lower-level learners in both pedagogical and non-pedagogical settings in Australia. He provides a technical analysis of this distinctive L2 learner turn construction and considers how this may be related to learning processes from a Vygotskian perspective.
- Simona Pekarek-Doehler and Gudrun Ziegler examine talk in bilingual science classrooms in an immersion setting in Switzerland. They reveal the interconnectedness of the multiple levels of talk, specifically the orientations to scientific content, linguistic form, socializing in the classroom community and the sequential organization of the lesson. Their socially situated perspective suggests that classroom language learning cannot be understood in isolation from socialization processes, participation frameworks and sequential organization.

Part 2 Identity and social action

Part 2 of the collection is centred around the issue of identity. The general argument is that language learning is a process of social identification. Learners are not only acquiring a new set of linguistic skills, but also developing a new identity:

- David Block calls for the socialization of Second Language Acquisition (SLA), echoing Ben Rampton's earlier call for a 'returned' applied linguistics (1997). Rampton argued that applied linguists needed a more eclectic approach to inquiry if they intended to explore real world problems involving language in the late modern age. This bigger toolkit means above all engaging with well-established social science disciplines such as social theory, sociology, politics, anthropology and history. Block extends the argument by suggesting that the analytic framework applied linguists use should be socially, politically and historically rooted and include globalization, multi-level models of migration and transmigration and multi-perspective post-structuralist approaches to identity.

- Viktoria Driagina and Aneta Pavlenko's joint chapter critically examines the notion of 'identity construction' in a foreign language context and discusses implications for applied linguistics theory, pedagogy and teaching materials. The identity repertories used by American learners of Russian and native Russian speakers are compared in order to understand what linguistic repertoires are made available to these learners in Russian language classrooms and what resources they draw on to perform selves in a foreign language.
- Zhu Hua develops the theme of identity construction by focusing on how L2 users present and construct the concept of 'self' in writing. Through an analysis of application letters in English as a Foreign Language (EFL) classes in an English university, she demonstrates that, despite the requirements specific to the genre, EFL learners can present themselves in different ways with a common goal of obtaining a place on a university course. These different ways of self-presentation are socioculturally situated and indicate the learners' cultural expectations.
- While most of the chapters in this part are focused on identity construction by L2 users, Jenny Miller's chapter looks at a different group, namely pre-service ESL teachers in an Australian university, and explores the issues of social constructions of teacher identity and language competence, the role of perception, particularly where international or non-native English-speaking pre-service teachers are concerned. The analysis highlights diversity within the group and the dilemmas faced by ESL teachers.
- Jean-Marc Dewaele investigates how social interaction affects pragmatic competence during the learning of a second language, arguing that the second language should not just be the abstract object of L2 instruction, but an effective tool for social interaction. He calls for an epistemological shift in gauging L2 users' pragmatic competence by taking into account their self-perceptions towards their own pragmatic competence.

Part 3 Multilingual and multicultural classrooms

Part 3 of the volume addresses the multilingual and multicultural practices of classrooms, particularly language use as social practice in the education of bilingual children:

- Jean Conteh reports a study of the skills and knowledge of bilingual Punjabi/English teachers in England and the ways in which they mediate classroom interaction with their pupils in the primary school. She examines the different kinds of knowledge and power available to the teachers and their pupils and the special space created by their bilingual discourse for the expression of particular voices.
- Nikhat Shameem studies the tensions between education policies and classroom practices in the use of languages in multilingual classrooms in Fiji. The study demonstrates that in many parts of the developing world,

language and education policies fail to reflect the multilingual and multicultural practices that exist among young learners.
- Juliet Langman and Robert Bayley track the language use and development of an adolescent immigrant in a US school context, and argue that, for many adolescent immigrants, the school context is not conducive to the development of English. They echo the argument put forward in Jean-Marc Dewaele's chapter, namely that formal classroom instruction contributes significantly less than social interaction to the development of pragmatic competence in the second language. The chapter raises a number of questions about language learning opportunities.
- Tony Young and Itesh Sachdev investigate learning style in a multicultural classroom setting in EFL organizations based in the United Kingdom, in particular, how teachers of multicultural classes perceive the pedagogical effectiveness of learning styles. Implications for pedagogy are discussed such as the caveats associated with cultural group profiling in training, validity and reliability of learning style assessment, and effective use of learning style indexing in learning and teaching.

The volume ends with a coda by Richard Young which pulls together all of the sections and themes of the collection into a single coherent framework of Discursive Practice. This is centred on an extended and multi-layered conception of context in social practices, with specific reference to language learning and teaching settings.

Acknowledgement

The editors would like to acknowledge funding received from Cambridge University Press and the British Association of Applied Linguistics for a seminar held in Newcastle University in July 2005.

Part 1
Interactional Foundations

2
Interaction and Constructs

Paul Seedhouse
Newcastle University

Introduction

There is currently considerable interest in the relationship between Conversation Analysis (CA) and Sociocultural or Social Constructionist (SC) approaches to language learning. This chapter analyses extracts of L2 classroom interaction to discover the extent to which SC constructs may or may not be manifest in the details of the interaction. If such constructs are evident, then how are they talked into being and how are they organized in interactional terms? Do they provide an adequate account of language learning in the L2 classroom?

First, some introduction to SC and CA is provided. The late 1990s saw a debate on a proposed 're-conceptualization' of Second Language Acquisition (SLA) (Firth and Wagner 1997, 1998; Gass 1998; Kasper 1997; Long 1997; Markee 2000; van Lier 2000). Some of the criticisms which Firth and Wagner (1997, 1998) made of SLA are as follows: SLA had neglected the social and contextual aspects of language use and their contribution to SLA processes. SLA was becoming a 'hermetically sealed area of study' (1998: 92) which was losing contact with sociology, sociolinguistics and discourse analysis in favour of a psycholinguistic focus on the cognition of the individual. There was an etic rather than emic[1] approach to fundamental concepts. The traditional SLA database was too narrow. Essentially the call was for a holistic approach which includes the social dimension and emic perspectives. Responses to Firth and Wagner (Gass 1998; Kasper 1997; Long 1997) generally suggested that, whilst CA was interesting, it had little or nothing to say about language learning or acquisition.

Since Firth and Wagner's (1997) article, a number of studies have been published which do incorporate social and contextual dimensions (e.g., Hall and Verplaetse 2000; Lantolf 2000; Ohta 2001) and which have established a school of sociocultural theory (SC) within SLA, based primarily on Vygotskian concepts. SC explores the interconnection of learning, language, interaction and society and offers a 'holistic perspective of language learning, where individual and social merge into one and where use and knowledge are indistinguishable' (Ellis and Barkhuizen 2005: 229). Deriving from psychology, SC tends to work top-down from Vygotskian cognitive constructs such as the *Zone of Proximal Development* (ZPD).

Deriving from sociology, Conversation Analysis (CA) is a methodology for the analysis of naturally occurring spoken interaction. CA practitioners aim 'to discover how participants understand and respond to one another in their turns at talk, with a central focus on how sequences of action are generated' (Hutchby and Wooffitt 1998: 14). CA always works bottom-up from data and is in principle agnostic in relation to learning theories. CA distinguishes between an 'etic' or external analyst's perspective on human behaviour and an 'emic' or participant's perspective and aims to develop an emic perspective. What CA means by an emic perspective, however, is the participant's perspective within the interactional environment in which the talk occurs.

At interest in this chapter is the extent to which CA and SC can be combined. Is CA able to provide evidence in relation to the process of learning and show how SC constructs are talked into being?

Conceptions of CA in language learning and teaching research

A number of publications since 1997 have therefore tried to establish what CA might be able to contribute to the study of language learning. Opinion is currently divided as to the relationship between CA and language learning and the status of CA. At the time of writing there are a number of competing and sometimes conflicting conceptions of how CA may or may not be employed in language learning and teaching research. From a temporal perspective, this lack of clarity is not a matter of major concern. CA itself only emerged in the 1960s, had no connection with learning and in its genesis dealt exclusively with monolingual English data (Sacks, Schegloff and Jefferson 1974; Schegloff, Jefferson and Sacks 1977). It is only in the period 2000–04 that publications have started to address the relationship between CA and language learning,[2] culminating in the special issue of the *Modern Language Journal* in 2004 (Markee and Kasper 2004). Seedhouse (2005) suggests that it now makes sense to identify two different approaches to the application of CA to the broad field of language learning and teaching.

In the *ethnomethodological CA approach*, data from language learning and teaching settings are approached in exactly the same way as any other data, following the principles and procedures described in introductions such as Hutchby and Wooffitt (1998), ten Have (1999) and Seedhouse (2004). If it is evident in the details of the interaction that the participants are orienting to language learning in some way, then it is legitimate to invoke this in the analysis. For example, Koshik (2002) reveals how teachers use the pedagogical practice of designedly incomplete utterances in order to initiate self-correction by learners. The analysis is not linked to any learning theory and Koshik states

(2002: 278) that her aim 'is not to evaluate the pedagogy but to describe an institutional practice, showing how practices of ordinary conversation can be adapted for specialized institutional tasks.'

This approach would argue that the very strength of applying CA to the field of language learning and teaching lies in the fact that it is neutral and agnostic in relation to learning theories and teaching methods and reveals an emic perspective. Unless it is evident that interactants are themselves orienting to a construct, it is not legitimate to invoke it in an *a priori* fashion. Therefore, linking CA to any theory of learning in abstraction from a specific interactional environment is an inherently etic undertaking.

The *sociocultural theory approach to CA* is currently attracting a great deal of interest as it has the potential to offer a systematic approach to how to study the process of second language learning. This approach seeks 'to use CA techniques as methodological tools that are in the service of different sociocultural theories of learning' (Markee and Kasper 2004: 495). Mondada and Pekarek Doehler outline the significant similarities between CA and sociocultural theory in a strong socio-interactionist perspective: 'both of these frameworks converge in insisting on the central role of contextually embedded communicative processes in the accomplishment of human actions and identities as well as of social facts' (2004: 504).

Young and Miller (2004), Brouwer and Wagner (2004) and Mondada and Pekarek Doehler (2004) propose to link a sociocultural view of development with a CA perspective on interaction. They apply to their data the notion of situated learning 'according to which learning is rooted in the learner's participation in social practice and continuous adaptation to the unfolding circumstances and activities that constitute talk-in-interaction' (Mondada and Pekarek Doehler 2004: 501). Young and Miller (2004) conduct a longitudinal observation of revision talk, show that the participation framework changed over time and reveal the processes by which the student moved from peripheral to fuller participation. Brouwer and Wagner (2004) suggest moving away from the typical SLA conception of language in terms of individual cognition and an input-output approach to the acquisition of discrete linguistic (typically syntactic or lexical) items. They propose instead to focus on the development of interactional skills and resources and conceptualizing language learning as a social process. They suggest that 'learning is situated; learning is social; and knowledge is located in communities of practice' and that 'learning not only takes place in the social world, it also constitutes that world' (Brouwer and Wagner 2004: 33).

The field of CA-for-SLA (Markee 2000) generally falls within this approach. The main difference with the previous approach is that the sociocultural theory approach to CA employs CA as a tool in the service of a theory of learning whereas ethnomethodological CA does not and is agnostic in relation to learning.

Data analysis

In this section I analyse extracts of L2 classroom interaction to examine the extent to which SC constructs may or may not be manifest in the details of the interaction. I also attempt to illustrate some of the issues and concepts previously discussed. A CA analysis would normally cover the areas described in Seedhouse (2004). Here, I do not present the initial stages because of space constraints. However, see Seedhouse (2004: 59–64) for a full analysis of data similar to Extract 1.

Extract 1
(The teacher has been asking learners to talk about their favourite movies)

```
1   L:  Kung Fu.
2   T:  Kung Fu? you like the movie Kung Fu?
3   L:  yeah ... fight.
4   T:  that was about a great fighter? ... a man who knows how to
        fight with his hands.
5   L:  I fight ... my hand.
6   T:  you know how to fight with your hands?
7   L:  I fight with my hand.
8   T:  do you know karate?
9   L:  I know karate.
10  T:  watch out guys, Wang knows karate.
```
                                                            (Johnson 1995: 24)

The analysis will be divided into three stages. *First*, what can we say about the learner's actual developmental level or current ability in L2? We can note in lines 3 and 5 that his grammatical resources are fairly limited. Nonetheless, the learner is able to make use of these limited resources to nominate a sub-topic (line 1), to develop the sub-topic (line 3) and to turn the discussion to his own fighting abilities (line 5). Although it can be challenging for children to interact with the teacher in a classroom setting, even in the L1, we can see that L is able to use the turn-taking and sequence organizations of the L2 proficiently. L constantly needs to analyse T's turns. From the learner's perspective, it is not just a matter of understanding the propositional content of what T says in the L2; it is also a matter of analysing what social and sequential action T is performing and what an appropriate social and sequential action in response would be. So we can see that L skilfully manages to co-construct meaning with T in the L2 from his limited grammatical resources.

Second, what can we say about the learning environment in terms of input to the language learning process and facilitation of upgrading as a result of the interaction? Line 6 reads: 'you know how to fight with your hands?' In CA terms this is known as embedded correction (Jefferson 1987: 95); that is, a correction done as a by-the-way occurrence in the context of a social action. We will break its contribution down into four points. First, the utterance places the sequence within the teacher's overall pedagogical plan for the lesson, which 'Was to allow the students to share their ideas and possibly generate some new vocabulary words within the context of the discussion' (Johnson 1995: 23). Second, it may promote positive affect and motivation in that the teacher engages with the ideas and personal meanings which the learner chooses to share and produces the conversational action of a confirmation check which validates the utterance. Line 6 also displays interest in the learner's extra-curricular abilities. It then demonstrates confidence in the learner by returning the floor to him with the question. Third, it makes it possible for the other learners in the class to follow the topic of the interaction (the others are explicitly addressed in line 10) and to receive correctly formed linguistic input. There is no evidence in the transcripts as to whether the other learners have done so or not. However, Ohta (2001) shows (by recording and transcribing the private talk of individually microphoned students in a classroom) that students *are capable* of using recasts in which they are not personally involved as negative evidence and of displaying uptake in their private talk. Fourth, and most importantly, there is positive evaluation of the propositional content of the learner utterance followed by an expansion of the learner utterance into a correct sequence of linguistic forms or embedded correction. In terms of input, the teacher provides a corrected version of the learner's turn in line 5 whilst retaining a focus on meaning. As Johnson (1995: 25) points out, this form of correction and expansion is highly reminiscent of adult–child conversation.

Third, what evidence is there of SC constructs in the detail of the interaction? The technique being used by the teacher in line 6 is often termed *scaffolding* (Johnson 1995: 75; Ohta 2005: 506) from a SC perspective. The SLA literature terms this action a recast and the instance in line 6 conforms to Long and colleagues' (1998: 358) definition of recasts.

Ohta defines Vygotsky's Zone of Proximal Development (ZPD) in relation to SLA in the following terms: 'For the L2 learner, the ZPD is the distance between the actual developmental level as determined by individual linguistic production, and the level of potential development as determined through language produced collaboratively with a teacher or peer' (Ohta 2001: 9). What we can see in this extract, then, is how a ZPD is talked into being through the organization of the interaction. Specifically, we see a neat juxtaposition of the learner's actual developmental level in line 3 (yeah ... fight) with the target native speaker (NS) level produced by the teacher in line 6 (you know how to fight with your hands?). We also see the learner producing, with the teacher's help, utterances which are moving up the scale in line 5 (I fight ... my hand) and line 7 (I fight with my hand). There is some evidence, then, of learner noticing and uptake of the embedded correction/scaffolding/recast in this case.

So from the perspectives of SLA psycholinguistic theory, L1 acquisition studies and Vygotskyan social constructivist theory there is agreement that such sequences are beneficial. A CA analysis demonstrates the same point. The distinctive CA contribution is to show how learning is constructed by the use of interactional resources and to explicate the progress of their learning and their intersubjectivity. In the case of Extract 1, then, a sociocultural theory CA analysis reveals a sequence including a ZPD and scaffolding.

In the analysis of Extract 1 we also noted that L2 classroom interaction can focus simultaneously on linguistic form and on meaning. Seedhouse suggests that L2 classroom interaction has a unique property, namely that language has a dual role as it is both the vehicle and object of instruction (2004: 183). This means that there is a reflexive relationship between pedagogy and interaction and this relationship is the foundation of the interactional architecture of the language classroom. In the extracts below we focus on the complex and ever-shifting relationship between linguistic form and meaning in the L2 classroom and consider whether concepts such as the ZPD, which are derived from L1 instruction, are able to do justice to this complexity.

In Extract 2, the learners are talking about what they had done the previous weekend. The setting is a language school in England.

Extract 2

1	L1:	and what did you do last weekend?
2	L2:	on Saturday I went on my own to Canterbury, so I took a bus
3		and I met L6 (.) he took the same bus to Canterbury. and in
4		Canterbury I visited the Cathedral and all the streets near
5		the Cathedral and I tried to find a pub where you don't see
6		(.) where you don't see many tourists. and I find one
7	T:	found
8	L2:	I found one where I spoke with two English women and we
9		spoke about life in Canterbury or things and after I came
10		back
11	T:	afterwards
12	L2:	afterwards I came back by bus too. and on Sunday what did
13		you do?
14	L1:	oh, er, I stayed in home
15	T:	at home
16	L1:	on Sunday I stayed at home and watched the Wimbledon Final.
17		what did you do on Sunday?

(Mathers 1990: 109)

The focus in Extract 2 is on personal meaning in that the learners are able to nominate and contribute new information concerning their personal experiences, and on fluency in that they are able to manage the interaction locally and by themselves. The evidence for this is that the learners use a *current speaker selects next speaker* technique to select another student in lines 12 and 16. The focus is also on accuracy and linguistic form in that the teacher corrects all errors of linguistic form, and in this extract the learners display uptake of the corrected forms in subsequent utterances. Although the teacher adopts a direct and overt repair technique which has a linguistic upgrading and scaffolding function, this does not result in the flow of the interaction being interrupted.

How does the teacher achieve this unobtrusive repair? According to Iles (1996), experienced teachers often engage in what she terms *camouflaging of repair*. This plays down the activity of repair so that it is less obtrusive and prominent, with the result that the flow of the interaction is not impeded. Some of the features of camouflage are as follows: the teacher produces the target form for adoption by the learner without any overt or explicit negative evaluation or indication that an error has been made. The teacher does not mark the target form out by loudness or decrease in tempo; there is narrow pitch movement and a lack of speech perturbation features. In other words, the teacher fits the repair as unobtrusively as possible into the prosodic environment of the learner's utterances so that the repair does not obtain prominence and does not become the interactional business. The correction can be treated as a by-the-way activity, and the interactional evidence is that the learners do treat it as a by-the-way activity, in that the corrections do not interrupt the flow of the interaction, with one exception. T's repair in line 15 causes L1 to backtrack in line 16 in order to form a linguistically complete sentence. However, this is a minor interruption of the interactional flow.

In Extract 2, then, we can see how a focus on both form and meaning is maintained by the teacher's employment of an unusual and specialized correction technique. The extract also illustrates the unique nature of L2 classroom interaction; in this case two interactants are having a seemingly 'everyday' conversation focused on meaning, whilst the only contribution of the teacher is to provide correction of errors of form. We can also note that there is clear evidence in Extract 2 of successful scaffolding by the teacher and of a ZPD in Ohta's (2001) terms, in that we can see a clear juxtaposition of actual developmental level with that achieved through collaboration with the teacher.

In the following extract a group of learners of mixed nationalities in New Zealand are discussing which of four potential recipients should receive a heart transplant. They are managing the interaction themselves and focus primarily on meaning and fluency until a problem with linguistic form impacts on communication in line 4.

Extract 3

1	L3:	they live in Australia the family?
2	L1:	( ) I don't know but they will go to Australia too. (.)
3	L3:	(1.0) okay

4 →	L1:	(.) and (3.0) another one for ( ) from <u>drug</u> (kʌm'pa:ni)
5	L2:	sorry?
6	L1:	from drug (kʌm'pa:ni) (laughs)
7	L2:	drug
8	L1:	drug drug <d-r-u-g> (spells word) the uh drug (kʌm'pa:ni)
9	L2:	what what is (kʌm'pa:ni)?
10	L1:	(kʌm'pa:ni)
11	L2:	(kʌm'pa:ni)
12	L1:	(kʌm'pa:ni)
13 →	L2:	(1.0) ah (' kʌmpəni)
14	L1:	yes (' kʌmpəni)
15	L2:	ah (.) from the drug (' kʌmpəni)
16	L1:	drug drug drug
17	L2:	yes but impossible for the parents to get ( )
18	L1:	drug (kʌm'pa:ni) know they know about this advertising (.)
19		so they will come to help this family this family (2.0) you know what I mean =
20	L2:	= no =
21	L1:	= drug (kʌm'pa:ni)
22	T: →	>can can I just right there-< it's (' kʌmpəni)
23	L1:	(' kʌmpəni) =
24	T:	= (' kʌmpəni) =
25	L1:	= (' kʌmpəni) =
26	T:	= (' kʌmpəni) yeah =
27	L1:	= yep =
28	T:	= yeah not (kʌm'pa:ni) (' kʌmpəni)
29	L1:	(' kʌmpəni)
		(16 lines omitted)
46	L1:	reasons against giving her a new heart, (1.0) uh (1.5) you
47		remember → drug (' kʌmpəni) ( ) family allowed drug (' kʌmpəni) give them money

(Loewen 2002 (5 December C12))

In Extract 3 a problem with linguistic form (mispronunciation of *company* with stress on the second syllable) causes a problem in communication for the learners which necessitates an incidental switch to a focus on linguistic form in lines 5 to 16. It is evident in line 9 that L1's mispronunciation has created a communication problem for L2. First of all, L1 and L2 jointly manage the repair without the help of the teacher, who is present. L2 initiates self-repair in line 9, then conducts other-initiated other-repair in line 13, with L1 displaying uptake of the repair in line 14. In line 17 the learners return to the meaning focus. However, although L1 was able to display uptake of the repaired item when the focus was on form (line 14), he reverts to the incorrect pronunciation (lines 18 and 21) when the focus shifts back to meaning and fluency. In line 22, T switches the focus back to form with other-initiated other-repair and L1 again displays uptake in lines 23 and 25. Subsequently, when the focus again shifts back to meaning and fluency, we find that L1 is now able to display uptake of the corrected item in lines 46–47. This extract is interesting in that L1 does not display continued uptake of a correction of linguistic form when performed by a peer, but does do so when it is performed by the teacher. Again, there is evidence of scaffolding in a ZPD in that we can see a clear juxtaposition of actual developmental level with that achieved through collaboration with the teacher.

The above extract demonstrates the fluidity of the interaction, with the focus switching instantly between form and meaning. It also demonstrates the importance of a contextual approach to repair (Seedhouse 2004: 142); a learner may be able to produce a linguistic item appropriately in one context but not in another. Uptake, then, cannot be demonstrated by repetition of an item in a form and accuracy context. Evidence of uptake is more convincing when a learner is able to produce the item independently when the focus is on meaning and fluency.

L2 classroom interaction involves a number of rather peculiar interactional sequences which are generated by the unique property (language as object and vehicle) and which need to be accounted for by any model of learning. In Extract 4 below we see a very strange teaching and learning sequence in which the teacher creates a 'fake' pedagogical focus; the real focus is camouflaged.

Extract 4

1	T:	good, um: (.) <u>Driss</u>, could you please repeat after me OK, (T speaks inaudibly)
2	L1:	I don't understand (laughs)
3	T:	don't you? repeat after me (T speaks inaudibly)
4	L1:	more loud please hhh
5	T:	pardon?
6	L1:	(.) .hh I don't understand,
7	T:	don't you? listen again, listen [again](inaudible)
8	L1:	[what-] what are you saying?
9	T:	(speaks inaudibly)
10	L1:	I: hh [.hh]
11	T:	[don]'t understand me?
12	L1:	I hhh don't understand (looks perplexed)
13	T:	oh that's terrible. I'll try Wafaa, Wafaa repeat after me repeat after me (T speaks inaudibly)
14	L2:	I don't hear you.
15	T:	no? (.) so what do you say?
16	L2:	(1.0) I beg your pardon but I don't understand
17	T:	I see, and what do you say then

18   *Interactional Foundations*

18 LL: you say ( ) you say could you ( ) could you please ( )
19 T: Mrs Khadraoui has got a good one here. Listen,
20 L4: yes, could you please er speak loudly?
21 T: pardon, would you mind repeating that please?
22 L4: could you please er (.) speak clearly and loudly?
23 T: yes of course Mrs Khadraoui, do excuse me. Yes (.) ↑OK and
24   erm (.) could you then write this on the board for me please. if you write this in your books please, OK? (T writes in tiny, unreadable
25   script; LL look perplexed)
26 L: (2.5) oh no
27 L: (2.0) we don't understand
28 L: we can't write anything
29 L: we can't
30 L: yes
31 L: please would you mind ( ) er writing ( )
32 T: listen, let's listen to Boujemaa- oh, she's got fantastic eyes hasn't she?
33 LL: (laugh)
34 L5: please er would you er: er mind writing er: more clearly?
35 T: certainly. excuse me. (T writes in large letters)
         (8 lines omitted)
43 T: OK er-, you've just been asking me to do things. (.) you've
44   just been asking me to do things. (6 lines omitted) OK I've got a cassette here I'd like you to listen to (.) now I
45   just want you to tell me (.) what the people say when they
46   ask someone to do something OK? listen.
                                    (British Council 1985, Volume 2: 17)

What the teacher is doing in the above extract is creating situations in which the learners have to make polite requests. This is stated explicitly in an interview with the teacher on the video:

> I'm going to: start off by putting them in a position where they need to make requests, er: the reason for doing this (.) is partly to find out how much they already know. (.) and also to see which structures they- they would choose to use.
>   (British Council 1985, Volume 2: 17)

The 'fake' pedagogical focus is for learners to repeat after the teacher (line 1) and copy the teacher's writing (line 25). The camouflaged real focus is for the learners to make requests to the teacher. However, he does not target particular linguistic forms, and in fact he says in the interview quoted above that he is interested in seeing which linguistic forms they use to carry out the function of requesting. Any linguistic forms which perform the function of polite requests would be acceptable, but the string must be correctly formed. It is clear from the teacher's repair initiations in lines 5, 15, 17 and 21 that the teacher is not accepting utterances on the basis of their communicative value; he keeps initiating repair until a learner produces the request function in a linguistically correct format. In the above extract the teacher's unusual behaviour flouts the norms of L2 classroom interaction and thereby creates a situation in which the learners feel the need to perform a communicative function (request) and must package the function in linguistically correct forms in order to do so.

The above extract also shows that an adequate model of instructed L2 learning must be able to portray the complex and sometimes eccentric relationship between pedagogical focus and patterns of interaction. Extracts 1 to 3 are of course convenient for a Vygotskian model of learning in that we can see evidence of juxtaposition between two levels of language development combined with teacher scaffolding. However, there are many different aspects to language learning and many possible approaches to language teaching. We should not limit ourselves to data which match neatly to a particular model of learning. Rather, we should consider a wide variety of data and be particularly interested in deviant cases such as Extract 4 above since these are particularly illuminating; as Heritage (1995: 399) puts it, deviant cases often serve to demonstrate the normativity of practices.

The unique property of L2 classroom interaction also means that two (or more) different languages are often used by the participants. Üstünel and Seedhouse (2005) suggest that code-switching in L2 classrooms is orderly and related to the evolution of pedagogical focus and sequence. Through their language choice, learners may display their alignment or misalignment with the teacher's pedagogical focus. This therefore creates an additional level of complexity which needs to be accounted for in our modelling of language learning processes.

Extract 5

1	T:	Ayvalik here
2		(0.5)
3		so twenty
4		(0.5)
5		twenty
6		(0.5)
7		twenty <u>good</u> persuaders
8	L5:	thank you
9	T:	persuade?
10		(0.5)
11		what was persuade?
12	L5:→	*ikna = etmek*
		[tr: to persuade]

13	T:	=//good sell of people okay, wonderful .hh this
14		time go back to your original partner
15		(0.5)
16		original?
17	L2:	=//*gerçek*
		[tr: real]
18	L5:	=//*ilk*
		[tr: the first]
19	L7:	=*orjinal*
		[tr: original]
20	T: →	yeah *ilk partnerinize geri dönüyorsunuz* (.) *beraber yazdığınız*
21		[tr: return to your first partner with whom you have written]
		((LL talk in English in groups))
		(7 minutes)

(Üstünel and Seedhouse 2005: 315)

Extract 5 above is taken from a post-task activity. In lines 1 and 7, the teacher comments on the task results. In lines 9, 11 and 16 the teacher initiates question turns that 'induce' the learners to code-switch, but she does not code-switch to Turkish herself. In line 12, S5 switches to the L1 to provide a translation of the L2 word and in lines 17, 18 and 19 three learners provide translations in the L1 of the L2 word 'original'. These learner turns display the learners' analysis of the teacher's pedagogical focus as being for them to CS to the L1. The teacher's follow-up turn in lines 13 and 20 provides positive feedback, which confirms that the learners had complied with the pedagogical focus. The data contain many such examples. In Extract 5 the teacher's utterance in the L2 has the pedagogical aim of the learners producing an utterance in the L1. The learners display affiliation to the teacher's pedagogical focus precisely by replying in the L1 and the teacher recognizes them as affiliative responses. Üstünel and Seedhouse (2005) suggest that it is only possible to understand and analyse code-switching in L2 classrooms by tracing how language choice relates to developments in sequence and the shifting pedagogical focus.

Conclusions

We have seen from the analysis that CA is able to illuminate some aspects of the relationship between interaction and language learning by revealing how learning is constructed by the use of interactional resources and by explicating the progress of their learning and intersubjectivity. In particular, the sociocultural theory approach to CA is able to provide some evidence of how SC concepts such as the ZPD and scaffolding might be actualized in L2 classroom interaction. This in turn provides a basis for developing a closer relationship between CA and SC.

However, an ethnomethodological approach to CA would point out that it is only relevant to invoke constructs when it is evident in the details of the interaction that the participants themselves are orienting to such constructs; there is no such evidence in the data we have seen above. From this perspective, linking learning theories to interaction is an inherently etic undertaking.

One possible criticism of current approaches to conceptualizing the ZPD in L2 learning is that it provides a 'prefabricated' relationship between learning and interaction which derives from L1 contexts and which fails to incorporate the unique property of L2 classroom interaction; that is, that language is both the vehicle and object of instruction. The analyses presented above have stressed the complex, fluid interplay between form and meaning, interaction and pedagogical focus; participants are orienting to multiple simultaneous concerns and code-switching may be relevant to the learning process. The other chapters in this section present interaction involving L2 learners in a similar light. In order to fully understand how instructed L2 learning occurs in classroom interaction, it will be necessary to portray the interaction holistically with the full multi-layered complexity of language use. Schegloff speaks of 'the embeddedness, the inextricable intertwinedness, of cognition and interaction' (1991: 152), which we might visualize as two intertwined strands. The problem with L2 classroom interaction is that a third strand is intertwined, namely language as object of the interaction. This creates an additional level of complexity, as we have seen in the analyses of extracts above. Our constructs and models need, therefore, to have this third strand built into them. Constructs such as the ZPD, then, would need considerable development to be able to cope with the unique property of L2 classroom interaction and the same point could hypothetically be made in relation to any construct which does not take as its starting point this unique property. So one possible future direction for sociocultural CA would be to develop the ZPD construct to incorporate the unique properties of L2 classroom interaction, the reflexive relationship between pedagogy and interaction, and the use of multiple languages.

Notes

1. See below for definitions of emic and etic.
2. See, however, Hatch, 1978a.

3
Handling Sequentially Inapposite Responses

Gabriele Kasper and Younhee Kim
University of Hawai'i at Manoa

Introduction

As a critical interactional resource to establish or re-establish shared understanding in talk-in-interaction, participants deploy various practices of repair organization. Repair can address any sort of problem in speaking, hearing and understanding, anywhere in the interaction, in any type of activity (Schegloff 1992b; Schegloff, Jefferson and Sacks 1977). It is precisely the availability of a robust mechanism for dealing with trouble in interaction that permits oral non-scripted language use to be as ambiguous, indirect, allusive, elliptic, incoherent and otherwise 'fundamentally flawed' (Coupland, Wiemann and Giles 1991) as it is and yet enable participants to manage their language-mediated activities largely successfully (House, Kasper and Ross 2003; Schegloff 1991). Following Schegloff and colleagues' (1977) seminal paper, a large volume of research attests to the ubiquity of repair in talk among linguistically expert speakers. Second language researchers working in the tradition of conversation analysis (CA) have been particularly interested in examining the formats and functions of repair in talk including second or foreign language speakers. The impetus for this focus comes first and foremost from the empirically sustained assumption that when shared linguistic resources are limited, mutual understanding may be at an increased risk, requiring more repair work from participants in order to manage their joint activities. A second line of inquiry into repair in L2 interaction takes its cue from second language acquisition research in the interactionist tradition, which accords repair initiated or completed by the trouble source recipient a critical role in L2 learning (Gass 2003). However, outside of classrooms (Seedhouse 2004) and other educational arrangements, other-completed repair, and especially other-repair of linguistic form, appears to be infrequent, while self-initiated repair in the same turn is most prevalent (Wagner and Gardner 2004). Speakers with less extensive L2 resources thus order their repair practices in the same way as expert speakers. Moreover, outside of language classrooms, repair targets the same types of trouble source regardless of participants' language expertise, that is, discursive events that threaten mutual understanding rather than linguistic errors. To the extent that linguistic form becomes the object of repair, it is typically initiated by the less expert speaker (Kasper 2004; Kurhila 2005; Wong 2005) or done as embedded correction (Brouwer, Rasmussen and Wagner 2004; Kurhila 2001).

While much of the CA literature on L2 interactions examines repair sequences (e.g., Egbert 2004; Egbert, Niebecker and Rezzara 2004; Brouwer, Rasmussen and Wagner 2004; Hosoda 2000, 2006; Kidwell 2000; Kurhila 2001; Mori 2004; Wagner 1996; Wagner and Firth 1997; Wong 2000), less attention has been paid to sequences that hearably (or visibly) display trouble in the interaction, yet where the participants pass up the opportunity for repair. Firth (1996) notes that in business interactions conducted in a lingua franca, participants may disattend to apparent misunderstandings and thereby maintain a sense of orderliness and normality of the interaction. Similarly, Wong (2005) observes that native speakers in informal conversation may other-initiate repair to clarify topical matters pertinent to the local interactional goal, but disregard grammatical, phonological and lexical errors in the trouble source turn. In quite different activities, participants thus prioritize the business at hand over dealing overtly with problems that do not pose a serious threat to intersubjectivity at the particular moment they occur (although a disattended trouble source may turn out to require repair further into the interaction, as Firth (1996) shows). For Firth, such practices instantiate the phenomenological concept of 'letting-it-pass', an interpretive procedure (Cicourel 1973) or method of practical reasoning (Garfinkel 1967) by virtue of which a hearer 'lets the unknown or unclear action, word or utterance "pass" on the (commonsense) assumption that it will either become clear or redundant as talk progresses' (Firth 1996: 243). As such, letting-it-pass is part of the interactional competencies that L2 users and their interlocutors bring to any interaction. The question at interest in this study is how the passing up of repair is deployed in conversations designed for language practice. In a large corpus of such interactions, we noticed that the learners' response turns were sometimes sequentially inapposite and could thereby be taken as 'misunderstandings' of the previous speaker's turn. Yet overwhelmingly such misunderstandings did not seem to be taken as such by the expert speaker or the other participating L2 learner. Conventionalized indicators deployed by misunderstood parties such as *I don't mean X* and *I mean Y* are very rare occurrences in our material. This observation propelled the general question we want to pursue in our chapter: how does an expert speaker handle sequentially misfitting response turns when she does not (overtly) treat them as misunderstandings?

Activity and participants

The activity in question can (etically) be categorized as a conversation arranged for the purpose of L2 practice and learning, in short, conversation-for-learning. Such activities owe their existence to language educators' long-standing concern that language classrooms may not provide learners sufficient opportunities for L2-mediated conversational interaction. In order to offer learners informal out-of-class experience in L2 use, some language programmes include scheduled small-group meetings between L2 learners and one or more expert (often native) speakers of the target language (Hauser 2005; Jung 2004; Kasper 2004). Mori and Hayashi (2006) report on a very similar, student-organized activity, referred to as 'conversation table'. The data analysed for this chapter were collected as part of a two-year longitudinal study of a conversation activity called *Gesprächsrunde* ('round of talk'), offered as a credit-giving assignment for students enrolled in German 101 to 202 at an American university. The students met with a bilingual speaker[1] of German (her native language) and English three times a semester, individually or in self-selected pairs. The only instruction given to the participants was to talk in German about whatever topic they liked for about 20 minutes. No 'German Only' policy was enforced, and in fact substantial code-switching is in evidence throughout the data.

Analysis

When the speaker of a response turn displays an understanding of the preceding turn, the speaker of that (first) turn has the opportunity in the following (third) turn to ratify or contest the previous speaker's understanding of the first turn. In the second case, the first speaker may do a third-position repair (Schegloff 1992b) on the previous turn and thereby treat the co-participant's understanding as a *mis*understanding. A characteristic way in which interlocutors display that a 'misunderstanding' in their talk has occurred is for the speaker of a first turn (T1) to claim that the understanding revealed by the speaker of the response turn (T2) is problematic and reformat the original utterance in some way that may improve its intelligibility (T3). The generic third-position repair is built of four components (Schegloff 1992b):

1. Repair initiation through particles such as *oh, no, oh no*
2. Agreement with/acceptance of the action at T2
3. Rejection of understanding displayed in T2, most commonly by the form *I don't mean X* or equivalent
4. The repair proper, commonly prefaced with the repair marker *I mean*. As such, the final component performs some operation on the trouble source turn that packages the repair speaker's claimed intention (at the moment of the repair) in a more intelligible or interpretable fashion. Such

operations include a rendition of the misunderstood utterance with improved clarity, a formulation contrasting with the one used by the recipient of the trouble source, a reformulation or paraphrase, a specification of the topical matter, or an explanation of the problematic action.

As Schegloff notes, any of these components can be absent in specific instances, although the fourth component is the least likely to be omitted. For the most part, the three ordered positions T1, T2, T3 coincide with the serial ordering of turns, but other turns can intervene – for instance, next-turn repair initiations – that alter the serial order though not the structural organization of the repair sequence. In interaction among linguistically expert interlocutors, typical trouble sources that third-position repair deals with include problems of reference and illocutionary force, literal versus figurative, serious versus non-serious meanings, or trouble of hearing and memory (Schegloff 1991, 1992b). A further type of misunderstanding, more common in talk including less expert speakers though not exclusively so, is that of linguistic form, as we will see in this chapter. The third-position repair in native speaker interaction in Extract 1 provides a case where the structural organization diverges from the serial ordering of the turns. B has called in a report to a fire department.

Extract 1 From Schegloff (1987, 1992)

T1	1	A:	Now what was that house number you said =
			= [you were-
T2	2	B:	= [No phone. No.
	3	A:	Sir?
T2–1	4	B:	No phone at all.
T3→	5	A:	No I mean the uh house number, [Y-
	6	B:	[thirty eight oh one?
	7	A:	thirty eight oh <u>one</u>

At turn 2/T2 B shows that he misunderstood the reference term 'house number' in turn 1/T1 as 'phone number'. After A's next-turn repair initiation (NTRI) at turn 3, B displays the same misunderstanding at turn 4 (T2-1). At turn 5/T3, A addresses the misunderstanding with a third-position repair, composed of a repair initiating component ('No') and the repair proper in the format 'I mean'+ contrasting reference term (house number versus phone number). In this repair sequence, the agreement/acceptance component and the rejection component are absent, and the NTRI displaces the repair T3 from the serially third turn.

In the *Gesprächsrunden*, we encounter many instances in which an L2 speaker hearably misconstrues the grammatically encoded meaning of the previous turn, specifically in answer turns to questions. Hence occasions for third-position repair to address sequentially inappropriate next turns arise frequently. However, it is very common for the L1 recipient of the answer turn not to address the sequential misfit in an overt manner. On other occasions the response turn does get a repair, but an NTRI rather than a third-position repair. Although some problem in that turn is addressed in this manner it is not the turn's sequential misalignment. Finally, in some instances the L1 recipient passes up repair entirely. We will examine each type of redressive action, including its absence, in turn.

Covert third-position repair

In the first cases of third-position repair we will examine, the repair speaker omits the components that would explicitly cast the L2 speaker's answer turn as a misunderstanding of the question to which that answer is addressed. The resulting action is a third-position repair *en passant*, reminiscent of embedded (as opposed to exposed) other-corrections (Jefferson 1987).[2] Extracts 2–4 provide different versions of covert third-position repair.

Extract 2 (T2 S21 S34)

```
442   D:    [und wohnst du bei deinen eltern?
             and live    you at  your   parents
             and do you live with your parents?
443         (0.5)
444   E:    ja.
             yeah
445   D:    ja?
             yeah?
446   E:    heh heh [heh
447   D:            [und wie kommst du morgens zur uni?
                     and how come     you morning to university
→                    and how do you get to school in the morning?
448   E:    ja
→           yeah
449   D:    fährst du  mit dem auto?
             drive you with the car
⇨           do you go by car?
450   E:    nein bus=
             no bus=
451   D:    =mit dem bus, (.4) a:h ok gehst du: schonmal in waikiki zum
             strand?
              with the bus     a:h ok  go    you sometimes in waikiki to
             beach
             =by bus, (0.4) a:h ok do you sometimes go to the beach in Waikiki?
452         (1.0)
454   E:    nein
             no
455   D:    nein
             no
```

The extract illustrates a recurrent type of misfit between a question and answer turn. Dagmar's question is formatted with an interrogative pro-form (447) yet Ellen's answer (448) treats it as a *yes/no* question (e.g., 'und kommst du morgens zur uni?' (*and do you come to school in the morning?*). The next turn (449) after Ellen's response affords Dagmar the opportunity to orient to Ellen's response as a 'misunderstanding' and take action to clear it up. For instance, she could recycle her question in a more audible format or specify the referential point. The sequence could thus run as follows.

Extract 2'

T1   D: [und wie kommst du morgens zur uni?
          and how come you morning to university
          and how do you go to school in the morning?
T2   E: ja
          yeah
T3   D: nein ich meine <u>wie</u> du zur uni   kommst
          no   I   mean <u>how</u> you to university come
          no I mean <u>how</u> you get to school

In the manner of Extract 1, such a repair format would make the misunderstanding salient through the repair initiator 'nein' and the repair marker 'ich meine'. However the only repair component in Dagmar's turn at T3 is the repair proper without a repair marker (449). The repair pursues the subject of how Ellen gets to school by narrowing the general topic[3] to a specific means of transportation that Ellen is likely to use: 'fährst du mit dem auto?/ *do you go by car?*'. This format facilitates Ellen's production of a sequentially fitting response as the question is minimally answerable by a 'yes' or 'no' token. The reformatted question proves effective. Not only does Ellen's answer (450) provide a disconfirming response, for which a bare 'nein' would be sufficient, she also specifies the means of transportation she uses (bus) and thereby contributes to the development of the active topic. Moreover, Ellen's response reveals more than her understanding of the immediately preceding question; it also shows her grasp of the pertinent component of Dagmar's sequence-initial question; that is, getting to university.

It might be argued that in the absence of the 'misunderstood' party's overt orientation to the sequentially inapposite answer through repair markers and the displayed recognition of a repair by the speaker of the misaligned answer there is no repair at all, and that Dagmar simply 'ignored' Ellen's answer. But such an analysis cannot account for the systematic relationship of Dagmar's turn in line 449 to her question (447). Turn 449 essentially reissues the same question in a more accessible format by performing two operations on the original version: changing its syntactic format from an interrogative pro-form question to a yes/no question, and specifying the referential focus. The reformatted question (T3) thus addresses Ellen's mishearing or misunderstanding (T2) through two of the operations of third-position repair, although the repair turn as a whole is designed in a covert, non-salient form. As the successful outcome of the sequence shows, covert third-position repair can be an effective method of handling inapposite answers.[4]

In Extract 2 the third-position repair *en passant* is located in an environment where the talk drifts from one topic to the next in fast succession. It could perhaps be surmised that the unexposed form of handling an L2 speaker's misunderstanding may be more prevalent when coherent topical talk is difficult to sustain. However the L1 speaker does not confine covert third-position repair to the more effortful interactions. In Extract 3 L2 speaker Cindy is in the midst of a long co-constructed narrative about her family and travel in California.

Extract 3 (T12 S37)

```
417   C:   ein uh sie hat ein (1.4) vier (0.7) four story house¿
           a uh she has a (1.4) four (0.7) four story house¿
418   D:   .hh vier etagen?=
           .hh four stories?
419   C:   =ja
           =yeah
420   D:   whoa::=
           whoa::=
421   C:   =mit ein basement¿
           =with a basement¿
422   D:   whoa [:: wie viele zimmer?
→          whoa [:: how many rooms?
423   C:        [ts.
424   C:   ja (.) so=
→          yeah (.) so=
425   D:   =ze:hn, zwanz[ig?
→          = ten, twen[ty?
426   C:                [uhm tch °oh(h)° (4.2) vier >uh< fünf
                        [uhm tch °oh(h)° (4.2) four >uh< five
427   D:   fünf [zimmer?
           five [rooms?
428   C:        [fünf zimmer. (.) u:nd ah upstairs, ist (0.4) tch uhm
                [five rooms. (.) and ah upstairs, is (0.4) tch uhm
429        drei (1.0) badroom?
           three (1.0) bathrooms?
430   D:   drei badezimmer
           three bathrooms
```

Excerpt 3 continues an ongoing sequence in which Cindy describes her grandmother's property in Ohio. In response to Dagmar's question about how many rooms the house has (422), Cindy answers with a 'ja' token, which can be heard either as an acknowledgement or an affirmative answer, neither of which is a sequentially appropriate answer to Dagmar's question.⁵ In the same way as Ellen in Excerpt 2, Cindy's answer orients to the prior turn as a yes/no question ('Hat das Haus viele Zimmer?' [*does the house have many rooms?*]) rather than a question initiated by an interrogative token. The prosodic format of Cindy's next turn-constructional unit (TCU) 'so' (delivered with German pronunciation) projects continuation of the turn-in-progress, but Dagmar cuts Cindy off by offering up a guess at the number of rooms for Cindy to confirm or correct (425). By pursuing a second-pair part to her yet unanswered question in this manner, Dagmar enables Cindy to give a sequentially fitting answer (426) without overtly orienting to Cindy's prior response (424) as inapposite. Yet similar to the unexposed third-position repair in Extract 2, Dagmar's reformatted question operates on the misconstrued earlier version by specification (exemplifying). As the repair only includes two numbers without any explicit referent, Cindy's relevant answer demonstrates that she retrieved the referent from the first version of the question (422). Following Dagmar's confirmation request (427), Cindy ratifies Dagmar's candidate understanding of her answer in an allusion-confirming format (Schegloff 1996a) and continues to add further details to her description of the house. Both participants actively develop the topic of grandmother's house in this fast-paced and animated sequence, with Cindy as the owner of the information taking the lead and Dagmar helping along.

The previous two extracts showed that the expert speaker recalibrated a misconstrued question in a covert third-position repair in two ways: syntactically by transforming a first question with an interrogative pro-form to a yes/no question, and referentially by narrowing the focus of the unanswered first question through specification and exemplification. In the following extract, the L2 speaker's inapposite second pair part generates a different version of covert third-position repair.

Extract 4 (T8 S37)

```
370   D:    und warum heisst der film radio?
            and why called the film radio
 →          and why is the film called radio?
371         (.)
372   C:    radio. ja =.
 →          radio. yeah =.
373   D:    = >°ja°<. was hat das mit radio zu tun? =
            yeah what has that with radio to do
 →          = >°yeah°<. what does it have to do with radio? =
374   C:    = ↑oh↓:: uh[m
375   D:               [ist da eine radio show? °radio°
                       [is there a radio show? 'radio'
```

376 C: nein.
         no
377 D: >'nein.'<
         >°*no.*°<
378 C: uhm, (0.3) he's (0.5) Cuba Gooding junior,
         uhm (0.3) he's (0.5) Cuba Gooding junior,
379   0.8) uh:m (0.9) liebs? (.)°l:iben?°
         (0.8) uh:m (0.9) loves?(.)°l:ove?°
380   (0.3)
381 D: liebt?
         loves?
382 C: liebt (0.4) uh <u>radio</u>
         loves (0.4) uh <u>radio</u>

Prior to the excerpt, Cindy was talking about the film *Radio* that she had recently seen. In response to Dagmar's question why that film is called 'Radio' (370), Cindy repeats the title of the film, 'radio' and adds a confirmation token 'ja' (372). She thereby treats Dagmar's prior turn as a request for confirmation rather than a topic-developmental question. Dagmar's rejoinder to the inapposite answer is a third-position repair that starts with an acknowledgement of Cindy's response ('ja'), delivered *sotto voce*. In the next component, the repair proper, Dagmar reformulates the misconstrued question with a version that semantically approximates the first version: 'was hat das mit radio zu tun?/ what does it have to do with radio?' (373). The repaired question format thus varies from the repairs we have seen previously in several respects: (1) The question type remains an interrogative pro-form question, with the interrogative pronoun changing from 'warum/why' to 'was/what'. (2) The referential scope and level of specificity remain virtually unchanged so that the trouble source and repair versions stand in a near-periphrastic relationship. (3) The repair version is more colloquial than the trouble source version and its format does not appear to facilitate comprehension, considering the complexity of the composite verb 'hat zu tun/has to do' and the opaque reference of the pronoun 'das/it'. But rather than displaying difficulties in processing the repair, Cindy's emphatically marked *oh*-response indexes that she does understand the reformatted question. Generically, the *oh* particle conveys that a speaker experiences a 'change of cognitive state' (Heritage 1984). With specific reference to response turns, Heritage argues that 'oh-prefacing uniformly conveys the sense that the prior question has occasioned a shift of attention (to the matter raised by the question)' (Heritage 1998: 327). Cindy's turn-initial = ↑oh↓:: may be proposing more than one attentional shift. It can be heard as a revision of her understanding of the trouble source turn (370) in light of the repair (373) (and could thus be glossed as 'now I see what you mean'), but also as suggesting that from *her* perspective the meaning of the film title is taken-for-granted knowledge and that Dagmar's inquiry about a self-evident matter appears as somewhat inapposite. The following hesitation token suggests that Cindy is getting ready to continue her turn with a substantive response, but Dagmar overlaps with yet another question version. This time the question is constructed on the same pattern as the repaired questions in Extracts 2 and 3, namely as yes/no question that embodies Dagmar's guess at what the film title might refer to ('ist da eine radioshow? radio?/ is there a radioshow? radio?', 375). Although in her next turn (376) Cindy does no more than disconfirm Dagmar's speculation, she takes up Dagmar's quiet repetition of her 'nein' token (377) as a solicit for elaboration and with Dagmar's assistance produces a detailed and successful explanation of the film title (378–81, continued beyond the end of the transcript).

In the following extract, the minimal acknowledgement component we saw in Extract 4 is extended into a repair sequence of its own, and the repair proper emphasizes the contrast to the trouble source as understood by the L2 speaker.

Extract 5 (T10 S37)

```
274   D:   wann ist er nach Kalifornien [gegangen?
           when is  he to    California gone
           when did he go to California?
275   C:                                 [uh:m fo:r: spring: break?
276        0.8) a[h
277   D:         [ach du   gehst zu den frühlingsferien na[ch
            oh   you go    in the spring break        to
            [oh you're going to California for
278   C:                                                  [ja.
                                                          [yeah.
279   D:   Kalifornien? [wann, wann ist er (.) von =
           California    when  when did he   from
           spring break?[when, when did he go from
280   C:                [°frühlingsferien°
                        ['spring break'
281   D:   = Hawaii nach Kalifornien gegangen? jetzt
             Hawaii to    California   gone     this
           = Hawaii to California? last
282        weihnachten im dezember?
           Christmas    in December
           Christmas in December?
283   C:   ja.
           yeah
284   D:   ah:
           ah:
```

In the sequence preceding Excerpt 5, Cindy was telling Dagmar that she has to spend Valentine's Day alone since her boyfriend moved to California. After some commiseration, Dagmar inquires when he went to California (274). Although Cindy's answer (275) only includes a temporal specification ('uh:m fo:r: spring break?'[6]), Dagmar's response (277) displays that she understood the answer to refer to Cindy's future plan to go to California rather than to the past event of her boyfriend's departure as projected by the question.[7] Prefaced by the change-of-state token 'ach/oh', Dagmar's response orients to the newsworthiness of Cindy's answer while disattending to its lack of sequential fit at this point. Instead, Dagmar does an NTRI, seeking confirmation of her understanding that Cindy is planning to go to California during spring break. While the NTRI is still in progress, Cindy delivers the confirmation (278) and completes the other-initiated repair. Without relinquishing her turn, Dagmar's next action does a third-position repair (the repair proper, 279) of the yet unanswered question (274). Although the repaired version ('wann wann, ist er (.) von hawaii nach kalifornien gegangen? jetzt weihnachten im dezember?/ when, when did he go to California? This past Christmas in December?') repeats the referential scope, syntactic format and lexical selection from the first question, it features several compositional details that were absent from the first version: The interrogative pronoun is made more salient through prosodic emphasis and duplication, the personal pronoun 'er/he' receives contrastive stress, the place reference 'nach Kalifornien/to California' is elaborated to 'von Hawaii nach Kalifornien/ from Hawaii to California', and following the syntactically complete question, Dagmar incrementally adds a guess at the month of the boyfriend's departure, 'jetzt weihnachten im dezember?/last Christmas in December?' By improving the recipient design of her question through various forms of specification, elaboration and enhanced clarity, Dagmar adopts a standard method of pursuing understanding of a previously misconstrued first pair part (Kasper, 2006b; Kasper and Ross, in press; Schegloff 1992b) yet without making the misunderstanding overt through repair markers. After Cindy ratifies Dagmar's understanding of the boyfriend's move to the mainland, an extended sequence continuing the topic of their separation and mutual visits ensues.

The third-position repairs in this section have in common that they are done without bringing the misunderstanding to the forefront of the interaction. They are composed either only of the repair proper, or of the repair proper and a preceding acknowledgement of the L2 speaker's answer. The repair initiating and rejection component, or a repair marker flagging the repair proper, are consistently omitted. These covert repairs – third-position repair redux, as it were – have distinct benefits. They help the L1 repair speaker to pursue a relevant and sequentially fitting response by improving the recipient design of the repair turn over that of the trouble source turn and in this way facilitate the L2 speakers' participation in the conversation. In all instances, the repairs enable the novice L2 speakers to understand the questions the second time around and provide sequentially appropriate answers that contribute to advance the topical talk. At the same time, covert third-position repairs forego the disaffiliative practices associated with overt third-position repair and so are more sensitive to the L2 participants' face concerns. One practice of handling sequentially inapposite responses is thus not to entirely pass up third-position repairs, but conduct them *en passant* in a non-salient manner.

We also saw a case where a problem in the immediately prior answer turn was addressed before the misunderstanding of the earlier question turn. In Extract 5, Dagmar first other-initiated repair on Cindy's answer in her (Dagmar's) next turn and only proceeded to tackle Cindy's misunderstanding after the NTRI had received a completion. In this way the canonical ordering of NTRI and third-position repair was maintained (cf. Extract 1) and different, sequentially separated trouble sources were addressed.

However on occasion sequentially misaligned answer turns remain unrepaired. As in Extract 5, the L2 speaker's answer turn may prompt an other-initiation of repair by the L1 speaker in the next turn that then becomes a focus of the interaction, with the result (unlike in Extract 5) that the misunderstanding is not taken up again. Finally, an inapposite next may go unrepaired entirely, as will be seen in the next section.

Passing up (third-position) repair

We saw earlier that L2 respondents to questions sometimes treat interrogative pro-form questions as yes/no questions. In Extract 6, the actual question format and the virtual answered question are reversed from the order seen in Extracts 2 and 3. Instead of:

T1: wh-question
T2: answer to virtual yes/no question

we now get:

T1: yes/no question
T2: answer to virtual wh-question.

Extract 6 (T3 S17 S34)

182	D:	was macht ihr heute abend?
		what do you today evening
		What are you guys going to do this evening?
183		(1.6)
184	E:	erm: (3.5) >I(h) d(h)on't kn(h)ow< (1.2) ich: (.5)
		erm: (3.5) >I(h) d(h)on't kn(h)ow< (1.2) I: (0.5)
185		(ju)st hausaufgabe I guess, =
		(ju)st homework I guess, =

```
186   D:    = hausaufgaben?
            = homework?
187   E:    en fernsehen
            an watching TV
188   D:    a:h fernsehen? (1.0) siehst  du gerne fern?
            ah watch TV              watch you like  TV
  →         a:h watching TV? (1.0) do you like watching TV?
            ((Dagmar nodding head during (1.0) pause)
189         (1.6)
190   E:    h:m:, (1.2) Everwood? [I guess
  →         h:m:, (1.2) Everwood? [I guess
191   D:                          [hm?
  →                               [hm?
192         (0.6)
193   E:    ich fernseh: Everwood,
            I watch Everwood,
194         (2.1)
195   D:    °e-° was ist das?
  →         °e-° what's that?
196   E:    Everwood? it's a (.3) programme
197   D:    a:h ein: (.) comedy?
            a:h a: (.) comedy?
198         (0.6)
199   E:    not really, [just a sho(h)w heh heh
200   D:                [nein?
                        [no?
201   D:    uh huh (.4) eine talk show?
            uh huh (.4) a talk show?
202   E:    uh-un (shaking head)
203   D:    hm (.) hm (.) ich kenne das nicht
            hm     hm     I   know  it  not
            hm (.) hm (.) I don't know it
```

In response to Dagmar's inquiry about the students' plan for the evening, Ellen brings up 'fernsehen/watch TV' (187). Dagmar seizes the opportunity for a new topic by asking a follow-up question, 'siehst du gerne fern? do you like watching TV?' (188). After a 1.6 second pause, Ellen produces a hesitation token 'h:m:' proposing that she is trying to assemble an answer, and after a further 1.2 second pause generates the name *Everwood*, with try-marking intonation (Sacks and Schegloff 1979) and followed by the epistemic stance marker 'I guess' (190). Ellen thus does not answer the actual question as to whether she likes watching TV but rather the virtual question of what programme she likes (e.g., 'was siehst du denn gern?/what do you like to watch?'). In overlap with the stance marker, Dagmar indicates that she did not understand Ellen's answer and initiates repair by issuing a 'hm?' token (191). As an 'open class next turn repair initiator' (Drew 1997), 'hm?' claims that something in the preceding turn is problematic for the producer of the token without identifying the particular problem. It is therefore unresolved at this point, whether Dagmar's other-initiation of repair targets the incomprehensibility for Dagmar of Ellen's entire response or proposes more specifically that she is unfamiliar with the show entitled *Everwood*. Ellen obviously understands the latter, as she repeats her answer in a syntactically complete (though ungrammatical) form (193). The continuing intonation of the last TCU ('Everwood,') suggests that Ellen's turn is not yet complete, but when Ellen does not resume her turn after a 2.1 second pause (194) Dagmar issues another repair initiation that specifically identifies the name 'Everwood' as the trouble source (195). Now switching to English for the remainder of the sequence, Ellen clarifies that *Everwood* is a television show. Further efforts to determine the genre of the show ensue, with Dagmar pursuing an answer through specifying questions that offer candidate television genres (comedy, 197; talk show, 201) for confirmation. Yet both questions get disconfirming answers from Ellen, leaving the generic categorization of *Everwood* unresolved and ending in Dagmar's explicit sequence-closing admission that she is not familiar with that programme. While Dagmar's problem in understanding the unfamiliar referent *Everwood* is addressed through her NTRI, the sequential misfit of Ellen's answer turn remains unattended.

In this segment, the L2 respondent misconstrues a (general) yes/no question about her stance towards watching television as a (more specific) question concerning her favourite programme. This mishearing may be sequentially induced because Ellen noted in the turn prior to Dagmar's question in line 188 that she was going to watch television that evening (187), a piece of information that Dagmar acknowledges as newsworthy in her response turn (188). After it had already been established that Ellen is a TV watcher, a possible (though demonstrably not the only possible) topic component to explore could have been the kind of programme or programmes that Ellen enjoys watching. Ellen's answer (190), bewildering as it turned out to be for Dagmar, is therefore predicated on a plausible sequential logic that appears to have taken precedence over the actual linguistic form of the question in Ellen's sense making.

Finally, in some instances a sequentially inapposite response gets no redressive interactional treatment at all. Extract 7 is a case in point.

Extract 7 (T2 S8 S17)

```
403   D:   ist die oper    hier in Honolulu gut?
           is the opera in Honolulu good?
404   A:   ja.
           yes.
405   D:   ja?=
           yah?=
```

406	A:	=uh, (.3) Hawaii opera hier ist gut.
		=*uh, (.3) the opera here in Hawaii is good.*
407	D:	a::h
408		(1.0)
409	D:	gehst du auch gerne in die oper?
		go you also gladly to the opera
→		*do you like to go to the opera too?*
410		(0.5)
411	Q:	nein.
		no
412	D:	nei[n? warum?
→		*n [o? why?*
413	Q:	[uh,
414		(2.3) (Q gestures as if trying to say something)
415	A:	heh heh heh
416		(0.3)
417	Q:	uh, ich (.5) ich habe uh (1.3) ein:, auto
→		*uh, I (.5) I have uh a car*
418		(0.6)
419	D:	o::h (.5) okay aber du <u>ma</u>gst klassische musik?
→		*o::h (.5) okay but you like classical music?*
420		(0.6)
421	Q:	ja:.
		yeah:.
422	D:	j[a?
		ye[ah?
423	Q:	[ich möchte classical music
		[I like/I would like to classical music.

In the sequence preceding Extract 7, the participants were talking about Adam's musical interests. It transpired that he plays saxophone in a band and enjoys going to the opera. In further elaboration of this topic component, Dagmar solicits opinions about the quality of the opera in Hawai'i (403). In ordinary conversation, such an inquiry would very likely generate an assessment and possibly an elaborative account of that assessment. However Adam only provides a minimal affirmative answer ('ja./yes.', 404) to Dagmar's positively slanted question. By repeating the answer token with rising intonation (405), Dagmar invites Adam to elaborate. Adam responds with a syntactically complete TCU ' = uh, (.3) Hawaii opera hier ist gut/. = *uh, (.3) the opera here in Hawaii is good.*' (406) that contributes to developing the topic by substituting the generic category term used by Dagmar 'die oper in Honolulu'/ the opera in Honolulu' with the (partial) name of the institution 'Hawaii opera'. Dagmar's acknowledgment (407) does not indicate that she noticed the difference in reference terms, which actually would have kept provided a resource for further talk about the activities of the company. In the absence of local knowledge, Adam's response may appear as a pedagogic exercise in 'speaking in complete sentences' with no topic developmental import, and this is how Dagmar seems to take it. When no further comment from Adam is forthcoming after a one second pause (408), Dagmar draws Quincy into the conversation by asking whether he also likes to go to the opera (409). In ordinary conversation, subsequent solicitations of opinions and personal preferences by second or third parties typically generate aligning or disaligning positions that explicitly build on the prior talk. Moreover, in the ongoing sequence Quincy's discourse identity up to this point had been that of a listener to his co-participants' talk about the topic addressed by Dagmar's question rather than that of an active contributor. His interactional competence as an ordinary conversationalist generally and the opportunity afforded by the participation structure of the preceding sequence specifically might have enabled Quincy to provide a substantive answer to Dagmar's question. Instead a sequence parallel to the previous one between Dagmar and Adam (403–5) develops. Quincy responds minimally with a negative answer token (411), which Dagmar repeats with rising intonation and thus invites further talk on the topic (412). But in contrast to her elaboration request in response to Adam's positive answer (405), she continues her turn by soliciting an account ('warum?/why?'). In overlap with Dagmar's repetition of the answer token, Quincy produces a non-lexical turn start-up token (413) and a hand movement (414) that appears to mediate his assembling of a turn although no vocal production is forthcoming at this point. It appears then that both Dagmar and Quincy orient to Quincy's negative answer regarding his going to the opera as an accountable action. An account would seem particularly well positioned at this point because Quincy's answer runs counter to Dagmar's positively tilted question and by implication disaffiliates Quincy from Adam.

Eventually, following Adam's sympathetic laughter and a further 0.3 second pause, Quincy incrementally constructs an answer turn 'uh, ich (.5) ich habe uh (1.3) ein:, auto (I have a car)' (417). The relevance of this turn as an account as projected by Dagmar's why-question (412) appears opaque. Perhaps constrained by his limited linguistic resources, Quincy offers no further talk that might make his turn more interpretable. After a bit of a pause (418), Dagmar acknowledges the information that Quincy owns a car as newsworthy, as indexed by the 'o::h' particle (419), but does not pursue the matter any further, nor does she probe its relevance as an account for why he does not like to go to the opera. Following a 0.5 second pause that separates the news receipt from the subsequent action in Dagmar's turn, the boundary marker 'okay' (Beach 1993; Schiffrin 1987) and the resumptive contrastive connective *aber* (but) (Park 1997; Schiffrin 1987) shift the talk back to the topic of classical music (419). The *aber*-preface of Dagmar's next question as to whether Quincy likes classical music produces a contrast between Quincy's earlier revelation that he does not like to go to the opera and Dagmar's following inquiry as to whether he likes classical music. Through its declarative syntax, prosodic emphasis of the verb 'magst/like', and positive mode, the inquiry conveys Dagmar's presumption that Quincy indeed enjoys classical music, and this expectation is met by Quincy's confirming answer (421). Further talk about the topic of music follows and Quincy's uninterpretable account is passed over.

Discussion

This chapter has examined cases in which an L1 recipient of an L2 speaker's sequentially inapposite answer turn does not address the misfit in an overt manner. Third-position repair, the standard practice of dealing with 'misunderstandings', is a common method in the data set, yet the repair is done in a covert manner that de-emphasizes the misalignment of question and answer – the 'misunderstanding – focusing instead on the 'constructive' elements of the repair that advance the talk. By selecting from the complete third-position repair apparatus the more affiliative components – acceptance or acknowledgements and the substantive portion of the repair proper – and omitting the less affiliative components – the repair initiator (no), the rejection (I don't mean x) and the repair marker (I mean) as a preface to the repair proper – the repair is made unobtrusively and carries less socially stigmatizing baggage. This would seem a particular advantage for interactions with novice L2 speakers. By repairing their 'misunderstandings' *en passant*, interlocutors can keep the repair activity to a minimum without passing it up entirely. As novice L2 users are regularly confronted with their 'problems' in L2 mediated interaction to a larger extent than might be necessary for developing their interactional competencies in L2 and their identities as L2 speakers, covert third-position repairs afford a useful balance between maintaining and advancing the interaction while simultaneously paying heed to L2 users as social beings with legitimate face concerns.

As noted earlier, third-position repair *en passant* bears resemblance to embedded corrections, an unobtrusive form of other-repair that has been described in talk between fully competent speakers (Jefferson 1987), second language interactions outside of language instruction (Brouwer, Rasmussan and Wagner 2004), and second language classrooms (Seedhouse 1997a and b, 2004). In L2 classroom interaction, Seedhouse found that exposed corrections – overt error treatment that occupies centre stage as interactional business – is teachers' dominant other-repair practice in form-and-accuracy-focused activities, whereas embedded corrections are prevalent in meaning-and-fluency contexts. These distributional patterns mesh well with our observations on covert third-position repair in the *Gesprächsrunden*. Although overtly addressed misunderstandings do occur on occasion, as in interaction between highly expert speakers, the German L1 speaker puts a premium on sustaining the flow of the conversation by advancing the talk in progress through third-position repair *en passant*, a method that pushes the L2 participants' understanding difficulties in the background while enabling them to contribute to further development of the talk. Along with embedded corrections, covert third-position repair would seem a useful teaching strategy for meaning-and-fluency focused classroom activities.

We also observed that on other occasions a sequentially inapposite response turn may get an NTRI rather than a third-position repair. As seen in native speaker interaction (Extract 1) and our *Gesprächsrunden* data (Extract 5), it is structurally possible for a response turn to be the object of an other-initiated repair in next turn as well as being implicated in a third-position repair. However there is also the possibility that the sequential misalignment of a response turn is passed over once the structurally prior repair initiated in next turn is brought to the fore of the interactional agenda. In the analysed case, the passed-over sequential misfit did not seem to have any detriment to the interaction, but a proper collection of cases would need to be examined to better appreciate the possible ramifications for novice L2 speakers and their co-participants engaged in conversation-for-learning.

Finally, we examined the case of an inapposite response on which the L1 recipient passed up repair entirely, perhaps because the relevance of that response to the question it presumably addressed was particularly obscure. From the two instances in which the L1 participant passed over the sequential incoherence of the first and second pair part, it appeared that 'letting-it-pass' served to sustain the current line of talk and keep the L2 participants actively engaged. Further cases will have to be assembled in order to understand in a more principled fashion in what interactional environments participants in novice L2 interaction pass up repair of sequentially inappropriate responses and what consequences such practices may have for the interaction at hand and its opportunities for L2 learning.

Conversation-analytic research on collections of different types of actions following misaligned response turns can contribute to the long-standing controversy over the pay-offs and drawbacks of 'trouble-shooting' (Aston 1986) in interactions with L2 speakers. Our study suggests that in conversational practice activities, unobtrusive or passed-up repairs of L2 speakers' inapposite responses have distinct advantages for sustaining and developing the topical talk. However in language teaching, maintaining and pursuing a somewhat relaxed version of mutual understanding as in the *Gesprächsrunden* may not always be in accordance with the institutional agenda. As the interactional organization and pedagogical purpose of classroom events are mutually constitutive and reflexively related (Seedhouse 2004), the methods by which third-position repair is (not) done by teachers and students in different activities require close scrutiny.

Acknowledgment

This chapter was supported in part by grant no. P229A020002-03, awarded under the Language Resource Centers program (84.229A) of the US

Department of Education. We thank Paul Seedhouse for his helpful comments on an earlier version.

Notes

1. The native speaker, Dagmar, was a graduate student in second language studies and a trained language teaching professional. She was not involved in the participants' German courses.
2. Third-position repair and corrections, a form of other-repair, are structurally and functionally distinct methods of repair organization. Corrections, located in second position after a trouble-source turn, treat an element in a previous speaker's turn as erroneous, minimally by replacing it. They address errors in *speaking*. Third-position repairs address problems in a preceding speaker's *understanding* of a first turn. Both types of repair interrupt the topical talk and shift the interactional focus to clearing up the problem. But just as corrections and third-position repairs can be done overtly, as the main business of the interaction, they can also be done in a covert, non-salient form. In embedded corrections, the repair is done in a manner that does not interrupt the action-in-progress. Line 6 in the extract below is an example.

T1 S27 S37

```
1   D:  hm (.) ehm was macht ihr gern am wochenende
        hm (.) uhm what do you like to do at the weekend
2   F:  mh
3   D:  auch schwimmen
        also swimming
4   C:  hehehe
5   F:  ja auch schwimmen (.) und fußball eh amerikaner fußball
        yeah also swimming (.) and football uh American football
6   D:  ah (to C) spielst du auch amerikanischen fußball?
→       ah (to C) do you also play American football
```

   In his answer turn in line 5, Frank used a wrong lexical category, the noun 'Amerikaner' (an American) instead of the adjective 'amerikanisch'. Dagmar first acknowledges Frank's answer as newsworthy and then asks Cindy whether she plays the same sport, using the correct adjectival form 'amerikanischen fußball'. Through this unobtrusive other-repair, Dagmar corrects the error without digressing from the topical talk (Brouwer, Rasmussan and Wagner 2004; Hauser 2005; Seedhouse 2004). We will come back to the parallel between embedded corrections and third-position repair *en passant* in the discussion section.
3. Subsequent questions following a problematic response to a first question are a common interviewer practice in oral proficiency interviews. Typically, the second question speficies or narrows the focus of the first and thereby facilitates the candidate's understanding (Kasper, 2006b; Kasper and Ross, in press).
4. Extract 2 also includes three common practices by which Dagmar acknowledges receipt of apposite answers through a form of repetition: by repeating a TCU from the preceding turn verbatim with rising intonation (445) ('trymarking', Schegloff, Jefferson and Sacks 1977); by repeating a TCU with a flat or falling intonation, indexing receipt (455); and by repeating the utterance partially with modification, as in the embedded other-repair (451) (Seedhouse, 2004).

5. 'Ja' in German is highly multifunctional and can also be used in turn-initial position as an utterance preface. Therefore it bears pointing out that the micropause following the 'ja' token precludes such a hearing.
6. The rising intonation does not appear to cast the turn as try-marked. Rather, it is a prosodic feature of Cindy's (age-graded?) variety of Californian English. As in many contemporary varieties of spoken English, the final rise indexes that the speaker considers the information so marked as not shared and new to the hearer. Prosody here serves as a resource for information management (McLemore 1991).
7. The cue for Dagmar to identify Cindy's answer as a mishearing is pragmatic and not available to the analyst from interaction-internal evidence. As the current interaction took place in February, a month or so before spring break, and Cindy's boyfriend already was in California at that time, Cindy could not have been referring to him but rather to herself.

4
Invitation Talk

Numa Markee
University of Illinois at Urbana-Champaign

Introduction

In Markee (2005), I investigated how off-task invitation talk that occurred during an English as a Second Language (ESL) class that was supposed to be discussing German reunification was achieved in the interactional context of what I have called elsewhere a zone of interactional transition, or ZIT (Markee 2004). ZITs may be understood as 'talk that occurs at the boundaries of different classroom speech exchange systems. ZITs are loci of potential interactional trouble, whose structural explication is of interest to both CA and SLA researchers, and also to teachers and teacher trainers' (Markee 2004: 584).

In addition, I showed in the 2005 chapter how difficult it was for the two learners who engaged in this invitation talk to maintain off-task talk in the face of ongoing, on-task talk by the rest of the class. Finally, I concluded with some general implications for socially contexted approaches to SLA such as conversation analysis-for-second language acquisition (CA-for-SLA).

In the present chapter, I have re-transcribed this off-task invitation talk to show how the same data may be re-analysed *post hoc* as a source of information that can be used for the purpose of qualitative, performance-based assessment of naturally occurring second language conversation. The use of CA techniques for performance-based assessment is currently an under-researched area in CA-for-SLA (though see Jacoby and MacNamara 1999; Lazaraton 2002; Young and He 1998), as is an analytic focus on ordinary conversation rather than on institutional talk (Firth and Wagner 1997; Wagner 2004. But see Brouwer and Wagner 2004, and Gardner and Wagner 2004, for the beginnings of research on second language conversation). These are both issues that need to be incorporated more fully into the emerging research agenda of socially contexted approaches to SLA (see, among others, Hall 2004; Kasper 2004, 2005, 2006; Markee 2000, in press; Markee and Kasper 2004; Wagner 2004; Young 2002; Young and Miller 2004).

More specifically, in the present chapter, I show how R attempts to invite M[1] to a party (actually, two parties), and how M initially resists this invitation. This analysis shows, on the one hand, how persistent R is in his attempts to get M to produce a preferred response to this invitation (i.e., an acceptance of R's invitation by M). And on the other, it shows how M skilfully resists acceding to this invitation until the very end of this off-task talk. As I argue in the Conclusions and Implications section of this chapter, this analysis therefore provides an empirical demonstration of how CA-for-SLA methodological procedures may be used for the purpose of assessing a particular aspect of R and M's co-constructed *interactional competence* (i.e., doing invitation/declination talk). In addition, following Crookes and Schmidt's (1991) definition of motivation in terms of 'choice, engagement and persistence, as determined by interest, relevance, expectancy, and outcomes', this analysis suggests that these behavioural techniques may also be used to investigate how motivational factors such as *persistence* are manifested as behaviour in and through talk (see also Markee 2001 for a preliminary conversation analytic treatment of motivation, and the interest evinced by Dörnyei 2005 in such an application of CA techniques to motivation research). Finally, I briefly consider the pedagogical implications of the analyses offered in this chapter.

Interactional competence

Following up on Hymes's (1972) original work on communicative competence, writers such as Hall (1993, 1995a, 1995b, 1997, 1999, 2004), He and Young (1998), Young (2002), Young and Nguyen (2002), and Young and Miller (2004) have been leaders in developing our theoretical understanding of the collaborative, intersubjective nature of interactional competence. Broadly speaking, these writers approach interactional competence from various sociocultural and/or functional-systemic perspectives. In my own work (Markee 2000, 2007), I treat interactional competence as an up-dated reformulation of Hatch's (1978b) Discourse Hypothesis. More specifically, in Markee in press), I suggest that:

> Developing interactional competence in a second language includes but goes far beyond learning language as a formal system, however this concept may be specified ... More specifically, developing this kind of competence in a second language involves learners orienting to different semiotic systems – specifically, the turn taking, repair and sequence organizations that underlie all talk-in-interaction, combined with the co-occurrent organization of eye gaze and embodied actions – and deploying these intersubjective resources to co-construct with their interlocutors locally enacted, and progressively more accurate, fluent, and complex *interactional repertoires* in the L2. These *interactional repertoires* – a concept which is derived from Hundeide's (1985: 306) notion of 'repertoires of typical episodes' – consist of the kinds of extended sequences of actions

discussed by Schegloff [1989] and illustrated by the work of Golato (2002, 2003, 2005) and Taleghani-Nikazm (2002a, 2002b) on compliment responses in German and English, and telephone greeting sequences in Persian and German, respectively.

As I also note in this paper, this formulation of interactional competence: (1) is native to CA-for-SLA; and (2) subscribes to a view of learners as highly knowledgeable social actors/learners, and not to what Gardner and Wagner (2004) have called a *deficit* model of language learning.

Research setting and participants

The talk analysed here consists of an off-task invitation to a party that was issued by R to M during a class whose official topic was the reunification of East and West Germany. The site of this audio/video-recorded interaction was an intermediate undergraduate ESL class of 12 learners, which was taught at a university in the United States during Spring Semester 1992. The class lasted for 50 minutes and was taught by T, who had also written the content-based unit that she was teaching. The methodology was task-based, and utilized small group work. T is a native speaker of English; R is a native speaker of Austrian German; and M is a native speaker of Sesotho, the official African language of Lesotho.

The data

The database for this chapter consists of 141 lines of audio/video-recorded talk which lasts for a total of 3 minutes and 32 seconds. For ease of exposition, the data are presented in eight consecutive fragments labelled Fragments 1a–1f. The interaction is transcribed according to standard CA transcription conventions (Jefferson 1984a), and also includes information about eye gaze and gesture using video framegrabs. An additional symbol unique to this chapter is: { } = talk from another conversation to the one that is being analysed.

Analysis

In Fragment 1a, we can see that the task of achieving off-task invitation talk is collaboratively achieved by R and M in the sequential context of a ZIT (Markee 2004); specifically, in the interactional space created by T as she checks whether students have finished a prior phase of small group work. T does not immediately move on to another activity. At the same time, R asserts that he and M have indeed finished their work (see lines 001–13). It is in this interactional space that R initiates the off-task invitation talk analysed in this chapter.

Fragment 1a

```
001   T:    OK ARE YOU ALMOST FINISHED.
002         (2.3)
003   R:    are we finished, you are
004         finished,
005         (1.0)
006   R:    ☺<I think. so.>☺ hhh
007         (0.3)
008   R:    huh=
009   M:    =h=
010   R:    =☺huh huh huh <I↓thi̲n:k so↓>☺
011   M:    huh huh huh huh ˙hhh
012   R:    ☺˙hhh oh no:.↓☺
013         (2.0)
014   M:    this writer has a
015         [rather- com- pli-]
016   R:    [I slept five ho- ]
017   M:    this is [co- ] writer has a
018   R:           [huh]
019   M:    complicated uh,
020   R:    yea:h[(h)]
021   M:         [h ] heh heh .hhh
022   R:    (what'd I say.)
023         (1.0)
024   R:    I'm so tired I slept five hours
025         that night
```
(Spring 1992: German Reunification Data)

More specifically, in lines 014–15, 017 and 019, M attempts to continue with their previous on-task discussion of the text that he and R have been reading, but R initiates some 'mock troubles talk' at lines 016, 022 and 024–25. I refer to this talk as mock troubles talk because the trouble that is reported is not talk that deals with real troubles, as previously reported in the literature (see Jefferson 1984b). Rather, it involves the pseudo-trouble of R apparently having had too much fun for his own good recently. In effect, R is really talking about unspecified exploits in his social life outside class. By designing the telling of exploits in this way, R is simultaneously able to 'not do overt boasting', while also seeking to obtain collaborative expressions of sympathy from M and thus subsequently draw M into doing off-task talk.

In Fragment 1b, after an initial trouble-relevant pause of 0.6 seconds in line 026, M produces preferred responses to this initiation of off-task talk by R when he aligns with R in lines 027 and 031–32. More specifically, M first expresses what may be analysed as mock sympathy through the use of a very

46 *Interactional Foundations*

exaggerated tone of voice in line 027. In lines 031–32, M then draws some of the logical consequences to be expected from R having slept only five hours on the night in question. Furthermore, M also claims in lines 035 and 037 to be perennially tired, presumably from the same general kinds of causes that afflict R. Finally, note also how M and R align to this mock troubles talk through the collaborative laughter tokens produced by both participants in lines 029, 032 and, in particular, lines 033–4.

Fragment 1b

```
026          (0.6)
027   M:     a:::h. ((M uses a noticeably
028          exaggerated tone of voice))
029   R:     °huh h ˙hhh°
030          (1.0)
031   M:     you're going to collapse I think
032          hhh
033   R:     huh ehh huh huh
034   M:     heh heh huhh ˙hhh (0.3)
035          [I'm ] always ↑ti:red↓-
036   R:     [°yeah°]
037   M:     ↑ti:red↓- no(h)-↓
```
(Spring 1992: German Reunification Data)

As Jefferson (1984b) has shown, a feature of troubles talk is that it is closure-implicative. Such talk is therefore frequently followed up by a so-called *pivot*, which introduces a change to a new topic. Note, however, that there is usually also a loose topical unity between the subject of the troubles talk and what immediately follows. This organization is clearly observable in Fragment 1c.

Fragment 1c

```
035          [I'm ] always ↑ti:red↓-
036   R:     [°yeah°]
037   M:     ↑ti:red↓- [no(h)-↓]
038   R:              [˙hhh ] I mean-
039          (1.0) >there are so many things,- <˙hh
040          d'you want to join a party-?
041          tonight? We have a party in
042          sherman hall.
043          (0.3) in our do:rm.
```
(Spring 1992: German Reunification Data)

More specifically, in lines 038–43, R begins a turn made up of several turn constructional units that are heavily repaired. R introduces the turn in line 038 with an in-breath. As shown in Figure 4.1 (Framegrab 1), M and R are

Figure 4.1 Framegrab 1

looking down at their desks as R does the in-breath in line 038 in overlap with M saying 'no(h)-↓' in line 037. R then says 'I mean-' in line 038. This phrase is not only cut off but is immediately followed by an intra-turn pause of 1.0 second.

As shown in Figure 4.2 (Framegrab 2), as R says 'I mean-', M shifts his eye-gaze to look at R. But by the end of the 1.0 second pause, R is still looking down at his desk.

As shown in Figure 4.3 (Framegrab 3), as R says ' > there are so' in line 039 (notice the increased speed of delivery), he also makes a slight sideways gesture with his left arm and also cocks his head to the left. The participants' talk, eye gaze and gestures so far all strongly suggest that something new is about to be introduced into the talk by R. Finally, after another preliminary in-breath in line 039, R produces the first version of his invitation in lines 040–3.

As shown in Figure 4.4 (Framegrab 4), the verbal delivery of this invitation is visually accompanied by R looking up to direct his eye-gaze at M and by R briefly touching M on the arm with his left hand. Thus, the talk in lines 038–9 is the pivot talk to the next topic; that is, the invitation to a party. The topical unity between the preceding troubles talk and the now current invitation talk may loosely be described as 'having a good time'.

The invitation talk that ensues lasts from lines 040–3. However, as we can see in Fragment 1d, R's invitation does not go well in at least two respects. First, the talk in lines 038–40 is not done as a recognizable pre-sequence that

48 *Interactional Foundations*

Figure 4.2 Framegrab 2

Figure 4.3 Framegrab 3

Invitation Talk 49

Figure 4.4 Framegrab 4

inquires into the potential availability of M to attend a party the same evening. And second, the lack of such a pre-sequence sets up the relevance of both participants having to deal with a potentially dispreferred declination of the invitation by M (Davidson 1984; Pomerantz 1984). And this is precisely what M eventually does in the arrowed turns of lines 093–105.

Fragment 1d

```
038   R:       ˙hhh I mean-
039            (1.0) >there are so many things,- <
040            ˙hh d'you want to join a party-?
041            tonight? We have a party in
042            sherman hall.
043            (0.3) in our do:rm.
                        .
                        .
                        .
093   M: →    =>°yeah.=it's bad.°<
094            (0.3)
095   M: →    I might (0.2) go there but uh (1.0)
096      →    [I have a busy   ]
097   R:       [°(yeah there is)°]
098   M: →    week (0.3) big project for next
```

50   *Interactional Foundations*

```
099  →         week=
100  R:        =a:oh. (0.3)] ˙hhh=
101  M: →     =monday 'ti:l.
102            (0.3)
103  R:        yeah > I have a
104            par[ty tomo:rrow <]
105  M: →        [°(wednesday)°] hhhhh
```
                          (Spring 1992: German Reunification Data)

More specifically, the way in which M declines R's invitation is initially quite abrupt (see line 093), and therefore requires a considerable amount of subsequent repair work to salvage his social relationship with R. This repair work is done as an account of the circumstances that prevent M from coming to the party. Note that this account *recapitulates* what members normally do *instead* of bluntly declining an invitation, thus downgrading the dispreferred nature of the response (Drew 1984). Nonetheless, M's response does function as a declination.

As shown in Fragment 1e, R is very persistent in trying to get M to respond to his invitation with a preferred acceptance response. That is, R uses the strategy of issuing several instances of what Davidson (1984) calls *subsequent versions* (SVs) of his invitation after he produces the initial first version (V1) of his invitation:

> by virtue of the fact that the relevance of [of the turn that follows an invitation] is acceptance/rejection, an inviter or offerer when faced with a silence may examine the initial formulation that may be adversely affecting its acceptability. Given such an analysis on the part of an inviter or offerer, he or she may then subsequently display an attempt to deal with the inadequacies of the initial formulation or offer and thereby to deal with the possibility of rejection. In the instances [provided by Davidson], the inviter or offerer, following a silence, produces what I shall call a subsequent version.
>   (Davidson 1984: 104)

More specifically, in lines 040–2, R issues V1 of his invitation. In light of M's repeated silences, non-committal passing turns or insertion sequences which request more information but which also function as delaying tactics (see the arrowed turns in Fragment 1e), R issues no less than nine SVs of his invitation. These SVs occur in lines 043, 048, 052, 057, 066, 070–1, 080 and 083.

Fragment 1e

```
040  R:   v1      ˙hh d'you want to join a party-?
041       v1      tonight? We have a party in
```

```
042            v1      sherman hall.
043          → sv1     (0.3) in our do:rm.
044                    (0.3)
045   M: →             uh huh,
046   R:               beginning at nine o'clock ↑pm↓
047                    ((listing intonation)).
048          → sv2     (1.0)↓free beer↑ ((listing
049                    intonation)).
050      →             (-  -  -  -  -  -  -  -  -  -[-  -  -  -  -  -      ])
051   M: →                                          [((M nods 3x))]
052   R:       sv3     ↓dan[cing↑]((listing intonation)).
053   M: →                 [uh    ] huhm, free, (0.3)
054                    [free,]
055   R:               [yeah] yeah,
056   M: →             (0.3) ((M nods 1x))
057   R:       sv4     there's a ↓[t]/ee/[t]/jay↑ ((listing
058                    intonation.))
059      →             (0.3)
060   M: →             ↓uh uh↑
061   R:               yeah::.
062      →             (1.0)
063   M:               so people are ☺dying for you.☺
064   R:               ☺↑yeah. [(h)]☺
065   M:                       [(h)] (hhh huh huh)
066   R:               in the ↑do::rm.
067      →             (0.6)
068   M: →             ˙hhhh hh
069      →             (0.3)
070   R:       sv5-6   ((sniff)) (0.3) so: (0.2) if you
071           sv7      ↑[v]ant- (0.2) to- ↑co:me
072      →             (1.0)
073   M: →             °uhm ok°
074   R:               ((sniff))
075   M: →             >°I alrea- uh°< = where is it
076                    (0.3) in the front?
077   R:               >in sherman ↑ha:ll<
078      →             (0.6)
079   M: →             [t]sherman hall. =
080   R:       sv8     = yeah (0.3) d'you ↑know where
081                    sherman hall is↓
082   M: →             ↑uh u::h↓
083   R:       sv9     yeah (0.8) ↑nine o'clock↓ it
084                    begins.
```

```
085        →         (1.3)
086   T:              {...}
087   M: →           where is it held, (0.3) what pa-
088        →         what part of (0.2) the hall.
089                  (0.3)
090   R:             it's in the lobby.
091   M: →           in the lobby.
092   R:             yeah =
093   M:             = >°yeah. = it's bad.° <
094                  (0.3)
095   M:             I might (0.2) go there but uh (1.0)
096                  [I have a busy   ]
097   R:             [°(yeah there is)°]
098   M:             week (0.3) big project for next
099                  week =
100   R:             = a:oh. (0.3)] ˙hhh =
```
                              (Spring 1992: German Reunification Data)

Notice that in the course of doing these SVs, R also seeks to build up the attractiveness of his invitation by listing the potential benefits of attending the party. For example, using the intonation characteristically adopted by members doing lists, R tells M that there will be free beer (SV3, line 048), dancing (SV4, line 052), and a DJ (SV5, line 057). But M repeatedly withholds doing a preferred acceptance response after these turns. In addition, as shown in Figure 4.5 (Framegrab 5), by line 075, M's body language also provides visual evidence that M is about to do a dispreferred declination of R's invitation.

Conversely, by the end of this fragment, R is becoming increasingly direct in making sure that M has all the possibly relevant information he needs, including the location of Sherman Hall (SV 11, lines 080–1) and repeating the time of the party (SV 12, lines 083–4). The form of this last turn does not just repeat the information that the party is at '↑nine o'clock↓' but 'fronts' this time component to the beginning of the turn for emphasis.

In Fragment 1f, we can see that when R's invitation to this first party seems to be failing in lines 095–105, he issues an invitation to a second party the following day in lines 103–4 and 107. More specifically, in lines 095–6, 098–9, 101 and 105, M is in the process of providing an account which explains why he cannot attend R's first party. In line 097, R starts his second invitation in overlap of M's account. But in line 100, the change of state token 'a:oh.' (Heritage 1984), which acknowledges receipt of the information that M has a 'big project for next week', allows R to redesign his invitation to the second party as an on-the-fly solution to the fact that M is busy on the date of the first party.

Figure 4.5 Framegrab 5

Fragment 1f

```
095  M:  I might (0.2) go there but uh (1.0)
096      [I have a busy    ]
097  R:  [°(yeah there is)°]
098  M:  week (0.3) big project for next
099      week=
100  R:  =a:oh. (0.3)] ˙hhh=
101  M:  =monday 'ti:l.
102      (0.3)
103  R:  yeah >I have a
104      par[ty tomo:rrow<]
105  M:     [°(wednesday)°] hhhhh
106      [HUHHH        ] HUHhh
107  R:  [if ↓you want↑]
```
(Spring 1992: German Reunification Data)

Although this second invitation also lacks a pre-invitation sequence, it goes much more smoothly than the first. As we can see in Fragment 1g, M responds to V1 of this second invitation (see lines 103–4 and 107) with loud (subsequently diminishing) laughter tokens in lines 106 and 108. R aligns with M by producing equally loud laughter tokens in line 108 which also slowly diminish in volume (see the arrowed turns). And in lines 110 and 112,

M and R further align with each other through the use of smiley voice, respectively (see the double arrowed turns). In lines 115–20, R proceeds to tell M who invited him, and concludes with SV1–SV2 in lines 122 and 124.

Fragment 1g

```
103   R:        v1    yeah >I have a
104              v1    par[ty tomo:rrow<]
105   M:                 [°(wednesday)°] hhhhh
106   →                  [HUHHH        ] HUHhh
107   R:        v1    [if ↓you want↓]
108   M: →              °huhh.°=
108   R: →              =↑GHU::GH huh huh↓ (0.6)↑ghu::h
110   M: →→           hhh. (0.3) ☺to↑morrow↓☺
111                   (0.3)
112   R: →→           ☺yeah.☺
113                   (0.3)
114   M:              ☺danie[lle is right. ]☺
115   R:                    ☺[the reason- ] >no no< the
116                   reason an u::h (↑[prastic]↓)party.☺
117                   (0.6) a girl invited me
118                   and- (0.6) and- (0.2) said-
119                   bring your ↑friends with you::
120                   ↓so ˙h
121   M:              ((M nods))
122   R:        sv1   {if you [v]ant.}
123                   {(0.3)}
124              sv2   {I- it's in:}
```

(Spring 1992: German Reunification Data)

As shown in Fragment 1 h, the only reason why M does not formally accept this second invitation in next turn is that M and R's off-task talk gets interrupted by T's question in line 125, which is directed at the whole class. Fifty four lines of whole class work then follow, which have been omitted from the transcript used here because they are not relevant to the present analysis (see Markee 2005 for the full transcript). In lines 126–31, another ZIT allows M and R to transition back to their off-task invitation talk. And in lines 132–40, just as the class is winding down, M and R agree (following M's initiative in lines 132–3 and 135) to get in touch by telephone after class so that M can get the details of where the second party is.

Fragment 1h

```
122   R:    {if you [v]ant.}
123         {(0.3)}
124         {I- it's in:}
```

```
125   T:    {U::H LET'S SEE. }
            {((39 lines of transcript omitted. M and R do not
            contribute to the conversation but they listen to
            it))}
            {((15 lines of transcript omitted, in which R
            makes an extensive contribution to the whole
            class discussion on German reunification))}
126   T:    °GOOD° (0.3) ok! (0.3) ARE WE
127         ↑FINISHED,
128         (1.6)
            {((3 lines of transcript omitted))}
            ((R looks up momentarily, catches T's eye and
            immediately looks down again)).
129   T:    are you almost finished, ((to M
130         and R))
131   R:    °yeah.° hhh ((sigh))
132   M:    °first make clear I still have-
133         my number so.°
            {((4 lines of transcript omitted))}
134   R:    °yeah°
135   M:    °I still have your number so- uh°
136   R:    °you can call me and then
137         [I can say you   ]
138   M:    [((M nods twice]))
139   R:    the the address of the party
140         tomorrow.°
141         ...
```

(Spring 1992: German Reunification Data)

Conclusions and implications

I have shown in this chapter how R and M achieve off-task invitation talk on a turn-by-turn basis. Perhaps because R is trying to transition to an illicit (i.e., off-task) topic during an ESL class, he fails to engage M in a pre-invitation sequence that would establish whether M was available to attend the first party.[2] The lack of a pre-invitation sequence, perhaps combined with the fact that M seems initially intent on continuing with the assigned topic, leads to considerable difficulties in the ensuing talk that is concerned with R's first invitation.

Despite the troubles that occur throughout this talk, the data show that R is remarkably persistent in trying to get M to accede to his first invitation.[3] He skilfully uses increasingly insistent multiple subsequent versions of his first invitation as resources to get M to accept his invitation. M equally skilfully avoids being pinned down by R, until R issues an invitation to the second party. Although R again fails to preface this second invitation with any pre-invitation talk, so that we might foresee that more trouble might occur during this second invitation sequence, R changes the recipient design of the second invitation in mid-turn. More specifically, he recasts this second invitation as a solution to the problem of M not being available for a party on Monday night – thus effectively undercutting the ostensible reasons for M's initial declination of R's invitation to attend the first party. The second invitation sequence is more successful, in that M and R agree to get in touch after the class so that M can find out where the second party is. But note that, while M has successfully preserved his social relationship with R, he has not actually committed to attending the second party during the course of this off-task talk.

In conclusion, I would like to argue that this conversation analysis of R and M's off-task invitation talk in fact constitutes a qualitative, performance-based assessment of R and M's interactional competence in ordinary second language conversation. More specifically, I have shown how R and M deploy highly sophisticated communication skills in real time to achieve the pragmatic actions of issuing and declining invitations, respectively. These actions not only contextually pre-suppose each other, they are collaboratively co-constructed by the two participants on a moment-by-moment basis.

Although R fails to produce any pre-invitation sequences, both participants are notably skilful in their ability to deploy turn-taking and repair practices with split-second timing to achieve their seemingly divergent conversational agendas. The same is true of their ability to coordinate eye-gaze, gesture and other embodied actions effectively with the unfolding talk.

Furthermore, this chapter also suggests that the behavioural techniques of CA-for-SLA may be used to carry out empirically based analyses of individual psychological factors such as persistence. This suggestion is obviously quite controversial, in that psychological and social accounts of cognition are often perceived to be divergent, even irreconcilable. Nonetheless, I believe that the analyses developed in this chapter have demonstrated that there may in fact be more common ground between psycholinguistic and conversation analytic accounts of individual differences, and that further research in this area is likely to prove quite fruitful.

Finally, the analyses of this naturally occurring, though pedagogically off-task, invitation talk raise some interesting questions about the quality of on-task classroom talk. As already noted, the talk reproduced in Fragments 1a–1h is highly sophisticated. In contrast, the kind of talk that is modelled in pedagogical treatments of invitations[4] is not only typically quite stilted but also much less complex in terms of its grammar of interaction. How, then, might materials writers and teachers develop tasks that engage learners in activities that force students to produce natural, well-formed invitation sequences[5] (or other similar extended pragmatic actions) as on-task talk in ESL or EFL classrooms?

In principle, the use of simulations and information gap tasks of various kinds is likely to generate classroom talk that *may* display at least some of these qualitative characteristics. But we are still very far from knowing how to *ensure* that simulations, information gaps and other tasks generate the kind of natural, well-formed talk exhibited by R and M. Speaking to these issues, I believe that the research methodology used in this chapter can not only provide assessment benchmarks of learners' interactional competence that are based on what second language speakers of English are *actually* able to do, as opposed to what we as ESL professionals *think* they can do. But in addition, this methodology could also potentially be used as a tool for iterative materials development/teaching implementation of on-task activities. Such an approach would entail adopting curricular practices that stress the importance of ongoing *revision* of tasks, based on empirical feedback that shows how participants co-construct language learning and teaching activities as social interaction. And this would represent a major, and much needed, shift in ESL curriculum theory (particularly in the area of English for Specific Purposes), much of which has traditionally been more interested in the *development* of materials rather than in their *implementation*.

Notes

1. In Markee (2005), I identified these participants as L11 and L9, respectively. However, in this chapter, I use abbreviations for their first names because I wish to emphasize that these participants' invitation talk is done as ordinary conversation (albeit as conversation that is overshadowed by pedagogical talk), not as learning talk. However, I continue to identify the teacher as T, because her talk (which is entirely peripheral to this analysis) is pedagogical in nature.
2. An empirical possibility worth exploring is that pre-invitations are not done in (Austrian) German. At my request, my colleague Andrea Golato kindly looked through her German conversation data to look for invitation sequences, as did Carmen Taleghani-Nikazm, but neither researcher was able to locate any empirical instances of invitation sequences in their data. However, their intuitions (if such an 'unCA' concept may be invoked in this chapter) are that German speakers do produce pre-invitation sequences in naturally occurring ordinary conversation.
3. Data from another part of the same lesson involving the same two speakers show that R is equally persistent during on-task interactions.
4. See, for example, the dialogues in the unit on invitations in *Speaking Naturally*, by Tillit and Bruder (1985).
5. By 'natural, well-formed' invitation talk, I mean talk which includes all three elements of invitations: specifically, pre-invitation, invitation and acceptance or declination sequences. Furthermore, such talk should exhibit the same kind of interactional complexity that we have observed in the empirical data presented in this chapter.

5
'Broken' Starts: Bricolage in Turn Starts in Second Language Talk

Rod Gardner
Griffith University

Introduction

Turn beginnings are pivotal positions in talk-in-interaction. Two of the fundamental orders of organization of talk converge at this point: turn-taking and sequence. First, speakers have to take a turn and claim the floor: they may have been selected, or may self-select, but however the floor is allocated to a speaker, there is pressure to begin one's turn at talk. Second, participants have to embark upon some action that has been made relevant (or has to be made relevant by the speaker) within the emerging sequence. If a participant has been selected to answer a question, then an answer is relevant, and this is so not at any time, but now. A delay in the answer quickly becomes an accountable action in itself. Similarly, if one has not been selected, but chooses to self-select, this needs to be done with reference to these same two orders: an appropriate time to begin the turn, and the production of an action that is designed to be conditionally relevant within the context of the emerging talk (Schegloff 1968). For first language speakers, the complex achievements of this moment generally, but not always, run off smoothly and automatically (though not necessarily effortlessly), but for second language speakers, familiar as they may be with turn-taking and action formation from their own first languages, such an apparently effortless launching of the turn may be impeded by the greater efforts they require to draw on the linguistic and interactional resources they need to construct the turn. They know how to talk, but, as second language speakers, they may not have automatic and easy access to the grammatical and lexical wherewithal to put together their turns. Temporality is inescapable, and the pressure is to produce the turn at the appropriate moment. If a second language speaker does not have the linguistic resources to do this immediately, they will have to draw on other means. This chapter investigates how some of those resources are used by second language speakers to launch turns, in particular those turns in which they struggle to begin.

Turn beginnings in first language

In order to address this question of second language speakers' struggles with (some) turn beginnings, it is useful to consider how first language speakers begin their turns. Turns have histories. They have a pre-beginning, somewhere before the production of the first sounds of the turn, and most usually during the course of the immediately preceding turn. They then get launched, become the current turn, then move towards their end, before becoming the prior turn. As Schegloff puts it, 'some next does not merely follow its predecessor temporally but is produced in some fashion by reference to it, to *it* in particular' (1979: 267). A next turn has to be built with reference to the 'sequential implicativeness' of the prior. Bearing this history in mind, what happens at the launching of a turn?

Schegloff (1996b) poses a number of research queries about turn beginnings, some of which are:

1. What are the successive elements of the Turn Constructional Unit (TCU) (of the opening of the TCU)?

TCUs are chunks of language that speakers may use to construct a turn at talk. According to Sacks and colleagues (1974), they may be sentential, clausal, phrasal or lexical. Ford and Thompson took this proposal further by positing that TCUs 'include intonational and pragmatic cues as well as syntactic ones' (1996: 137), and that 'these three types of cues converge to a great extent to define transition relevance places (TRPs) in conversations' (p. 171); that is, places at which change of speaker legitimately occurs according to the provisions of the rules of turn-taking as proposed by Sacks and colleagues (1974). Thus a speaker not only has to construct a turn at talk, but also has to time the beginning of the turn so as to orient it to the prior speaker's turn completion, the TRP. This necessitates prediction of possible completion points, so that a speaker can gear up for a turn (e.g., by breathing in). There may also be interactional elements occurring before the start of the turn that project a turn's beginning, such as change in posture, turn of the head or shift in gaze. These pre-beginnings (Schegloff 1996b: 24) to a turn may be followed by the actual turn-beginnings, which may or may not coincide with the actual start of the TCU; for example, there may be a first verbal element such as a turn-holding 'uhm' or a conjunction, which are turn initiating (or turn beginning) without being turn launching (or turn starting). There may also be vocalizations such as throat-clearings, audible or merely visible lip-partings, audible or inaudible in-breaths. (Schegloff 1996b; Sacks, Schegloff and Jefferson 1974: 719). Alternatively, when the prior turn reaches completion there may be a silence, which can have a range of implications: it may be a harbinger of a disagreeing turn (Pomerantz 1984), or of a repair initiation (Schegloff 2000), or it may precede a delicate topic (Lerner 1999), all of which are regularly delayed. After this, one may find the first words that launch the turn itself.

2. Where do these elements occur?

This is a question for research, but one might surmise that some non-vocal elements, such as gaze shift or head turns, are likely to occur early in the pre-beginnings of a turn while the prior turn is still in progress, whereas vocalizations such as throat-clearing would tend to be closer to the turn beginning, and in-breaths may be the last action before the launching of the turn. Pauses might then occur after the launch of the turn, for example at a point of syntactic incompletion, where there would be 'maximum grammatical control' (Schegloff 1979), and thus less chance of loss of the speaker's turn.

3. Which elements 'advance' the TCU, which 'retard' it?

Once the turn has been launched, it may proceed smoothly to TCU completion and the next transition relevance place. On the other hand, as Goodwin (1981) has shown, the lack of gaze of an intended recipient may curtail the progress of the turn until gaze has been secured, and lead to repetition of initial elements, cut-offs, pauses, alveolar clicks, or the use of *uh(m)*s. Such 'retarders' might also occur if a turn-beginning is overlapped by another speaker, with hitches such as cut-offs, stutters, prosodic changes and repetitions after the overlap resolution (Schegloff 1987).

4. What are the grammatical relations between the elements?

This question, according to Schegloff (1996b) concerns not just the relations of lexical and syntactic features, but also, for example, the places at which in-breaths, clicks, *uh(m)*s, pauses, repetitions and repairs occur. In-breaths, for example, have their home as the first audible element of the turn, and repetitions follow some already uttered element in the turn.

5. What effect does self-repair in the TCU have?

Schegloff (1979) has shown how self-repair affects the course of a turn in progress by subverting the syntax embarked upon at the beginning of the turn, with implications for where, for example, the next TRP occurs, and thus the length of the TCU in progress. Self-repair can provide an occasion for avoiding potential troubles that may arise in the course of the current turn. They necessarily occur after the beginning of a turn, though they might occur very soon after the beginning of a turn.

   In terms of how turns get allocated, an incoming speaker may be selected by the prior speaker or may self-select. In the former case, the next TCU begins its state of incipiency once the next speaker has been selected (e.g., by means of naming, gaze, relevance of prior TCU to the selected speaker). In such cases, the incoming speaker will mostly locate the turn-beginning with reference to the transition relevance space at a possible end point of the previous TCU, which may come some time after next speaker selection, or may be more or less coterminous with it.

In the case of a next speaker self-selecting, there are different pressures on the incoming speaker. This is turn allocation under rule 1b, one of the rules of turn-taking proposed by Sacks and colleagues: if the next speaker is not selected by the current speaker, 'then self-selection for next speakership may, but need not, be instituted; first starter acquires rights to a turn, and transfer occurs at that place' (1974: 704). This 'first starter' provision means that following this rule 'motivates any intending self-selector to start as early as possible' (Sacks, Schegloff and Jefferson 1974: 719). This may account for what they call 'appositionals' (*well, and, but, so*, etc.) being 'extraordinarily common' (p. 719) at turn beginnings, as the incoming speaker is under pressure to come in as early as possible to secure the turn to satisfy the constraints of TCU beginnings, and doing so 'without revealing much about the constructional features of the sentence thus begun; that is, without requiring that the speaker have a plan in hand as a condition for starting' (p. 719).

The incoming speaker, whether other- or self-selected, then has the job not just to produce a TCU, with all its internal features (the words and grammar and other interactional resources), but also to do the work that shows how it fits (or doesn't) with the prior talk (or other contextual features). After the first 'word' of the new TCU there may be a smooth production of a TCU, and the early part of the TCU is a locus where links to the previous TCU may be located: these can be lexical (repetition of words from the previous turn, words from the same semantic field, intonational continuation or some other prosodic link), or by grammatical tying (cf. Sacks 1992: 349–51). Alternatively there may be what Goodwin (1981) has termed a phrasal break; that is, a cut-off just after the launch of the TCU, followed by a silence, a common purpose of which is to attract the missing gaze of a co-participant.

Thus a turn start has to locate by some means the new turn in relation to the prior talk (or some other contextual feature), and also project what is being launched by the TCU under construction. The prior turn may project a single TCU (such as a brief acknowledgement with a response turn, or a brief answer to a question) or a multi-unit turn (such as an extended accounting, or a story). A brief acknowledgement or newsmarker may occur as an 'only' in its turn, or may precede a more substantial second TCU in the turn. The new turn may be a relatively simple, brief, agreeing turn, or may be a more complex, extended disagreeing one.

Whatever the design and length of the turn being embarked upon, it is the home of an action, which is the crux of what a turn is about for speakers. This action is located in a turn, and that turn is located within a coherent sequence of turns. The material embodiment of the action within the turn is created through grammar and words and the other bits and pieces that go to make up turns. As can be seen from the above, the turn-beginning is the locus for a great variety of possible conduct, and a crucial point for establishing speakership and launching a recognizable relevant next action. Seen in this way, it is no wonder that second language speakers regularly show disfluencies at the beginnings of their turns.

Turn beginnings in a second language

Learner turns at talk are often characterized by broken starts, or bricolage: using whatever is interactionally available to launch a turn, whilst grappling with the forms of the language to achieve whatever it is the speaker is trying to say, whether that be an ordering of elements of an utterance, or finding specific lexical items. Language learners, almost by definition, do not have the full range of grammatical and lexical resources to accomplish all the tasks they may need to do in a fluent and effortless manner. As Swain notes:

> In speaking or writing, learners can 'stretch' their interlanguage to meet communicative goals. They might work toward solving their linguistic limitations by using their own internalised knowledge, or by cueing themselves to listen for a solution in future output. Learners (as well as native speakers, of course) can fake it, so to speak, in comprehension but they cannot do so in the same way in production ... To produce, learners need to do something; they need to create linguistic form and meaning and in doing so, discover what they can and cannot do.
>
> (1995: 127)

This is the view from the application of linguistic competence, so to speak, but as Schegloff, Ochs and Thompson note, 'grammar is part of a broader range of resources – organizations of practice, if you will – which underlie the organization of social life, and in particular the way in which language figures in everyday interaction and cognition' (1996: 2).

When we look at the language of second language speakers, and their struggles with language, it is important to see these struggles not simply as attempts to use grammar and lexis, but as an emerging and developing ability to engage socially in the world. On the other hand, it is necessary to recognize that the level of development of their grammar and lexis will affect the production of their turns, the ways in which they accomplish the actions they are engaged in, and how these actions are embedded in the broader interaction. The objective of this chapter is to begin to characterize the ways in which second language turns are regularly produced, and more specifically, how features such as hesitancy, repetition, abandonment and reformulation are used as resources by second language speakers, and to explore learners' conduct in social interaction in the language they are learning, in this case English.

The data used for this study is from two sources. First there are four lessons involving Korean EFL learners at an intermediate level in private language schools in Seoul, Korea (though evidence from the recordings suggests that some of these learners would better be characterized as being at pre-intermediate level). These are two small 'conversation' classes (one with two students, the other with seven), each with an English first language teacher from North America. Seventy-five minutes from these lessons have been closely transcribed. These have mostly been selected as some of the 'most conversational' sections of the lesson; that is, there is discussion rather than attention to language forms or vocabulary. The second data source is a Sydney restaurant conversation involving three first language speakers of Australian English, and two advanced second language speakers of English, a German and a Brazilian, who were visiting Sydney at the time. Forty-seven minutes of this conversation have been closely transcribed. The first of these, the classroom, is a site for institutional talk, and the second, the restaurant, is an occasion for ordinary conversation. This distinction has implications for many aspects of interactional conduct, including turn-taking, lexical choice, sequence organization, the overall structure of the interaction, and turn design (Drew and Heritage 1992). For example, in a classroom lesson, turn-taking is typically asymmetrical, with the teacher in greater control, whereas in the restaurant conversation, other factors notwithstanding (e.g., first vs. second language speaker participants), each has equal rights to claim a turn under Sacks and colleagues' (1974) rules of turn-taking. However, although the *purposes* of the turns constructed by the speakers in each of these situations may be different (e.g., for 'learning' in the classroom, for 'social relations' in the restaurant), the speakers still have to construct their turns using the resources they have, and the focus of this paper is how second language speakers regularly struggle to construct their turns.

The findings of this study are that the second language speaker, in a characteristic broken-start turn, begins the turn haltingly. The start of the turn is often delayed, (cf. Wong 2004). This may be by silence in the inter-turn space, or by turn-holding tokens such as *uhms* (called 'silence fillers' by Jefferson 1983). There may also be a turn-beginning that is abandoned, a repetition of some initial element (cf. Carroll 2004), intra-turn pauses after the turn has begun, sound stretches on an initial item, slow delivery of the talk, a next turn repair initiation, stutters and occasionally some other prosodic marking, such as soft talk, tremulous voice, throat-clearing noises, or even by abandonment of the whole turn. What then happens regularly is that the initial hesitancy terminates some way into the turn, and the rest of the turn is delivered relatively fluently and smoothly. Given the patterns of hesitancy and fluency in such turns, it is argued that the hesitancy is a result of the speaker being engaged in planning and designing the whole turn.

Of course, not all second language speaker turns show these bricolage characteristics. Some turns are delivered smoothly from the start, whilst others will be abandoned or avoided. A possible reason for the former is that the second language speaker does not struggle with the turn because there is a confluence of trouble-free (inter)actional factors and undemanding grammatical circumstances – for that particular speaker on that particular occasion. For the latter it may be that interaction and grammar converge in such complexity that the production of a turn, on this occasion, is beyond the limits of the second language speaker. The interesting question for the study of second language learning is whether those turns that reach termination after a broken start are loci of a zone of proximal development (cf. Vygotsky 1978), or 'pushed output' (cf. Swain 1985), or even, if you will, of the 'output' side of Krashen's 'i + 1' (Krashen 1985). In other words, it is, I think, worth looking at these broken starts with the possibility in mind that these may be a place at which learning is taking place.

The first extract is an example of a fairly typical bricolage turn. This comes from early in a lesson with an American teacher and two female Korean learners. In these classes the focus is on fluency, though some grammar points are often raised. In this extract, the learners have been asked to say something about what they have been doing in the previous few days. Ann begins by announcing that there were three funerals at the church with which she is associated.

Extract 1 (BS-A8-K-TR8:111)

```
001   T-Ken:    Alrigh- uh- u:hm. (0.9) so you
002             voluntee:r:ed- (0.2) *to::* (0.8) a::h to
003             attend a- (0.2) funeral ceremony.
004   S1-Ann:   Yea:h. (.) fun'ral ceremony[y.
005   T-Ken:                               [Mm:.
006   S1-Ann: -> ·hhh U:m ↑last wee:k-h (0.5) ↓uhm: (0.8) kh
007           -> uh ↑dere ↓we:re (0.3) ↑sree funerral:s; (.)
008           -> in duh churchh.
009   T-Ken:    Mm:?
010             (0.3)
011   T-Ken:    Oh; < thre[e ↑funerals?]
012   S1-Ann:             [s:r:ee funer ]rals.
013   S1-Ann:   Yes-h
```

The teacher begins with a formulation of what they had been talking about so far: a resumption after a brief interruption of their talk (a problem with the camera). The topic is well established, and I take the teacher's turn to be a nomination of Ann to continue talking on the topic. Initially, Ann confirms the formulation, the teacher acknowledges, and, without delay, Ann launches her next turn.

Note how she starts her turn in line 6: the first element is an in-breath, a perfectly normal start. This is followed by a slightly lengthened turn-holding *um*, which tells the others that she is in her turn. Nothing has been said so far, but she has diminished the likelihood of competition for the floor from the teacher or her fellow student. This is followed immediately by an expression of time, *last week*, thus further securing her turn: she now has launched a TCU with a first lexical element. This allows her to pause at what Schegloff (1979) terms a 'point of maximum grammatical control'. For the next 2.2 seconds she says nothing more that is substantial: she hesitates in a fairly major way, with a half-second silence, another turn-holding *uhm*, a silence of 0.8 seconds, a guttural noise *kh*, and a brief turn-holding *uh*. There is also some, though not very marked, sound stretching (drawl), another resource for slowing down the turn.

Typically, as Jefferson (1989) has shown for ordinary conversation, a turn with a silence of about one second or longer would be vulnerable to incoming talk from another participant, but here Ann deflects potential incoming speakers with two turn-holding tokens (the *uhm* and the *uh*), and a brief guttural noise (the *kh*). Neither silence is allowed to grow beyond a second. In fact in the whole Korean EFL data set, only seven intra-turn silences (or pauses) in 57 broken-start turns are allowed to grow to beyond about 1.2 or 1.3 seconds, despite this being institutional talk in a pedagogical setting (remembering also that these examples are taken from 'conversational' segments of the lessons). In the restaurant conversation, there are a mere five pauses that are longer than just over a second in 70 turns. Overall, in these turns, there are over 420 pauses of silence. So here we see a very strong orientation, even in these troubled starts, to keeping silences down to around a second. The silences are kept down, mainly, by turn-holding *uhm*s and sound stretches.

From this point, Ann delivers the rest of the turn relatively smoothly, albeit with elements of second language speakership in the pronunciation. There are two brief pauses (of 0.3 seconds and a micropause). In this latter part of the turn, another vulnerability can occur. Jefferson has shown that one locus for simultaneous talk caused by an incoming speaker starting well before a transition relevance place is what she calls progressional or hitch overlap: as she puts it, 'hitches generate recipient activities' (1983: 27), by which she means if a speaker pauses in their turn, or begins stuttering or repeating, these are loci where current recipients might begin talking. If we consider that most of these turns by second language speakers with broken starts become much more fluent once they are underway, then we can see that the vulnerability to incursion by another speaker is reduced. Thus designing a turn so that it is hearably launched (with a turn-holding *uhm* and/or an initial lexical element), then pausing at a point of maximum grammatical control (sometimes massively so), but not allowing silences to grow beyond about one second, and then launching the rest of the turn relatively fluently, the chances of losing the turn to an incoming speaker are greatly reduced. Looking at Extract 1, we see massive hesitancy in the early part of the turn, and relative fluency in the latter part.

It can also be noted that there were no words in this turn that would have caused Ann difficulty, as all the words that come after the slow start were ones she had been using earlier in this passage of talk. Broken-start turns by second language speakers which are part of planning a whole turn need, of course, to be distinguished from word searches, which are a regular feature of first language talk (cf. Goodwin and Goodwin 1986; Hayashi 1999; Lerner 1996; Schegloff, Jefferson and Sacks 1977). For English, word searches indicate trouble in producing the next item, typically through sound stretches, cut-offs, turn-holding markers such as *uhm*, and pauses, which are the same resources used by these second language speakers in their broken starts. Indeed for English, Lerner notes that 'many turn units that end up containing word searches are designed in such a way that the search is placed near the end of the unit' (1996: 262). This may be something which distinguishes these second language bricolage turns, where the hesitancy is very regularly at or soon after the beginning of the turn, with the remainder of the turn being relatively fluent. With this in mind, it may be claimed that Extract 1 is an example of a struggle to produce the complete turn, involving whole-turn planning and not a word search.

In fact, in word searches, unlike the typical second language broken-start turn, the hesitancy and struggle with expression can occur anywhere in the turn. One task is to demonstrate criteria for distinguishing between these two types of turn. The second example involves an advanced second language speaker, Edina, in the restaurant conversation, who does a number of tries to find the country name *Persia*.

Extract 2 (BS-B35-XcultBurgess:2054)

```
001   Colin:     I mi:gh' check , = [that's dre]a:dful.
002   Roberta:                     [ Yea::hn. ]
003              (2.1)
004   Edina:     -> Today I ta:lked to a gi:rl;=
005              -> ↓f:ro:m:::::; (1.1) Pe:rsiuh? (0.5)
006              -> °Pe:rsiuh.°
007   Colin:     > Whu- fr-[fr'm whe:re,]= ↑sorry? <
008   Denise:              [W h e: r e ; ]
009   Edina:     Pe:rzien:¿
010              (1.1)
011   Denise:    Persia:¿
012   Edina:     (Ira:n),= Pe:rsia¿
013   Denise:    Pe↑r[sia.
014   Colin:         [Oh;= ↑Pe:rsia.
015              (.)
```

The reason for considering this to be a word search is that the hesitancy does not come initially, as the turn starts fluently. The hesitancy begins with a long sound stretch on *from* and a silence, then a try-marked *Persiuh* (rising terminal pitch direction), with German pronunciation. She follows with more tries, including the actual German word, *Persien*. When Denise recognizes the country in 011, Edina comes back (though hearing is uncertain) with an alternative name *Iran*, and then, benefiting from the scaffolding supplied by Denise, with a more native-like version, *Persia*.[1] It can be seen here that the problem word is, as Lerner predicts, placed not only near, but at the end of the turn.

The phenomenon of broken starts in the turns of the second language speakers, such as the one seen in Extract 1, was found to be commonly present in the data used in this study. These struggles with turn beginnings occur most commonly when second language speakers are asked a question (usually by the teacher or a first language speaker) requiring an extended answer or invited to produce some other kind of telling, though they also occur, to a lesser extent, when the second language speaker self-selects. As we saw in the first extract, there appear to be two steps in the construction of these turns: first the speaker takes the turn, following rule 1(a) as formulated by Sacks, Schegloff and Jefferson (1974: 704): 'if the turn so far is so constructed as to involve the use of a "current speaker selects next" technique, then the party so selected has the right and is obliged to take the next turn to speak, no others have such rights or obligations, and transfer occurs at that place.' Second language speakers, though, will often have a problem at this point, with a clash occurring between the requirements of the turn-taking system to speak when selected, and a possible difficulty in being able to say what they want to say (formulate the action they have been asked to undertake), due to their being learners with developing grammars and vocabulary. They regularly deal with this clash by demonstrating their presence in the turn, and their attention to the interactional requirements and developments, through the use of a variety of resources, such as those set out above. So the second step is to hold their turn, using these resources until they have designed the turn sufficiently for a coherent response – or not.

Regularly, though, second language speakers will produce turns that are fluent throughout, as in Extract 3. The class had been discussing basketball in Canada. The teacher is a Canadian national. Dean, whose turn in lines 007–8 is targeted, is one of the most active students in this class, and his proficiency is amongst the highest, based on the evidence from the recordings.

Extract 3 (BS-K-TR12:810)

```
001   T-Barry:    so I wa:n' >everyone so but- (.) ↑C:anada
002               is ay uh- very importent country.
003               (0.8)
004   S?:         Mm-h.
005   S7-Dean:    Hhuh ·hhuh (.) huh
```

```
006   T-Barry:      fer tha:t rea:s[on.
007   S7-Dean:  ->            [Actuarry (.) ↓duh:
008             ->  baske'ball is not- popul'r in °Can'da°.
009                 (0.6)
010   T-Barry:      uh- it's ↑s:tarding ↓tuh be more po:pular. <
011                 b't we only have a few tea:ms,
```

Barry, the teacher, is claiming that Canada is an important country in the history of basketball because the inventor was Canadian. Dean responds to this with what is, at least in some respects, a dispreferred, challenging turn, because the implication of what he is saying is that Canada is at least in some respects not so important, as it is not a popular sport there. Dean starts early in terminal overlap with the teacher's turn, and then delivers his turn fluently from the start, with only a micropause at the beginning, and some minor sound stretching on *duh*. One reason for the fluency is Dean's relatively high proficiency. The words and structures of this turn are at a level he can deal with. Basketball is the established topic, and the words 'popular' and 'Canada', as well as 'actually', appear to be within his established personal lexicon. Furthermore, the grammatical construction, with subject, copula verb, complement adjective and simple prepositional phrase, does not present problems for him. It can also be noted that he has self-selected here, rather than been selected by the teacher. This would have given him the opportunity – which he may or may not have used – to plan his turn well before his start, as he was not put on the spot by having to produce a turn immediately. We might say that rather than being in his 'zone of proximal development' (Vygotsky 1978), this turn is within his 'zone of comfort'. So if the words and structures required for the production of a turn and action are within the speaker's capabilities, then the utterance is likely to be produced fluently (though often relatively slowly compared with first language speakers). If the turn requires words and structures that are at or near their current capabilities, then broken-start turns are more likely to be produced. If speakers' current capabilities are not sufficient for them to produce a fluent turn, then it is likely that the turn will either be abandoned completely, or the first attempt will be abandoned, and another – usually simpler – way of producing the turn will be attempted. It may also be the case that a turn is avoided altogether, which is difficult if the speaker has been selected, but is likely to go undetected if not.

In fact, abandoned turns do not occur at all in the data set. Extract 4 is the closest to such a case. This comes from a more pedagogical sequence in the Korean EFL data. Hopi has been selected by the teacher to produce an evidential sentence using 'it looks as if', or 'X is supposed to be'.

Extract 4 (BS-K-TR14:678)

```
001   T-Barry:                 [Y:ou have to talk aboud a
002                  reputa:tion;= some- specific thing:. (0.2)
```

```
003                  talk about E:rin's (fla:t);
004                  (6.2)
005    S4-Hopi:      American peo:ple:, (0.7) ↓u:h (5.0)
006                  u::*::h* hhooh (.) going:- (.) a:h_ (1.0)
007                  easy- (0.2) u- (1.2) uh- (0.4) two:-u (.) –
008                  u- (1.0) two American;= people:, ·hhh go to
009                  be:d, (.) und- *u-* (.) uh-wid duh [sa:me be:t; ]=
010    S?:                                              [-eh hih hih]
011    S4-Hopi:      =°-as°h i:f-u dey hafto- (0.4) s:tudy'ng (0.4)
012                  bible:.
013                  (0.3)
014    S?:           hhh-hh huh-huh-huh (.) ·hhh h[hh
015    T-Barry:                                   [↑O:↓ka:y;=
016                  ↑that's ↓good-.
017                  (0.4)
```

Initially there is a very long inter-turn gap of over 6 seconds. Then the turn not only gets off to a broken start, but it remains broken well into the turn. First a lexical element is uttered (*American people*), after which there is a pause, a turn holding *uh*, and then a massive 5-second pause, which projects a possibly worse than normal trouble with the turn start. Such a massive intra-turn pause is unlikely to occur in ordinary conversation. Indeed, in the restaurant conversation the longest intra-turn pause is 2.8 seconds, and that is by one of the first language speakers. The pause in this extract is a marker of its institutionality: the participants here are oriented to providing learners with space and time to produce their turns.

Without going into a detailed analysis of Hopi's turn, what follows is highly troubled, with numerous pauses, cut-offs, turn-holding *uhm*s, several self-repairs. But even here, it can be noted that the end of the turn is produced relatively fluently, from line 8 to 12. One way of considering this turn is that the broken start is very extended, lasting more than 16 seconds.

Conclusion

In this chapter I have presented evidence of a distinctively second language speaker turn construction, in which the turn beginnings are hesitant, starting with a turn-holding *uhm* or an initial lexical item or phrase, which is then typically followed by a range of turn-retarding elements such as further *uhm*s or other non-lexical sounds such as throat clearings, cut-offs, and pauses of silence, and less frequently self-repairs. Rarely do the silences extend beyond a little more than just over a second. Such broken starts appear to occur only if the utterance being produced is at or beyond the speaker's zone of proximal development. These troubled starts always, in the data to hand, sooner or later get going and become more fluent. This suggests that the broken starts are used to plan the turn: to put together the words and structures required to do the action being undertaken, and overwhelmingly, a resolution of the trouble is achieved by the intermediate and advanced second language speakers used in this study.

It is also the case that most, but not all, broken starts occur when the speaker of the turn has been selected by another; in other words, when there has been no time to plan the turn. These speakers have to deal with a number of contingencies. Because they have been selected to speak next, they are required to produce a turn immediately, but they also have to construct a relevant next action using the linguistic (phonological, lexical and morphosyntactic) and interactional resources to hand. They do on occasion receive help from the teacher or other learners, as can be seen in Extract 2, but regularly, particularly in the classroom, they are given space to struggle through to the end without any verbal help or scaffolding from the other participants. If they do not have immediate access to the linguistic resources, they will show their availability to talk by non-linguistic means, until they are ready to produce the turn more fluently.

The purpose of this chapter has not been to argue that bricolage turns *are* sites where learning takes place, but to identify a regularly occurring type of turn construction in second language speaker talk. It has also focused on the struggle to construct the turn, rather than the (at least equally important) sequence in which the turn occurs. It is, nevertheless, important to consider how bricolage turns might be sites of learning. Lantolf and Thorne (2006) provide a theoretical basis for approaching the problems of understanding how second languages develop, and what follows is indebted to them. As Ellis says, 'if we want to understand language acquisition, first we need to be able to observe language acquisition' (1999: 31). In a similar way to how 'private speech' (Ohta 2001) might be seen as evidence for acquisition, these bricolage turns, in which a speaker is not yet capable of fluent production, may be a place where 'acquisition' comes close to being observable. The hesitations, restarts, re-formulations, and self-corrections we see in these turns may be evidence for this. The second language speaker would appear to be at an interface between the already established level of development in language, and the zone of proximal development; that is, the 'level of potential development' (Vygotsky 1978: 86). This level is achieved under the guidance of those who know more: teachers and other first language speakers, or more capable peers. Bricolage turns are not *beyond* their speakers' capabilities, as these turns do in fact get spoken, but, as Vygotsky puts it, they are in a 'process of maturation', 'in an embryonic state', and can be seen as ' "buds" or "flowers" of development rather than the "fruits" of development' (1978: 86–7). As Dunn and Lantolf put it, 'L2 learning is about gaining the freedom to create', and 'accents, (un)grammaticality, and pragmatic and lexical failures are not just flaws or signs of imperfect learning but ways in which learners attempt to establish (new) identities and gain self-regulation through linguistic means'

(1998: 427). If internalization, the way in which 'humans gain control over natural mental functions by bringing externally (socioculturally) formed mediating artefacts into thinking activity' (Vygotsky 1978), is occurring in these bricolage turns, it is as an emergence of 'active, nurturing transformation of externals'; that is, expression mediated through the artefact of language, 'into personally meaningful experience' (Frawley 1997: 95).

Thus these broken-start turns can be seen as potential loci for learning. These are places where second language speakers are not producing readily available chunks of language in fluent turns, but are struggling with their language. They are in the spotlight in the interactional space of shared cognition, pushing their output to its limit.

Note

1. An important question here is whether this is a potential site of learning. There are grounds for claiming that this word is within Edina's zone of proximal development, as she shows that she 'almost' has it. She is helped ('scaffolded') by Denise, she imitates her pronunciation, and the question is whether through this she then internalizes the pronunciation of the word. These issues are taken up in the conclusion.

6
Doing Language, Doing Science and the Sequential Organization of the Immersion Classroom

Simona Pekarek Doehler and Gudrun Ziegler
University of Neuchâtel and University of Luxembourg

Introduction: talk-as-activity

Nothing is real unless it is observed.
(based on Erwin Schroedinger, *Mind and Matter*, 1958)

Second language talk admittedly is not quite like first language talk. This, however, does not mean that second language (L2) speakers do radically different things from first language (L1) speakers, neither does it imply that second language talk needs to be analyzed according to different principles than first language talk (see the papers collected in Gardner and Wagner 2004). One interesting fact is that second language speakers, along with first language speakers, when engaging in talk-in-interaction, also engage in accomplishing locally relevant, interactionally coordinated activities; they are active co-participants in organizing both the communicative contents of talk as well as the activities accomplished by talk. Thereby, they also participate in creating occasions for learning.

In this chapter, we are interested in the interconnectedness of these different organizational levels of second language interaction as they are deployed in an accountable way within a specific interactional situation, namely the bilingual science classroom. The analysis of the interconnectedness of 'doing science', 'doing language' and sequentially organizing activities demonstrates that the traditionally accepted separation for second language interactions between work or focus on communication – that is, the exchange of some communicative content – on the one hand, and work or focus on language (or language forms), on the other hand, is misleading. By categorizing communication on the mere basis of its contents, such a binary distinction hides from our observation relevant characteristics of second language interaction, some of which are crucial to (our understanding of) how participants jointly configure occasions for learning.

Our opening quotation, taken from the seminal work of Erwin Schroedinger, one of the founders of modern quantum physics, resonates with Harvey Sack's point about the primacy of empirical observations for any theorizing or understanding of social interaction (cf. Sacks 1984: 25, and 1992: 271). This type of observation – be it related to the physical or to the social world – can, and often does imply going beyond generally assumed categories, dichotomies or frameworks of analysis. Our empirical investigation of how 'doing science' and 'doing language' are accomplished throughout courses of jointly managed activities in the foreign language classroom states the case for reconsidering the nature of these very doings as well as some of the analytical categories at hand.

This is most visibly the case as regards the very separation between focus on communication on the one hand, and focus on language form on the other. One major concern within the extended literature operating with the binary notion of 'focus on form' *versus* 'focus on communication'[1] (for overviews, see Doughty and Williams 1998; Gass 1997; Oller 2005; but see Bange 1992, for a different argument) is the question as to what extent and on behalf of which language features attention is drawn to 'form' (or 'forms') in second language interaction. To briefly illustrate this point, let us look at Extract 1, taken from a longer segment (Extract 2, Section 3). In this segment taken from a biology lesson, the class is reviewing the phenomenon they were studying during the last lesson.

Extract 1

C: = Class, J: = John, P: = Peter, T: = Teacher, X: = Xenia

51 T: which creature is it
52   which kingdom or which group was it,
53 X: °it is a unicellular°=
54 T: =it is unicellular good, (.) what
55   is the other word for this
56   unicellular organism, (.) [peter
57 P: [(it is) protist . hm=
                              (immersion UB1GL1, 040202_1)

Following a binary view of focus on form and focus on communication, the extract can be interpreted as comprising in the first lines a stretch of talk focusing on content (51–53/54), which then occasions a focus on form: the content-focused reply of the student (53) triggers a change of the teacher's orientation from communicative content to form(s) (54) which in turn leads to an extended focus on form (54–7), centred on vocabulary.

We believe that while such a binary vision of communicative content on the one hand and form(s) on the other hand – and even more so communication on the one hand and focus on forms on the other – might be useful for practical purposes within a more pedagogically motivated perspective on interaction in the classroom (e.g., Lightbown 1998), it clearly underestimates the complexities of the interactional work that is being accomplished in second language interactions.

Two major assumptions underlie this vision. The first is a definition of language learning as the acquisition of linguistic forms. This is mainly seen through the analytic focus many studies put on the object of form-negotiations (e.g., lexicon, grammar, see Extract 1), rather than on the communicative mechanisms which underlie such negotiations, which trigger them or which configure occasions favouring their occurrence. These, however, might be a central component of what the learner has to develop in order to both communicate and further learn the language. The second critical point is a view of communication that reduces it to the mere exchange of communicative contents, according to which talk is characterized as 'talking about' linguistic or non-linguistic objects, while considerations about *talk-as-activity* are completely left out of the picture. These assumptions, then, along with the very dichotomy of 'focus on form' and 'focus on communication', reflect a view of language (and language learning) as primarily being (about) form(s) which goes hand in hand with a view of communication as information transfer. Our own position strongly contrasts with this view.

The reason for rejecting any dichotomy between content-focused and language-focused talk lies in a fundamental characteristic of talk: *talk-about* does not equal *talk-that-does* (Schegloff 1992a), as has been widely documented in CA research. That is, talking about a given content can imply (and in fact regularly does imply) a wide range of activities far beyond mere talk about that content: it can involve regulating role-relationships, categorizing each other as novices or experts, managing agreement or disagreement, moving into or out of specific activities and so on. The explicit content of talk ('talking about X') is only one potential indicator of what participants actually orient to: participants may orient toward language without explicitly focusing on language (this has for instance been evidenced in the extensive literature on embedded corrections, going back to Jeffersons's 1987 seminal paper; see most recently Brouwer, Rasmussen and Wagner 2004). Also, participants may orient toward academic content or pursue other activities, while highlighting problems of grammar or vocabulary (which, as we will see, is the case for Extract 1). For L1 conversation, Goodwin (2000), for instance, has shown how repair can function to attract gaze, Schegloff (1996b) how repeats of linguistic tokens from another speaker's turn can deploy agreement and, in another paper, how same-speaker recasts serve to manage turn-taking (Schegloff 1987). As regards second language interaction, several studies have evidenced how the manipulation of linguistic objects is intrinsically linked to methods for achieving co-participation and co-membership (Kasper 2004; Kurhila 2004;

Mondada 1999; Wagner 1998) and more generally to dealing with the organization of interaction (Markee 2004; Mori 2004).

As a consequence, rather than focusing in this chapter on talk as content or language(-form(s)) as two distinct and distinguishable levels of (classroom) talk *per se*, we are interested in *how participants' 'doing science' and 'doing language' are interconnected*, and – maybe more importantly – *how these very doings are organized to accomplish other types of locally relevant activities, including configuring occasions for learning*. By doing so, we wish to shed light on some ways in which language, and in particular participants' orientation toward language, is embedded in and structured by the wider practices of talk-in-interaction. One interesting aspect of the empirical site (the immersion classroom) we are studying here is that it is explicitly designed for embedding second language related work into the study and discussion of some academic subject matter. Our analysis pursues two closely related objectives:

First, we wish to provide empirical arguments that strongly relativize a binary and unidirectional view of the orientation toward content on the one hand and toward language form(s) on the other. With this objective in mind, we will concentrate on the following two issues:

- How are doing science and doing language sequentially organized in the second language classroom? What methods do participants deploy in order to move from one to the other or to manage simultaneous orientation toward both? And how do they deal with the problem of coordinating their mutual orientation toward doing the same thing; that is, being engaged in some kind of jointly agreed upon activity?
- How do participants, by deploying the relevant methods for doing science and doing language, also engage in doing other things, especially configuring activities for learning by, for example, enacting themselves as learners or experts, students and teachers, moving from one topic or activity to the other or coordinating their mutual activities?

On this basis, and second, we wish to provide further empirical grounds that feed into a radically different understanding of language use and language learning from the one sketched above – an understanding of learning as a socially situated practice that is currently advocated by interactionally and socioculturally oriented approaches to second language acquisition.

The immersion classroom and beyond: learning-as-activity

Within second language research, the immersion or bilingual classroom seems to hold a special place as it is often said to overcome the aforementioned dichotomies, and more generally the 'language-as-system' instructional orientation, by allowing for a more integrated view of working on language, communicating and also socializing in a given linguistic and social context. Thereby, the immersion classroom provides a zooming effect on the deployment of activities, and in particular what is largely labelled 'communicative activities', within the second language classroom in general.

It may be (as our first observations suggest) that the specific intensity of such interrelations is particular to more advanced classrooms as regards the target language. More importantly, exactly with regard to advanced learners, such interrelations are a central characteristic of instructional settings far beyond the immersion situation. As a matter of fact, very similar findings have been provided for more traditional classrooms within communication-oriented activities (cf. Mondada and Pekarek Doehler 2004, and Pekarek Doehler 2002, for advanced French second language literature discussions in traditional high-school L2 instruction).[2]

The somewhat poor outcomes of traditional language classroom teaching methods contributed to implementing the now common practices of both communicative activities in the second language classroom and (at least partly) bilingual classrooms, especially in upper levels of secondary schools. The essentially linguistic and acquisitional motivations for immersion classrooms do not contribute to highlighting the interactional work that is being done throughout a lesson, nor do they point to the interrelation of language and academic work that it involves. This very fact is reflected in the dominant research in the field (cf. Baker 1996; Tarone and Swain 1995) that only recently started to systematically explore the interrelationship between linguistic and non-linguistic (i.e., academic) knowledge (see Mercer's 1995 study and more recently Gajo 2001, as well as Kress et al. 2001). However, systematic fine-grained interactional studies of this interrelation and of the relations between linguistic and academic work are still lacking (but see Kanagy 1999).

As to our own purpose here, we view the immersion classroom as an empirical site that allows us to investigate certain issues that are centrally at stake in many second language settings, namely the situated coexisting orientation of participants toward language, content and sequentially organized activities.

With this analytic focus, and in line with the general orientation of the contributions collected in this volume, this chapter wishes to feed into recent discussions within and between conversation analysis and sociocultural theory on the complex organizational patterns that underlie second language instructional activities, and hence configure opportunities for learning. One of the pervading empirical observations emanating from this line of research is that instructional 'tasks', and hence classroom practices, emerge as locally configured, jointly negotiated and sequentially organized activities (Coughlan and Duff 1994; Mondada and Pekarek Doehler 2004; Mori 2002; Ohta 2001; Pekarek Doehler 2002; Ziegler 2004) – that is, they emerge as tasks-as-activities that do not strictly – and sometimes do not at all – follow pre-planned tasks-as-workplans. This implies, for instance, that the learner's participation in the organization of activities, in the configuration of participation frameworks, in the negotiation of identities or membership categorizations, and in the sequencing of actions is coextensive with his co-participation in the configuration of instructional activities and learning opportunities. Also, what we see at stake in second language learning is essentially the development of a sociocultural competence through the continued participation in oral practices of a group (see Hall 1993; Lantolf and Pavlenko 1995), which is in line with Lave and Wenger's (1991) notion of learning as participation; we understand the empirical site of our study – the immersion classroom – as a locus of both language and school socialization.

Doing science, doing language and sequentially organizing activities

In this section, we present a detailed analysis of a lengthy extract of interaction taken from a larger database which consists of eight immersion classroom lessons that have been tape-recorded over a period of 12 months, with a three- to four-month interval. All lessons come from the same class that was split into two equal groups of about ten students each, so that the teacher taught each lesson twice. It is a high-school class in German-speaking Switzerland, participating in a pilot programme that leads to a so-called bilingual high-school degree: students follow selective branches in English (in our data: biology) while they attend other branches in German. Students are 15–16 years old and have had traditional English instruction for three to four years.

The following extract (extract 2), which includes extract 1 (section 1) is taken from the first minutes of a biology class. The class opens with clarifications about an upcoming exam and then moves on to identifying the biological phenomenon to be discussed.

Extract 2
A: = Anna, B: = Ben, C: = Class, D: = Daniel, J: = John, M: = Michelle, P: = Peter, T: = Teacher, V: = Vicky, X: = Xenia

20 T: ahm: and also (.) the contents of this
21   test will not include (.)
22   classification, so this is a bit °lighter and° (.)
23 A: will be [not?
24 B: [no/
25 T: not classification (1.6)
26   are there any questions about the test,
27   (2.0)
28 A: °question°
29   (2.6)

30	T:	nadine did the test copy come in, (.) have
31		you got the test
32	N:	°mmh=h°
33	T:	°cause later you (can come) come we can talk
34		i will show you about this°
35	B:	°( )°
36		(1.2)
37	T:	okay . so we will continue
38		on looking at living organisms (.)
39		can you remind me WHICH? (.) organism
40		do- did we look
41		at in the practicum (.) last time (.)
42		can you remember what it was?
43		(0.4) what was this little organism, JOHN?
44	J:	[pariKium]
45	T:	yes, (.) in english pronunciation
46		(it')s- (.) < paramecium >
47		(.) yeah john? good,
48		yes: and what sort of (.) creature
49		do we call this, (.)
50	C:	((noise 2.5))
51	T:	which creature is it
52		which kingdom or which group was it,
53	X:	°it is a unicellular°=
54	T:	=it is unicellular good, (.) what
55		is the other word for this
56		unicellular organism, (.) [peter
57	P:	[(it is) protist (.) hm=
58	T:	=protist yes good protist, this is
59		one term that you see used
60		for a unicellular organism good protist (.) or
61		protista is
62		another word we (could have mentioned),
63		(0.4) (.) okay? so we are
64		going to look at a more dangerous (.)
65		protist (.) unicellular organism
66		today in a theory lesson, (.) because (with)
67		these dangerous cuts won't really
68		want to see it under a microscope
69		°yes° it's dangerous (.) ahm and: it causes
70		malaria (.) what is
71		malaria, (1.3) vicky=
72	V:	=ah it's a disease
73	T:	yes, (.) what kind of disease or

74		what symptom what do you know
75		about malaria (.) °anything else about
76		malaria° (2.0) perhaps eh michelle
77	M:	ehm it's a fever i think [°and it°
78	T:	[yes
79	M:	and it comes from time to time again
80	T:	good yes . ahm: there are regular
81		temperatures the person or
82		fever the person suffers
83		from good (.) ahm: any other ideas about
84		malaria (2.4) nadine
85	N:	ehm it goes from person to person
86		by a fly °I think°
87	T:	yes (.) it is transported we call this
88		transportation by a vector . it it-
89		what kind of fly: or insect is it,
90	D:	mosquito
91	T:	well done (.) it is (.) the mosquito, (0.2)
92		so this mosquito carries
93		this unicellular organism which creates
94		this temperature or fever (.) in
95		a person, (.) so we are going
96		to have a look (.) at (.) this unicellular

(immersion UB1GL1, 040202_2)

Extract 2 shows a complex embeddedness of various orientations toward linguistic forms and negotiations of such forms within the sequential organization of both contents (i.e., talk about biological organisms) and activities. The analysis that follows shows how this negotiation contributes to configuring the organizational patterns of the segment, spreading from more macro-level organization to more micro-level organization:

1. the sequential organization of – and transition between – activities;
2. the interconnectedness of linguistic and academic work;
3. the normative formatting of students' contributions.

Although the three dimensions are praxeologically indissociable, we will, for reasons of clarity, discuss each point separately.

The sequential organization of activities

The whole segment is structured into three major activities (i.e., sequences of closely interrelated actions): clarifying the terms of the upcoming exam in lines 20–36, reviewing what has been done before by the class in lines 37–62 and moving, in two steps, into the core activity of the segment, namely the discussion of a specific unicellular organism in lines 63–96. It is noteworthy that the transition between these activities is tightly interwoven with the identification of specific scientific terminology. Three moments are relevant in this regard.

The segment starts with a typical closing of a previous activity (26–9; see Schegloff and Sacks 1973) where the teacher first offers the floor for further questions (i.e., unmentioned mentionables, line 26), then, after two longer pauses (27, 29), places himself a last mentionable (a side-comment addressed to Nadine in lines 30–4) and finally, after yet another pause (36), transitions by means of *okay* and micro-pause to the next activity. This activity is being opened by means of the teacher's naming of the topic of the upcoming science-talk, namely living organisms, introduced by *so* and the explicit mention *we will continue on looking* (37/38). The very labelling of the topic of talk (which in fact is the general theme of the lesson) combined with other cues functions here as a resource for moving into the general activity of doing science, after the closing down of the activity of organizing the exam.

Doing science itself is organized in several steps. It starts with a retrospect in lines 39 and 40 on what the group has discussed before. John is invited to name the organism that the class was discussing (43). John's providing the name (44) is first ratified by the teacher's *yes* (45), but then becomes an object of repair: *in english pronunciation (it')s- (.) paramecium* (45/46). This is an other-initiated other repair, which interestingly is postponed, being preceded by a ratification plus a micro-pause. The repair by means of rephrasing is itself multi-layered, as we will see below (section 'The normative formatting of students' contributions'). Xenia is then invited to name the group this organism is part of, which she does at line 53 (*unicellular*) and finally Peter is solicited to specify it (*protist*, 57). All three of these terms are thus provided by students and ratified by the teacher. The orientation toward naming; that is, providing linguistic labels for the organisms under discussion, is clearly highlighted by the teacher's metalinguistic comments (*what is the other word for this unicellular organism* in 54–6; *yes this is one term that you see used for a unicellular organism* in 58–60; *or protista is another word we (could have mentioned)* in 60–2). The orientation toward language is also highlighted by means of the embedded correction at line 54, where the teacher recasts the student's *it is a unicellular* (53) as *it is unicellular* (see section 'The normative formatting of students' contributions').

While these elements reveal the metalinguistic focus of the sequence, and most prominently of the teacher's actions, they are clearly embedded in a larger activity related to a scientific topic. As a matter of fact, we have here a situation where the explicit and implicit orientation toward linguistic form, including vocabulary, pronunciation (45–6) and grammar (54), is a functional element in reviewing the scientific content of what has been studied in the class before. More importantly, the terminology provided by the student is used by the teacher in order to transition to a next activity: after ratifying and commenting on the term *protist* (58–62), followed by a slight pause, the teacher takes up exactly the two technical terms that have been provided by the students in order to announce the plan for the current lesson: *okay so we are going to look at a more dangerous (.) protist (.) unicellular organism today in a theory lesson* (63–6). Note that this transition is closely mapped onto the previous one at lines 36–8: *pause + okay + so + announcement of the next general activity*. On this basis, the teacher introduces the larger theme of the lesson: *malaria* in line 70. Here, again, the naming of the scientific entities under discussion, by means of the precise terminology provided by the students, serves as a stepping-stone for transiting from one activity (providing a retrospect on what has been done before) into another, moving toward the core issue of the current lesson (namely discussing the phenomenon of malaria).

Finally, the teacher's open questions with regard to malaria that follow (°*anything else about malaria*°, 75–6; *any other ideas about malaria*, 83–4), combined with the low voice on the first of these, foreshadow a potential move toward further specifying the exact topic the lesson is going to deal with. Indeed, in a similar way as before, the identification, by the students, of what malaria is (77–9; 85–6) leads up to the identification, by the teacher, of the vector of malaria, namely a unicellular organism carried by a mosquito. This very organism is presented as the object of the lesson: *so this mosquito carries this unicellular organism which creates this temperature or fever (.) in a person, (.) so we are going to have a look at this unicellular . . .* (92–6). (We will come back to the negotiation sequence in these lines.)

What the analysis reveals so far is this: throughout the segment, the linguistic labelling systematically functions as a pivot around which are organized not only the moves from subject matter to subject matter, but also – and more interestingly – the transitions from one activity to the other. This provides a first piece of evidence for the interconnectedness between participants' orientation toward scientific terminology and the sequential organization of the classroom activities.

The interconnectedness of academic and linguistic work

One further noticeable – though not surprising – aspect of the quoted segment is the fact that orientation toward language form, including vocabulary, pronunciation and grammar, and orientation toward scientific content are tightly interwoven. This has already been mentioned above with regard to the embedded correction on the determiner at lines 53–4, the scope of which is the grammatical category of *unicellular*, passing from a (non-standard) nominal use in line 53 to the habitual adjectival use in line 54. This interconnectedness of the participants' orientation toward language form and the orientation toward scientific content is most visibly deployed in the closing lines of the extract, between lines 85 and 96. After malaria has been identified by Michelle as a fever, the teacher opens the floor for other ideas about malaria (84). After a short pause, Nadine provides a first answer: *ehm it [malaria] goes from person to person by a fly* (85–6). The answer is then ratified by the teacher's *yes* (87) and rephrased as *it is transported* (87). This very rephrasing functions as an embedded correction, replacing the word 'go' by the more technical term 'transport', and leading up to the even more technical nominalized expression *transportation by a vector* (88), which is exposed as a metalinguistic comment by the preceding *we call this . . .* (87). In a second step, the teacher asks for further specification of another part of Nadine's answer, namely 'fly': *what kind of fly: or insect is it* (89). An answer is immediately provided by Daniel (*mosquito*, 90) and ratified by the teacher's *well done* (91). Here again, the teacher produces an embedded correction, by recasting *mosquito* in terms of *it is (.) the mosquito*, (91). His repair is oriented both to the standard English form of a NP – namely [article + N] – as an answer within the local context of the immediately preceding question, and to the scientifically relevant generic form (*the mosquito*), marked by the generic use of the definite article. This is a symptomatic moment testifying for the inseparability of doing science and doing language and the teacher's (and students') simultaneous orientation to both. Immediately after this, the teacher goes on to rephrase the whole issue in more technical terms in lines 92–5 and identify the unicellular organism carried by malaria-transmitting mosquitoes as the very object of the lesson.

In sum, then, the extract shows a clear orientation to linguistic forms, both as regards lexicon (*go -> transport -> carry; fly -> mosquito*) and as regards grammar (*a unicellular -> unicellular; mosquito -> the mosquito*). This orientation to form is embedded in a larger scientific project, which, in turn is used as a functional element within the problem of how to organize transitions from one activity to another (see section 'The sequential organization of activities').

The normative formatting of students' contributions

Finally, let us go back in more detail to the internal organization of the activities and the actions they are composed of, starting with the teachers rephrasing (in lines 45–7) of John's initial answer (*[pariKium]* in 44). What is at stake here is not simply the correct linguistic form (i.e., pronunciation), nor the correct answer, but the format onto which the answer is mapped: the student's single-word answer is rephrased as a complete clause. There is further sequential evidence supporting this interpretation in what follows: the [it is] + [X]-format is repeatedly taken up by the students (53, 57, 72, 77), it is ratified by the teacher in line 54; if the format is not provided (as with *mosquito* in 90), it becomes the object of repair by the teacher (*the mosquito*, 91). What is at stake, then, is the students' 'doing being a student' so to say; that is, their recognition of, and compliance to, the appropriate interactional format (i.e., ways of tying answers to questions) in which they are to provide scientific answers in correct linguistic forms. Most interestingly, throughout the sequence, the [it is] + [X]-format appears recurrently to highlight key technical terms. It is indeed the crucial locus for such terms: its recurrence is such that when one adds up its instances, the result is an outline of the key-notions identifying the issue under discussion: [Paramecium] (46) being an organism that belongs to the group of [unicellular]s (53/54), also being called [protist]s (57) among which is the vector of malaria, which in turn is a [disease] (72), a [fever] (77) carried by a [mosquito] (91). The bracketed items are all provided in the [it is] + [X]-format, the first and last within the teacher's repairs, the others directly by the students.

In sum, then, the focus on a specific syntactic format within which answers are being produced – a format which significantly is here a part of the classical IRE (*initiation-reaction-evaluation*, cf. Mehan 1979) formatting of classroom interaction – provides a third type of evidence for the interplay between orientation toward doing language and orientation toward doing science. Most importantly, it documents the fact that each of these orientations as well as their interplay are constitutive of – and shaped by – processes of classroom socialization: doing language, doing science and doing being a student/a teacher are tightly and ostensibly interconnected.

Discussion and conclusion

The preceding analysis clearly shows that orientation to linguistic form within the immersion classroom is embedded in larger scientific projects (e.g., identifying and discussing biological organisms) and serves the participants as a resource for interactionally organizing the classroom activity (moving from providing a retrospective summary of the previous lesson to identifying the issue to be addressed in the present discussion and then to opening the core of the discussion). In sum:

- The analysis provides evidence for *the interplay between participants' orientation toward language form and their orientation toward academic content*. These orientations are not connected by a one-way relationship, but each feeds into the other: participants' orientation toward language form contributes to the elaboration of precise scientific contents; this orientation toward language is in turn structured by the wider practices of talk-in-interaction.
- The analysis also documents *a tight interconnectedness of participants' orientation toward the language–science interplay on the one hand and the sequential organization of classroom activities on the other*. Most strikingly, we see that the interactionally established and sequentially organized labelling of scientific topics at talk recurrently functions as a stepping-stone not only for moving from subject matter to subject matter (i.e., at the level of talk-about), but

also – and more interestingly – for moving from one activity to another (i.e., at the level of talk-that-does).
- The analysis finally reveals the students' and teacher's joint orientation toward a specific formatting of the students' contributions. In particular, the focus on a specific syntactic format onto which second pair parts (mostly answers provided by the students) are mapped provides further evidence for the interplay between orientation toward language form and orientation toward academic work. It also documents the fact that *either of these orientations and their interplay are constitutive of – as well as shaped by – processes of classroom socialization: doing language, doing science and doing being a student/a teacher are tightly interconnected* within situated processes of activity organization in the classroom.

What is at stake, then, with these observations, is not the mere deconstruction of a categorical distinction between 'focus on form' and 'focus on communication'. This would be banal, in some sense at least, as it should be obvious that formal tasks in the classroom, for instance, are regularly organized as interactional exchanges, and hence based on what we might call a communicative focus on form. What is crucial here, on the contrary, is the very complexity of talk-in-interaction as both, a site of potential learning and the very object of second language acquisition.

The analysis of one lengthy extract taken from an immersion classroom has allowed us to zoom in on patterns that are at work in other, more traditional L2 classroom settings. In fact, Mondada and Pekarek Doehler (2004) discuss one very similar example, taken from the advanced French L2 classroom, where the focus on form is a crucial step in the elaboration of a more precise interpretation of a piece of literature; it involves a reconceptualization of content that would otherwise not take place in the same way. This is taken by the authors as evidence for the intertwining of various competencies and types of knowledge as well as for the situated, socially configured nature of classroom tasks. This observation is in line with the present study. On the one hand, the analysis shows that tasks – that is 'tasks-as-activities' (cf. section 'The immersion classroom and beyond') – are multi-layered, involving linguistic, socio-interactional, and institutional work that is dealt with by the participants in a mutually coordinated and sequentially organized way. On the other hand, the tasks' targets – that is, the potential objects of learning (including language competence) – are fundamentally permeable to each other: working on the refinement of linguistic means, working on a better description and analysis of the scientific (or more generally thematic) object at hand, and formatting one's contributions according to appropriate interactional and morphosyntactic patterns within the communicative culture of the classroom are intrinsically interconnected, both as practical accomplishments and as objects of potential learning. Within the empirical data presented here, they are the observable underpinnings of the interrelation between doing science, doing language and doing being a learner.

Such observations go hand in hand, both on the level of analytic procedure as well as theoretical consequences, with a radical rethinking of the traditional conception of learning and language competence as such. By closely looking at the sequential unfolding of 'doing language' and 'doing science', we have revealed some of the complexities that are linked to dealing with learning as a socially situated practice. This meets a distinctly sociocultural turn in SLA which rejects a twofold dominant assumption according to which, as Gardner and Wagner have recently put it, 'language is primarily form' and 'acquisition is individual cognition' (2004: 2). According to this position, learning cannot be abstracted, neither conceptually nor analytically, from the organization of action, participation frameworks and from socialization processes (see Firth and Wagner 1997; Hall 1993, Mondada and Pekarek Doehler 2000, and the papers in *The Modern Language Journal*, 88/4, 2004). It is exactly in this sense that understanding the joint and local configuration of learning situations is crucial to understanding learning. Language learning is understood as learning to deal with locally organized and sequentially structured discourse activities and hence rooted in the learner's participation in organizing talk-in-interaction, such as configuring participation structures or sequencing activities. This highlights the importance of a socially situated view of language, instruction and learning, in which learning objects are inseparable from the local management of – to use Paul ten Have's words – 'the procedural infrastructure of situated action' (1999: 37; see also Pekarek Doehler 2005; Young and Miller 2004).

By closely looking at the sequential unfolding of 'doing language' and 'doing science', we have observed, in this chapter, some of the complexities that are linked to dealing with learning situations as loci of a socially situated practice – a practice that encompasses communicating, language learning and academic learning as well as socializing in the classroom. What this boils down to in the light of the preceding remarks is this: as a characteristic of talk-in-interaction, the multi-layeredness that we have observed – involving jointly dealing with communicative contents, working on language, sequentially organizing (classroom) activities and socializing as a student and/or learner – is not only part of the processes of learning, understood as developing the ability to participate in the sociocultural practices of a group, such as a specific classroom community. It is also fundamental to the object of learning a second language, and hence a crucial aspect of language competence itself.

Notes

1. The term 'focus on form' has been introduced by Long (e.g., Long, 1991) to refer to the incidental attention speakers pay to language form when encountering communicative problems. Focus on form is part of sequences of interactional

negotiation and has been intensely studied within the Interaction Hypothesis framework. The term is also used by Ellis (e.g., Ellis, Basturkmen and Loewen 2001) in a wider sense, including instances when speakers pay attention to form; for example, pre-emptively, without encountering communicative problems. The binary view underlying current applications of the notion of focus on form has been most recently worded by Ellis, Loewen and Basturkmen as follows : 'We characterize focus on form episodes as including brief 'time-outs' from the effort to communicate'(2006: 136).

2. A similar study is currently being conducted which provides more evidence for this being the case in English as a Second Language *beginner* classrooms (Pekarek Doehler and Ziegler, in preparation); see also Ziegler and Mutz 2003.

Part 2
Identity and Social Action

7
Socializing Second Language Acquisition

David Block
University of London

Introduction

Some ten years ago, Ben Rampton (1997) wrote about 'retuning' applied linguistics, moving the field in the direction of more multidisciplinary and interdisciplinary approaches to the study of language-related problems in the real world. In making such a suggestion, Rampton was following Del Hymes, who proposed a reformulation of sociolinguistics some 25 years earlier. Specifically, Hymes (1974a) argued for three changes to sociolinguistics. First, sociolinguists should study language as not only a linguistic phenomenon, but also a social one, examining social problems and language use in addition to the formal features of language. Second, sociolinguistic research should be socially *realistic*; that is, it should be based on data collected from existing speech communities. Third and finally, sociolinguistic research should be *socially constituted*, beginning with a discussion of how the social emerges out of a concern for function, before moving to explore how formal features of language are organized to serve the social.

One part of Hymes's call for a change in sociolinguistics became very influential among those interested in language teaching and learning. I refer here to his notion of communicative competence, understood as the knowledge not only of formal aspects of language, but also appropriacy; that is, whether and to what degree utterances in a particular language are formally possible, feasible, appropriate and done (Hymes 1974a). Communicative Competence became foundational to the great paradigm shift in language teaching worldwide, Communicative Language Teaching (Brumfit and Johnson 1979; Brumfit 1984), which in recent years has evolved into Task-Based Language Teaching (Ellis 2003). In addition, when Second Language Acquisition (SLA) research began to catch up with language teaching, from about 1980 onwards, it very selectively and partially took on board a part of Hymes agenda. Thus, as I note elsewhere (Block 2003), SLA researchers began to show an interest in conversation analysis, in particular the notion of adjacency pairs. They were also influenced by the field of ethnomethodology, in particular Garfinkel's (1967) analytical principle of sticking closely to the data collected, while rejecting, for the most part, any reference to social categories such as social class, gender or ethnicity in their analysis. Finally, they took on board the concepts of 'speech event' from Hymes's (1974b) ethnography of speaking, 'speech act' from the work of Searle (1969) and 'cooperative principle' from the work of Grice (1975).

However, this early move in the direction of a socialization of SLA research was to be brief, partial and incomplete as researchers immediately attempted to apply what they had learned from sociolinguistics to what SLA research had produced up to 1980. On the one hand, there was a perceived need to convert Krashen's (1981) Comprehensible Input Hypothesis into a more complete framework which could be empirically tested. On the other hand, there was a growing belief that while comprehensible input was no doubt a necessary condition for SLA to take place, it was deemed to be insufficient on its own. Researchers sought a theory which could take into account interaction (e.g., Long 1981) and output (e.g., Swain 1985), while accommodating key SLA phenomena such as transfer, staged grammatical development, the systematicity of interlanguage and variability. In addition, such a theory had to reconcile the relative roles of Universal Grammar and cognition (information processing) and also have something to say about the influence of individual psychological variables, such as learning style and motivation.

The most noteworthy outcome of research which attempted to cater for Hymesian sociolinguistics in the modest manner described above, while taking into account the key findings from SLA research as of 1980, is Susan Gass's (1988, 1997) Input-Interaction-Output (IIO) model. This model is an embellishment of the work of other scholars, most notably Michael Long (1996), who began writing about what he terms the 'Interaction Hypothesis' in the early 1980s (e.g., Long 1981). Gass's model is powerful because it can take on board what the authors of SLA textbooks (e.g., Doughty and Long 2003; Ellis 2007; Gass and Selinker 2001; Lightbown and Spada 2006; Mitchell and Myles 2004) have identified as the key issues in SLA; that is, the different SLA-related phenomena outlined in the previous paragraph.

Nevertheless, what is an impressive and powerful model for mainstream SLA researchers does not necessarily seem impressive and powerful when viewed from a more socially informed perspective which draws heavily on sociology, social theory and current sociolinguistics research. My 2003 book, *The Social Turn in Second Language Acquisition*, was an attempt to take apart and analyse the SLA embodied in Gass's model, framing the 'second', the 'language;' and the 'acquisition' in new and different ways. In doing so, I was, following Rampton (1997), bringing to bear on SLA research a bigger 'toolkit' than is normally the case. I was also making a case for a move towards SLA research which engages with the fuzzy and unclear social, cultural, historical, political and economic aspects emergent in and around second language learning, rather than sweeping them to the side as 'interesting but not relevant'. Such a move would be in keeping with the Hymsean tradition.

A few years on, I propose in this paper to explore further what bringing a bigger toolkit to bear on SLA might mean in practice. I begin by reproducing an exchange taking place in a London workplace between a Colombian migrant and two of his British colleagues. This exchange is part of a larger database which was foundational to my study of Spanish-speaking Latinos (hereafter, SSLs) as an emerging ethnolinguistic group in London (Block 2006, 2007a, 2007b). Here, however, I frame the exchange as potential second language learning activity which I view from a variety of angles. These angles range from more SLA-friendly frameworks such as 'negotiation for meaning' to current work on globalization and migration.

My point is that any exchange which might count as potential second language acquisition activity can and should be analysed not only at the micro/local interactional level (in the here and now), but also with regard to extra-interactional factors. These factors include the biography of the individual language learner, his/her membership in different communities of practice – that is, groups of people who come together to engage in common goal-oriented activity (Lave and Wenger 1991) – and broader macro-social phenomena such as global migration. Only in this way can we apply the bigger toolkit and move towards multi-layered understandings of SLA. The pay-off is a more complete understanding of SLA, including an understanding of why, for example, so many second language learners seem to develop only a partial communicative competence in the target language.

A workplace conversation with second language acquisition potential

I begin with an excerpt from a conversation recorded in the reception area of a public building in central London in early 2004. The participants are Dan (D), Carlos (C) and Bob (B). Carlos and Bob worked in the building at the time of the conversation while Dan was a recently retired ex-workmate. The key figure for the discussion that follows is Carlos, a Colombian migrant who had been living in London for 2 and a half years at the time of the recording.

Extract 1

1   D: I feel a bit rough like I've got a bad cold and ( ) and erh (1)
         I can't shake it off I've had it for over a week so I thought I'd
         come up to town a bit ((Phones ringing in background)) oh, gosh
         thought I'd come down
2   C: yeah?=
3   D: =and we had a poor performance/ 'cause see he can't get down very
         often so he booked the tickets about four weeks ago=
4   C: =and it was easy game for Chelsea
5   D: I know ( ) (1) and really I felt so rough I didn't feel like
         going but I thought don't want to let im down

6   C: yeah=
7   D: =cause what I've been taking and carrying this cold and then they played like that awful!=
8   B: =poor=
9   D: =yeah, very poor=
10 B: [no
11 C: he] was very poor performance for Chelsea=
12 D: =but a lot of the play=
13 B: =[yeah
14 C: yeah]
15 D: °°we're not scoring the goals we're not scoring the goals I can't make it out not scoring many goal°°
16 B: ( )
17 D: yeah but last Wednesday I mean ( ) I got the fucking shivers and I that day all of a sudden I couldn't stop shivering even though it wasn't that cold really=
18 C: =yeah
19 D: I just had the fucking shivers later then I went to see the doctor and me own doctor's been ill funnily enough so I see another doctor (2) and he examined me and said 'no, don't seem too bad' so he says 'no use in giving you any antibiotics' HE WASN'T EVEN GONNA GIVE ME ANY MEDICINE
20 C: ((laughing))
21 D: I said well what about you know cause I've been taking lemsips and all [that
22 C: that's] that's the worse really=
23 D: =and like last night I took a fucking Lemsip before ((In the background, Bob asks if he can help someone who has come to the reception counter)) about ten o'clock in bed (2) and uh about two in the morning I've got this fucking cough. Oh I couldn't shake it off (2) Oh, I just feel terrible.

First, I need to address the question of whether or not this exchange counts as an instance of second language acquisition. Susan Gass (1998) has argued that there is a distinction to be made between second language acquisition and second language use, the former referring to a focus on the language used in interactions and the latter focusing on the act of communication taking place. However, as some authors have noted (e.g., Firth and Wagner 1998; Block 2003) separating acquisition from use is not at all straightforward. Here I take the position that for migrants like Carlos, the acquisition of English will never really stop and that every instance of English language use in his day-to-day life is potentially an instance of English language acquisition.

Examining Carlos's contributions to this exchange, I see several things worthy of mention. First, in turn 2, he provides an appropriate enough interjection – 'yeah?' – that splits Dan's opening statement about his cold and travelling to London to see a Chelsea football match. In turn 3, Dan begins with an assessment of the match – 'we had a poor performance' – and then shifts to how difficult it is for him and his friend to travel from their homes north of London to Stamford Bridge in west London to see Chelsea matches. Carlos interrupts the latter half of Dan's intervention to add his own assessment of the match in question in turn 4: 'it was easy game for Chelsea'. However, Dan carries on talking about travelling to London as opposed to the match and Carlos provides a backchannelling 'yeah' in turn 6, to keep the conversation going. In turns 7–10, Dan and Bob make comments about the match and Carlos again attempts to come back into the conversation in turn 11 with an appropriation of Dan's statement about Chelsea having had a 'poor performance'. Carlos and Bob then collaborate with Dan who defines Chelsea's problem, dramatically whispering 'we're not scoring the goals' in turn 15. However, in turn 17, Dan returns to the topic of his cold. Carlos follows him in this topic shift, laughing when Dan loudly condemns his doctor's reluctance to prescribe him medicine for his cold. Carlos adds his own wisdom about taking Lempsips instead of prescribed medicine when he says 'that's the worse really' in turn 22. The exchange ends with Dan launching into a long account of his battles with his cold.

Viewed from a discourse management point of view, Carlos appears to do a good job of acting as an active co-participant in this conversation. He gives Dan plenty of space as the central figure in the exchange, but he intervenes appropriately along the way, both in terms of content and function. He also balances his interventions well with those of the third participant, Bob. What he says is grammatical, although he omits the article in turns 4 and 11, refers to the match as 'he' in turn 11 and uses 'worse' instead of 'worst' in turn 22. The latter anomaly could be a case of repeating what he has heard ('worse' is not uncommon usage in this context) or it could be a question of pronunciation, not producing the word-final phoneme /t/.

Many SLA researchers would be more interested in this exchange as an example of two native speakers of English conversing with a non-native and how the conversation is managed from a negotiation for meaning point of view. Negotiation for meaning refers to 'the process in which, in an effort to communicate, learners and competent speakers provide and interpret signals of their own and their interlocutor's perceived comprehension, thus provoking adjustments to linguistic form, conversational structure, message content, or all three, until an acceptable level of understanding is achieved' (Long 1996: 418). Looking at the conversation in this light, we see that information exchange flows smoothly with no hiccups. Thus, there do not appear to be any overt adjustments to linguistic form, conversational structure or message content. Nevertheless, there is some evidence that Carlos has acquired a new lexical item when in turn 11 he appropriates the expression 'have a poor performance', introduced by Dan in turn 3, albeit inaccurately as 'he was a very poor performance'.

Generically, this conversation seems more like the small talk at work described by sociolinguists (e.g., Coupland 2000) than an information exchange. Holmes categorizes such talk at work along a scale ranging from 'core business talk', that is, 'relevant, focused, often context bound, on-task talk, with a high information content' (2000: 36), to the Malinowski-inspired 'phatic communion', that is, talk which is 'independent of any specific workplace context, which is 'atopical' and irrelevant in terms of workplace business, and which has relatively little referential content or information load' (2000: 37). In between core business talk and phatic communion, there is 'work-related talk', that is, talk relevant to the business context, but not strictly relevant to the task at hand, and 'social talk', that is, talk which is about socializing on the job rather than work. In the case of Carlos's conversation with Dan and Bob, we witness an example of social talk. There is nothing work-related in the conversation but talk is about something: Dan's cold, travelling to London and the Chelsea match. Carlos's performance in this exchange points to his command of this workplace speech genre.

Thus far, I have attempted to show how different micro-analyses of this one exchange can tell us things about Carlos's language use and the acquisition opportunities that arise from this language use. However, these micro-analyses keep us at the level of exchange and they do not allow us to construct a more complete version of the communicative event in question. In order to do the latter, we need to ask and attempt to answer questions that distance us from this exchange in terms of space and time. One such question concerns who Carlos is in terms of his personal biography and his identity as an English speaker.

Carlos's story and his English-speaking identity

Carlos grew up in a working-class family in a small city located in the southwestern part of Colombia. He studied philosophy and eventually became a philosophy lecturer at a university in Colombia. By the late 1980s, he was married and he had two children from this marriage, which ended in 1991. In the late 1980s and early 1990s, Carlos was very active in leftist political movements working in opposition to the Colombian political and military establishment. On more than one occasion he was imprisoned and on two occasions he visited friends in London to avoid difficulties with the Colombian authorities. During his second visit, in 1991, he met Kelly, a British national, whom he married soon after. Their son, Eduardo, was born in 1992. Carlos, Kelly and Eduardo lived in Colombia together between 1992 and 2001. Their life was middle class: Carlos had his university post and Kelly worked as a Spanish/English translator. After more than eight years in Colombia, Kelly wanted to be close to her family in London again and there was some concern that Eduardo would never learn English, given that the couple spoke only Spanish at home. In autumn 2001, Carlos, Kelly and Eduardo moved to London.

In migration theory terms, Carlos is part of the larger emigration of Colombians to the United Kingdom in the past 15 years for political, economic and security reasons (Bermúdez Torres 2003; Block 2006; Dempsey and Lema 1998; McIlwaine 2005). His particular migration has been facilitated by the fact that he is married to a British national. As regards his migrant identity, he is difficult to categorize. On the one hand, he lives his life in London as an expatriate Colombian; that is, as someone who has chosen to live abroad for an extended period of time, but who knows that whenever he wants, he can go back to Colombia (Block 2006). Alternatively, Carlos might be seen as a transmigrant; that is, someone who 'organize[s] [his] daily economic, familial, religious, and social relations within networks that extend across the borders of two nation-states' (Fouron and Glick Schiller 2001: 60), in this case, Colombia and the United Kingdom. However, while Carlos does maintain some contact with events in Colombia, particularly political events, he does not, as I note below, show any propensity to participate in Colombian transmigrant social spaces in London, organized around, for example, playing football on Sunday in particular parks, salsa dancing, festivals and so on.

As regards his English language skills, Carlos's profile is perhaps not typical of many university-educated Colombians. Throughout his formal education, he studied French as a matter of protest against what he perceived as the imposition of English as the international language by the United States. In addition, as I note above, he and Kelly never spoke in English during the time they lived in Colombia. The lack of contact with English during his lifetime meant that upon his arrival in London in 2001, he spoke hardly any English and this meant, in turn, that he could not find any employment beyond low-level manual service jobs. In this sense, he was effectively declassed when he arrived in London, falling from professional middle class to unskilled low-level service provider overnight.

Although I never assessed Carlos's English language proficiency in a rigorous manner (e.g., using language tests), I have heard enough of his English to be able to describe it, in general terms, as good enough for him to do what he needs to do on a day-to-day basis in London. His on-the-job conversations, both social (see above) and more work related, are handled with ease. He is particularly adept when dealing with professionals, such as doctors and lawyers, as the following phone conversation with a barrister suggests:

Extract 2

Note: / indicates the end of a turn

> Good morning sir (.) can I speak to Mr Fulham please/ (.) oh right good morning sir/ (.) I'm Mr Carlos Sanchez/ (.)/ Carlos Sanchez / (1)/ yes (.) you was on my flat yesterday/ (.) in our place yesterday/ (.)/ you was yesterday

in my place in ((Provides his address))/ (.)/ no/ (.)/ ah (.) yes/ (.)/ I received the notice/ (1)/ erm/ (.)/ ( ) yeah OK ((Laughing))/ (.)/ yeah erm/ (.)/ yes/ (6)/ sorry Mr Coram/ (.)/ yeah/ (.)/ yeah/ (.)/ yes sir/ (.)/ yeah/ (.)/ yes sir/ (3)/ but I yes I yes yesterday we were in erm erm hearing because I / (.)/ in the court/ (.)/ yes sir erm/ (.)/ yes sir erm we were in an appeal we made erm (.) with the erm (.) home office/ (.)/ yes and we spent all the day there because/ (.)/ yes we started at 10 o'clock and we spent all the day there/ (1)/ yeah/ (12)/ yes that's fine/ (10)/ yes please/ (4)/ yeah/ (8)/ yes sir/ (12)/ yes/ (4)/ yes/ (4)/ OK could you let me know when exactly? because in that in that/ (1)/ no/ (3)/ yeah/ (5)/ yeah

Unlike the migrants in studies such as Bremer and colleagues (1996) and Goldstein (1996), Carlos is not intimidated by contacts with individuals in gate-keeping posts, such as immigration authorities, or professionals, such as doctors or lawyers. Indeed, when talking about his interactions with people in positions of power, he says that he feels that he is dealing with his equals. He explains:

... la experiencia mia anterior, digamos academica... te da confianza para ir al médico, por ejemplo, para hacer un poco las cosas en tu vida normal. Pero es un poco sentirse como afianzado en esa situación intellectual que te permite como ganar la confianza. Y he pensado también o he visto que la gente que no tiene, digamos, ese sustento ... es más débil, es más vunerable ...

... *my previous experience, let's say academic... gives you confidence to go to the doctor, for example, to kind of do things in your normal life. But it's a little like feeling strengthened by that intellectual situation that allows you to gain confidence. And I have thought about this and I have seen how the people who don't have, let's say, this support ... are weaker, more vulnerable.*

(Carlos, 4/12/03)

What Carlos refers to here is a matter of social class linked to his background as an academic and the considerable cultural and social capital (Bourdieu 1977b, 1984) that comes with this background. In recent versions of Bourdieu's oft-cited capital metaphors (e.g., Skeggs 2004), cultural capital is seen as an array of ever-evolving sociosemiotic resources that individuals draw on in contacts with others. These resources are about exhibiting the behavioural patterns (e.g., accent and attitude) valued in society, being associated with particular artefacts (e.g., knowing the 'good' books, having the right academic qualifications, having a tastefully decorated flat) and being connected to certain institutions (e.g., university and professional associations). Meanwhile, social capital relates directly to these institutional contacts. It is about the connections to and relationships with less, equally or more powerful others: the greater the cultural capital of these others, the greater the social capital accrued by knowing them.

Carlos's case may be seen in terms of the considerable cultural capital and social capital that he is able to draw on as resources in his contacts with professionals and in other institutional encounters. However, these resources are mediated more by Spanish than English, or better said, are more 'invokable' in Spanish than in English. Given this state of affairs, it is interestingly to note that Carlos exhibits little or no desire to make up the difference between his Spanish-mediated and English-mediated selves. Indeed, it seems that his contacts with English, in which he is often not able to give as much of himself as he would be able to do in Spanish, have not had the effect of making him want to improve his English beyond his current level. His declassing, from university lecturer to porter, thus has not been a sufficient impetus to increase his contact with English and seek more opportunities to develop his communicative competence in this language. In short, he feels little sense of personal investment in English (Norton 2000); that is, he does not engage in conversation in English with a view to increasing his cultural and social capital in this language.

This lack of interest in developing his English language skills is, in part, due to how he experiences most of his contacts in English. These contacts take place at work and they are either brief service encounters with the general public (e.g., 'Where is the loo?') or more casual conversations with his English-speaking colleagues, such as the one with Dan and Bob reproduced above. Regarding the former type of exchange, Carlos for the most part acquits himself well, especially because such contacts tend to be short, generally involving only a few turns. By contrast, his more informal conversations with colleagues are more extensive, although they are, as Carlos explains, no more rewarding for him.

Indeed, in the English-mediated, white, working-class and male-dominant atmosphere in which he worked, Carlos found that he had little in common with his fellow workers. He was Colombian, mixed race in British census terms, a university lecturer by profession and not completely familiar with the kind of masculine subject positions adopted by his colleagues. As we see in the exchange with Dan and Bob, it was only football that he could talk about with his colleagues with any degree of enthusiasm. However, even with football, he could not always keep up with his colleagues as his account of the conversation with Dan and Bob suggests:

> Estoy escuchando y ya hay una parte de la conversación, que yo te digo, la pierdo porque la otra persona con quien habla ... tiene el problema, es tartamudo, y luego su dicción, la forma de pronunciar, es muy cortante, y pierdo ya el ánimo, el interés, en la conversación. Entonces los dejo ya entre ellos allí. Yo estoy allí pero ... ((encogiéndose de hombros))
>
> *I'm listening and there is a part of the conversation, that I tell you, I lose it because the other person he is talking to ... he has this problem, he stutters, and then his diction, how he pronounces, its very sharp, and I lose spirit, interest, in the*

*conversation. So, I just leave them there, to talk between themselves. I'm there but
...((shrugging))*

(Carlos, 6/2/04)

Carlos as Spanish-speaking Latino or cosmopolitan Spanish speaker

Carlos thus manifests a lack of engagement with and affiliation to English, and indeed he expresses a high degree of alienation towards most of the speakers of English with whom he comes into contact. Carlos might have been expected to seek potentially more rewarding contacts with fellow Colombians, or beyond Colombians, Spanish-speaking Latinos. However, when asked about this prospect, he was rather categorical, maintaining that he did not really see himself as part of such a community:

Es curioso, David, porque trabajo en contacto con Colombianos básicamente, y latinos en general. Pero por fuera, y estando ya en casa, no queremos el contacto con más latinos, supuestamente porque queríamos desarrollar más mi inglés o porque el niño también hablara mas inglés. Pero creo que [el contacto con SSLs] no está funcionando al final del dia [porque] son personas que tienen objetivos muy precisos. Por ejemplo, ellos necesitan trabajar un numero de horas por dia, que no les permite hacer una vida social muy amplia tampoco. Y luego, ya el tipo de actividades sociales a que ellos acuden, a mi no me interesan, por ejemplo, que es ir a beber y ir a bailar y ir a comer una comida que he comido durante todos los años de mi vida... no puedo compartir este tipo de cosas porque no, o sea no me llegan...

It's funny, David, because I work in contact with Colombians basically, and Latinos in general. But away from work, and being at home, we don't want contact with more Latinos, supposedly because we wanted to develop more my English or so that our son also could speak English. But I think that [the contact with SSLs] doesn't really work at the end of the day [because] they are people with specific objectives. For example, they need to work a certain number of hours a day, which does not allow time to have a very broad social life either. And then I'm not interested in the type of social activities that they go to, for example, going out drinking, going out dancing and going out to eat a type of food that I have eaten every year of my life. I can't share this type of things just because they just aren't enough...

(Carlos, 12/9/03)

In effect, it is once again Carlos's cultural and social capital that make him feel very different from the majority of SSLs with whom he comes in contact at work. On the one hand, he is university educated, with a middle-class lifestyle. On the other hand, through his wife, he has access to social networks denied to most migrants. By contrast, most of these SSLs, to whom Carlos refers to in the third person, have not studied at university and they live a marginal life in London in social, economic and political terms.

As I note elsewhere (Block 2006), Carlos's political consciousness pushed him towards contact with fellow SSLs, for example when he and his wife Kelly would attempt to help them solve some of their day-to-day problems. However, his background as a university lecturer, along with his more cosmopolitan lifestyle, pushed him in a diametrically opposed direction, away from the majority of his compatriots and towards better-educated, middle-class Spanish speakers. He explains:

> ... por casa vienen unos amigos españoles que tienen profesiones, que están desarrollando otro tipo de actividades, diferente a los latinos y claro es un nivel un poquito más interesante. También vienen a casa unos amigos argentinos que trabajan en esto de psicologia y algunos son profesores. Entonces es un poquito diferente ...
>
> *Some Spanish friends come round who have professions, who are engaging in another type of activities, different from the Latinos and obviously it's a slightly more interesting level. Some Argentinian friends also come round who work in psychology and some of them are teachers. So it's a little different ...*
>
> (Carlos, 12/9/03)

Carlos, thus, is an individual who is comfortable carrying out his life as much as possible in Spanish. In this sense, he adopts a form of cultural and linguistic maintenance. However, this maintenance is more cosmopolitan in nature, its reference point more a transnational community of university-educated Spanish speakers than a sense of being a Colombian or SSL in London. In other words, it is transnationalism more related to social class and language than to nationality (or geographical region) and language.

In discussions of how the forces and flows of globalization impact on the movement of people around the world, David Harvey's (1989) concept of 'time-space compression' is often invoked. Time-space compression means that via advanced technology and transportation, people can be in either physical or technologically mediated contact with one another much faster and more effectively and efficiently than has ever been the case in the past. The impact of this time-space compression has meant that the world is coming to be organized less vertically, along nation-state lines, and more horizontally, according to communities of shared interests and experiences (Perlmutter 1991). Thus there are progressively more and more communities which transcend nation-state boundaries and individuals who in much of their lives feel more allegiance and affinity to these communities than they do to the nation-states in which they reside. These communities are based on a long list of shared experiences and orientations, such as: tastes in fashion, music, cinema, literature and so on; beliefs and opinions; and lifestyle options. In Carlos's case, the community of affiliation is based on international Spanish language and culture.

Importantly, Carlos's affiliation to Spanish and well-educated cosmopolitan speakers of Spanish has had an impact on his English language development in that it has allowed him to reserve important parts of his day-to-day life – his family and his social life – for Spanish, not English. Because his English language use is confined primarily to the workplace, and because his workplace communication is in no way fulfilling, Carlos remains stabilized as a more or less competent speaker of English for the kinds of things he needs to do in English on the job. In a sense, there is not much in his input, shaped by some of the social factors I have mentioned in this section, that is challenging enough to push him towards richer and more sophisticated English language use. At the same time, as I note elsewhere (Block 2007b), he has not made any effort to use the kind of colloquial language that is typical in his colleagues' speech, such as the numerous morphological variations on the word 'fuck'. Indeed, his English generally seems to be relatively bland as regards the use of expletives and other forms of emotional language that are deemed so important to the individual's sense of self in a language (Pavlenko 2006a).

Conclusion

In this chapter I have made a modest attempt to expand the analysis of an exchange by a second language learner, Carlos, moving from the more microlinguistic level to broader issues related to his background and his life in London. My aim has been to suggest to the reader how the application of a bigger toolkit to the analysis of second language learning opportunities might illuminate our understanding of the learning process, providing us with information about what such opportunities mean to the individuals involved. Examining some – though certainly not all – aspects of Carlos's life, we come to understand that his exchanges at work with colleagues are not particularly important to Carlos as second language learning opportunities. However, they do not work as second language learning opportunities for reasons that are very different from those found elsewhere in SLA research focusing on adult migrants.

For example, in her research with five migrant women in Canada, Bonny Norton (2000, 2001) examines issues of power in exchanges involving native and non-native speakers of English. She challenges the assumption made in much SLA research that 'those who speak regard those who listen as worthy to listen, and that those who listen regard those who speak as worthy to speak' (Norton 2000: 8), while focusing on how the women in her study developed subject positions as what Bourdieu (1977b) calls 'legitimate speakers', that is how they come to be accepted and fully functioning members of the different communities of practice (Lave and Wenger 1991) with which they engage in their day-to-day lives. What Norton found was that all five women to varying degrees and in different ways struggled to move from peripheral participation in the communities of practice with which they engaged to full participation and their acceptance as valid and valued community members.

For Carlos, however, acceptance in the English-mediated communities of practice with which he engages is not a salient issue. Nor does it seem to have ever been a goal for him. The contrast with Norton's informants is that he does not feel a need to develop this status with his co-workers or just about anyone else he comes into contact with in English. He is perfectly able to feel satisfied and confident about himself as a valid and valued interlocutor through his day-to-day use of Spanish at home, with friends and sometimes on the job. His strong affiliation to the imagined international community of educated Spanish speakers ultimately trumps all else as regards his ethnolinguistic identity.

The point in all of this is that a micro-analysis of Carlos's exchange with his two work colleagues would show us something about the development of his communicative competence within the conversation (or lack thereof) and presumably a selection of such examples, spread over several months, would show longer term development. Such research could be linked to theories of SLA, whereby certain interaction patterns and events are deemed to lead to acquisition more than others. This would provide an answer to the why question: Why did Carlos develop or not develop his communicative competence within these exchanges? However, such research would not provide us with answers to the same why question moved outside the micro-level of linguistic interaction. Why, for example, in exchanges recorded over period of several months, did Carlos seem to make little progress, in linguistic terms, in pragmatic terms *and* in terms of his affiliation to and identification with English? SLA researchers moving slightly outside the level of the interaction, might adduce any number of individual factors, ranging from age to a lack of integrative motivation. However, as Pavlenko (2002) notes, these socio-psychological constructs prove to be relatively confining and deterministic in so much research and crucially, they tell us very little about individuals as social beings with social identities. Following Cole (1996) and others working within a sociocultural framework, we need to work at several levels, simultaneously, or, in any case, in a back-and-forth manner. Thus we need to be attentive to: (1) the micro-genetic, that is changes occurring in the individual's mental functioning over the span of weeks, days, hours or even seconds; and (2) the ontogenetic, the individual's cognitive and psychological development over a lifetime. In addition, we need to add a third layer which encompasses larger social dimensions such as social identity, migration as a global phenomenon, engagements with different communities of practice, and so on.

Nearly two decades ago, Leo van Lier noted that in all research context must be delimited at some point, as researchers cannot take on board everything:

> Context may be regarded as extending, like ripples on a pond, in concentric circles from any particular action or utterance. At some point we will have to draw a line and say: this is as far as we shall look.
> (van Lier 1988: 10)

What I propose here is that in SLA research, we draw this line as far from the utterance or interactional level as possible, as we seek ever-more sophisticated understandings of second language acquisition.

8
Identity Repertoires in the Narratives of Advanced American Learners of Russian

Viktoria Driagina and Aneta Pavlenko
Pennsylvania State University and Temple University

Introduction

One of the central goals of foreign and second language (L2) learning for many, albeit not all, learners is self-translation; that is, the ability to present oneself in complex and diverse ways as one would do in the native language, yet in terms understandable to target language speakers. In cases of typologically similar languages and culturally similar communities, the achievement and display of this ability may pass unnoticed, but when the linguistic and cultural gap between the two speech communities is wide, self-translation becomes a daunting task (Pavlenko 1998, 2001, 2004).

What opportunities to master new self-representation resources are offered to students in foreign language classrooms? In a recent paper, 'Identity Options in Russian Textbooks', Shardakova and Pavlenko (2004) analysed two popular introductory Russian-language textbooks with regard to two types of identity options: imagined learners (targeted implicitly by the texts) and imagined interlocutors (invoked explicitly). They found that imagined learners were invariably able-bodied white heterosexual middle-class young people, members of the international elite, while their imagined interlocutors were upper- and middle-class members of Russian intelligentsia. Based on the results of their analysis, the authors argued that the books did not fully reflect the linguistic, social, ethnic and religious diversity of contemporary Russian society, nor did they address the full range of students in North American classrooms, obscuring the presence of Asian, Latino and African-American students, gay and lesbian students, disabled students, working-class students, or, for that matter, women.

The authors further argued that the biases, omissions and oversimplifications found in the texts 'represent lost opportunities for cross-cultural reflection; they may also negatively affect the students and deprive them of important means of self-representation' (Shardakova and Pavlenko 2004: 25). Notably, however, the researchers' analysis was limited to the textbooks.

In the present chapter, we will examine identity repertoires in the speech of advanced American students of Russian.

Research design

Objective. The aim of the present study was to examine resources for identity construction available to advanced American learners of Russian. While recognizing that linguistic repertoires are complex conglomerates of semantic, morphosyntactic, pragmatic and discursive resources, due to space constraints we will limit our discussion to a single resource, namely identity terms used by the learners to construct their own and others' identities. We will identify the range of terms used and the contexts in which they were used, compare the uses of identity terms by learners and native speakers of Russian in the context of the same task, and try to understand the sources of the students' difficulties and errors.

Method. To investigate the uses of identity terms we adopted a *corpus-based approach* to the study of learner language. In this approach, data are collected from a group of learners (here, advanced American learners of Russian) and from native speakers of the learners' L2 (here, Russian) similar to the learner group in terms of sociodemographic and socio-educational variables. The use of the native Russian corpus allowed us to identify the range of language variation in the target language and to judge the learners against a real, rather than an idealized, reference group. In the concluding section we will return to the implications of using such a native speaker standard.

In selecting among different types of data we could have collected, we chose *elicited life stories*, that is, narratives about participants' personal experiences elicited through the use of a structured life story questionnaire, which asked questions about participants' childhood and school memories, family, friends, and career choices and aspirations (see Appendix 1). In doing so, the interview prompted the participants to categorize and name themselves and others involved in their life trajectories.

Participants. The interviews were collected from two groups of participants:

1. Thirty native speakers of Russian (21 females, 9 males) who had only minimal knowledge of either German, English or French, ages between 18 and 21, undergraduate students at Tomsk State University, Russia; and
2. Thirty advanced American learners of Russian (15 females, 15 males), undergraduate and graduate students enrolled in sixth- and seventh-level and in graduate-level Russian courses in the intensive immersion programme at the Middlebury Summer Russian School, Middlebury College, Vermont, United States.

The age range of the learners was wider than in the native speaker corpus: 19 participants (9 females, 10 males) were between the ages of 19 and 24 (mean = 22.2), 11 participants (6 females, 5 males) were between the ages of 28 and 56 (mean = 35.7). While the students differed in the length of study of the language (range 1–16 years, mean = 5.3), their skills were relatively similar. On a 7-point Likert scale where 1 equaled 'poor' and 7 'native-like', most saw themselves as best at reading (mean = 4.9) and weakest at writing (mean = 4.2) with listening (mean = 4.7) and speaking skills (mean = 4.3) somewhere in between.

Data collection and analysis. To collect the data for the study, we chose to conduct oral interviews, rather than elicit written answers, because oral narratives are more representative of spontaneous speech. Each participant was interviewed separately by a native speaker of Russian using the same protocol. All interviews were tape-recorded and subsequently transcribed by a native speaker of Russian. Identity terms were identified, counted and then subjected to thematic analysis which allowed us to separate them into three thematic categories (for lists of identity terms produced by each group see Appendixes 2 and 3). Because nouns constituted by far the largest category of identity terms in the narratives, they were chosen as the target lexical category for the analyses. Where relevant, however, we will extend our discussion to the uses of adjectives, noun phrases, suffixation and so on.

The uses of identity terms by the two groups were analysed both quantitatively and qualitatively. The quantitative analysis examined the influence of the native language on the narrative length and the size and richness of the identity lexicon. The qualitative analysis considered similarities and differences in lexical choices made by native speakers and learners of Russian, and allowed us to identify clusters of identity terms that caused difficulties for the learners. Throughout the analysis, we distinguished between *lemmas* (units of meaning or words) and *tokens* (lexical items or lexemes).

Results

Quantitative analysis

A Kolmogorov-Smirnov test revealed that all of our data (life story length, proportion of identity term tokens per narrative) are normally distributed; the additional F-test showed no differences in variances between the native speaker and the learner corpora in reference to the above specified parameters. We therefore used parametric statistics (independent sample t-test and analyses of variance (ANOVA)) to analyse the data. Table 8.1 summarizes the comparison of the American learner corpus and the Russian native speaker corpus in terms of size and lexical richness of identity vocabulary.

Table 8.1 Size and lexical richness in the life story corpora

	N of words	N of identity term lemmas	N of identity term tokens	Lexical richness of the identity lexicon
Russian corpus n = 30	32,015 mean = 1,067.2	147 mean = 4.9	1,160 mean = 38.7	0.13
American learner corpus n = 30	24,225 mean = 807.5	124 mean = 4.1	780 mean = 26.0	0.16

In terms of narrative length, we found significant differences between Russian monolinguals and American learners ($t = 2.61$, $df = 58$, $p < 0.05$), with the American group producing shorter life stories (mean = 807.5 words, $SD = 409.7$) than the Russian group (mean = 1067.2 words, $SD = 356.1$). An ANOVA confirmed the significance of the language group effect ($F = 6.8$, $df = 1$, $p < 0.05$). This result is particularly interesting because in the analysis of elicited fictional narratives from the same two groups of participants, learners' narratives were significantly longer than those of native speakers of Russian ($p < 0.003$) (Pavlenko and Driagina 2007). One possible explanation is that the learners may have felt more comfortable with elicited fictional narratives, a task similar to picture and film descriptions required of them in their Russian classes. According to the comments made in the interviews and in the debriefing procedure, some students had little or no experience with self-translation in a coherent narrative format, with the focus on the content rather than on particular lexical items or grammatical structures. Their experiences with life story telling were often limited to tasks eliciting personal utterances in the form of a list (e.g., Things I like) or a dialogue; for example:

(1) Мою семью? Ой, сколько раз я сделал этот диалог. С первого класса.

(My family? Oy, how many times did I do that dialogue. From the first grade on [what the speaker means here is 'from the first Russian class on'].)

(Paul[1], 20, international affairs major)

American learners also used fewer identity term tokens than Russian monolinguals (780 vs. 1160), but there was no significant difference between the two participant groups in terms of proportion of identity-term tokens in the overall corpus ($t = 0$, $df = 58$, $p = ns$). The learners' overall identity lexicon was somewhat more limited than that of the Russian speakers (124 vs. 147 lemmas); however, the richness of the identity lexicon was slightly higher in the American learner corpus that in the native speaker corpus (0.16 vs. 0.13). Therefore, quantitatively, the learner and the native speaker corpora were not significantly different from each other in terms of identity vocabulary employed in the life stories.

Qualitative analysis

Our qualitative analysis tells a somewhat different story. The analysis consisted of two steps. First, we applied thematic analysis, which allowed us to subdivide our identity term corpus into three categories: (a) family membership, age and gender; (b) profession, occupation and class; and (c) other social affiliations and characteristics. We then compared the uses of terms in each category in the native speaker and in the learner corpus both quantitatively and qualitatively, and in the learner corpus we also analysed lexical choices in terms of correctness and appropriateness (for a full list of identity terms used by the two groups, see Appendixes 2 and 3).

Family membership, age and gender

Identity terms related to family membership, age and gender constituted the largest group in both corpora. In the native speaker corpus, 26.5 per cent of all identity lemmas and 53 per cent of all tokens fell into this group. In the American learner corpus, it was 25 per cent and 55.5 per cent respectively. Analysis of the learner corpus shows that the learners were well familiar with Russian kinship terms and used them appropriately and correctly (with the exception of the lemma *kuzen* 'cousin' which is an archaic borrowing, not used in Modern Russian). They also demonstrated the mastery of basic age distinctions, differentiating, for instance, between *devochka* 'little girl', *devushka* 'young woman', *zhenshchina* 'woman' and *staruha* 'old woman'.

There are also, however, subtle differences in the use of family membership terms between the two participant groups. To begin with, the learner corpus is limited to kinship terms and forms of address. In turn, the native speaker corpus also contains a number of collective nouns which delineate belongingness to one's circle of family, relatives and close friends: *rodnye* (a language-specific term referring to 'people related by blood or very close spiritually, emotionally'), *rodnia* (a related and more colloquial term synonymous to *rodnye* or *rodstvenniki* 'relatives'), *blizkie* ('circle of the closest, dear people'), *lubimye* ('loved ones'). These collective nouns, derived from adjectives signifying affection, function not simply as kinship terms but as emotional membership references, saturated with feelings of closeness and intimacy. As seen in examples below, they were employed by Russian speakers to sustain the emotional warmth of passages in which they discussed their family members:

(2) Я всегда с-с большой гордостью говорю о своей родине, то есть я туда приезжаю, у меня открывается второе дыхание, буквально вот эта вот природа, вот это вот успокоение, изобилие фруктов, то есть

родные, близкие, друзья, которые меня/э то есть с которыми я уже
поддерживаю отношения теплые, именно с детских лет . . .

(I always speak about my motherland with-with great pride, that is, I
come there, I get a second wind, literally this nature, this this serenity,
abundance of fruit, that is [dear] relatives (*rodnye*), close ones (*blizkie*),
friends (*druzia*), who/uhm, with whom I keep a warm relationship,
precisely from childhood . . .)

(Lera, 20, engineering major)

(3) Семья . . . ну . . . семья у меня интересная, все любимые, мама, папа,
братик . . . младший.

(Family . . . well . . . my family is interesting, all my loved ones (*lubi-mye*), Mom, Dad, little brother (*bratik* DIMINUTIVE) . . . younger.)

(Olga, 20, engineering major)

Native speakers of Russian also favoured adjectives from which these collective nouns are derived. Thus, adjectives *rodnoi* ('related by blood or spiritually'), *lubimyi* ('loved, beloved') and *blizkii* ('close') frequently appeared as modifiers of such terms as *drug* (friend), *druzia* ('friends'), *otnoshenia* ('relationship'), *brat* ('brother'), *gorod* ('town'), *chelovek* ('person'), *ludi* ('people') (55 tokens). As mentioned earlier, *rodnoi* ('close, native') is an untranslatable Russian word that presents a person as a blood relative even if they are not an actual member of the family in question; this meaning also extends to metaphoric usages of the word, bringing in emotional overtones absent from the English term 'native' (Levontina 2005; Wierzbicka 1997); for example:

(4) Я очень люблю своих родителей, скучаю, потому что уже четыре
месяца их не видела, все равно домой тянет, как . . . ну все равно . . .
хотя, конечно, Томск уже как бы стал родной дом.

(I love my parents very much, miss them, because [I] haven't seen
them for four months now, [I] still really want to go home, well . . . still
. . . although, of course, Tomsk already became like home [*rodnoi dom*,
literally 'native, related/ kin home'].)

(Sasha, 20, engineering major)

Interestingly, while American learners did not use the nouns in this semantic
domain, they are beginning to appropriate the adjectives: we found 11 tokens
of *rodnoi*, *blizkii* and *lubimyi* in their narratives; for example:

(5) А может быть десять лет назад мои родители, то есть мама и отчим,
переместились в Вашингтон . . . , так что я не знаю новый дом так

хорошо. Так что для меня, я считаю, что как бы родной дом или семейный дом, это первый дом все-таки для меня.

(And maybe ten years ago my parents, that is mother and stepfather, moved to Washington ..., so I don't know the new house that well. So for me I consider that the native home (*rodnoi dom*) or family home is still the first house for me.)
(Ben, 31, graduate student in Slavic languages and literature)

Another feature that differentiates the native speaker corpus from the learner corpus is the use of kinship terms, such as *dedushka* ('grandpa'), *diaden'ka* ('uncle'; colloq.), *teten'ka* ('auntie'; colloq.) and *bratok* ('brother'; colloq), in reference to non-family members. Levontina (2005) comments that the metaphor of kinship is widely used in colloquial Russian for a variety of affective purposes, most often to signal a warm quasi-kin relationship, and at times also to signal a somewhat dismissive attitude; for example:

(6) Я бы хотела там поработать. Тем более как бы у нас специалистов таких с высшим образованием нету, ну там уже как бы все такие старые тетеньки работают, ну, есть как бы перспективы наверно.

(I would like to work for a while there. Especially because we are lacking such specialists with higher education, well, it's like old ladies [*teten'ki*; literally *aunties*] are working there, so there is a future in this, probably.)
(Larissa, 20, engineering major)

Similar trends are seen in the use of diminutives and expressive derivation. Native speakers of Russian use more diminutive nouns when speaking of others in their circle than do American learners (19 tokens vs. 5 tokens, excluding nouns that are inherently diminutive in form, e.g., *devochka* ('girl'), *babushka* ('grandmother')). This difference in usage once again reflects a linguistic and cultural difference: While there are some diminutives in English (e.g., Mommy, kiddie, auntie), in Russian the use of diminutives and expressive derivation of personal names (e.g., *Elena > Lenochka* ('little Helen')) is widespread, diminutive suffixes play a prominent role in personal interactions by signalling feelings of warmth, affection and intimacy (Wierzbicka 1984, 1992); for example:

(7) У меня мама, папа, есть еще младший братишка, на четыре года меня младше, Павлик.

(I have Mom, Dad, there is also a little brother (*bratishka* DIM.), four years younger than me, *Pavlik* [< Pavel, expressive derivation].)
(Lena, 20, business and management major)

A few learners, however, have begun to appropriate these language- and culture-specific uses of diminutives; for example:

(8) Если моя мама расстроилась или что-то случилась, со/собака знает и сразу к ней подходит и 'Не плачь, мамочка, пожалуйста'.

(If my Mom is upset or something happened the do/dog knows and right away comes to her and 'Don't cry, Mommy [*mamochka*, DIM], please'.)

(Laura, 23, Russian major)

Overall, however, we see that advanced learners in our study use kinship-, age- and gender-related terms appropriately in their literal meanings, but do not yet have mastery of their metaphoric extensions to non-blood relatives, of the nouns in the semantic domain of *rodnoi/blizkii* ('close one'), and of affective uses of the kinship terms, diminutives and expressive derivation.

Profession, occupation and class

The second category of identity terms in our analysis is profession or occupation of the life story protagonists (42.2 per cent of all lemmas and 16 per cent of all tokens in the native speaker corpus, and 47.5 per cent and 23.7 per cent respectively in the learner one). The American learners used 50 different Russian terms for various professions and occupations, closely approximating the breadth of the native speaker lexicon. At the same time, 22 per cent of the terms (41 tokens) were used by the learners inappropriately. These errors can be subdivided into three types. The first type involves formal errors, whereby the learners distort the phonological or morphological form of the word; for example:

(9) Я вырос в много местах ... да, я жил в семь штатах. потому что мой отец был *цветощик / цветощиком, он работал в церковь/в церкови.

(I grew up in many places ... yes, I lived in seven states, because my father was *tsvetoshchik* /*tsvetoshchikom* [should be *svyashchennikom* ('minister')], he worked at the church/at the church [changes the ending].)

(Jeff, 24, graduate student in international studies)

The second type involves cases where learners simply lacked the appropriate terms and code-switched to English in order to fill their lexical gaps; for example:

(10) И моя старшая сестра ... она ... работает кем-нибудь. Она была *social worker.

(And my older sister ... she ... works as someone. She was a *social worker*.)

(Paul, 20, international affairs major)

(11) Да, а моя мама она работала/она была учитель американской истории, но и потом, она, ну, после мой брат родил/родились/ родился он/она больше не работала / ну она работала как, я не знаю как сказать, с налогами, не знаю, *consultant* или что-то ...

(Yes, and my mother she worked/she was a teacher of American history, but and later, she, well, after my brother was bo/born/born she/she no longer worked/ well, she worked as a, I don't know how to say, with taxes, I don't know, *consultant* or something ...)

(Laura, 20, Russian major)

(12) А у меня брат есть, просто человек такой ((смеется)). Ааа но он будет стать *lieutenant* в армии ...

(And I have a brother, simply such a person ((laughs)) Aah but he will become a *lieutenant* in the army ...

(Mark, 21, Spanish major)

The learners also experienced lexical difficulties in discussing class issues, appealing to circumlocution and direct speech to overcome vocabulary limitations and to transmit the American notions of class; for example:

(13) Ой, мой отец он работает плотником и он владелец своего бизне:са. Он более-менее успешный, более-менее богатый, но мы/мы как средний класс. Мы не как 'О, мой отец только врач, и моя мама *юрист*. Мы средний класс'. Это как настоящий средний класс. И у нас есть *минивэн* и так далее.

(Oy, my father, he works as a carpenter and he is the owner of his business. He is more or less successful, more or less rich, but we/ we are middle-class. We are not like 'Oh, my father is only a doctor, and my mother a *iurist*. We are middle-class.' This is real middle-class. We have a *minivan* [lexical borrowing] etc.)

(Paul, 20, international affairs major)

Interestingly, while *iurist* is one possible translation of the term 'lawyer', in the present context it does not work, because the core meaning of the term *iurist* is a 'legal specialist' or 'legal consultant'. To convey the notion of a 'wealthy lawyer', the speaker would need a different word, *advokat* ('defence lawyer'). This error, stemming from the fact that the English-language category of 'lawyer' is quite broad while the corresponding Russian domain is more differentiated, exemplifies the third category, semantic errors.[2]

Somewhat unexpectedly, the learners – undergraduate and graduate students themselves – made the most errors when using academic terms. For instance, Russian differentiates between 'secondary school students' (*ucheniki, shkol'niki*) and 'college or university students' (*studenty*). Consequently, when describing their secondary school experience, native Russian speakers used such terms as *odnoklassnik/odnoklassnitsa* ('male/female classmate'; 17 tokens), *shkol'nik* ('schoolchild'; 1 token), and *uchenik* ('pupil'; 2 tokens). It is only in discussions of their experiences in higher education that they used the word *student* ('college/university student'; 7 tokens). In English, on the other hand, the term 'student' has a very broad semantic scope, referring not only to college and university but also to secondary school students. It is not surprising, then, that several American learners committed first language (L1) transfer, mistakenly extending the use of the Russian word *student* to pre-college studies, both in secondary school and even in the nursery school (12 erroneous tokens); for example:

(14) ... я/я был *студентом немецкого языка и я/я всегда хотел изучать ц/самый странный язык, и когда я был на/в школе, это был немецкий, и сейчас в колледже я/я изучаю русск/русский язык ...

(... I/I was a *student* of German, and I/I always wanted to study the st/ strangest language, and when I was in/at school, it was German, and now in college I/I study Russian ...)

(George, 20, history major)

(15) Но я был неплохим *студентом, и когда мне было одиннадцать лет, я начинал как специальную школу как для особенных хороших *студентов литературы и истории и социальных вещей и социальных/ социальных ученых или что-то, не знаю.

(But I was not a bad *student*, and when I was 11 years old, I began a special school, for particularly good *students* of literature and history and social things and social/social scholars or something, I don't know.)

(John, 20, history major)

The learners also misused the term *professor* (20 tokens, all erroneous). This term is also only a partial cognate of the Russian word *professor*. In English, 'professor' may function as a rank term and as a form of address for a variety of college- and university- level instructors. In Russian, on the other hand, the use of the term is limited to those occupying the rank similar to that of a full professor in the United States or a Chair in the United Kingdom. School teachers are referred to as *uchitelia* ('teachers') or *prepodavateli* ('instructors') and college faculty as *prepodavateli* ('instructors'); for example:

(16) Ну, мама преподавателем – она работает преподавателем в моей же школе, где я учился.

(Well, Mom is a teacher [instructor] – she works as a teacher [instructor] at the very school where I studied.)

(Aleksei, 21, engineering major)

The learners, however, once again committed semantic extension driven by the L1 transfer and used the term *professor* to refer to their university instructors or even school teachers, as in the discussion of high school below:

(17) Я была отличная *студентка и ... я много читала и я любила рисовать и ... разговаривать конечно. И я/всегда *teacher/*тичеры *профессоры всегда были сердиты на меня.

(I was an excellent *student* and I ... read a lot and I liked to draw and ... talk of course. And I/always *teachers* ... *teachery* [lexical borrowing], *professors* were angry at me.)

(Mary, 20, Russian area studies major)

While it is understandable that such partial cognates may lead to semantic extension in beginning students of Russian, it was unexpected to discover that these errors systematically appear in the speech of advanced students. Most introductory and intermediate textbooks present students with a full set of terms referring to students and teachers, or at least differentiate between college and secondary school students and instructors (e.g., Kagan and Miller 1996; Martin and Zaitsev 2001; Morris, Vyatyutnev and Vokhmina 1993; Rosengrant and Lifschitz 1996). Kagan and Miller (1996: 395), for instance, differentiate between *shkol'nik/shkol'nitsa* (elementary school student), *uchenik/uchenitsa* (school student), *student/studentka* (college student), and *aspirant/aspirantka* (graduate student).

Without further inquiry into acquisition of these terms it is impossible to determine precisely why these distinctions have not been acquired by the students in our study yet the data strongly suggest that further attention needs to be paid to the teaching of these identity categories. Considering the centrality of academic terminology for the students' presentation of self, we argue that, in order to avoid fossilization of semantic extensions, academic identity terms – and in particular false and partial cognates – need to be introduced in the teaching materials early on, repeatedly, and in a contextualized and contrastive manner that helps the learners to differentiate systematically between different types of students and teachers and thus avoid misunderstandings in communication with their Russian interlocutors.

Other social affiliations and characteristics

The third category in our study involved references to social affiliations and characteristics (29.3 per cent of lemmas and 31 per cent of tokens in the native speaker corpus, and 27.5 per cent of lemmas and 20.8 per cent of tokens in the learner corpus). Both native speakers and American learners of Russian employed a wide variety of terms to refer to their own and others' social affiliations and characteristics, although native speakers demonstrated a slightly more diverse lexical repertoire than the learners (43 vs. 34 lemmas respectively).

The learners also exhibited three types of errors in references to social affiliations. The first type of error was semantic extension, this time in the domain of friendship. Native speakers of Russian systematically distinguished between different types of friends and acquaintances, such as *drug/podruga* ('close male/ female friend'; 158 tokens), *znakomyi* ('acquaintance'; 33 tokens), *priyatel'* ('person one is in a friendly, affectionate relationship with'; 5 tokens) and *tovarishch* ('comrade, friend, mate'; 2 tokens); for example:

(18) Ну у меня так, я могу сказать, что у меня в принципе больше не друзей, а приятелей, таких очень близких мне людей / таких друзей очень близких у меня мало как бы. Ну вот приятелей, знакомых много, есть с кем пойти, там, повеселиться, но чтобы с кем-то такие вот были очень близкие отношения таких людей мало.

(Well, I can say that actually that I have more *priyateli* rather than *druz'ya*, it's like very close/such close *druz'ya* I have very few. But I have many *priyateli, znakomye*, I have people to go out with, to have fun, but to have a very close relationship with, I have very few such people.)

(Larissa, 20, engineering major)

The use of these terms by the speaker reflects a central characteristic of Russian discourse, frequently discussed by linguists – categorical distinctions made between close friends (*drug/podruga*) and various types of acquaintances (Shmelyov 2005; Wierzbicka 1997, 1999). In contrast, in English the word 'friend' has a much broader semantic scope and can be used in reference to close friends and recent acquaintances alike. In accordance with the English-language pattern, American learners of Russian used the terms *drug/podruga* 54 times, with only one mention of *znakomyi* and *priyatel'*.

Similar to the case of academic identity terms, this performance reflects L1 transfer of a conceptual category delineated by English into Russian: the learners are either unable or unwilling to utilize the full Russian lexicon of friendship. While it is the learners' choice whether or not to attend to the specificity of social relationships in their speech, they should be made aware of the importance that Russians place on identifying someone as a friend: overuse of the term *drug* (friend) can lead to misunderstanding, awkwardness or perception of the speaker as a shallow person by the Russian interlocutors.

The second set of errors involved substitution of ethnic and national identity nouns with adjectives; for example:

(19) Моя мама сама русская, *белорусская ...

(My mother herself is Russian, *Belorussian* [should have been белоруска) ...)

(Steve, 24, graduate student in Russian)

(20) ... ну в моей школе все были *итальянские и это был итальянский район ...

(... in my school everyone was *Italian* [should have been итальянцы] and it was an Italian area ...)

(Kate, 23, graduate student in Russian)

(21) Ой, у меня большая ирландская семья, это не редко в Нью-Йорке. Ты еврей, *ирландский или *итальянский, если ты живешь в Нью-Йорке. И русский конечно ...

(Oy, I have a big Irish family, this is not a rarity in New York. You are a Jew, *Irish* or *Italian* [should have been ирландец или итальянец], if you live in New York. And Russian of course ...)

(Paul, 20, international affairs major)

These category errors also stem from transfer, as English uses the same words as ethnic and national identity adjectives and nouns, both single and collective. Russian, on the other hand, has distinct nouns and adjectives in this category (e.g., *frantsuz/frantsuzhenka*: 'French (person)' (noun, masc. and fem.), *frantsuzy*: 'the French' (collective noun), *frantsuzskii/frantsuzskaia*: 'French' (adjective, masc and fem)). The most notable exception in Russian is, in fact, the word 'Russian' itself, where the same form *russkii* (masc.)/ *russkaia* (fem.) is used both as a noun and as an adjective. In the majority of the other cases students are asked to learn corresponding adjectives and nouns. Yet, even though they are warned against confusing the two categories and offered the appropriate vocabulary from the introductory level on, for some learners the confusion between structural categories persists.

The third set of problems involved cases where translation equivalents do not exist or at least are unfamiliar to the students. In these cases the students resorted to code-switching in characterizing people; for example:

(22) Был очень трудно из-за того как я/меня считали как *scapegoat*, что и дети как всегда смеялись на меня.

(It was very difficult because I/I was considered a *scapegoat*, and children always laughed at me.)
(Laura, 20, Russian major)

(23) Она самая умная/ самый умный человек в моей семье ... Но она очень, но она большой *nerd*, и ей так чуть-чуть грустно в школе.

(She is the smartest/the smartest member of my family ... But she is very, she is a big *nerd*, and it is somewhat sad in school for her.)
(Paul, 20, international affairs major)

We are not however concerned about this code-switching, especially becausethe switches appeared in interviews with a speaker bilingual in Russian and English. It is quite possible that in conversations with Russian speakers who are not fluent in English, the learners would express these meanings differently, for instance, appealing to circumlocution.

Discussion and conclusions

To sum up, the American learner corpus in our study contains numerous instances of correct and appropriate uses of identity terms referring to kinship, profession, social affiliations, age, gender, looks and personality. At the same time, the learners' usage differs qualitatively from that of native speakers of Russian, exhibiting the following distinguishing characteristics: (a) semantic and conceptual transfer evident in semantic extensions; (b) structural transfer; (c) lexical gaps evident in instances of code-switching and lexical borrowing; (d) narrow, and mainly literal, scope or reference; and (e) reduced affective range. The finding that the students have a reduced affective range of identity terms, seen in the lack of mastery of metaphoric uses of kinship terms, diminutives and expressive derivation, is consistent with our overall finding that advanced American learners of Russian have difficulties with authentic emotional expression and description in their L2 Russian (Pavlenko and Driagina 2007).

Together, these errors and weaknesses signal three main problems in self-translation and self-representation. The instances of code-switching and lexical borrowing suggest that sometimes the learners do not know how to map their own reality appropriately onto the Russian semantic map. This is a common problem that stems not only from lexical gaps but also from social and cultural differences between the two speech communities. Second, taken together, lexical gaps, the lack of metaphoric extensions, and reduced affective range suggest that the students have a somewhat limited array of resources at their disposal, which is also to be expected in the case of classroom learners. A more disconcerting problem is presented by the cases where students map their own reality inappropriately onto Russian, as seen in the transfer of the all-encompassing L1 categories 'friend', 'lawyer', 'professor' and 'student' into the L2. These instances of semantic and possibly conceptual transfer reflect a lack of understanding of the internal structure of important Russian identity categories, all of which are more semantically differentiated than their English counterparts.

Unfortunately, we have been unable to elicit any references to race, sexuality or (dis)ability. It is unclear whether these references did not occur because of the students' lack of relevant vocabulary, because of the limited scope of our questionnaire, or because of the students' perceptions of these topics as irrelevant or taboo. Consequently, we were unable to address Shardakova and Pavlenko's (2004) arguments about the effects of omission of this vocabulary in the Russian textbooks. We did, however, identify an even more important problem – the fact that semantic and structural non-equivalences lead to difficulties in acquisition and use even for those identity terms that are well-represented in the textbooks.

A major limitation of the corpus analysed here is the lack of any descriptions of negotiation of identities with Russian-speaking interlocutors. This limitation is intentional and can be explained by our criteria for participant selection. Because we were interested in learners who acquired their identity repertoires primarily through classroom instruction, our learner group included only a few learners who had any experience in the Russian-speaking context. In order to see how cross-cultural contact is perceived and experienced, and how it transforms and expands learners' identity repertoires, future studies could examine identity repertoires of American learners before, during and after a study abroad experience, where most, if not all, will have had numerous attempts at self-translation in interactions with Russian interlocutors.

Another limitation of our findings is the exclusive focus on identity terms and, more specifically, nouns. While we found this focus to be extremely informative and well-linked to presentation of the terms in foreign language textbooks, in future studies it would be important to consider a full range of semantic, morphosyntactic, pragmatic and prosodic self-presentation resources used by the students.

We also realize that the approach taken here can be seen as an imposition of native speaker standard, and perhaps even of monolingual bias. We argue, however, that this approach is in fact consistent with the multicompetence model and the L2 user perspective (Cook 2002). To begin with, we take an emic – that is, student – perspective on the goals of our study, which is consistent with the L2 user approach (Pavlenko 2002). The participants in our study do want to be compared to native speakers of Russian, not because this is who they want to be, but because these are their prospective interlocutors with whom they have to reach an understanding. And since semantic errors outlined above will affect communication, the students are interested in knowing where and how they can fine-tune their uses and interpretations of identity terms.

Second, in accordance with the multicompetence perspective, we acknowledge the hybrid and multilingual nature of their repertoires and do not exhibit concern with formal errors that do not affect communication, nor with code-switching and lexical borrowing. Rather, we are concerned with 'hidden' semantic errors whereby students impose their own worldview onto the new reality and miss out on the opportunity to learn new ways of presenting and interpreting identities.

Most importantly, in line with the multicompetence model, we are concerned with self-translation, that is with ways in which L2 users of Russian appeal to their linguistic repertoires to translate what is often untranslatable, their identities as Americans, into Russian. We do not expect that they will create artificial Russian identities for themselves. Rather, we are concerned with providing them with adequate means of self-expression and with alerting them to conceptual non-equivalences.

Our inquiry suggests that to acquire a fuller range of Russian identity terms and thus new interpretive repertoires, the learners will need a variety of consciousness-raising and noticing activities focused on cross-linguistic differences between Russian and English identity terms. For the learners to internalize the terms non-equivalent to English, more opportunities must be created in the classroom to discuss topics relevant to their lives and identities and more space for tasks that appeal to their motivation and ignite interest in expressing themselves through the means of the Russian language.

Notes

1. To protect the confidentiality of participants, all names have been changed.
2. Without further inquiry we cannot decide whether all of these errors also represent the case of conceptual transfer, consequently, we will use the more moderate term 'semantic'.

APPENDIX 1

Life Story Interview Guide

1. When and where were you born?

2. Please tell me about your childhood.

3. When and where did you go to school?

4. Please tell me about your school years.

5. Where were you and how old were you when the Soviet Union ceased to exist? (Only for Russian participants)

6. Please tell me about ways in which you managed life in the Soviet Union and ways in which you managed life in Russia. (Only for Russian participants)

7. Please tell me about your current educational status and your future plans.

8. Please tell me about your career plans and why you decided to choose your particular career.

9. Please tell me about your family.

10. Please tell me about your friends.

APPENDIX 2

Identity Terms in the Russian Corpus

(Total lemmas = 147, tokens = 1160)

Family membership, age and gender (lemmas = 39; 26.5%; tokens = 616; 53%)	Profession, occupation, and class (lemmas = 65; 44.2% tokens = 184; 16%)	Other social affiliations and characteristics (lemmas = 43; 29.3% tokens = 360; 31%)
бабушка (grandma) 32	автомеханик (auto mechanic) 1	болельщик (sports fan) 1
близкие (close people) 2	администратор (administrator) 3	братки (*col.*, gangsters) 1
близняшки (*dim.*, twins) 1	аудитор (auditor) 2	выпускники (alumni) 1
брат (brother) 57	бакалавр (bachelor) 3	гражданин (*masc.*, citizen) 1
братик (*dim.*, brother) 1	бандит (bandit) 1	друг (friend) 128
братишка (*dim.*, brother) 2	бухгалтер (accountant) 2	земляк (fellow-townsman) 4
взрослые (adults) 6	водитель (driver) 5	знакомый (*masc.*, acquaintance) 33
девочка (little girl) 12	воспитатель (pre-school teacher) 2	индивидуум (individual) 1
девчонка (*dim.*, girl) 3	врач (doctor) 3	иногородняя (*fem.*, person from out of town) 1
девушка (young woman; girlfriend) 17	директор (director) 5	
	диспетчер (dispatcher) 1	иностранец (*masc.*, foreigner) 1
дед (grandfather) 4	двоечник (poor student) 1	казах (*masc.*, Kazakh) 1
дедушка (grandpa) 7	домохозяйка (housewife) 1	казахстанец (*masc.*, citizen of Kazakhstan) 1
двоюродный брат (male cousin) 3	заводила (ringleader) 1	
дочка (*dim.*, daughter) 2	завуч (school head-master) 3	коллега (colleague) 2
дочь (daughter) 2	инженер (engineer) 25	коммунист (communist) 1
дяденька (*col., dim.*, man) 1	инспектор (inspector) 1	личность (persona, personality) 3
жена (wife) 4	историчка (*col.*, history teacher) 1	любимица (*fem.*, favorite) 1
женщина (woman) 10	консультант (consultant) 1	люди (people) 53
любимые (loved ones) 2	лидер (leader) 2	народ (*collective*, people) 2
мальчик (boy) 7	лингвист (linguist) 1	одногруппник (*masc.*, group-mate in university) 6
мальчишка (*dim.*, boy) 6	маляр (house-painter) 1	одногруппница (*fem.*, group-mate in university) 2
мама (Mom) 86	медик (medic) 1	
матушка (*dim.*, Mom) 1	менеджер (manager) 7	

мать (mother) 8
муж (husband) 5
мужчина (man, male) 4
отец (father) 25
папа (Dad) 50
парень (guy, boyfriend) 16

племянница (niece) 1
ребенок (child) 45
родители (parents) 151

родные (relatives) 1
родня (*col.*, relatives) 1
родственник (relative) 8

сестра (sister) 21
сестренка (*dim.*, sister) 7

сын (son) 4

тетенька (*col., dim.*, woman) 1

метролог (metrology engineer) 2
механизатор (mechanical engineer) 1
механик (mechanic) 2
милиционер (militia man) 1
начальник (boss) 2
нянечка (*dim.*, care-giver) 1
охранник (guard) 2
переводчик (interpreter) 1
повар (cook) 1
президент (president) 2
преподаватель (teacher; instructor) 9
программист (programmer) 1
прораб (work superintendent) 1
психолог (psychologist) 2

рабочий (worker) 3
радиооператор (radio technician) 1
руководитель (manager) 8
сертификатор (certifier) 1
специалист (specialist) 4
стандартизатор (standard controller) 1
стоматолог (dentist) 1
строитель (construction worker) 3
студент (student) 4
токарь (turner) 4
тракторист (tractor driver) 1
тренер (coach) 1
управленец (administrator, manager) 2
управляющий (manager) 1
ученик (pupil, student) 2

одноклассник (*masc.*, classmate) 13
одноклассница (*fem.*, classmate) 4
октябренок (young pioneer) 1
отличник (*masc.*, straight-A student) 1
отличница (*fem.*, straight-A student) 1
пацанка (*col., fem.*, tomboy) 2
первопроходец (explorer, inciter) 1
пионер (pioneer) 2
подруга (female friend) 28
подружка (*dim.*, female friend) 2
приятель (*masc.*, friend) 5
проказник (*masc.*, mischievous child; prankster) 1
ребята (guys, friends) 2
россияне (Russian citizens) 1
русский (*masc.*, Russian) 1
советчик (*masc.*, mentor) 1
сосед (*masc.*, neighbor) 3
соседка (*fem.*, neighbor) 1
тёзка (namesake) 1
товарищ (*masc.*, friend) 2
томич (resident of Tomsk) 4
трудоголик (workaholic) 1

человек (human being) 38

(Continued)

Family membership, age and gender (lemmas = 39; 26.5%; tokens = 616; 53%)	Profession, occupation, and class (lemmas = 65; 44.2%; tokens = 184; 16%)	Other social affiliations and characteristics (lemmas = 43; 29.3% tokens = 360; 31%)
	учитель (*masc.*, teacher) 19 учительница (*fem.*, teacher) 8 фармацевт (pharmacist) 1 футболист (football player) 1 химик (chemist) 2 шахтер (miner) 2 швея (seamstress) 1 школьники (schoolchildren) 1 шофер (driver) 1 штукатур (plasterer) 1 экономист (economist) 5 электрик (electrician) 3	

Note: *dim.* = diminutive form; *col.* = colloquial; *collective* = collective noun; *fem.* = feminine noun; *masc.* = masculine noun.

APPENDIX 3

Identity Terms in the Learner Corpus

(Total lemmas = 124, tokens = 780)

Family membership, age and gender (lemmas = 31; 25%; tokens = 433; 55.5%)	Profession/occupation (lemmas = 59; 47.5%; tokens = 185; 23.7%)	Other social affiliations and characteristics (lemmas = 34; 27.5%; tokens = 162; 20.8%)
бабушка (grandma) 17	*автор (author, used in the meaning of writer = писатель) 1	американец (*masc.*, American) 9
близнец (twin) 1		американка (*fem.*, American) 1
брат (brother) 68	адвокат (lawyer) 4	англичанин (Englishman) 2
внук (grandson) 1	актер (actor) 2	*белорусская = белоруска (Belarusian) 1
девочка (little girl) 6	аспирант (graduate student) 4	
девушка (young woman; girlfriend) 4	балерина (*fem.*, ballet dancer) 1	блондин (*masc.*, blonde) 1
	банкир (banker) 1	ботаник (*coll*, nerd) 2
дедушка (grandpa) 16	врач (doctor) 3	гуманист (humanitarian) 1
двоюродный брат / сестра (cousin) 5	губернатор (governor) 1	*заво̀дила = заводила (ringleader) 1
дочка (*dim.*, daughter) 3	дипломат (diplomat) 1	друг (friend) 40
жена (wife) 4	доктор (doctor) 1	еврей (Jew) 3
женщина (woman) 11	журналист (journalist) 1	знакомые (acquaintances) 1
кузен (*book.*, male cousin) 1	инженер (engineer) 2	иммигрантка (*fem.*, immigrant) 1
	исследователь (researcher) 2	
мальчик (boy) 9	кандидат (candidate) 1	иностранец (*masc.*, foreigner) 2
мама (Mom) 57	медсестра (nurse) 1	*итальянский = итальянец (Italian) 2
мамочка (Mommy) 1	менеджер (manager) 3	
мать (mother) 6	музыкант (musician) 3	*ирландский = ирландец (Irish) 1
*молодижь (youth) 2	официантка (waitress) 1	любитель (fan) 1
муж (husband) 2	пастырь (preacher) 1	люди (people) 27
отец (father) 37	пенсионер (*masc.*, pensioner) 3	наркоман (drug addict) 2
отчим (step-father) 2	пенсионерка (*fem.*, pensioner) 2	
папа (Dad) 33	переводчик (interpreter) 5	немец (*masc.*,) German 1
парень (guy; boyfriend) 1	*печатальник (printer) 1	подруга (female friend) 13
*подростник=	первокурсник (freshman; also used incorrectly to refer to first grader = первоклассник) 2	подружка (*dim.*, female friend) 1
подросток (teenager) 1		приятель (*masc.*, friend) 1
ребенок (child) 29		русский (*masc.*, Russian) 4

(Continued)

Family membership, age and gender (lemmas = 31; 25%; tokens = 433; 55.5%)	Profession/occupation (lemmas = 59; 47.5%; tokens = 185; 23.7%)	Other social affiliations and characteristics (lemmas = 34; 27.5% tokens = 162; 20.8%)
родители (parents) 55	писатель (writer) 2	сосед (*masc.*, neighbor) 5
родственник (relative) 3	плотник (carpenter) 1	соседка (*fem.*, neighbor) 1
сестра (sister) 49	поэт (poet) 1	украинка (*fem.*, Ukrainian) 1
старуха (old woman) 1	президент (president) 2	феминистка (*fem.*, feminist) 1
сын (son) 5	преподаватель (*masc.*, teacher; instructor) 10	хулиган (hooligan) 2
тетя (aunt) 2		человек (human being) 28
троюродные братья и сестры (second cousins) 1	преподавательница (*fem.*, teacher; instructor) 6	чемпионка (*fem.*, champion) 2
	программист (programmer) 2	*чек=чех (*masc.*, Czech) 1
	*профессор (full professor) 20	шатен (person with brown hair) 1
	психотерапевт (psychotherapist) 3	*nerd 1
	работник (employee; worker) 1	*scapegoat 1
	репетитор (tutor) 2	
	редактор (editor) 2	
	режиссер (movie director) 3	
	секретарь (secretary) 1	
	секретарша (*fem.*, secretary) 2	
	*социальный ученый = социолог (sociologist) 1	
	специалист (specialist) 2	
	спортсмен (*masc.*, athlete) 2	
	спортсменка (*fem.*, athlete) 1	
	студент (student) 31 (out of these 12 *студент = ученик, pupil)	
	судья (judge) 3	
	танцор (dancer) 1	
	ученик (pupil, student) 1	
	учитель (*masc.*, teacher) 12	
	учительница (*fem.*, teacher) 14	
	*цветощик = священник (minister) 1	
	футболист (football player) 1	
	художник (artist) 3	
	художница (*fem.*, artist) 1	
	школьники (schoolchildren) 1	

*юрист (lawyer) 1
*consultant 1
*lieutenant 1
*photographer 1
*social worker 1

Note: book. = bookish; *dim.* = diminutive form; *col.* = colloquial; *collective* = collective noun; *fem.* = feminine noun; *masc.* = masculine noun; * word used inappropriately

9
Presentation of 'Self' in Application Letters

Zhu Hua

Birkbeck, University of London

Extending the argument proposed earlier in Part 2 of this volume that language learning is a social action, this chapter looks at the socialcultural construction of the concept of self in application letters by L2 users. I will argue that while there are specific conventions for genres, writing in all genres is in essence a process of self-presentation. The writers' social-cultural background will inevitably affect the way that ideas, information and arguments are presented in a piece of writing.

The role of culture

The role of culture in second language writing has long been acknowledged, though opinions differ with regard to the extent to which culture shapes second language writing. Strong support for the role of culture in second language writing comes from the Sapir-Whorf hypothesis of linguistic relativity (Sapir 1921) and Kaplan's seminal work on contrastive rhetoric (Kaplan 1966,1988). Since Kaplan's study, a huge number of studies have emerged investigating culture-specific writing patterns in languages such as Arabic, Chinese, Japanese, Korean, German, Finnish, Spanish, Czech and so on (for review, see Connor 1998; Silva 1993; and for a more recent one, see the selected bibliography published periodically in the *Journal of Second Language Writing*). In a recent study, Hinkel (2002) compared 68 syntactic, lexical and rhetorical features in essays written by advanced non-native speakers with those of native speakers enrolled in first-year composition courses. These studies attributed perceived differences between second language writing and native speaker's writing to differences in cultural conventions and linguistic influence from first language (L1).

Some researchers have argued that the differences in cultural conventions are, directly or indirectly, influenced by a wider social context, in particular, the pedagogical approach dominant in a particular culture. The educational system and strategies of learning and the way children learn to read and write in L1 all play a role in shaping the way people write in L2. Carson (1992), for example, noted that in countries such as Japan and China, rote-learning is widely used in literacy development and 'there is a strong belief that the path to lively and creative writing styles lies in internalizing others' styles'. Nisbett (2003) also argues that there seem to be differences between 'Easterners' and 'Westerners' in their fundamental assumptions about the inclination to use rules. Different cultures may also have different expectations of writer and reader responsibility. Hinds (1987) found that Japanese writing depends heavily on readers to work out the link between different sections, while English writers are expected to provide transitional statements.

Some researchers attempted to adopt a cognitive model of writing to explain cross-cultural differences in second language writing (Flower and Hayes 1981, Nystand 1989). In this model, writing is not a linear process where a writer starts with ideas and plans and then puts these ideas and plans to paper. Instead, it is seen as consisting of four interactive components: task, environment (i.e., the audience and the context), the writer's long-term memory (retaining relevant information about the topic, environment and writing plans), and the composing process itself (i.e., a discursive process of generating, organizing and translating ideas into texts). Cross-cultural differences in writing are evident when the composing process in the first language is transferred to or influences the second-language composing process (see Krapels 1990, for a review of L2 composing process research).

While studies of the cultural influence on writing succeed in acknowledging and highlighting differences between second language users' and native speakers' writing, some argue that when it comes to genres (i.e., a class of communicative events linked by shared purposes recognized by members of a discourse community, Swales 1990), such as CV, job application cover letter, grant proposal book review, etc), culture has very little role. For example, Bhatia (1993) argued that since genres are highly structured and conventionalized with constraints on allowable contributions in terms of intent, positioning, form and functional value, many of the professional and academic genres, particularly in research and science, are of the homogenous type. These writings are universally conventionalized to such an extent that even in their cross-cultural realizations, they rarely show any variations and therefore students are expected to follow these conventions despite the different cultural orientations they may have. While arguing for the conventionalized nature of genre, Bhatia (1993) also noticed that business genres seem to be an exception to the rule in that cross-cultural variations have been found to exist in sales promotion letters and job application letters. In particular, in the case of job application letters, East-Asian applicants seem to favour three strategies: self glorification, adversary-glorification and self-degradation. They tend to put forward unsupported claim of their own superiority, based simply on feelings or desires (self-glorification); sing praises to the organization of the prospective employer (adversary-glorification); or downgrade the current situation they are in either in terms of financial or academic resources. However, apart from this exception, Bhatia (1993) argued that genres seem to be very much culture-free (Bhatia 1993). The question is: does culture truly have little role in genres, in particular, in academic genres? To answer this question, we need to address the role of social context in writing first.

Writing/genre as social action

The role of social context in writing has been overlooked until the 1980s, when a social action model of writing, influenced by a Hallidayan Systemic Functional view of language to some extent, began to emerge. Concepts such as context, situation and discourse community have been expanded to incorporate a social constructivist element (Bizzell 1982a, b). In particular, the notion of discourse community was seen as a particular discursive space joining writers, texts and readers together. It 'foregrounds the socially situated nature of genre and helps illuminate something of what writers and readers bring to a text, implying a certain degree of inter-community diversity and intra-community homogeneity in generic forms' (Hyland 2003).

With such a shift, genre has ceased to be static and deterministic. Instead, it is seen as purposeful, socially situated responses to particular contexts and communities, and keys to understanding how to participate in the actions of a community (Miller 1984; also see a different definition of genre in the previous section). Evidence supporting this view comes from many perspectives. Some studies found that the writers' plans, goals and other process-based strategies are dependent on the particular purpose, setting and audience of writing (Heath 1983; Odell and Goswami 1985) – a practice that seems to have been dominant in standard textbooks used by schools in the past century. Prior (1995) argues that writing tasks are not static; instead, they are explicitly and implicitly negotiated throughout between the instructor and the student. Some studies examined writers' identity and the reader/writer power relationship. Starfield argues that

> Whether consciously or not, [student] writers textually convey a sense of who they are ... as well as their understanding of who their potential reader is.
>
> (2004: 69)

Kubota (2003) extends this discussion to gender, class and race, arguing that it is often the case that little attention is given to these categories in discussions of second language writing, when so many writers are women, and so many second language teachers are women.

Genre as a social-culturally situated phenomenon and this study

If we accept that genre is a form of social action and the concept of discourse community is embedded with socially situated dynamics, the role of culture in genres needs to be revisited, since discourse communities, apart from being constantly negotiated between writers and readers, cannot be free of cultural interpretations. Similar to any other group of people sharing core cultural values and beliefs, a discourse community shapes and is shaped by core cultural values and beliefs and ideologies of writers and readers by whom these values and beliefs are reproduced, transmitted, negotiated and potentially changed when writers interact with readers in discourse. For example, when writers are negotiating their identity and power relationship with their readers through writing as a form of social action, they need to present an image of their self. The very concept of 'self' and how to present self are found to have cross-cultural variations. Using the Twenty Statement Tests, various researchers (e.g., Bond and Cheung 1983; Cousins 1989; Markus and Kitayama 1991; Triandis, McCusker and Hui 1990) in social psychology have found that self in 'Eastern' cultures is defined by social membership (e.g., I'm a student of this University, I'm from China, etc.) while Western cultures seem to favour an independent self by referring to individual attributes (e.g., I'm 35, I'm fit, etc.). The different orientations towards self have been associated with individualism–collectivism constructs in that content of the self includes more group-linked elements in collectivist cultures than in individualist cultures (Triandis, McCusker and Hui 1990). However, there is little research on whether and how second language users adapt to the way native speakers present themselves in writing.

Extending the social action model to second language writing, I aim to focus on the sociocultural nature of genre in this chapter. By comparing the way advanced second language users construct self with that of native speakers in the context of the genre of the studentship application cover letter, I would argue that genre is not only a form of social action, but also subject to cultural interpretation. It is a social-culturally situated phenomenon.

In the following sections, I will review briefly the research on the application letter as a genre and to provide the rationale for the cross-cultural comparison framework adopted in the study.

Application letter

The present study focuses on a specific genre, namely studentship application letters, where the main purpose of writing is to promote one's abilities, skills, knowledge, experience and so on, in order to obtain financial support while taking into consideration the stakeholder's requirement (the specification of the studentship can be found in Appendix 1 together with a sample application letter in Appendix 2). Though there seem to be very few direct studies on studentship application cover letters, some findings are available on job application cover letters (e.g., Bhatia's 1993 findings discussed at the beginning of this chapter). Anecdotal evidence on cross-cultural variations in CV and job applications is abundant from guidebooks on how to find a job in another country. In *The Global Resumé and CV Guide*, Thompson (2000) highlighted different cultural practices associated with CVs and cover letters. According to the guide: in Japan, the job application or *rirekisho* is a handwritten two-page form that is purchased from the local stationery store; in Korea, it is important to state on your CV if you are the eldest child in the family; in Sweden, your CV should be signed by someone who can attest that what you wrote is true; in China, if you are looking for a job in a place far away from your home, you need to state if you intend to take your family as the employer needs to assess the suitability of the assignment location for a family in terms of spouse's job and children's schooling. While handwritten cover letters and attaching a photo to resumés are not considered appropriate in the United States, it is acceptable in countries like the Netherlands. Though studentship application letters and job application letters are not exactly the same, they share a number of similarities; for example, both are intended to be persuasive and capture the attention of the reader.

Cross-cultural comparison framework

Though a huge number of cross-cultural studies have emerged in the past 40 years, very little attention has been paid to the rationale and potential caveats behind different approaches used by cross-cultural comparative studies. The pros and cons of each approach will be discussed briefly in this section in the hope that results of this study will be interpreted in an appropriate context.

Perhaps, the most popular and intuitive one in cross-cultural comparative studies is to compare country by country, as 'geographical' and 'political' entities. In some studies, several countries or places are grouped together to compare with another group of countries or places. For example, the broad dichotomy of East versus West, the frequent grouping of Mainland China, Taiwan, Hong Kong, Korea and Japan as East-Asian, or the use of Arabic to refer to all the Arabic-speaking countries. One such example is Nisbett's book (2003) entitled *The Geography of Thought: How Asians and Westerners Think Differently – and Why*. Though intuitively easy to use, this approach is at the risk of overgeneralization, since it tends to dismiss linguistic and cultural differences between countries or places grouped together, or equate geographical/political entities with cultural groupings.

Another approach is to use cultural dimensions or orientations to differentiate each culture. Hofstede's (1997) widely cited five cultural dimensions (i.e., individualism vs. collectivism; high vs. low power distance; masculinity vs. femininity; high vs. low uncertainty avoidance; and long-term vs. short-term orientation) examines each country from a multi-perspective and places each country/culture on a continuum (cf. dilemmas in Trompenaars and Hampden-Turner 1998). One of the strengths of Hofstede's framework lies in the strong connection between each dimension and communicative behaviour in different contexts (e.g., work, family life, education, politics, etc.). Relevant to this study on job application cover letters, Hofstede argued that people from individualistic cultures tend to use an explicit or direct approach instead of being indirect and they say 'I' instead of 'we'; people from high power distance cultures regard language as signs and symbols of power and they show respect for hierarchy; people from masculinity cultures tend to emphasize achievement, leadership and control; and people from high uncertainty avoidance cultures go for ambiguity rather than accuracy.

The weakness of these dimensions or orientations is that they run the risk of reducing the complexities of a given culture into a framework that, if interpreted inappropriately, promotes stereotyping. However, imperfect though these two approaches may be, they provide a starting point for cross-cultural comparison and therefore will be used in this study.

Looking at these different approaches, it suggests the following questions for our research into studentship application letters:

1. Are there quantitative and/or qualitative differences between second language writers' and native speaker writers' presentation of self in the context of the genre of studentship application letters?
2. If so, can these differences be accounted for by their cultural orientations?

Data

Participants

The participants of the present study are students from one master-level module taught in the University of Newcastle upon Tyne, United Kingdom. The participants' cultural background and each country's scores in Hofstedes' cultural dimensions (i.e., power distance, individualism, masculinity and uncertainty avoidance) are summarized in Table 9.1. All international students have an IELTS (International English Language Testing System) score of at least 6.5 to qualify for a place in the programme.

Task

As part of an assignment for a module on Language and Cross-Cultural Communication, participants were asked to write an application cover letter for a postgraduate research studentship in a number of areas such as French studies, English, Archaeology, History, Linguistics and so on, advertised by a UK university at jobs.ac.uk (see Appendix 1 for the advertisement). They have been informed that the letter would not be marked, but they needed to bring the letter with them when they came to the lecture on Cross-Cultural Differences in Writing. Altogether 55 letters were collected after

Table 9.1 Participants' distribution and cultural orientations*

Place of origin	No.	Individualism	Power distance	Masculinity	Uncertainty avoidance
Britain	3	89	35	66	35
Canada	1	80	39	52	48
China	28	15	75	50	35
France	1	71	68	43	86
German	1	67	35	66	65
Greece	4	35	60	57	112
Hong Kong	2	25	68	57	29
Japan	3	46	54	95	92
Libya	5	38	80	53	68
Malaysia	1	26	104	50	36
Netherlands	1	80	38	14	53
South Korea	1	18	60	39	85
Sweden	2	71	31	5	29
Taiwan	3	17	58	45	69
Total	55				

1. The scores are cited from Hofstede's cultural dimension framework (for more info on the framework, see the website at: http://www.geert-hofstede.com/hofstede_dimensions.php)
2. Long-term orientation vs. short-term orientation to life seems to have very little implication on the writing style and therefore is not referred to in this study.

the lecture as the database for the study. The average length of the letters was 405 words.

Coding scheme

All the sentences in the application cover letters are coded using the following scheme.

Code	Category	Example and Note
A	Name	The applicant's self-introduction; e.g. 'I'm XX.'
B	Ethnic membership	The applicant's place of origin; e.g. 'I'm from Taiwan'.
C1	Current qualification	'I'm currently completing an MA programme'.
C2	Past qualification	'Prior to my MA, I studied Applied Linguistics for my first degree.'
D1	Current work experience	'I'm currently working as language teacher'.
D2	Past work experience	'I worked as interpreter for The Women's Congress in Beijing'
E1	Research area	'I'm interested in studies of cultural core values.'
E2	Research publications	'I have published one article on the role of Greek women in families.'

F1	Professional affiliation	'I'm a member of MECCA.'
F2	Achievements	Awards, special recognition, promotion, leadership role, etc.
G	Physical traits	Age, height, gender, etc.
H1	Motivation: preferences	Application is out of personal preferences and interests.
H2	Motivation: career aspiration	Application is for career development.
H3	Motivation: financial situation	Application is for financial benefit.
I	Adversary-glorification	Claim of the superiority of the institution
J	Self-glorification	Subjective claim of one's own superiority
K	Discourse markers	Presupposition markers such as 'of course', 'obviously'; hedges such as 'actually', 'probably', 'somehow'; emphatics such as' indeed', 'really'
L	Personal hobbies	Personal hobby such as travelling, train-spotting, sports
M	Other strengths	Advantages not covered by above categories such as language abilities, familiarity with the system
N	Personality and attitude	Personality and attitude such as warm-heartedness, hard-working, enthusiasm, etc.

If there is more than one category in one sentence, the sentence will be coded as a multi-category. If two or more subsequent sentences are elaborating on the same category, these sentences will be coded as one category. Examples are:

1. I recently graduated from the University of XX with a degree in archaeology, where I was president of Archaeology Society and a member of Archaeology Association in XX (cited from Participant 04).
2. I completed my first degree in the University of XX on the subject of Greek History and Philosophy. The course covers a wide range of modules such as Greek Literature, Cultural Studies, European Unions, Research Method, etc. (cited from Participant 42).

Using the coding scheme, the first sentence will be coded as C2 (past qualification), F2 (achievements) and F1 (affiliations); the second sentence will be coded as C2 (past qualification).

Results

In terms of quantitative analysis, the percentage of people using each category of self-statement was calculated. One-way ANOVA on the frequency of use of various categories by participants from different cultures was conducted to examine the interaction of the four culture dimensions under study and categories of statements about self in the context of the studentship application letter. Each category is also examined qualitatively in terms of group trends and individual variations. In particular, the use of categories is compared between the largest group of subjects; that is, Chinese students, and British students as native English speakers.

Quantitative analysis

1. Overview of use of each category
   Figure 9.1 shows the percentage of participants using each category in the coding scheme. The most frequently used category is current qualification: 80 per cent of the subjects (44 out of the total number of 55) used this category and the least used category is the one referred to as 'other strengths': only one subject mentioned this category in the application letter (Appendix 3 provides the raw figures of number of participants using each category).
2. One way ANOVA on frequency of use of various categories by participants.

Table 9.2 summarizes the ANOVA result on the frequency of use of various categories of self statements in relation to the subject's cultural background.

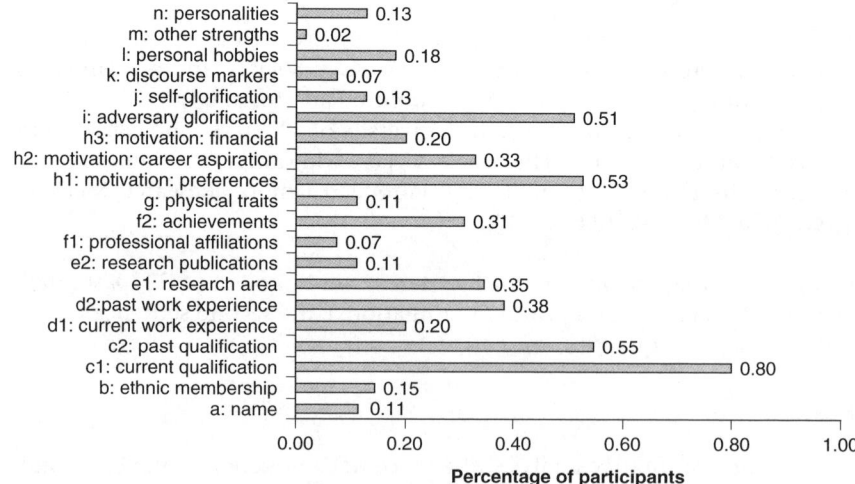

Figure 9.1 Percentage of participants using each category

Table 9.2 One-way ANOVA on Culture X Category

Category	Code	F value			
		Individualism	Power distance	Masculinity	Uncertainty avoidance
Name	A	0.572	0.808	0.788	0.362
Ethnic membership	B	1.744	2.016	1.994	1.737
Current qualification	C1	1.325	1.358	1.042	1.234
Past qualification	C2	5.235***	4.944***	1.966	5.024***
Current work experience	D1	0.697	0.609	0.517	0.365
Past work experience	D2	1.451	1.491	1.571	1.234
Research area	E1	0.857	0.876	0.820	0.833
Research publications	E2	0.886	0.996	0.992	0.876
Professional affiliation	F1	1.056	0.876	0.695	1.018
Achievements	F2	10.158***	0.855	0.850	10.063***
Physical traits	P	0.074	0.083	0.077	0.060
Motivation: preferences	H1	0.507	0.488	0.345	0.468
Motivation: career aspiration	H2	2.240*	0.748	2.165*	1.824
Motivation: financial situation	H3	2.419*	2.290*	0.763	2.374*
Adversary-glorification	I	1.342	1.806	1.098	0.776
Self-glorification	J	0.470	0.529	0.488	0.371
Discourse markers	K	0.667	0.490	0.239	0.290
Personal hobbies	L	1.893	1.393	1.393	0.060
Other strength	M	1.414	1.428	1.393	2.231
Personality and attitude	N	0.740	1.370	1.357	0.507

Note: * $p < 0.05$; ** $p < 0.01$; *** $p < 0.001$

Significant interactions are found between cultural dimensions and frequency of use of self statements. Specifically:

- Participants from cultures with a high individualism index are more likely to mention their past qualification, achievements and career aspirations, and less likely to talk about the need for financial support.
- Participants from cultures with a high power distance index are more likely to mention their past qualification and the need for financial support.

- Participants from cultures with a high masculinity index are more likely to make statements about their career aspiration.
- Participants from cultures with a high uncertainty avoidance index are more likely to mention their past qualification, their leadership role and other advantages such as familiarity with the subject, language ability, familiarity with UK teaching and learning style and so on. They are also more likely to mention the need for financial support.
- No interaction is evident between cultural dimensions with categories including ethnic membership, personal physical traits, target-glorification, self-glorification, and use of discourse markers.

Qualitative analysis

Table 9.3 compares the way Chinese and British students used each category. Since there were 28 Chinese participants and only three British participants, the raw number of persons who used a particular category is given rather than a percentage, and caution needs to be taken when interpreting and comparing the group trends. The findings from Table 9.3 can be summarized as below:

1. No significant differences have been found between the two groups with regard to self-introduction (i.e., Category of Name). A number of people from both groups (4 from the Chinese group and 1 from the British group) mentioned their names in the studentship application letter.
2. Some Chinese students mentioned their ethnic membership, while no one from the British group mentioned it. This is understandable, since the application was meant for a UK university, and ethnic membership is therefore less salient to British applicants.
3. All the British students and a majority of the Chinese students (23 from the Chinese group and 3 from the British group) mentioned their current qualifications and past qualifications. However, Chinese students tended to introduce their past qualifications before current qualifications. For example, one Chinese student wrote, 'I studied English language for my BA degree during 1999–2003. After graduation, I had an opportunity to study an MA in Cross-cultural Communication in XX.' Similarly, more Chinese students mentioned their past work experience than current work experience.
4. In terms of research interests, publications and professional affiliations, no significant differences are found between these two groups.
5. Though nearly half of the Chinese and British groups mentioned their achievements, a few Chinese students used 'self-glorification' strategy and made subjective claim of their achievements. Examples are: 'I have got "good" marks on these modules'; 'I am a graduate in English with "excellent" academic record in my credit'. Although these statements may be facts, unfortunately they sound less convincing without further clarification from the applicants on the criteria of being 'good' or 'excellent'. In

Table 9.3 Comparison of Chinese and British groups

Code	Category	Chinese		British	
		Examples	No of persons (total no is 28)	No of persons (total no is 3)	Examples
A	Name	I'm XXX.	4/28	1/3	I'm XXX
B	Ethnic membership	I'm from China as an overseas student.	5/28	0/3	None
C1	Current qualification	At present I am enrolled in a full time MA programme in cross-cultural communications and International management.	23/28	3/3	I'm currently enrolled to begin a postgraduate course in linguistics at the University of X to begin in September 2005.
C2	Past qualification	I was awarded the BA degree with distinction in History in XX University in 2002. 'I majored in English language Literature for my BA degree…. During my last year of studying MA in cross-cultural communication at XX, I had the choice to explore further and deeper the intercultural perspective.	16/28	3/3	Prior to my current course I studied at the University of X in the Department of Language and linguistics. I feel that this first degree gave me a firm grounding in order to pursue my current degree into this specific area and will also serve me as a good preparation for the research I intend to pursue.
D1	Current work experience	I am working for Professor of Applied Linguistics currently, by who I have learned a great deal about research methods.	7/28	1/3	I'm also the owner/manager of Business Language and Communication Consultants in XXX.

Table 9.3 (Continued)

Code	Category	Chinese			British		
		Examples	No of persons (total no is 28)		Examples	No of persons (total no is 3)	
D2	Past work experience	In the final year of my degree programme, I have worked for my department as a research assistant. My duties were to find out some translation failure in daily lives and study them with the aid of contrastive analysis. I hope this working experience can equip me with the research skills that meet your requirement.	12/28		I was trained as a TEFL instructor and am experienced in TOEFL and IELTs.	1/3	
E1	Research area	My speciality is children's literature.	12/28		I now focus no the cultural implications of meeting and negotiating in English as well as the theories of speed reading and successful business writing.	2/3	
E2	Research publications	I also have written about 3 research articles, all of which have been published in scholarly journals.	4/28			0/3	
F1	Professional affiliation	I recently graduated from the University of Newcastle with a degree in archaeology, where I was president of archaeology society and a member of Archaeology Association in Newcastle.	2/28		I'm a member of SIESTER.	1/3	

F2	Achievements	I have got good marks on these modules.	13/28	1/3	I'm currently achieving averaging distinction level marks across all subjects and would be happy to provide you with written references from the relevant lectures.
G	Physical traits	I'm 22.	1/22	0/3	
H1	Motivation: preferences	I'm particularly interested in the research area that the university offers: theatre and publishing history. I would enjoy being a postgraduate student here as well.	18/28	2/3	As well as extending my existing knowledge, it has also allowed me to study an area which has been of interest to me for some time now in a formal manner. Linguistics has always been a great interest of mine. I wish to achieve a greater understanding of the hidden patterns of communication; identifying what is, and ……. I believe that these things will be essential for good and important communication skills.
H2	Motivation: career aspiration	I believe that researching on linguistics in your University can be a challenging work and benefits my future career. I believe that the university will prepare me for a successful and challenging career in the communication.	12/28	1/3	

Table 9.3 (Continued)

Code	Category	Chinese		British	
		Examples	No of persons (total no is 28)	No of persons (total no is 3)	Examples
H3	Motivation: financial situation	But due to my financial situation, I cannot afford the tuition fee, since I belong to a very poor family and my parents are not financially to pay for heavy expenses on my studies. I sincerely wish that I can grab this opportunity and will not let the financial difficulty become the obstacle of my further study. As I have no other financial source to support my study in UK, your assistance would be very important to me.	7/28	1/3	I'm applying for the AHRB scholarship as I truly believe that this will contribute effectively to my studying and will help to relieve the obvious and inevitable financial burden that affects any University student nowadays, undergraduate, or postgraduate.
I	Adversary-glorification	I understand that the University of X has an international reputation for the excellence of its research and the majority of its schools and departments achieved a score of 5 or 5* in the recent RAE. I also learnt from my degree supervisor that your school has a high reputation in academia. The teaching staff and learning facilities are one of the best in UK. This is the major reason why I choose to study in your university.	16/28	0/3	

J	Self-glorification	I am a graduate in English having a shining academic record in my credit.	7/28	0/3
K	Discourse markers	Obviously, I have had a systematic study on linguistics. Actually, I have already got an offer ….	4/28	0/3
L	Personal hobbies		0/28	1/3 Outside of studying I am involved in various activities both related and non-related to my course, including being a student rep as well as taking part in various sporting activities such as cross-country running and practising Tai Chi.
M	Other strengths	I have learned Germany for two years. …These foreign language learning experiences have helped me to understand the purpose of Linguistics research to a higher extent. I have the maturity, skills and abilities to further my research in your prestigious university.	7/28	1/3 I believe that I have the necessary maturity, responsibility and self management skills in order to undertake a position as this. I feel that I am able to manage a healthy balance between my work and private life and could be an asset to your department.
N	Personality and attitude	I have progressed well in lexicographical editorial works and advanced my communication skills to a high level, because of my warm-heartedness and hard working. I believe my enthusiasm is evidenced in my involvement in voluntary activities and in my employment achievements so far.	5/28	0/3

contrast, British students tend to provide reference points. In the example given in Table 9.3, when the student makes a claim that he achieved 'distinction' across all subjects, he also offers to provide written references from the module leaders, which makes his claim sound more convincing.

6. Opposite to self-glorification, several Chinese students undersold themselves in their cover letters by using words such as 'basic', 'introductory' to describe their course work and ability. Examples are: 'these subjects had equipped me with the basic language and linguistic knowledge'; 'I'm capable of carrying out research under your guidance.'
7. With regard to the purposes of applying for the studentship in a particular subject area, more Chinese students tend to present that their application is out of personal interest and preferences than career aspiration.
8. Though students from both the Chinese and British groups mentioned that the studentship would help with their financial situation, the approach was different: Chinese students seemed to 'sell' their personal circumstances, while the British student seemed to seek the readers' empathy on the overall financial burden carried by university students nowadays.
9. A significant difference existed in the usage of adversary glorification. A majority of Chinese students praised the university they are writing to. Some of them repeated the research strengths of the university mentioned in the advertisement. In some letters, the strength or superiority of the university is presented as a reason for the students to study there. One Chinese student wrote, 'I decided to choose your school to continue my study because I know that the linguistics studies in your school are very famous.'
10. Four Chinese students used 'discourse markers' such as 'obviously', 'actually' in their application.
11. No significant differences existed with regard to 'personal hobbies' and 'physical traits'. Only one British student mentioned his personal hobby and only one Chinese student mentioned his age.
12. While none of the British students mentioned their personality and attitude, a few Chinese students described themselves as 'hard-working', 'warm-hearted', or 'enthusiastic'. The word 'enthusiasm' is used consistently by a few students where 'interest' might have been sufficient. Examples are: 'my enthusiasm about linguistics began from my interest in English'; 'this is an ideal studentship for me given my enthusiasm for research job'. In addition to personality and attitude, some of the Chinese students also mentioned their language ability, familiarity with the system and learning style.

Apart from these, several Chinese students also pressed for a favourable decision by claiming that they have already had an offer from somewhere else. For example, one student said in the letter: 'Actually I have got a place in a postgraduate programme on Applied Linguistics from a famous university in China.

However, we know that you University have an international reputation for the excellence of its research and achieved a high score in the recent RAE.'

Discussion

This study compares both quantitatively and qualitatively advanced second language writers' and native speaker writers' construction of self in the context of the genre of studentship application cover letters. It provides insight into differences in the way people from different cultures present themselves in a particular context and whether and how their self-presentation is affected by the conventions of another culture.

The existence of significant interactions between cultural dimensions and frequency of use of different categories of self-statements in the application letter and the subsequent comparative study of Chinese and British students both suggest that cross-cultural variations exist in the way people present themselves across different cultures even in a highly structured and conventionalized context such as a scholarship application letter. These differences are manifested at different levels. For example, at the group level, participants from countries with a high individualism index, where an explicit or direct approach is preferred, are more likely to mention their past qualification, achievements and career aspirations, and less likely to talk about the need for financial support; participants from countries with a high power distance index are more likely to mention the need for financial support; participants with a high uncertainty avoidance index are more likely to mention their past qualification, their leadership roles and other relevant advantages.

At a micro-level, the 28 Chinese and three British students included in the sample adopted different approaches when they tried to stress the need for financial help: Chinese students seemed to emphasize their personal circumstances more while British students tried to evoke empathy by referring to the overall less ideal financial arrangement for university students. These two groups of students also differ in their perceptions on the qualities that will make them 'good' candidates: Chinese students tend to describe themselves as 'hard–working', 'warm-hearted' and 'enthusiastic' – qualities that are deemed very important in China, but less so in the United Kingom. Another difference lies in the sequence in which these two groups of students present past and current qualification and work experience. Chinese students tend to mention their past work experience or qualification prior to their current ones, probably because the Chinese language prefers linear and chorological presentation.

Cross-cultural variations also exist in the strategies used by both the Chinese and British groups to negotiate with the audience of the application letter. A majority of Chinese students praised the university they were writing to by mentioning or repeating the strengths of the university referred to in the advertisemen ('target-glorification' in Bhatia's terms). This is in tune with the Chinese notion of 'politeness', which is equated with either an individual's desire to be pleasant to others in daily social interaction, or of showing respect to others by virtue of their higher status, older age and so on (Zhu, Li and Qian 2000). However, when it comes to describing their own achievements, Chinese students very often either over-sell themselves by making subjective claims about their achievements or under-sell themselves by down-grading them. It may be the case that, as second language users, some Chinese participants are not familiar with the pragmatic connotations associated with some lexical items such as 'basic' and 'introductory', and discourse markers such as 'obviously', 'actually' and 'by the way'.

Apart from providing evidence for cross-cultural variations in genre, the findings further suggest that identity and self-presentation are constantly shaped by context. People consciously or unconsciously decide which aspects of identities are salient according to social-cultural conventions in a particular context. For example, contrary to expectation, this study did not find that people from a collectivistic culture are significantly different from an individualistic culture in using group membership, personal traits and the like. Both the Chinese and English groups used 'self-introduction' at the beginning of the application, due to their perceived need to establish who they are at the beginning of an application letter.

Conclusion and implications

This study examines the role of culture in genres and demonstrates that writing, even for a much conventionalized purpose, is in fact a social-culturally constructed phenomenon. It is a process by which writers have to negotiate constantly between various constraints; for example, writers' cultural orientations, writers' perceived purpose and conventions of the writing, readers' expectation, writers' perceived readers' expectations, and writers' perceived power relationship with readers. In addition, it also shows the changing nature of self in that different saliency values can be assigned to different aspects of identity.

These findings will have various implications for teaching and learning to write in a second language. Learning to write in a second language is not only about learning how to construct grammatically correct sentences and how to present ideas and information, but also (perhaps more importantly) a process of negotiating between various elements. These elements or constraints include second language users' cultural orientations towards self, communities and society, among others; their changed cultural orientations due to exposure to the new culture; the power relationship with the audience of the writing and writing conventions for a particular discourse community. As a result, some unique characteristics of second language writing emerge and exist. These unique features need to be acknowledged and addressed not only in the education context but also in a wider social context.

APPENDIX 1

Scholarship Advertisement

> The University of [Name]*
> Research studentship in Arts and Humanities
>
> Applications are invited for up to twelve postgraduate research studentships in the following areas: Archaeology; Classics, Critical Theory, English; Film, Theatre and Television; Fine Art; French Studies; German Studies; History; History of Art and Architecture; Italian Studies; Linguistics Science and Applied Linguistics; Medieval Studies; Music; Philosophy; Typography: History and Theory.
>
> The University has an international reputation for the excellence of its research and the majority of its Schools and Departments achieved a score of 5 or 5* in the recent Research Assessment Exercise.
>
> Full and part-time research studentships are available covering UK/EU fees and maintenance at the rate paid by research councils. Interdisciplinary applications and applications from overseas students are welcomed. Applicants will be expected to apply for, and accept if offered, AHRB, SAAS or ORS Studentships or other sources of external funding to attend this University, although applications are welcome from candidates who do not have access to any other funds.
>
> Further information and applications forms my be obtained from: [Name], Senior Administrative Officer (Postgraduate), Faculty of Letters and Social Sciences, The University of [name], Postal Address + Email address. Please state research areas in which you are interested.
>
> Applications should be received by Monday 25 February 2005.

*Note: All names are removed from the appendix.

APPENDIX 2

Sample Application Letter*

> Dear Sir
>
> I'm writing to apply for the postgraduate studentship for year 2004–5. The field that I'm interested in is 'Linguistics'.
>
> I am a student who graduated in XXX for my BA degree. In my first degree, I studied in the field of Translation and Chinese and also studies some linguistics subjects during the past three years. These subjects had equipped me with the basic language and linguistic knowledge. After the BA degree, I know that having the knowledge of linguistics can help us to have effective communications with all kinds of people. Therefore I am really interested in this subject and would like to continue my further study at your school.
>
> Moreover, I have worked as a freelance translator for two years. In this working experience, I had come across many practical linguistic problems which I need to overcome. The job does not only give me the experience of work, but also let me have more interest on linguistics study.
>
> I decided to choose your school to continue my study because I know that the linguistics study in your school is very famous and I am sure that with this post-graduate year, I will learn as much as I can and will benefit for my future.
>
> Thank you for reading my application letter. Please kindly consider my application and I look forward for your reply.
>
> Yours sincerely
>
> XXX

Note: All grammatical and lexical errors remain unedited in the sample letter.

APPENDIX 3

The Raw Figures of the Participants Using Each Category

Category	No. of participants	Percentage of participants
a: name	6	0.11
b: ethnic membership	8	0.15
c1: current qualification	44	0.80
c2: past qualification	30	0.55
d1: current work experience	11	0.20
d2: past work experience	21	0.38
e1: research area	19	0.35
e2: research publications	6	0.11
f1: professional affiliations	4	0.07
f2: achievements	17	0.31
g: physical traits	6	0.11
h1: motivation: preferences	29	0.53
h2: motivation: career aspiration	18	0.33
h3: motivation: financial situation	11	0.20
i: adversary glorification	28	0.51
j: self-glorification	7	0.13
k: discourse markers	4	0.07
l: personal hobbies	10	0.18
m: other strengths	1	0.02
n: personalities	7	0.13

10
Identity Construction in Teacher Education

Jennifer Miller
Monash University

What's in a name?

When I first met my two classes of English as a Second Language (ESL) pre-service teacher education students in 2005, I could see and hear that they were a very diverse group, linguistically, ethnically and culturally. Early in the year, and for the second year running, the office organizing the fourth year practicum placements took a call from a school requesting that no ESL pre-service teacher *with a foreign name* be sent to their school for the practicum. Although legally on thin ice, the school was in fact making a claim about the English language competence of native speakers in ESL classrooms, and the assumed lack of competence of those from linguistically diverse backgrounds. In an age of globalization and given the hugely diverse population of Australia, where a quarter of the population were born elsewhere, I found this a bizarre request. The assumption that the student teachers' names might be an index to their language use and competence seemed appalling, yet also required an empirical response. In any case, in this cohort Susie Sakamoto was a red-haired Aussie; Katelin Fisher was half-Chinese; Elodie was Belgian and spoke only Flemish and Japanese at home; and Imaniji Obenyo was an English-speaking monolingual from Kenya. Their names would not have helped anyone 'pick the Anglo'. I have used pseudonyms here, but retained the 'ethnicity of the name', so to speak. How did the pre-service teachers construct their own identities? And how might these identities inform schools, native English-speaking students, teacher educators and others?

My final year ESL pre-service classes seemed to constitute a clear exception to studies showing that Australian teachers are 'overwhelmingly Anglo-Australian' (Santoro and Allard 2005). The catalyst for the study had been an unlikely phone call. I wanted to look at this group of students, and to document how their diversity, their identities and language use were socially constituted within a range of ESL programme contexts. This seemed imperative to build a more critical understanding of language teacher education and also to problematize practice (see Pennycook 2004). Who gets to be an ESL teacher? What is the programme like for those whose first language is not English? In this chapter, I look first at the theory of social language use and identity, including the positioning of native speakers in educational contexts. I then provide a brief contextual background on ESL in Victoria, and outline the diversity represented within my two classes of ESL teacher education students (n = 45). The third section of the chapter presents data from an extended email exchange between myself and Julia (pseudonym), a Chinese student, who reflects at length on the issues of language competence, identity and the interactions she experiences in her practicum school. Finally, I draw implications from the study for ESL teaching and learning and more broadly for teacher education.

Social constructions of identity, language learning and teaching

Many recent critical works have stressed the important link between discourse and identity, with identity now conceptualized as a process of continual emerging and becoming. Unitary labels and hard binary oppositions are rejected in favour of the conception of multiply faceted identities, 'points of temporary attachment' (Hall 1996: 6), which are fluid, dynamic, contradictory, shifting and contingent. While identities may be partly constituted through language, race, education, gender, community membership, class, kinship and so on, Giddens proposes that identity 'forms a trajectory across the different institutional settings of modernity' (1991: 14). The word 'trajectory' evokes concepts of movement, evolutionary development and change – all of which are coherent with contemporary conceptualizations of identity and also language learning and use. In the introduction to their book, *Critical Pedagogies and Language Learning*, Norton and Toohey sum up key aspects of these conceptualizations as follows:

> Advocates of critical approaches to second language teaching are interested in relationships between language learning and social change. From this perspective, language is not simply a means of expression or communication; rather, it is a practice that constructs, and is constructed by, the ways language learners understand themselves, their social surroundings, their histories, and their possibilities for the future.
>
> (2004: 1)

Much recent writing and research has helped us understand better the complex sociocultural contexts of ESL learners and their teachers today (Block in this volume; Hawkins 2004; Miller 2003, 2004; Norton and Toohey 2004; Pavlenko and Blackledge 2004; Driagina and Pavlenko in this volume), and the importance of identity in the ways languages are acquired and used. This works constitutes a more interdisciplinary and socially informed approach, which draws on a highly eclectic theoretical and epistemological base

(Block 2003; Roberts 2001). This shift also corresponds to the broadening of traditional SLA perspectives on language learning and teaching to include a knowledge of discourse and social theory, along with the problematization of issues and constructs such as communicative competence, identity and representation, diversity and ethnicity, agency, access and audibility, the native/non-native binary and standard language (Miller 2003). The traditional SLA focus on the input-interaction-output process has given way to more discourse-based critical sociocultural perspectives, which attend to the contexts and social conditions of language use, to representational resources and processes of interpretation, including ideological aspects of these. For example, Norton (2006) uses a range of sociocultural perspectives to explore the notion of identity.

In a move to incorporate critical perspectives, a number of researchers draw on the sociological theory of Pierre Bourdieu (1977a, 1991), who provides key notions of embodied social capital, including linguistic capital, and the role of the social and institutional legitimizing process which admits, devalues or rejects the capital of 'outsiders'. The notion of legitimacy as part of the nexus between identity and language use is a powerful one, and has been used in critical TESOL work to make what Pennycook calls 'explicit social critique' (2004: 329), for example around the issue of discrimination, as well as a case for social change. Pennycook argues that another approach to critical work is that of *problematizing practice*, 'a perspective that insists on casting far more doubt on the categories we employ to understand the social world' (2004: 329), while maintaining issues of power, identity and discourse as central. In a similar vein, Kubota (2004) advocates that *critical multiculturalism* must be a part of language education, to counteract what she calls *difference blindness*, which serves to mask racism, discrimination and inequality.

Native speakers, standard English and ESL teaching

Although the traditional SLA native-speaker/non-native speaker binary and assumptions about native speaker competence have been contested for some years (Higgins 2003; Leung, Harris and Rampton 1997; Lippi-Green 1997; McKay 2003), institutions and teachers are often complicit in promoting a standard language ideology which rejects or marginalizes certain varieties of English. In their assessments, scales measuring second language proficiency frequently reserve the highest levels for those who are near-native or native-like in their production and understanding of the language. Higgins writes that 'The act of labeling speakers as belonging to the categories native speaker (NS) and non-native speaker (NNS) implicitly underlies much of what TESOL professionals do' (2003: 615). In the TESOL work place, non-native speakers often face discrimination based on accent and credibility problems (Maum 2002). Lippi-Green reminds us that standard language and non-accent are abstractions, and that the opposite of standard appears to be non-standard or substandard, and that 'these terms automatically bring with them a unidirectionality and subordination which is counterproductive to a discussion of language variation in linguistic terms' (1997: 60). The deconstruction of conventional notions of native speaker competence is also stressed by Leung, Harris and Rampton (1997), who emphasize that majority language speakers are also done a disservice by the assumption that they speak, and are affiliated to, an undifferentiated standard English. They replace the blunt notion of native speaker competence with the concepts of *language expertise* (linguistic and cultural knowledge), *language affiliation* (identification and attachment) and *language inheritance* (connectedness and continuity).

It is no accident that the contestation of concepts such as native speaker and standard language has occurred at a time of unprecedented mass global movements of people. Immigrants, refugees, a globalized workforce, a vast body of mobile international students, and the prominence of English as *the* international language have rendered unworkable concepts which were forged in a simpler time. The vast majority of English language teachers around the world are now 'non-native' users of English (Matsuda and Matsuda 2001) and numerous scholars have taken on the challenge of rethinking the terminology, theory and principles of research involving such speakers (Braine 1999; Davies 2003; McKay 2003).

The research interest in non-native or bilingual teachers of English has also burgeoned since the 1998 formation of an international professional organization for non-native English speakers in TESOL (NNEST; http://nnest.moussu.net/). The term NNEST is also used to represent non-native English-speaking teachers. However Maum (2002) identifies a division between those who support such a nomenclature, highlighting the differences of these teachers as strengths, and those who oppose it, believing that such a term reinforces the dichotomy between native and non-native, and could reify discriminatory practices. McKay also draws attention to the unhelpfulness of distinguishing between native and non-native teachers, arguing: 'Such an approach is not productive in examining the benefits of bilingualism and biculturalism in the teaching of EIL' (2003: 9). Although she extends notions of culture in her paper, the problem remains around those two words – bilingualism and biculturalism – terms that presuppose that some people have two languages or two cultures, which clearly understates and oversimplifies the case. This is how we remain trapped in our words, in our categories and in our names for things.

Critically however, McKay writes that 'it is time to recognize the multilingual context of English use and to put aside a native speaker model of research and pedagogy' (2003: 19). How do we do research in globalized multilingual contexts? In a world characterized by increasing diversity, dislocation, social and cultural inequalities, Apple suggests these conditions are 'best seen through a process of "repositioning" ourselves, that is, by seeing the world from below, from the perspectives of those who are not dominant'

(1996: ix), a process already evident in critical sociocultural studies of language learning and teaching.

The study

This study looks at issues of identity and language use, and the perceived relationships between these in a very diverse cohort of ESL teacher education students. It focuses specifically on the problem of non-native speaker identity and competence in relation to teaching English as a second language in Australian high schools. On the surface the group was ethnically and linguistically quite diverse, as outlined in the introduction. Data sources to explore this diversity included a questionnaire (N = 37) and an extended email correspondence with Julia, a Chinese student. The questionnaire contained language background details and two open-ended questions, as follows:

A. If English is not your first language, comment on any issues you feel you have or that you have experienced in regard to teaching ESL.
B. What is your view of the statement, 'Only native speakers of English should teach ESL'?

The emails from Julia were unsolicited, but during her practicum she wrote extensively to me, around 2500 words of reflection on language, and her perceptions of identity and teaching during this period. I replied each time, and as I perceived the significance of this communication, sought permission to analyse and use these email texts. To analyse the questionnaire data, I made numerical tallies of categories from the first questions. For the open-ended questions I then coded key themes and issues, and mapped them across data from other students to find interrelated areas of interest (Miller and Glassner 1997). For the emails, I used a discourse analytic approach, since the framework of the study views discourse as situated, and implicative of social roles and identities. The text analyses draw on key concepts from discourse analysis as used by Gee (1996) and Luke (1998).

Overview of the class

Table 10.1 shows the diversity of languages and backgrounds of this ESL cohort, which has a more diverse profile than classes in other curriculum methods such as Maths, Science, History or Music for example. It will be seen that students from diverse language backgrounds may gravitate to the teaching of ESL as it reverberates with their prior experience of learning English, or sometimes because they do not have undergraduate degree majors in other subject areas. The first item refers to *names*, as this was the issue which prompted the study, as outlined in the introduction.

Table 10.1 The ESL cohort (N = 37)

Categories	Number	Percentage
Students with 'Anglo-Australian' names	12	32%
Students who use English only at home	13	35%
Students who do not use English at home	5	13%
Students for whom English is not the L1	13	35%
Students whose parents are from language backgrounds other than English	16 (both parents); 8 (one parent)	64%
Students not born in Australia	16	43%
Languages represented in this group*	19	
Countries of origin	14	
Born or have lived overseas	28	76%
Australian-born students who speak a LOTE (languages other than English)	13	35%
Students who speak 3 languages	14	38%

* English, Japanese, Flemish, Mandarin, French, Greek, Italian, German, Tamil, Arabic, Cantonese, Chinese dialect, Indonesian, Spanish, Hakka, Creole, Estonian, German, Armenian.

The table reveals that only a minority of 12 students 'look like Anglo-Australians on paper', and that the majority are multilingual, with 13 from 'other' language backgrounds, and 13 having learned other languages in Australia, such as Japanese or German. A minority use only English at home, emphasizing the linguistic diversity and diverse language competence within the group. The table shows that the ESL curriculum cohort here is far more diverse than the general population of pre-service teachers (see Santoro and Allard 2005), with 19 languages between them. So what did they have to say about the language issues raised in the questions on native and non-native speaker competence?

You don't have to be a native speaker but ...

One pre-service teacher called the view expressed in Question B 'an archaic way of thinking'. Several participants stated that being a native speaker was less important than spoken fluency, 'near-native' fluency, or a 'strong command' of English, as evidenced in the following three comments:

> I don't think that you need to be a native speaker but I do feel that you need to be fluent in the way you speak because you are a model for the students.
>
> (IDNO 4)
>
> Disagree. I do believe, however, that teachers of ESL should have a sound knowledge of grammar, and near-native fluency.
>
> (IDNO 12)

> Non-native speakers who have a strong command of English should be allowed to teach ESL.
>
> (IDNO 18)
>
> I totally disagree: only competent speakers, readers and writers (all combined) of English, be they first, second or third language users, should teach ESL.
>
> (IDNO 17)

I found it interesting that in all the references to fluency, grammar and competence in the surveys, there is no mention of linguistic competence beyond the level of surface grammar. There were no explicit attempts to tie grammar to discourse, genre or cultural forms, although the final comment above refers to 'competent speakers, readers and writers of English'. The assumption of most pre-service teachers seems to be that grammatical accuracy is a primary criterion needed to teach English. Some referred specifically, however, to pedagogical competence, the ability to teach.

> I think a teacher of any nationality should be able to teach English as long as they are competent to do so.
>
> (IDNO 8)
>
> Being able to teach ESL is more important than being a 'native speaker'.
>
> (IDNO 32)

Another student made a point of delinking both the notions of native speaker and linguistic competence, and also native speaker and pedagogical competence. She wrote:

> This statement makes me feel very uncomfortable. It's like saying only Japanese people can/should teach Japanese. I've had some brilliant non-Japanese teachers teach me Japanese – I had no problems learning Japanese quickly & accurately. As long as people have the correct understanding/ grasp of English, then this is fine.
>
> (IDNO 16)

What remains fuzzy here is what is meant by a 'correct understanding/ grasp of English'. However her position that non-native speaking teachers of a language can sometimes teach it very effectively is unequivocal, and has also on many occasions been my own experience as a teacher and teacher educator. The reverse, namely that native speakers of English or other languages were appalling teachers of their L1 has also been true at times.

The advantages of being a non-native speaker, and of foreign language learning

The two comments below are from an Anglo-Australian pre-service teacher and a Japanese one. They reiterate and extend the point made above about the strengths of non-native teachers. I have reproduced the comments without any changes.

> My knowledge of English grammar comes almost entirely from having learned French. I would therefore assume that in many cases, people for whom English is their second language have a better grasp of English grammar than most native English speakers! Furthermore, ESL teachers with ESL backgrounds would have a better ability to empathize with students and a better understanding of the difficult areas of English.
> (IDNO 20)

> I understand why some people strongly agree with this statement, However non-native ESL teachers still have some advantages. I respect non-native (Australian) LOTE Japanese teachers; they have such a logical way of thinking and understanding of linguistic rules, instead of intuition of a language that we native speakers have. Of course I am still learning English and my overall linguistic knowledge & sociocultural knowledge in/of English might still not quite good enough, but I regard the fact that I'm still learning English, as a positive thing. I know exactly how learners feel when they learn, make a mistake, speak English and so on. I know some common difficulties in learning English (especially for Asian (Japanese) students), because I have experienced those difficulties too.
> (IDNO 15)

The first teacher suggests that the advantages for teachers 'with ESL backgrounds' include a formal knowledge of grammar, and the capacity to empathize with learners in meaningful ways. Aiko (pseudonym), the second teacher quoted, reveals the flip side of the same coin, arguing that Australian teachers of Japanese have a logical and formal linguistic knowledge of Japanese which is more helpful in teaching than native speaker intuition. It is not an either/or thing, however – formal knowledge of a second language in the absence of fluency, or for the Japanese teachers, native speakers' intuition in the absence of pedagogical skills. There is a fine interplay between linguistic competence in a language and pedagogical competence, and neither can be compromised if learners are to learn. Unlike any of the 24 pre-service teachers who speak English as their L1, Aiko states that learning English entails both linguistic and sociocultural knowledge, and the process itself allows her to identify directly with learners' experiences. It is noteworthy that this articulate and productive comment comes from someone who claims 'learner' identity and status.

Reservations about being a non-native speaker of English in the classroom

Not all felt as confident as Aiko that ESL backgrounds could be an advantage. In the comments below, I indicate country of origin and length of residence in Australia, as these have some bearing on a personal sense of competence, confidence and identity.

> Teaching Yr 11 international students (especially texts such as short stories or creative writing) was quite a challenge. I felt I did not have enough preparation doing it but was a good learning school [sic].
> (b. Belgium, 10 years in Australia, IDNO 1).

> At times I have problems in speaking grammatically correct sentences.
> (b. Sri Lanka, 5 years in Australia, IDNO 6)

> I feel I have some problems with grammar because I have never learnt English grammar before.
> (b. HK, 17 years in Australia, IDNO 7)

> Pronunciation, fluency, grammar are issues for me.
> (b. Japan, 5 years in Australia, IDNO 14)

> Although I believe that ESL teachers who are not native speakers have some advantages in teaching in a way, I sometimes feel anxious about teaching ESL.
> (b. Japan, 2.5 years in Australia, IDNO 15)

Only the first statement draws attention to the specialized knowledge associated with teaching specific genres in English, which ESL teachers must do in the senior school. The next three relate to grammar and grammatical accuracy, and it is worth noting that the person who had lived for 17 years in Australia had missed out on grammar instruction (an endemic problem for students in this country), while the Japanese student teacher in the final comment had only been here two and half years, but did not mention problems with grammar. This was in fact Aiko, who, despite her short stay in Australia, was one of the most eloquent and competent students in my class. My view is that anxiety in the teaching practicum is utterly normal, but Aiko related it not to normal and predictable feelings, but to the question of her not being a native speaker of English. That is, anxiety is linked in her perception to English native speaker competence rather than to being a novice teacher. This will arise again in the case study of Julia below, to which I now turn.

A case study – Julia

Julia is a Chinese international student who has studied in Australia for almost two years. Prior to and during the practicum round, she wrote over 2500 words in emails to me, reflecting on her experience. In what follows I look at three themes of identity from different perspectives. In the first two of these, concerning the notions of teaching contexts and lesson preparation, I juxtapose the views of Julia and myself as mentor. In the third theme on practicum supervision, Julia reports on the comments of her supervising teacher and her responses to these, and I offer an alternative response. That is, identities here represent the competing constructions of novice (Julia as pre-service teacher), mentor (myself as teacher educator) and teaching supervisor (experienced teacher). In terms of my own identity, I should add that although now an academic, I spent over 20 years in language classrooms, years which have had a powerful bearing on the ways I view the world of teaching and learning.

Theme 1 Hard to be in the context

In my pre-service ESL classes, I often stress the importance and potential of using current media texts which are relevant to students as the basis for intensive language work. At the start of her practicum, Julia did this, using a tabloid newspaper. It targeted the right age group and a topical issue. Here is her comment about the result:

> ... with the Yr 8, I chose a one-page article 'Teens turn to dietary boosters' from last week's *Herald Sun*. Originally, I assumed it would be interesting for them since it talks about body image, how teens start to use dietary supplements to look better. But once I start to teach, I feel it might not be the case. They are not aware of these, and I am not sure how to make them aware or involved in it. I went back to the library to search for teenage magazine, hoping to find something relevant to the topic ... I do find some, but then not knowing how to incorporate.

Here is the painful discovery of a complex and difficult issue in teaching. Teenagers may not be interested in media texts, or even aware of current media debates, and choosing a topic involving their age group is no guarantee of their motivation to read or explore an issue. This was also a pedagogical problem. Her instinct was that colourful teenage magazines might appeal more, but then she was unsure how to integrate new texts. What she pinpoints next is that the text and the classroom are both embedded with meanings which may not be obvious or easy to grasp. She writes:

> My supervisor is very kind and helpful. But sometimes, I just feel myself hard to be in the context, of the text, of the classroom, since stuff that I

need to be in the situation are beyond me. I'm learning, not only ESL teaching but the language as well.

Recall here Gee's (1996) definition of discourses as 'ways of being in the world'. In Julia's experience, it is hard to *be* in the context of the text and of the classroom, in one way an almost existentialist conclusion. She is learning the discourses of English and of teaching, but claims 'the stuff that she needs' is *beyond* her. What stuff is this?

First, there is social and cultural knowledge about the students and the supervising teacher's normal practices. Second, there is pedagogical knowledge about how to choose and adapt texts to build a coherent teaching sequence, and also teaching skills. Third, the texts themselves contain sociocultural meanings which may or may not be recognized by students, or by Julia. It is a truism that texts are socially situated, with layers of historical, political, cultural and social meanings. Julia's short time in Australia and English language issues are perhaps part of her problem, but logic and common sense tell us that any pre-service teacher, regardless of language background, could have experienced these problems. Choosing appropriate material, scaffolding it for processing by students, and seeing layers of meaning in context and text are complex, demanding high levels of knowledge and skill. When I asked in a reply how the context of vocabulary posed a problem for her, she answered:

> It's a drawback for me because I used to learn English words without context, therefore when now it's my turn to explain words to my students such as 'toting the latest models of mobile phones', 'cyber bullying' or even as simple as 'telecommunications', I feel it hard. But as all coins have two sides, in another perspective, it helps me to look at the problem from ESL students' position. What I have experienced may be what they did and are experiencing now. How can we help them most to grasp vocabulary by providing a variety of real-life contexts one word can be used in, and same with text?

Julia here identifies the decontextualized approach to English learning that she had experienced in China, and recognizes that 'the English word in Australia' may require extra layers of understanding. On a more positive note, she adds to what her peers in the pre-service class had stated about heightened empathy for learners. Ironically, she asks and then answers her own question in the final sentence, a sophisticated understanding for a beginning teacher and one certainly not realized by all. However, overall, Julia attributed superior knowledge about language and teaching to native English-speaking teachers, as seen in the next theme, on lesson preparation.

Theme 2 The purpose of lessons

Lesson planning is a constant focus in the pre-service ESL curriculum course, with purpose of lessons, sequence, resources and strategies all playing central roles. In the following excerpt, Julia describes two lessons on body image and fashion:

> How can I improve? If this morning's class has a more clear purpose – to learn vocab of the news article and its structure and sequence, this afternoon, while I am doing the video of 'Interviews with fashion magazine editors and models', we basically break it down to several episodes and students watch it and fill in worksheets of comprehension questions. I made all the questions and tried to design them with a focus on key ideas and info, but when the lesson finishes, if I am asked what the kids get, I am not quite sure. Is it to understand the interviews, get more ideas about how media look at this issue etc. ... But it seems to me I am just bombarding them with materials or ideas without a very clear central line. Then if for one lesson the purpose isn't well defined then the logical linkage between each lesson and the coherence of the whole unit will be even worse.

Implicit in her opening question is the belief that she should be doing better. She suggests the morning's lesson using a news article had a clearer purpose and focus, related to vocabulary and generic structure. She also gives the purpose of the video lesson, namely comprehension of the key ideas and information. The second half of the text however is full of self doubt, shown by the phrases 'I am not sure', 'it seems to me I am just bombarding them with materials and ideas', and concluding that logical links between lessons and the cohesion of the larger unit could be lost if her purposes are not always clear. As her lecturer, I felt happy that she articulated key aspects of teaching in this way, and wished some of the other students were as perceptive and reflective. Experienced teachers, including myself, don't always do these things well. Who has not bombarded their students with material and ideas, without a pre-designed clear purpose and cohesive tie to what goes before and after? Was it Julia's assumption that native-speaking teachers did not experience these difficulties? This becomes clearer in the third and final theme below.

Theme 3 The teaching supervisor

In the comments below, we hear the voice of Julia's supervising teacher in the school, not directly, but reported in an email, along with Julia's response to the comments. These comments were, however, reliably represented, as a version of them appeared in Julia's final practicum report which was written by the supervisor.

My supervisor's comments usu. include:

1) should be assertive and directly address students who are distracted or switched off;
2) should make chances of facilitating interesting discussions thus keep the momentum of the lesson, don't let it drag;
3) the structure of the lesson is most important, always introduce at the beginning and wrap up at the end.

Till now, I failed to do all these.

For the first one, I have an obstacle at heart, feeling not fully accepted; not knowing what is the most appropriate words or 'good English' to deal with behavioural students, fear of being ignored thus not making myself heard by others.

For the 2nd, keeping admiring native-speaking teachers who can improvise wise and interesting comments on the spot, which relates to the students and the society and thus contributes to the lively atmosphere of the lesson; being quite frustrated since the topics chosen by myself 'body image' 'animal talk' 'mobile phone' are not my expertise, some of which I am not concerned about. Thus, the lesson drags on.

3) Surely I understand the significance of structure (a concise beginning and a strong ending almost weigh half of the lesson). But each time, when the bell goes, I just can't clear and raise my voice, summarize what happens today, what is to be expected tomorrow, ask them to quietly sit down and wait, and dismiss them when the bell goes, as if I were the boss. But I am not, that's what i feel, and that's why it's so hard for me to assert myself. If you are, you are. If you are not, even if you pretend to be, you are not. Perhaps I am too sensitive and self-preoccupied.

These comments on teaching are wonderfully rich and perceptive. Logically, she tackles the three suggestions of her supervisor, namely the need for assertiveness in the classroom, the need to maintain pace and interest, and the need for competence in the procedural structure of a lesson. Her responses are poignant, filled with the language of emotion. She names her 'obstacle at heart', a combination of fears of not being accepted and of being ignored and unheard, her admiration of 'native-speaking teachers', her frustration, sensitivity and incapacity to pretend to be what she is not.

On observing her teach, Julia's supervising teacher made the suggestions above, as any competent and well-meaning supervisor might do. Few would question that control of the lesson and the class are primary goals for pre-service teachers. Yet in light of Julia's thoughts and feelings about these suggestions, both the suggestions and Julia's expectations seem somewhat idealized. She observes that native-speaking teachers 'can improvise wise and interesting comments on the spot, which relates to the students and the society and thus contributes to the lively atmosphere of the lesson'. Again, many pre-service and experienced teachers struggle with such improvisation. Similarly, exemplary lesson conclusions are, in my experience, somewhat thin on the ground. Julia herself identifies the complex multi-tasking control this requires – 'when the bell goes, I just can't clear and raise my voice, summarize what happens today, what is to be expected tomorrow, ask them to quietly sit down and wait, and dismiss them when the bell goes.' The fact is, after 20 years of teaching, I often didn't get this right, and there are myriad contextual reasons why.

Julia's comment on lesson endings is very insightful, highlighting that one cannot pretend to be 'the boss' if one is not. This was in response to an email from me, in which I suggested part of the game was acting *as if you were* confident and competent, that looking and sounding the part might be enough to start with. The reality is far more complex of course. This is an identity issue to do with accrued cultural and symbolic capital, which cannot be easily faked before a class full of adolescents, watching and listening for the slightest slip-up. Julia had recognized you need 'good English' for students with behavioural problems. But while language competence should not be underestimated in teaching, this was not in fact a major problem for Julia. There are no recipes for good teaching, or an easy practicum. Language use, context, sociocultural meanings and identities all come into play in what is clearly far more complex than the facile binary of native English speaker or non-native English speaker might suggest. What can we understand as teacher educators from Julia's experience, and the way she so ably represented it?

Implications of the study

The views and experiences of these pre-service ESL teachers raise a number of identity issues which are of concern for teacher educators and schools. The cultural and linguistic diversity of this cohort of pre-service ESL teachers stands in contrast to the more homogeneously white and middle-class nature of groups in other mainstream content areas (Santoro and Allard 2005). As a group, they highlight the complex relationship between English language competence and pedagogical competence, presenting the clear view that being a native speaker of English is not a valid criterion for selecting teachers of English.

The group also emphasized the value of their diversity (and specifically bilingualism and biculturalism) in the teaching of ESL students. The gains they recognized were in terms of the grammatical knowledge and increased levels of empathy for culturally and linguistically diverse students. What remains unclear, and a question for future research is what students understood by the need for 'a strong command of English'. No one would argue that a language teacher should be less than competent in their skills in, and knowledge of, the language which they teach but what this means and the ways in which these skills and knowledge are reflected in pedagogical understandings has received little attention.

The case of Julia presents a more nuanced view of the construction of identity for pre-service teachers from diverse language backgrounds. She offers us an example of language as 'a practice that constructs, and is constructed by, the ways language learners understand themselves' (Norton and Toohey 2004: 1). She outlines three problems she faces in her teaching, namely her being a non-native speaker of English, her lack of the social and cultural knowledge she assumes native speakers possess, and her sense of not being in charge. She constructs these problems primarily as a function of her being and speaking Chinese. Her supervising teacher constructs her as a novice teacher who needs to focus on behaviour and lesson management. Although I have not analysed my email responses to Julia here (see Miller, in press), as teacher educator and mentor I constructed her problems as those of almost all beginning teachers in challenging classrooms. Building the necessary capital and levels of pedagogical competence to be recognized as legitimate in a school by both students and other teachers takes a great deal of time. And although I was unconvinced that her Aussie colleagues were all conveying 'wise and interesting comments' to their classes, Julia's perceptions of feeling diminished in comparison to native-speaking colleagues were very real to her.

Looking at competing constructions of identity in language classrooms is perhaps one way to problematize practice, as Pennycook (2004) suggests. I viewed her reflectiveness as a powerful way of teacher knowing and learning (Johnson 2006), and a critical 'discovery' for me was the value of the way the writing allowed her to process her lived experience in classrooms in a very sophisticated way. Burton (2005) reminds us that practising teachers seldom write about TESOL teaching, lacking time, support, confidence and recognition. Although the teaching practicum can be a fraught time for pre-service teachers, reflective emails could be built into programmes, and texts such as Julia's analysed for their insights into teaching and identity. Although lecturers may also not have time to reply to 25 students in depth, the way lies open for pre-service teachers to respond to each other, along with their lecturers.

At the time of writing this chapter, I am also marking a small truckload of assignments from postgraduate TESOL students and pre-service teachers. There are myriad examples of non-native English-speaking students who are more critically analytical, more reflective and more engaging in the ways they write about language and teaching than many of their native English-speaking peers. It is hard not to buy into the NS–NNS dichotomy, but I would like to tell ALL pre-service teachers on our courses that no assumptions can be made based on language background. I would like to tell practising teachers and administrators that culturally and linguistically diverse students often have qualities that strengthen their practice and potential in classrooms. And I would like to tell the school that rang hoping to avoid a 'foreign' pre-service teacher that they are seriously short-changing themselves.

11
Context and L2 Users' Pragmatic Development

Jean-Marc Dewaele
Birkbeck, University of London

Introduction

The immigrant starting a new life in a new language is usually prepared for a culture shock. However, the shock may come from an unexpected corner. Linguistic skills in the new language may have been learnt at school in the home country, and the immigrant may have been the best student in the language class, and may therefore be quietly confident in his/her capacity to communicate, but the brutal immersion in authentic interactions in that second language (L2) may suddenly reveal unexpected problems. Jemma, a 22-year-old student who filled out our questionnaire on bilingualism and emotions (Dewaele and Pavlenko 2001) wrote the following comment concerning her study abroad experience and her gradual acquisition of pragmatic competence in German through social interaction:

> Jemma (English L1, French L2, German L3): During my year in Germany I felt for the first few months that I had completely lost my identity. I was slow to understand, I could not express precisely what I meant and could not shape my verbal persona nor could I make jokes or entertaining remarks as I had no shared frame of context. I felt alienated and painfully frustrated and became very depressed. By the time I had finished my year however, I had sufficient command of the language to express myself and my character, to make jokes and even use comic catchphrases.

Crystal defines pragmatics as 'the study of language from the point of view of users, especially of the choices they make, the constraints they encounter in using language in social interaction and the effects their use of language has on other participants in the act of communication' (1997: 301). Jemma provides us with exactly that point of view of the L2 user (cf. Cook 2002a). Her feeling of rage arose from the lack of choices offered to her in her new language, her lack of ability to control the effect of her language on others, and the false projection of self because of this pragmatic handicap. She realized that her pragmatic competence in German lagged far behind her pragmatic competence in English. In German she had not yet fully mastered the illocutionary acts (realizing her intention in producing an utterance, e.g., an apology or a joke), and she was therefore still struggling with the perlocutionary act (i.e., the intended effect of an utterance on the hearer, like making the hearer laugh) (Austin 1962). Only towards the end of her stay did Jemma feel that her pragmatic competence in German allowed her to project a more accurate image of herself.

Many long-established immigrants who learnt an L2 in a foreign language class do remain uncertain about their levels of pragmatic competence. This uncertainty typically involves the exact emotional force and perlocutionary effects of swear words and taboo words (cf. Dewaele 2004a, b). Veronica Zhengdao Ye, for example, who emigrated from China to Australia (see Ye 2003) also reports on the surprise expressed by English-speaking Australians when she uses English swear words (personal communication):

> I belong to the group of people who are brought up with the notion that swearing is uncivil. And I have NEVER used swear and taboo words in my L1. But I do use words in English which native English speaker would consider uncivil to use, such as 'shit' and 'pissed off'. I could not use them exactly because I do not have the same sense of emotional weight of these words as do the NSs. My only clue of how 'strong' these words are was from people's reaction when I used them. My friends are often astonished when I use them, because they say that I do not look like the person who could say those words. When I use them, they say that they knew I feel very strong about something. I myself don't mind using those English swear words, as when I use them, I have fun of being another person for a moment!

Another interesting observation that emerges from linguistic autobiographies is the perception of the L2 as being somehow more remote, more detached and less emotional than the L1 (Pavlenko 2005). Nancy Huston, an Anglo-Canadian author who emigrated from Calgary to Paris as a student, became an established writer of novels and essays in French. She became a highly regarded French intellectual and started writing in English only later in her career. Despite her high level of proficiency and her constant use, French remains at best a neutral tool of communication for Huston:

> Oui, je crois que c'était là l'essentiel: la langue française (et pas seulement ses mots tabous) était, par rapport à ma langue maternelle, moins chargée d'affect et donc moins dangereuse. Elle était froide, et je l'abordais froidement. Elle m'était égale. C'était une substance lisse et homogène, autant dire neutre. Au début, je m'en rends compte maintenant, cela me conférait une immense liberté dans l'écriture – car je ne savais pas par rapport à quoi, sur fond de quoi, j'écrivais.

(Yes, I think that was the essential thing: compared to my mother tongue, the French language was less burdened with emotion and therefore less dangerous. She was cold and I approached her coldly. She was uniform. It was a smooth and homogeneous substance, one might say neutral. In the beginning, I realize now, this conveyed an enormous liberty to me in writing – because I didn't know with respect to what, or against what background I was writing.)
(*Nord perdu*, 1999: 63, cited in Kinginger 2004: 171, Kinginger's translation)

Pragmatics research in the second language acquisition context

Kasper and Rose (2001, 2002) choose Crystal's definition of pragmatics as the basis of their study on pragmatics and second language teaching. They argue that Crystal's view of pragmatics as the study of communicative action in its sociocultural context is perfectly suited to a second language acquisition (SLA) context. The term 'communicative action' is broad enough to cover a wide range of variables, including speech acts, but it also includes 'engaging in different types of discourse and participating in speech events of varying length and complexity' (Kasper and Rose 2001: 2). One traditional dichotomy in the study of pragmatics is the distinction introduced by Leech (1983) and Thomas (1983) between pragmalinguistics and sociopragmatics. While the former refers to resources for conveying communicative acts and interpersonal meanings, the latter focuses on 'the sociological interface of pragmatics' (Leech 1983: 10) concerned with 'the social perceptions underlying participants' interpretation and performance of communicative action' (Kasper and Rose 2001: 2). Kasper and Rose note that teaching sociopragmatics is much more challenging than pragmalinguistics. While pragmalinguistics is 'akin to grammar in that it consists of linguistics forms and their respective functions' (Kasper and Rose 2001: 3), sociopragmatics 'is very much about proper social behaviour, making it a far thornier issue to deal with it in the classroom' (p. 3).

One of the issues that have been hotly debated in the last decade is that of classroom-based learning of pragmatics in the L2. Bardovi-Harlig and Do?rnyei (1998) looked at the effects of the learning environment and proficiency on learners' awareness of pragmatic and grammatical errors in the L2. They found that learners in a foreign language setting showed a higher awareness of grammatical errors while the learners in the second language setting were better at spotting pragmatic errors, and rated them as more severe. In a replication of the previous study, Niezgoda and Ro?ver (2001) compared Czech EFL and Hawaiian ESL learners. They found that the learning environment was not the most important variable affecting learners' pragmatic awareness, although Hawaiian ESL students also had higher awareness of pragmatic errors. A number of researchers have shown that a focus on interactional and pragmatic norms in the classroom through consciousness-raising strategies has a positive effect on interlanguage development (cf. Liddicoat and Crozet 2001; Lyster 1994).

Other researchers such as Kinginger and Farrell (2004) and Kinginger and Belz (2005) have shown that study abroad can offer L2 learners the opportunity to seek out authentic interactions with native speakers (NSs) of the target language (TL), and hence put into practice what had previously been learnt in a classroom. Kinginger and Farrell (2004) found a rapid growth of meta-pragmatic awareness among their eight American students studying in France. The participants became much more aware of the social indexicality of pronouns of address in relation to age-peers. In a follow-up study based on two participants, Kinginger and Belz (2005) found that the development and awareness of the use of pronouns of address reflects the nature of the language learning experience. The participant who engaged in frequent interactions with NSs of French in a variety of social contexts developed a much greater awareness of the social meaning of the *tu* form than the other participant for whom interactions with NSs was limited to service encounters.

Jeon and Kaya (2006) carried out a meta-analysis of 13 quantitative studies (out of a pool of 34 studies) that considered the development of L2 pragmatics in classroom settings. Results of the meta-analysis showed that the effectiveness of direct pragmatic instruction is large and trustworthy (Jeon and Kaya 2006: 191). Long-term instruction in pragmatics (i.e., more than five hours) was found to have larger instructional effects than short-term instruction (i.e., fewer than five hours). This is in contrast with grammar-related features which can be taught and learnt in much shorter time-spans (Jeon and Kaya 2006: 202).

Methodological and epistemological problems in SLA pragmatics research

What the different types of pragmatic research within an SLA or multicultural context have in common is that they aim to measure individuals' pragmatic competence and compare it with the monolingual NS norm. How indeed can one decide what is 'proper social behaviour'? The literature on interlanguage pragmatics (see Barron 2003 for an overview) discusses the advantages and disadvantages of different data elicitation techniques such as Discourse Completion Tests (which is still the most popular instrument, cf. Jeon and Kaya 2006), role-plays and interviews.

We would like to argue that there are several problems with this approach: first, it has been pointed out (Cook 2002a; Grosjean 1992; Pavlenko 2005) that we need to get rid of the monolingual bias in applied linguistic research. If we accept that L2 users are legitimate, multicompetent users of L2 (cf. Cook 2002a), does it matter whether or not they conform to some NS norm? L2 users' deviations from the NS norm are not necessarily examples of pragmatic failure. Another question concerns the intentionality of the deviation from the NS norm. Pragmaticists looking at L2 production data may unconsciously want to attribute deviations from the NS norm to gaps in pragmatic competence, or transfer from other languages. However, L2 users may intentionally violate pragmatic rules, just as L1 users do. The L2 user who appears rude for not apologizing in a specific situation may be expressing dissatisfaction consciously. The lack of an apology is not a pragmatic failure in that case. In other words, it is very difficult for pragmaticists working on L2 production data to guess what the communicative intention of the L2 user was and hence to decide whether something was an error or not, whether a deviation was intentional or not.

The second serious problem that researchers in L2 pragmatics face is the definition of the NS norm (cf. Davies 2003). Different communities of practice have different sets of unwritten rules concerning appropriate behaviour. Against what set of rules should we compare the data from our L2 learners and L2 users?

The third problem relates to the amount of evidence needed to draw conclusions. In other words, can any data gathered in the course of our linguistic investigations ever be sufficient to claim that an individual has acquired 'pragmatic competence' in an L2? Is there any guarantee that the appropriate apology in the L2 produced in role-play or written down on the Discourse Completion Questionnaire (DCT) would indeed be used in an authentic communicative situation? Can we ever generalize fragmented findings to make any definitive announcement about an individual's pragmatic competence? One could wonder whether such an enterprise is inherently doomed to failure as it seems to imply that linguistic systems are stable and that competence in the L2 progresses linearly.

Pragmatics through the eyes and the heart of the L2 user

Rather than focusing on specific communicative actions as reflections of pragmatic competence in the L2, we propose to look at the phenomena illustrated in the extracts by Jemma, Ye and Huston, namely the perceptions L2 users have of their ability to communicate and their relationship with the L2. As Huston puts it, the capacity to be moved by 'pur plaisir de la parole' ('the pure pleasure of speech') (*Nord perdu*, 1999: 61, cited in Kinginger 2004: 208), to which one could add the capacity to move other people by appropriate use of the L2. The L2 users' perceptions and affective states related to their life-long communicative experience in different languages may give us a better, more general view of their pragmatic competence. Indeed, at some point the fluency and accuracy of long-term L2 users may reach an equilibrium point, and judgments of proficiency and success will probably be determined more by the relative ease with which communicative intentions are translated in the L2, rather than a concern about pronunciation, vocabulary, grammar and fluency in the L2. We can compare multilinguals' perceptions and affective states in their different languages, thus avoiding the need for an L1 control group. We share the focus on participants' social perceptions with Kasper and Rose (2001), but we add affect to the equation, propose a different epistemology and methodology, and focus on L2 users rather than L2 learners.

The present study will focus more particularly on the effect of one independent variable, the context of acquisition – more specifically the amount of authentic communicative interaction during the acquisition of the L2 – on self-reported levels of oral and written proficiency, communicative anxiety and perceptions towards the L2 among 1579 adult multilinguals from around the world.

The rationale for the study is to investigate to what extent purely formal classroom instruction contributes to the development of pragmatic competence in the L2. In other words, does the L2 classroom provide learners with a rich enough source of social interactions? By comparing levels of pragmatic competence of former classroom learners with those of former learners who combined formal instruction with extra-curricular interactions in the L2, and naturalistic learners, we will be able to determine the impact of classroom interaction on the development of pragmatic competence in the L2.

Hypotheses

This chapter will test the following two hypotheses:

1. Levels of self-perceived pragmatic competence will be higher in the L1 than in the L2.
2. Mixed and naturalistic second language learning will result in higher levels of self-perceived pragmatic competence compared to purely formal classroom instruction.

Method: data elicitation instrument

The web-based form of the Bilingualism and Emotion Questionnaire (Dewaele and Pavlenko 2001) was used to collect information on multilingualism and the communication of emotions. The questionnaire was advertised through several listservers and informal contacts with colleagues around the world. The first part of the questionnaire contained 13 questions relating to participants' gender, age, education level, ethnic group, occupation, languages known, dominant language(s), chronological order of language acquisition, context of acquisition, age of onset, frequency of use, typical interlocutors, and self-rated proficiency scores for speaking, comprehending, reading and writing in the languages in question. The second part of the questionnaire consisted of 13 closed-ended Likert-type questions on language choice for the expression of various emotions with various interlocutors, on code-switching behaviour in inner and articulated speech, on the use and perception of swear-words, on attitudes towards the different languages and, finally on communicative anxiety in the different languages. The last part of the questionnaire presented 5 open-ended questions which asked about emotion and verbal behaviour. Only data relating to the participants' L1 and L2 was used in the quantitative analysis.

Participants

A total of 1579 multilinguals (1114 females, 465 males) contributed to the web questionnaire database used in the present study. The participants spoke a total of 77 different L1s. Anglophone NSs represent the largest group (n = 433), followed by NSs of Spanish (n = 162), French (n = 159), Chinese (n = 136), German (n = 131), Dutch (n = 96), Italian (n = 66), Finnish (n = 38), Catalan (n = 36), Russian (n = 35), Portuguese (n = 34), Swedish (n = 24), Greek (n = 21), Afrikaans (n = 14), Danish (n = 14), Japanese (n = 14), Welsh (n = 11) and Polish (n = 10). The remaining 138 participants share another 57 languages: Albanian, Arabic, Armenian, Basque, Bengali, Boobe, Bosnian, Bulgarian, Cheyenne, French Creole, Croatian, Czech, Esperanto, Estonian, Faroese, Farsi, Frisian, Galician, Gujarati, Hebrew, Hindi, Hungarian, Ibo, Icelandic, Indonesian, Irish, Korean, Latvian, Lingala, Lithuanian, Luganda, Lugwara, Luxembourgish, Macedonian, Malay, Malinke, Marathi, Norwegian, Oriya, Punjabi, Romanian, Rwandan, Serbian, Serbo-Croatian, Sindhi, Slovak, Slovene, Sudanese, Tagalog, Taiwanese, Tamil, Turkish, Ukrainian, Vietnamese, Wobe, Yiddish and Zulu.

The most frequent L2 is English (n = 727), followed by French (n = 304), Spanish (n = 146), German (n = 99), Dutch (n = 49), Italian (n = 33), Catalan (n = 24), Russian (n = 21), Swedish (n = 17), Greek (n = 15) and 44 other languages with smaller number of speakers.

The mean age of onset of learning was 8.6 yrs (SD = 6.2) for the L2. The L2 was defined as the second language to have been acquired. The participants consisted of 323 bilinguals, 376 trilinguals, 377 quadrilinguals and 503 pentalinguals.

Participants are generally highly educated with 160 having a high school diploma, 539 a Bachelor's degree, 454 a Master's degree, and 421 a doctoral degree. Ages ranged from 16 to 73 (Mean = 34.3; SD: 11.5).

Independent variable: context of acquisition

The effect of authentic language use with NSs of the TL on the acquisition of sociolinguistic and pragmatic competence has been clearly demonstrated (for overviews, see Dewaele 2004c, 2007). The studies showed that after their stay abroad or after prolonged contact with NSs, the L2 users approximated to the NS norm on a range of sociolinguistic and pragmatic variables. It thus seems that living abroad for an extended period does something unique to the learners' usage which classroom input does not.

Table 11.1 Distribution of participants according to context of acquisition of the L2

Context of acquisition	n	%
Instructed	664	43.8
Mixed	630	41.5
Naturalistic	222	14.6
TOTAL	1,516	100

Three types of contexts of acquisition were considered and ordered according to the amount of extra-curricular contact with the TL: (1) instructed context (i.e., formal classroom contact only); (2) mixed context (i.e., classroom contact + naturalistic contact); and (3) naturalistic context (i.e., no classroom contact, only naturalistic communication outside school).

The distinction between the three contexts is obviously quite crude. More fine-grained categories could have been used for the instructed context to distinguish between 'foreign language-classrooms', where the TL is the instructional target, and 'immersion classrooms', where the TL primarily serves as the medium for teaching non-language subject matter.

We observed in Dewaele (2005a) that learning and teaching practices at school have considerably evolved over the years, and still vary widely both geographically and socially, but they all share one aspect, namely that the learning happens within the confines of classroom walls, in the presence of a teacher and classmates, and that an official programme has to be followed. The notion of 'naturalistic context' refers to a wide range of ways in which one can learn a language naturalistically. They all have in common that the learning process was not intentionally guided by a particular teacher or programme, but developed gradually and spontaneously through interaction with speakers of the TL.

Table 11.1 shows that roughly an equal number of participants learned their L2 through an instructed or a mixed context, with a smaller number learning the L2 naturalistically. Sixty-three participants did not provide this information.

Dependent variables: self-perceived competence in the L1 and L2

Self-perceived competence is a person's evaluation of their ability to communicate (McCroskey and McCroskey 1988). It is a judgment that reflects a sum of various aspects of the L2 including perceived competence in grammar, phonology, lexis, syntax and especially pragmatics among experienced L2 users. It is probably also influenced by past traumas or successes in the L2, as well as recent experiences in intercultural communication.

Self-perceived competence was measured through 5-point Likert scales. Questions focused on self-perceived competence in speaking, comprehending, reading and writing a language:

Table 11.2 Distribution of participants according to self-perceived proficiency in the L1 and L2

Proficiency	Speaking		Comprehending		Reading		Writing	
L1	n	%	n	%	n	%	n	%
Minimal	23	1.5	20	1.3	28	1.8	43	2.8
Low	27	1.7	11	0.7	26	1.7	52	3.3
Medium	38	2.4	29	1.8	46	2.9	78	5.0
High	143	9.1	108	6.9	117	7.5	153	9.8
Maximal	1,342	85.3	1,403	89.3	1,347	86.1	1,235	79.1
TOTAL	1,573	100	1,571	100	1,564	100	1,561	100
L2								
Minimal	77	4.9	53	3.4	42	2.7	81	5.2
Low	128	8.2	86	5.5	94	6.0	172	11.1
Medium	235	15.0	166	10.6	151	9.7	275	17.7
High	443	28.2	414	26.4	392	25.2	435	28.1
Maximal	686	43.7	848	54.1	878	56.4	587	37.9
TOTAL	1,569	100	1,567	100	1,557	100	1,550	100

On a scale from 1 (least proficient) to 5 (fully fluent) how do you rate yourself in speaking, comprehending, reading and writing your L1/L2? Possible answers include: (1) Minimal, (2) Low, (3) Medium, (4) High, (5) Maximal.

Not surprisingly, a very high proportion of participants feel maximally proficient in the L1, and this proportion is slightly lower for the L2 (see Table 11.2).

Communicative anxiety in the L1 and L2

MacIntyre and Gardner defined foreign language anxiety as 'the feeling of tension and apprehension specifically associated with second language contexts, including speaking, listening, and learning' (MacIntyre and Gardner 1994: 284). The effect of communicative anxiety on performance in the L1 is much weaker than performance in the L2. The authors concluded that the 'potential effects of language anxiety on cognitive processing in the second language may be pervasive and may be quite subtle' (1994: 301).

Data on communicative anxiety was obtained through the following closed question, based on a 5-point Likert scale, and formulated as follows:

> How anxious are you when speaking your different languages with different people in different situations? (Circle appropriate number, 1 = not at all, 2 = a little, 3 = quite anxious, 4 = very anxious, 5 = extremely anxious).

Information was requested for the L1 and the L2 of the participant in the following situations: speaking with friends, with colleagues, with strangers,

Table 11.3 Distribution of participants according to communicative anxiety in the L1 and L2

Communicative anxiety	Friends		Colleagues		Strangers		Phone		Public	
	n	%	n	%	n	%	n	%	n	%
L1										
Not at all	1,348	88.0	1,129	76.6	1114	73.5	1,134	74.4	775	51.8
A little	117	7.6	241	16.4	291	19.2	273	17.9	412	27.6
Quite	21	1.4	52	3.5	62	4.1	63	4.1	186	12.4
Very	17	1.1	25	1.7	26	1.7	30	2.0	77	5.2
Extremely	28	1.8	26	1.8	22	1.5	25	1.6	45	3.0
TOTAL	1,531	100	1,473	100	1515	100	1,525	100	1,495	100
L2										
Not at all	990	66.3	713	49.8	710	47.3	602	40.5	369	25.4
A little	383	25.7	486	33.9	506	33.7	476	32	458	31.5
Quite	90	6.0	173	12.1	203	13.5	283	19	334	23.0
Very	18	1.2	39	2.7	60	4.0	91	6.1	188	12.9
Extremely	12	0.8	22	1.5	21	1.4	35	2.4	105	7.2
TOTAL	1,493	100	1433	100	1,500	100	1,487	100	1,454	100

on the phone, and in public. The data in Table 11.3 show that participants report experiencing communicative anxiety in the L1, especially in more stressful situations, but that greater numbers of participants report higher levels of communicative anxiety in the L2.

Perceptions of the L1 and the L2

Attitudes and perceptions towards languages and their speakers strongly affect their motivation, acquisition and use (Do?rnyei 2003). These attitudes and perceptions towards languages are determined by a complex interaction of societal, historical and individual variables. The perception of emotional characteristics of a language is usually linked to higher proficiency in that language (Dewaele 2004d).

The perceptions of participants towards their L1 and L2 were captured through the following closed question, based on a 5-point Likert scale, and formulated as follows:

> Here are some subjective statements about the languages you know. Please mark to what extent they correspond to your own perceptions. There are no right/wrong answers. (My L1 / L2 is ... useful, colourful, rich, poetic, emotional). Possible answers included:
>
> 1 = not at all, 2 = somewhat, 3 = more or less, 4 = to a large extent, 5 = absolutely.

Table 11.4 Distribution of participants according to perception of the L1 and L2

Perception	Useful		Colourful		Rich		Poetic		Emotional		Cold	
L1	n	%	n	%	n	%	n	%	n	%	n	%
Not at all	9	0.6	23	1.5	13	0.8	45	2.9	33	2.1	915	61.7
Somewhat	41	2.6	52	3.4	30	1.9	107	6.9	109	7.1	323	21.8
More or less	99	6.3	182	11.8	141	9.1	225	14.6	208	13.5	137	9.2
To a large extent	219	14.0	372	24.2	325	21.0	304	19.7	353	23.0	56	3.8
Absolutely	1192	76.4	908	59.1	1035	67.0	860	55.8	833	54.2	51	3.4
TOTAL	1,560	100	1537	100	1,544	100	1,541	100	1,536	100	1,482	100
L2												
Not at all	10	0.6	22	1.4	21	1.4	74	4.9	59	3.9	777	53.1
Somewhat	57	3.7	80	5.2	69	4.5	151	9.9	174	11.4	369	25.2
More or less	93	6.0	261	17.0	236	15.3	310	20.3	330	21.7	202	13.8
To a large extent	266	17.1	507	33.0	470	30.6	393	25.8	406	26.7	75	5.1
Absolutely	1126	72.6	665	43.3	742	48.2	597	39.1	551	36.3	40	2.7
TOTAL	1,552	100	1,535	100	1,538	100	1,525	100	1,520	100	1,463	100

A majority of participants choose the statement 'absolutely' to describe their L1 (with the exception of 'coldness', with which most disagree). These proportions of highly positives is slightly lower for the L2 (Table 11.4).

Distribution of the data

A series of one-sample Kolmogorov-Smirnov tests revealed that the values for self-perceived competence, communicative anxiety and perceptions of the languages are not normally distributed (Kolmogorov-Smirnov Z values vary between 8.1 and 19.3 for the different variables, all $p < 0.0001$). As a consequence, non-parametric Wilcoxon Signed Ranks Tests were used instead of a paired t-test. Kruskall Wallis analyses were used as non-parametric equivalents to multivariate analyses to examine the effect of the independent variable on levels of self-perceived competence, communicative anxiety and perceptions of the languages.

Results

The Wilcoxon Signed Ranks Tests reveal that for the three sets of dependent variables reflecting pragmatic competence, the scores are significantly higher in the L1 of participants than in their L2 (see Tables 11.5, 11.6 and 11.7).

Table 11.5 Comparison of self-perceived proficiency scores in L1 and L2 (Wilcoxon Signed Ranks Test)

	Speaking	Comprehending	Reading	Writing
Z	−22.06	−20.82	−16.59	−19.07
Asymp. Sig. (2-tailed)	0	0	0	0

Table 11.6 Comparison of communicative anxiety scores in L1 and L2 (Wilcoxon Signed Ranks Test)

	Friends	Colleagues	Strangers	Phone	Public
Z	−11.26	−12.89	−14.03	−17.43	−16.66
Asymp. Sig. (2-tailed)	0	0	0	0	0

Table 11.7 Comparison of language perception scores in L1 and L2 (Wilcoxon Signed Ranks Test)

	Usefulness	Colorfulness	Richness	Poetic character	Emotionality	Coldness
Z	−2.01	−8.32	−10.88	−9.37	−10.27	−4.60
Asymp. Sig. (2-tailed)	0.044	0	0	0	0	0

Mean scores for perceived proficiency in speaking, comprehending, reading and writing are significantly higher in the L1 than in the L2 (see Figure 11.1).

The perceived emotional attributes of the L1 are judged to be significantly stronger than those of the L2 (the difference between L1 and L2 for the only non-emotional attribute, usefulness, is smaller but still significant) (see Figure 11.2).

Finally, levels of communicative anxiety are significantly lower in the L1 compared to the L2 in all situations (see Figure 11.3).

The effect of the context of acquisition was found to have a highly significant effect on the three sets of independent variables reflecting pragmatic competence. The effect was most significant for self-perceived proficiency (see Table 11.8), followed by communicative anxiety (see Table 11.9), and finally for perception of the L2 (see Table 11.10).

Participants who learned the L2 in an instructed context do not rate themselves as being as proficient as the participants who learned the L2 in a mixed or naturalistic context (see Figure 11.4).

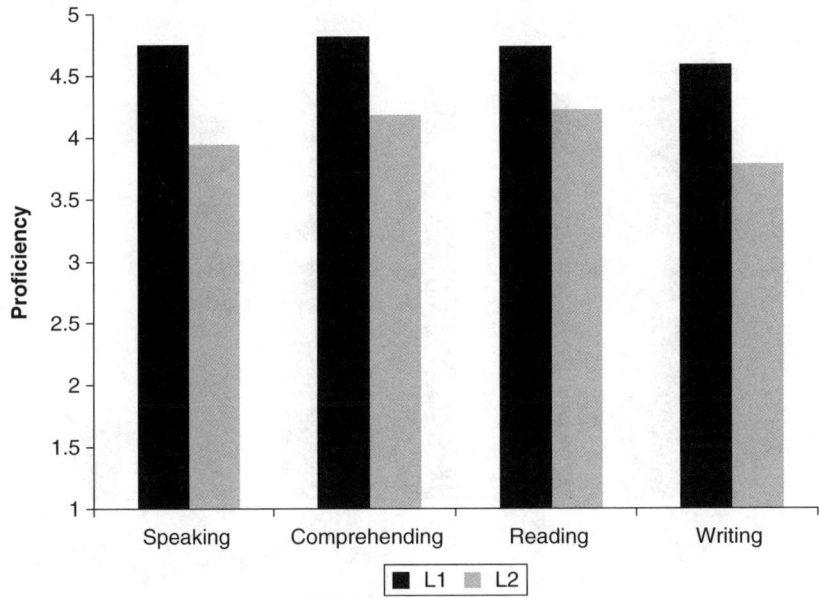

Figure 11.1 Mean self-perceived proficiency scores for L1 and L2

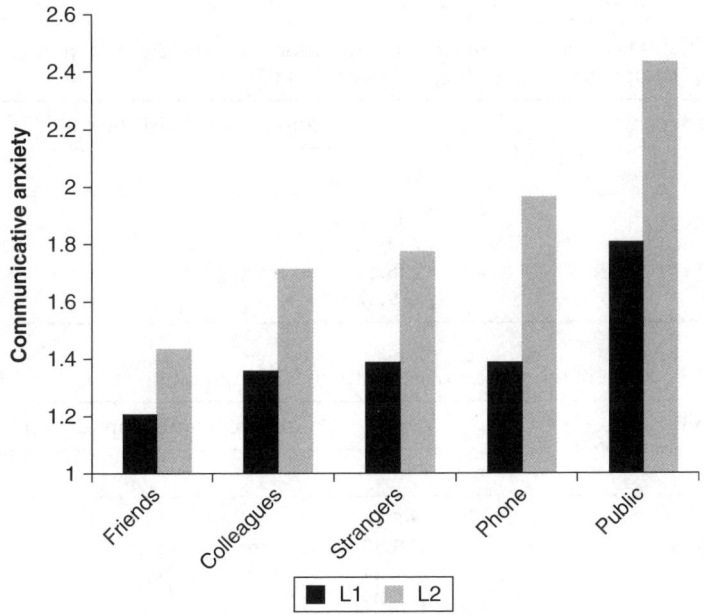

Figure 11.2 Mean communicative anxiety scores for L1 and L2

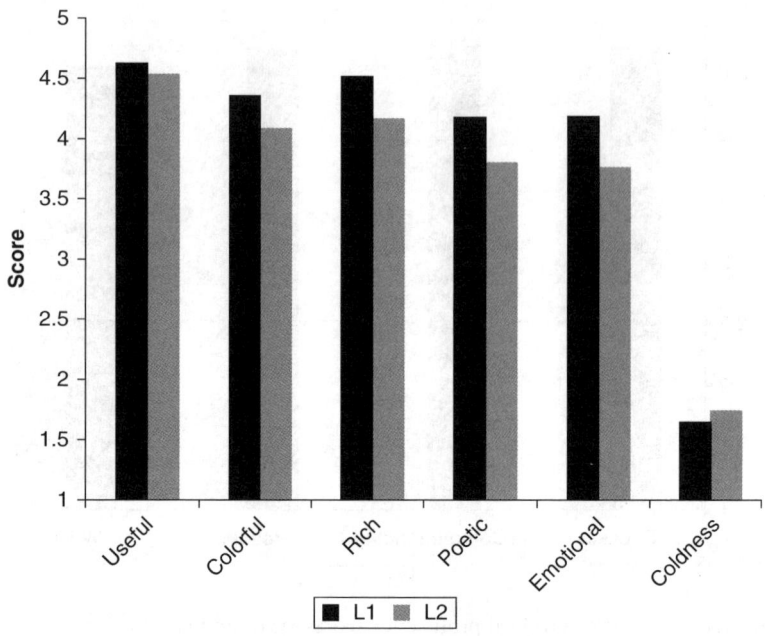

Figure 11.3 Mean language perception scores for L1 and L2

Table 11.8 Effect of the context of acquisition on self-perceived proficiency in speaking, comprehending, reading and writing in the L2

Proficiency	Context of Acquisition (df = 2)	
	Chi²	p
Speaking	207.16	0
Comprehending	223.12	0
Reading	136.17	0
Writing	129.37	0

Table 11.9 Effect of the context of acquisition on communicative anxiety in the L2

Situation	Context of Acquisition (df = 2)	
	Chi²	p
Friends	66.17	0
Colleagues	88.82	0
Strangers	90.44	0
Phone	101.09	0
Public	61.95	0

Table 11.10 Effect of the context of acquisition on language perception scores in the L2

Perception	Context of Acquisition (df = 2)	
	Chi^2	p
Usefulness	26.33	0
Colorfulness	19.39	0
Richness	9.32	0.009
Poetic character	14.31	0.001
Emotionality	26.26	0
Coldness	40.26	0

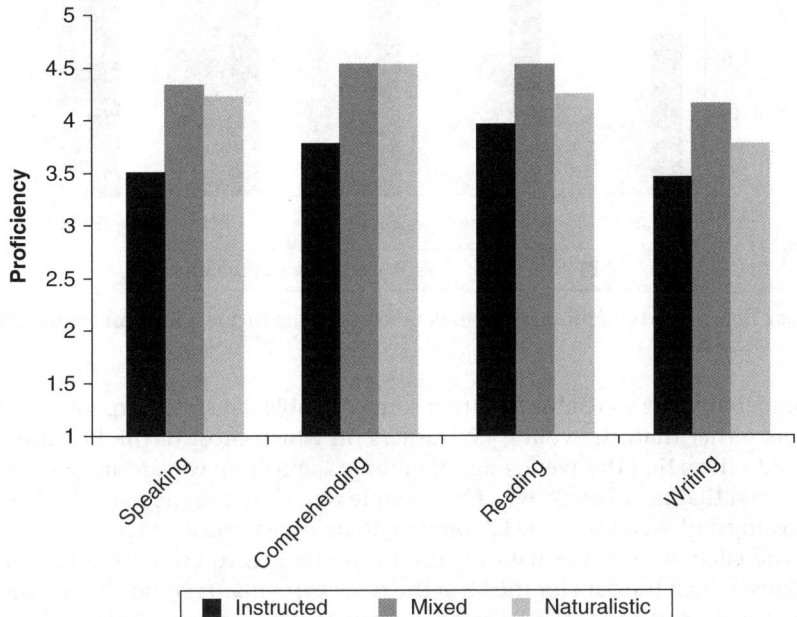

Figure 11.4 Mean self-perceived proficiency scores for instructed, mixed and naturalistic learners in L2

These instructed learners also suffer more from communicative anxiety (see Figure 11.5) and do not rate the L2 to be quite as useful or as powerful as far as the affective characteristics are concerned (see Figure 11.6).

Discussion

By considering participants' perceptions and feelings about language and communication in these languages as a reflection of their pragmatic

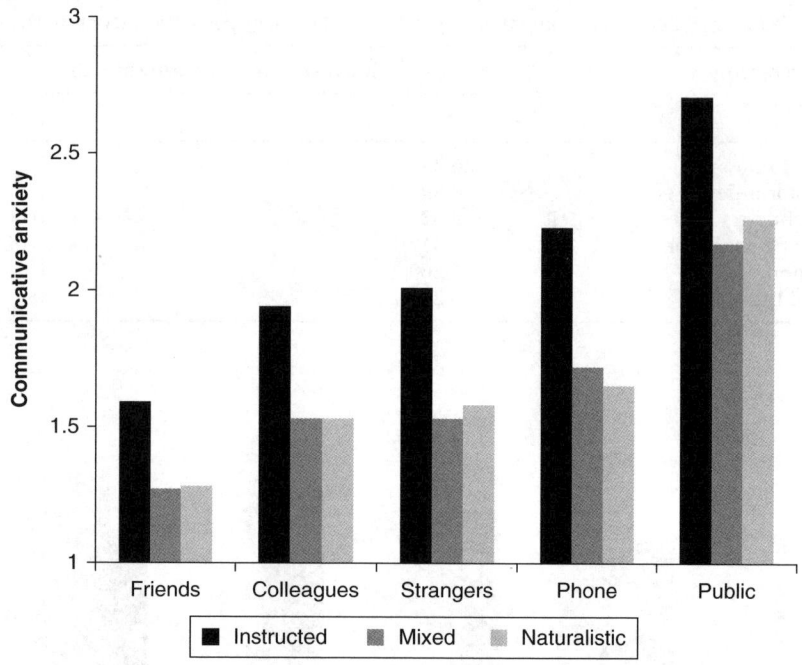

Figure 11.5 Mean communicative anxiety scores for instructed, mixed and naturalistic learners in L2

competence, we were able to gather some valuable data from experienced L2 users rather than the young L2 learners on which most of the literature is based. Given that the average age of onset of acquisition was around 8 years of age, and that the average age of the sample was 35, the participants had been learning and then using the L2 for more than 25 years on average.

The elicitation of the data for the L1 allowed us to establish a base-line against which the data for the L2 of the same participants could be compared. Our first hypothesis was confirmed, namely that participants feel more proficient and more at ease in their L1, and that the L1 is perceived as being more powerful in all respects compared to the L2. This finding nicely confirms the observations from Jemma, Ye and Huston. These three women had sufficient knowledge of grammar, vocabulary and phonology to communicate adequately with NSs of the TLs. They felt frustrated at the difficulty they experienced trying to juggle with words in their L2, especially when they compared their L2 performance with their L1 performance. They seemed to realize that uncertainty about the emotional strength and illocutionary power of words and expressions in the L2 hampers the control over perlocutionary effects in specific situations. The joke in the L2 might fall flat, the use of L2 swear-words might elicit unexpected reactions from interlocutors, the L2 might remain

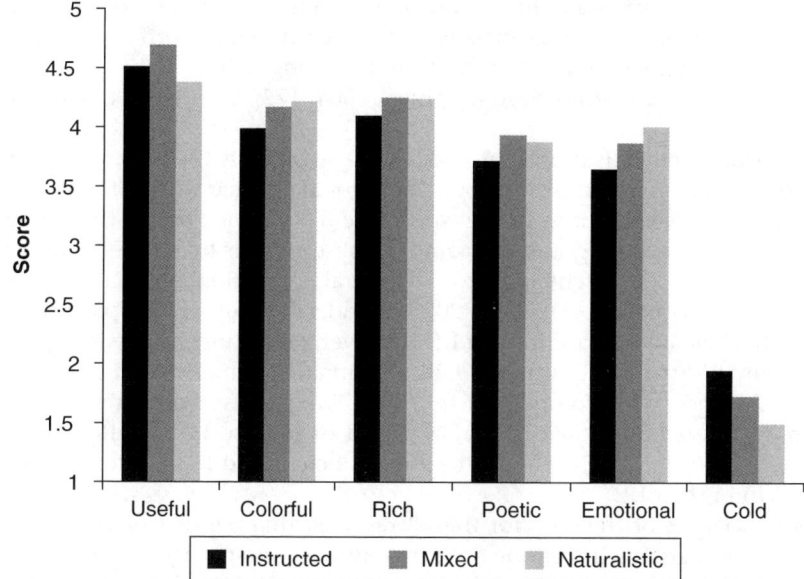

Figure 11.6 Mean language perception scores for instructed, mixed and naturalistic learners in L2

too detached to be moved by it (possibly because L2 words lack the emotional connotations, cf. Harris, Gleason and Ayçiçegi 2006) and to move other people with it. One could argue that once the L2 user can feel the pure pleasure of language, that person may indeed have attained a very advanced level of pragmatic competence in the L2.

It is important to avoid easy generalizations though. First, the L2 user can attain a very high level of pragmatic competence in certain domains, in certain modes, but it does not necessarily extend to all domains and modes. Huston, for example, would not have become an established writer in France if her command of the written language was only average. In other words, her command of written L2 is probably superior to that of most French NSs. And yet she writes that she experiences great difficulty in expressing anger orally in social interactions:

> il y a toujours quelque chose de ridicule à s'emporter dans une langue étrangère: l'accent s'empire, le débit s'emballe et s'achoppe ... on emploie les jurons à tort et a travers ....

(there is always something ridiculous about getting carried away in a foreign language: the accent gets worse, the rhythm runs off and stumbles ... you use the wrong swear words in the wrong way ...)

(quoted in Kinginger 2004: 172; Kinginger's translation)

The second generalization that needs to be avoided is the belief that pragmatic competence and perception of emotional characteristics of the L2 will be lower for every L2 user in the world. We have argued before that significantly higher averages, and concomitant observations by L2 users, show us general trends that might apply to the general population, but that it is in no way a law of nature (Dewaele 2005b). Indeed, most of our participants reported being dominant in their L1. However, for a minority of participants, typically L1 attriters (Dewaele 2004d), pragmatic competence in the L2 had overtaken pragmatic competence in the L1. These L2 users preferred the L2 to express affect and to swear after a period of intense L2 socialization (cf. Pavlenko 2004a, 2005). They felt more proficient and less anxious in their L2 than in their L1.

The analysis of the data for the L2 revealed that context of acquisition, which gives a rough indication of the amount of extra-curricular contact with the L2 during the learning of the L2, continues to exert a strong influence after more than two decades of L2 use (on average). In other words, the type of context in which an L2 is learned permanently affects the perceived level of pragmatic competence in that L2. L2 learners who learned the language strictly within the classroom walls feel significantly less proficient in that L2, are more anxious and have a weaker bond with the L2 compared to the learners who used the language more outside the classroom. This clearly demonstrates that if the L2 is not used as an authentic tool of social interaction during the learning process, progress will be hampered and the ultimate level of pragmatic competence will be felt to be lower than that of L2 users who did use the L2 effectively during the learning phase. It seems that the quicker an L2 learner becomes an L2 user, the more likely it is that that person will attain high levels of pragmatic competence.

We are of course fully aware that context of acquisition is only one independent variable, and that many other interrelated variables determine levels of pragmatic competence. The variables could be grouped according to the individual's linguistic history (age of onset of acquisition), the individual's current exposure to the different languages (frequency of use, degree of socialization, network of interlocutors), or the individual's social and psychological characteristics (age, gender, education level, level of emotional intelligence). Previous studies based on the same database or on sub-samples of it have focused on language choice for the expression of anger (Dewaele 2006); swearing (Dewaele 2004a); perception of emotional force of swear words and taboo words (Dewaele 2004b); the effect of context of acquisition on language choice for swearing and perception of emotional force of swear-words

(Dewaele 2005a); the link between Trait Emotional Intelligence and communicative anxiety (Dewaele, Petrides and Furnham 2006) and variation in self-perceived oral proficiency (Dewaele, forthcoming). In sum, what emerged from these studies is that context of acquisition clearly affects pragmatic competence in the foreign language but that is by no means the only variable to do so. Other social, historical, psychological characteristics of L2 users also determine their pragmatic competence.

Conclusion

The specific aim of this chapter was to investigate the effect of social interaction during the learning of an L2 on pragmatic competence. A highly significant effect of context of acquisition was found on the three constituent parts of pragmatic competence in the L2: self-perceived proficiency, communicative anxiety and perception of the characteristics of the L2. The amount of authentic use of the L2 during the learning of the language is clearly crucial in attaining a high level of pragmatic competence, and its effect remains detectable several decades after the end of the active 'learning phase'. The didactic implication is that the L2 should not just be the abstract object of L2 instruction, but an effective tool for social interaction in the L2. Extra-curricular contact with the L2 through holidays or study abroad periods would seem most useful in helping transform the L2 from an abstract set of grammar rules, speech acts and vocabulary items, into a new channel into which communicative intentions can be formulated without constraints.

The present study rests on the argument that one way to gauge pragmatic competence is to consider what experienced L2 users think and feel about their past performance in the L2, but they have been ignored so far in pragmatic research despite Kasper and Rose's definition of sociopragmatic competence as 'the social perception of participants' (2001: 2). We have advanced a number of arguments for this epistemological shift. By considering L2 users' feelings and thoughts about their communicative experience in the L2, rather than a limited number of communicative actions, one can shed a new light on the objective on pragmatics, namely taking the point of view of the L2 users in a L2 sociocultural environment (cf. Crystal 1997).

This new approach also allows the researcher to avoid the tricky question of deciding on the status (intentional or non-intentional) of deviations from some abstract NS norm. Also, by comparing self-perceptions in the L2 to self-perception in the L1 of the same participants, the problem of comparing apples and pears can be avoided.

The use of the web questionnaire allowed us to gather data from adult L2 users from all over the world. This ethnic, cultural, linguistic and social diversity ensures that the data are not overly influenced by local factors or particular forms of L2 teaching. The advantage of gaining breadth with this approach is obviously counterbalanced by the lack of detail. We are certainly not claiming that micro-level pragmatic research on L2 production should be abandoned. We simply argue that an alternative macro-level perspective is possible, and that it can yield generalizable results.

Part 3
Multilingual and Multicultural Classrooms

12
Bilingualism in Mainstream Primary Classrooms

Jean Conteh
University of Leeds

The author acknowledges the invaluable contributions of Safina Hussain and Ishrat Dad to the writing of this chapter.

Introduction: living multilingually

' ... when the teacher asks me to translate for someone who can't understand, I feel proud ...'
'... when you're learning English, it feels like you're helping somebody ....'
'... I'd like to have more languages in school ...'

These are snippets from a conversation which I had with a group of Year 6 pupils – four boys and four girls – in their classroom in a primary school in the north of England. Among them, the children spoke, read and wrote most of the languages of their local community; English, Urdu, Punjabi, Bengali, Gujarati. They were also learning French in mainstream school, and most were learning to read the Koran in Arabic in local mosques. The girls explained how they also went to a class in the mosque to learn how to write Urdu from a female teacher, and they compared her systematic approach to teaching grapho-phonic correspondences in Urdu script to the ways their mainstream teacher had taught them phonics in English in the Literacy Hour. All the children had recently gained Level 4 in their SATS (the Standard Attainment Tasks done by all pupils in England at the end of primary school; Level 4 is the benchmark for 11-year olds), and some had attained Level 5. They were soon to leave primary school to begin their secondary education.

For about 30 minutes, we sat and talked about languages, of the ways they used the different languages in their repertoires for a wide range of purposes at home and at school; writing letters in Urdu to relatives in Pakistan, speaking Bengali to their grandparents at home, helping the teacher out in class by interpreting for a child new to English. They talked about how Simon,[1] a 'white' boy in the class, enjoyed learning words in Punjabi – one of the boys suggested that he was 'a bit jealous' of the fact that they spoke languages which he could not understand. They joked about swapping words in different languages with each other when the teacher wasn't listening. One boy, Rashid, spoke confidently about how he had almost completed learning the Koran and described what this entailed. He also explained at length why it was important to be good at English, but ended his contribution to the conversation with the uncompromising declaration:

'... you should take pride in your own language ...'

While the children experienced this rich language diversity in their daily lives, the language which dominated their mainstream classroom contexts was English. Some of their mainstream teachers were no doubt curious and may even have expressed positive attitudes about the languages their pupils used outside school, but there was no way that they were able to recognize their importance for their learning of the National Curriculum in school. Towards the end of the discussion, I asked the group of children if they had ever heard the word 'bilingual', and whether they knew what it meant. It did not seem to be a familiar word, or one that had strongly positive connotations for them. One boy said that he had heard of it, and thought it had something to do with 'bilingual support'.

In the ways they describe how they use the different languages in their repertoires, switching and mixing easily and naturally as they move between home, community and school and among all the different people who constitute their everyday social networks, these eight children are no different from thousands of other second- and third-generation 'ethnic minority' children and adults living in British cities today. They live in multilingual contexts, constructing their identities through their social practices as members of multilingual communities. But, paradoxically, they are part of a wider society which constructs itself as unequivocally monolingual (Leung, Harris and Rampton 1997; Blackledge 2004). This monolingualism is reinforced in official educational discourses in England where the labels used for different languages and their speakers contain them in specific and separate contexts and position them in hierarchical relationships with English and with each other; *EAL, second language learners, mother tongue, first language, second language* and so on. Such terminology does nothing to capture the multilingual social and cultural realities of the Year 6 children who took part in the above conversation, which are similar to those of most ethnic minority pupils in schools in England. Similarly, it does nothing to reflect the professional and personal experiences of the growing numbers of bilingual teachers who are beginning to take their places in primary classrooms in England. When they take up positions as newly qualified mainstream teachers, they will have had virtually no advice or even recognition in their training of their bilingualism or of ways in which it could be used as a positive tool in their teaching (Conteh 2007a).

Bilingualism and education policy: a 'rich resource' or lost opportunities?

Thirty years ago, the Bullock Report, speaking of inner-city 'immigrant' communities, suggested that:

> ... their bilingualism is of great importance to the children and their families, and also to society as a whole.
> (DES 1975: 293)

and encouraged us to:

> ... see it as an asset, as something to be nurtured, and one of the agencies which should nurture it is the school.
> (DES 1975: 294)

However, it is well documented (e.g., Bourne 2001; Conteh 2006) that, from Bullock onwards, policy responses to the presence of bilingualism in mainstream schools have been contradictory and confusing. It is, on the one hand, constructed as a 'rich resource' and 'an asset' (NCC 1991: 1) but it is also seen as a phenomenon that threatens to disrupt the naturalized practices of primary classrooms and so needs to be controlled and contained, as Bourne argues:

> ... while there is an available discourse in primary education of 'valuing' the languages children bring to school, it may be much harder to introduce these languages into the routines of classroom practice in a way which does not challenge the construction of reality in that classroom.
> (2001: 257–8)

Two significant outcomes of this muddled approach to policy are the total separation of mother tongue teaching from mainstream contexts and the deployment of bilingual support assistants in mainstream classes. These were both strongly advocated in the Swann Report (DES 1985). Introduced at a time of social unrest and uncertainty in Britain when cohesion was high on the political agenda, this was part of the integrationist 'Education for All' ideology of the 1980s. Prior to Swann, in Britain as in other parts of Europe, there had been various small-scale projects investigating the role of the mother tongue in teaching and learning in primary schools (e.g., Fitzpatrick

1987; Tansley 1984). In the light of the Swann Committee's anxieties about the possible divisive effects of any kind of 'separate' provision in language education, funding for projects such as these came to an end.

But, paradoxically, this has led to an even greater separation than the one which it attempted to prevent. Currently, a wide gulf exists between so-called supplementary (or complementary or community) schooling and mainstream schools. In multilingual cities throughout the country, the range of out-of-hours, community-based schooling is huge; in Bradford, for example, there are almost 80 such language schools and classes. But very few mainstream teachers have much idea about what goes on in them, although pupils from their classrooms may attend such classes for several hours a week. In addition, since the 1980s, there has been virtually no research at all into the possible role of community languages in children's learning and achievement or into the potential of bilingual education in England. Indeed, as Bourne (2001: 263) points out, the only model of so-called 'bilingual education' we have in the United Kingdom, in Wales, is not really bilingual at all, but in practice is usually a case of the two languages being used in parallel.

The second key policy initiative strongly supported by Swann, the appointment of bilingual support assistants, became important as the policy of withdrawal to separate ESL classes or language centres for learners new to English came to an end and they were moved into mainstream classes. The support assistant's role was characterized by Swann as:

> ... providing a degree of continuity between the home and school environment by offering psychological and social support for the child, as well as being able to explain simple educational concepts in a child's mother tongue, if the need arises, but always working within the mainstream classroom and alongside the class teacher.
>
> (DES 1985: 407)

Bilingual assistants have been a key aspect of the construction of the 'transitional' model of bilingualism (Cummins 2001) which has developed in primary classroom practice over the years. This model was further reproduced through the course of the 1990s, which saw the introduction of the National Curriculum and the National Literacy Strategy (see Barwell 2004, for a critical review). Martin-Jones and Saxena (1995, 1996) present examples of talk from multilingual primary classrooms which illustrate the typical ways in which transitional bilingualism was (and still is) played out in the interactions among support assistants, pupils and class teachers. As Bourne (2001: 256) argues, 'monolingual definitions of "bilingual support" remain dominant despite the introduction of bilingual adults into the classroom.'

A big change currently being brought about in primary schools is the introduction (or re-introduction) of so-called 'modern foreign languages' into the curriculum. The *Languages for All: Languages for Life* strategy (DfES

2002) lays down – with a strong hint of *déjà vu* – long-term objectives aimed towards introducing language learning at Key Stage Two for all pupils by 2010. Statutory guidance is spelt out in the *Key Stage 2 Framework for Languages* (DfES 2006). In the 2002 document, it is just about possible to detect the recognition of the idea that there may be links between modern foreign languages and 'community' languages. There is the suggestion that children who are already bilingual, such as the eight children whose conversation began this chapter, could be at an advantage in their learning of French, German or Spanish in school, compared to monolingual learners. There is also even the hint that speakers of community languages could have a contribution to make to developing England as a nation of 'multilingual and culturally aware citizens' (DfES 2002: 5).

But the statutory *Framework for Languages* does not support these ideas. It provides virtually no opportunities for teachers to use or develop links between the different languages which may already be represented in their classrooms as a support for children's learning of new languages, or to develop genuinely bilingual approaches in their teaching. The old contradictions between celebrating language diversity, but in no way systematically promoting its cognitive potential, echo throughout the document. There are three strands of activity for each year of Key Stage Two; *Oracy, Literacy* and *Intercultural Understanding*. The oracy and literacy activities, in general, are in the well-established foreign language teaching tradition, providing interesting opportunities for extensive repetition and reinforcement of the target language. The *Intercultural Understanding* strand is different, offering a mix of different 'cultural' activities such as the following:

- Compile a list of languages spoken within the school.(Year 3, p. 29)
- Listen to authentic songs linked to celebrations and learn a few key phrases. (Year 4, p. 41)
- Follow a simple recipe and prepare a dish. (Year 5, p. 53)
- Create a multi-media presentation using simple sentences to present information about another culture. (Year 6, p. 64)

In general, they seem to embody a fixed and static model of culture and cultural interchange, failing to recognize its attributes as a fluid medium through which social relationships, including learning, are mediated. All too depressingly, the familiar old 'saris, samosas and steel bands' approach to cultural diversity seems to live on. Despite the positive hints in the 2002 strategy, there is no suggestion of the possibility that the languages which children bring from home could be a positive starting-point for their learning of new languages, and no advice given for helping children to make links between the known and the unknown. Indeed, the opposite view is implied; concern is expressed that 'children for whom English is a second or additional language' may need to overcome 'potential barriers to learning'

(DfES 2002: Part 2, p. 11). The introduction of language teaching into Key Stage Two could be an opportunity for pupils who already have knowledge of, and access to, different languages to further develop their language repertoires. In turn, monolingual learners could gain greater awareness of the language diversity that is around them. Instead, the policy-makers already seem to be apologizing for the problems it might cause. There is the real risk of:

> ... schools successfully transforming fluent speakers of foreign languages into monolingual English speakers, at the same time as they struggle, largely unsuccessfully, to transform English monolingual students into foreign language speakers.
> (Cummins 2005: 586)

Bilingualism and the cultures of mainstream primary classrooms

In England, the culture of primary classrooms is still strongly influenced – albeit often at an intuitive level – by the child-centred philosophy of the Plowden Report (Central Advisory Council for England 1967), built on the Piagetian model of the child as 'lone scientist' who progresses through fixed stages of development, often without the need for adult intervention. The teacher's role is to facilitate and monitor this process. Alongside this, we have a powerful discourse of 'good primary practice' where the teacher assumes overall responsibility for what is happening in her (in the vast majority of cases) classroom. Any other adults present take on supporting roles, their positions in the hierarchy clearly visible to the children. Within such a framework, Bourne (2001) shows how difficult it is for 'good' primary teachers to come to terms with the fact that they cannot understand the languages of the children they are teaching, suggesting that the presence of such children in their classroom 'is tantamount to admitting that they cannot carry out their fundamental role competently' (Bourne 2001: 258). How much harder must it be for them to accept that another adult, entering their space, may be able to meet the needs of those children in ways which are not available to them. It is not surprising then that primary classrooms remain largely monolingual spaces, despite the longstanding presence of bilingual support assistants. Languages other than English are seen as marginal, of no relevance to anyone else but the few pupils who may speak them.

But despite their relegation to the margins, there is some evidence that bilingual assistants can have positive effects on their pupils' learning. Martin-Jones and Saxena (2003) present some telling examples of ways in which assistants, when they have the space to use the full range of languages which they share with their pupils along with their knowledge of local and cultural contexts, are able to develop classroom interaction which extends different kinds of affordances for learning than those which occur with monolingual teachers who do not share the same 'funds of knowledge' (Moll et al. 1992). In classrooms where bilingual assistants and teachers work together in partnership, the potential for learning can be greatly enhanced. But, most often, the assistant's role is constrained by her position in the primary classroom hierarchy and such potential is not realized.

Things may change as the numbers of bilingual qualified teachers in mainstream schools slowly increases. Over the past few years, the Government has introduced several initiatives to raise the numbers of such teachers and claims are made for their positive effects on the achievements of ethnic minority pupils. But these claims are, as yet, unsubstantiated. Questions of how bilingual teachers can establish themselves as equal professionals with bilingualism as part of their professional repertoires within the prevailing monolingual system remain unanswered. The potentials and possibilities of bilingual pedagogies remain unexplored. Investigating the skills and knowledge of mainstream bilingual teachers is an underdeveloped area of classroom research in England, actual evidence of bilingual teachers' work in classrooms is very rare. Creese (2005) provides detailed evidence of the work of bilingual EAL teachers in secondary classrooms. Conteh (2007a) reports on bilingual primary teachers' views on their bilingualism as an aspect of their professional identities and as a possible pedagogical tool, and also provides evidence of bilingual interaction between a teacher and her pupils in a complementary class. In the following sections, I provide some evidence of one teacher's use of code-switching in a mainstream classroom, discuss her own views on its value for her teaching and learning and consider the implications. As Mercer indicates (2001: 250), code-switching is sometimes regarded as a 'somewhat controversial' teaching strategy, but can be used in complex and currently little understood ways as part of 'special bilingual techniques' to enhance children's understanding of the curriculum.

A case study – one primary teacher's bilingual interactions with her pupils

Meena is an experienced, bilingual Key Stage 2 teacher. She was employed at the time the data in this chapter were collected in an EMA (Ethnic Minority Achievement)-funded post in a large, ethnically diverse primary school, the school attended by the children whose conversation was reported at the start of this chapter. About 70 per cent of the children in the school shared her first language, Punjabi, and several other South Asian languages were represented. Meena's brief – like most other EMA teachers in England – was to help raise the achievement of ethnic minority pupils. She worked alongside class teachers in Years 4–6, but time for shared planning and review was very restricted. What she actually did for most of the time was work on her own with class-sized groups of children on Geography, History and D&T activities, to help the teachers cover the National Curriculum. In the following paragraphs, I consider one of Meena's lessons, which I observed and audio-recorded. I first give an overview of it from my observations, and then discuss in detail some examples of Meena's use of code-switching in her teaching.

The lesson was Geography and lasted 45 minutes. The class was Year 4, with 25 children, about 15 of whom had Punjabi as their first language and the rest were (or appeared to be) monolingual. One child, who had recently come from Denmark, was fluent in both Danish and Punjabi, and was quickly learning English. The content of the lesson was taken from the 'knowledge and understanding of places, patterns and processes' theme, and aimed to meet the requirement for studying two localities; one in the United Kingdom and one in 'a country that is less economically developed' (National Curriculum online). Packaged resources covering different countries are readily available for such lessons, and a popular set for schools with significant numbers of pupils from Pakistani heritage backgrounds covers the Swat Valley in Pakistan and includes a well-produced video. The assumption seems to be that the material might relate to the community lives of the children, but this is often not the case as it deals with quite a remote part of Pakistan which is not very familiar to them. Meena, however, had quite extensive knowledge of the context in Pakistan, as well as of the home backgrounds of the children in England, so her teaching was informed by this cultural and social knowledge. Her main stated aim was to raise the children's awareness of the differences and similarities between what they saw on the video and the community in which they lived in West Yorkshire. The lesson time was mostly taken up with the whole class together watching sections of the video, interspersed with questions and discussion.

In the process of the lesson, Meena code-switched between English and Punjabi at least seven times for extended exchanges and at other times more briefly. Although the code-switching was clearly marked, it was smoothly incorporated into the overall texture of the lesson with no apparent dissonance between one language and another. At the first occurrence of code-switching, one or two children turned and looked at me, as if to check my reactions. After that, no one took any notice of me, and they gave their (almost) full attention to their teacher. The interactions in Punjabi took place between Meena and individual or small groups of children, and some of these went on for quite some time. The other Punjabi-speaking children all seemed to listen intently to what was taking place, and the 'monolingual' children sat quietly, apparently paying attention. At times, the child to whom the Punjabi was directed replied in the same language, and at others in English. Once or twice, Meena encouraged a child to 'say it in Punjabi' when they seemed to be having difficulty expressing themselves in English. One or two children, such as the new child from Denmark, were specifically targeted, and at one point Meena held a fairly extended dialogue with another child. My overall impression was of an orderly and well-run lesson, with complex exchanges intended to include all of the children in the room. English was dominant, but Punjabi had a definite place.

I transcribed the lesson and analysed the instances of code-switching which took place with the help of Meena and another bilingual teacher. They listened to the audiotape of the lesson, and I asked them their views on it, using the following questions:

1. What were the teacher's purposes in code-switching?
2. What were its effects on the children?

I have used their comments to inform the analysis presented below.

Most of the code-switching was aimed at providing support for individual children, or for checking that the children understood what was going on. But one or two examples seemed to be different, as I explain below. Two examples of code-switching are discussed in the following paragraphs.

In the transcripts, the regular text shows what was said in English, the text in bold shows what was said in Punjabi, and the italicized text provides a gloss of this in English.

What were the teacher's purposes in code-switching?

A: Extending thinking. The first example happened early on in the lesson. It shows how Meena used Punjabi as a linguistic support for the children, and a means of amplifying points being made, in the same way as the teacher described by Camilleri (1994) and referred to by Mercer (2001: 251). Through her use of Punjabi, Meena provides access to the content of the lesson and reinforces and extends points which had already been introduced in English. When the children had seen a few minutes of the video, she stopped it, and initiated a discussion about the words 'different' and 'similar', which she had introduced in English at the start. She asked the class for a definition of 'similarity', and the following exchange ensued.

Extract 1

001	Meena:	What is a similarity?
002	Child:	Something the same as
003	Meena:	The same as ... right .. Similarity **ai jarai**
004		**cheese tako thai .. dree cheese ai nal barabar**
		Similarity is when two things are equal and ...
005		Differences **kai ik ke thako thai usnay**
006		**koi aithai duee khol khani**
		differences means when one thing has something but the other one doesn't

```
007                Give me one example that we can look at,
008                of a similarity, so that I know that you
009                understand the word.
```

In introducing the idea of 'the same as' (line 002), it is possible that the child is linking the word 'similarity' with 'simile', which is something she may have come across in other subjects. Meena, possibly aware of this, switches to Punjabi to give a more detailed explanation of the key words 'similarity' and 'difference' than she has previously done in English. Afterwards, she returns to English to address an instruction to the class as a whole. In her reflection on the lesson, Meena commented that one of her key purposes in code-switching is to ensure that important concepts are understood by the children, and this seems to be the case here. Meena's explanation of 'similarity', beginning in line 003, serves to correct the misconception which she suspects the child holds of the word, and also extends and enriches the definitions of two key concepts in the lesson for other children in the class.

B: Establishing professional identity and using 'funds of knowledge'. The second example of code-switching is much more complex and – I argue – illustrates more about the teacher's professional identity than her conscious strategies to support the children's learning. Towards the end of the lesson, a sequence on the video shows the inhabitants of the Swat Valley bartering crops they had grown for goods in a nearby town. By this point, Meena – as she told me afterwards – was anxious to prevent the children forming the view that the lives of the inhabitants of the Swat Valley were totally different from their own and of no relevance to them. To try to explain the idea of bartering, she introduces the notion of buying things 'on tick' from the local corner shops, a practice she knew was common in communities such as the children lived in. She begins a sustained conversation which involves several children and moves back and forth between Punjabi and English:

Extract 2

```
001    Meena:      When you ... I know that ... jilay thusa rai ami
                   thayabba
002                janay na dukarnay par paysay ar vacth danay ..
                   dukarn
003                daray .. koi .. jraay khusa nay kol
                   When your mum and dad go to the 'corner shops' and they pay the
                   shopkeepers, do they pay the shopkeeper there and then .. I mean
                   the shops that are near you
004    Child 1:    No, they can give ....
005    Meena:      Kay karnai?
                   What do they give?
```

006 Child 2: **Paysay daynay na**
They give money
007 Meena: **Paysay sarai day nay?**
Do they give all the money?
008 Child 3: No ... (unintelligible)
009 Meena: Who said 'no'? What does your mum do when she goes to the
010 shop? **Paysay daynay ... kai kithabay par liknay saab kithab**
Do they pay (upfront) or do they write it in a book, i.e., 'all your goods'
011 Child 2: **Paysay daynay nah**
They pay
012 Child 3: **Liknay thay paysay daynay**
They write it and pay
013 Meena: I know ... I know ..

What Meena is doing here is sometimes described as 'cultural bridging'. Her access to the funds of knowledge of both the community in the United Kingdom and in Pakistan leads her to make links in her own mind between trading carried out in small corner shops in West Yorkshire and by farmers in Pakistan, and she tries to form the bridge for the children. In the course of this, she uses Punjabi vocabulary which, afterwards, she said she was quite surprised she had used. For example 'dukarnay' in line 002, which the teachers translated as a 'hut', but said was the 'cultural' word for a corner shop, and 'saab kithab' in line 010, which they translated as 'something like a book for all your goods'. Meena's surprise arose because she said that such vocabulary was not the most commonly used for the ideas she was trying to communicate and she pointed out that some of the Punjabi-speaking children may not have understood the words, but they would have understood the cultural connotations.

Meena felt she did not achieve her aim of drawing out the commonalities between Swat and West Yorkshire. This is probably correct, as the idea of buying 'on tick' may not have been as familiar to the children as she thought. But what she clearly did do, from my viewpoint as observer, was to include the whole class in the bilingual discourse which developed. The speed and pitch of the children who spoke in the extract above reveal their emotional engagement. The Punjabi was somewhat rhythmic with the repetition of sounds such as 'ay' in '... thay paysay daynay' and so on. I noticed that, as the conversation developed, several of the non-Punjabi speaking children were focusing intently on what was happening and repeating the rhythmically reoccurring Punjabi words to themselves. Perhaps Meena did not totally succeed in getting the children to appreciate how cultural practices in West Yorkshire corner shops reflected those in markets in north Pakistan, but what she did achieve was important for the children and for her professional identity as a bilingual teacher. She succeeded in placing bilingualism at the centre of the discourse processes in her classroom, at least for a while. Her role and status as a teacher gave her the right to claim the space for this to happen, and her language and cultural knowledge provided her with the substance. All the children in the class were part of the bilingual discourse, it was not just restricted to a small group on the margins.

What were its effects on the children?

But the important question remains – what are the children, and particularly those who do not speak Punjabi, learning from episodes of code-switching such as these in their classrooms? It could be argued, possibly with some justification, that such bilingual exchanges exclude those pupils who do not understand the words being spoken, and can impair their access to the curriculum. This might be true if it were the case that the whole content of the lesson were contained in such exchanges and the children had no other input, which of course it is not. There was the video, supporting written material and also extensive discussion in English. There is not much risk that the monolingual children's access to the curriculum content was impaired. Indeed, I would argue, they had the added advantage of participation in some of the processes through which 'legitimate knowledge' (Apple 1993: 46) is socioculturally constructed and mediated – which demonstrate how it is, emphatically, about them. Although it is undoubtedly true that the 'Anglo' and 'Asian' children in Meena's class do in many ways inhabit different language and cultural communities outside the classroom, their lives do intersect to some extent; they live in the same streets, visit the same shops, at times take part in the same social events. So, their experience of the cultural practices which Meena referred to in her discussion may not be so different. Meena's attempt at cultural bridging would have some resonance for all the children present.

In addition – and perhaps more importantly – I suggest that while the words may be strange, the lessons offered by the introduction of Punjabi into the classroom interaction are broad and powerful, going beyond the semantic and syntactic aspects of the language itself. Although the children in the class and their families live in close proximity, there is not much personal and social communication across ethnic groups, a factor identified as significant in many of the analyses of the causes of the social unrest in towns and cities like Bradford (e.g., Ouseley 2001: 11). For the non-Punjabi speaking children, their direct experience of the language diversity of the community is probably very limited; little more than shop signs, labels, notices and overheard conversations. So for them, in their classroom, to hear sustained exchanges in a language which is normally marginal to their everyday experiences provides an important lesson in awareness of language and cultural diversity. This is a positive factor for their learning generally as well as something which helps to promote a more inclusive whole-school ethos and contributes to wider community cohesion (Conteh 2003: 120–1).

Some concluding comments: primary classrooms, cultures and pedagogies

> Primary classrooms are social worlds of their own, creating specially sorts of identities and ways of behaving for those who enter them.
>
> (Bourne 2001: 256)

Sociocultural theoretical frameworks (Lantolf 2000) have introduced into discussions of teaching and learning the illuminating and now widely accepted notion that interactions between teachers and pupils are important sites for the co-construction of knowledge and the enhancement of pupils' chances for success. A parallel, but perhaps not so well understood idea to this is that they are also sites for negotiating personal and cultural identities. Cultural psychologists such as Cole (1985, 1996) suggest that teachers (and other adults) and learners view and mediate experiences in classrooms through the lenses of their personal and cultural histories, and that in their classroom conversations, the individual and the social come together and 'culture and cognition create each other' (Cole 1985: 147). Cummins (2001: 1–2) leaves us in no doubt as to the potential transformative power of the conversations between teachers and learners:

> When powerful relationships are established between teachers and students, these relationships frequently can transcend the economic and social disadvantages that afflict communities and schools alike in inner city and rural areas.
>
> (2001: 1–2)

He argues that it is only when the 'deep structure of relationships between educators and culturally diverse students' become oriented towards 'empowerment' rather than reproducing the 'coercive relations of power operating in the wider society' that the culture of the classroom can be transformed and genuine equality of opportunity can become a possibility (Cummins 2001: 136).

There is no doubt that, in a system which recognizes the potential of and supports the development of their bilingualism as an element of their professional expertise, bilingual teachers could have much to contribute to the kind of transformative teaching and learning advocated by Cummins. Research into their professional experiences and practices is crucial, and will have theoretical and practical implications for mainstream classrooms in England. Practically, it will contribute to the development of models of teacher professionalism for a culturally and linguistically diverse society. Theoretically, it will contribute to greater understanding of the ways in which culture plays out in interactions between teachers and pupils, and how a lack of attention to the cultural dimensions of classroom interaction can lead to communication breakdown and possibly to educational failure. It will feed into the growth of 'culturally responsive pedagogies' which, as Osborne (1996) shows, offer so much potential for education systems that strive to provide genuine equality in diversity. And, although the focus of this chapter has been on bilingual teachers, as Osborne emphatically declares in his first assertion (1996: 289), such pedagogies can be available to all educators, not just those who share the language and cultural backgrounds of their pupils.

Note

1. The names of all participants in the study referred to in the chapter have been anonymized.

13
Social Interaction in Multilingual Classrooms

Nikhat Shameem
Newcastle University

Introduction

This chapter looks at the differences between education policy and classroom practice in the use of languages in multilingual primary school classrooms. In many parts of the developing world current in-country language and education policies or written curriculum documents do not necessarily reflect the ways in which languages are learnt and used among young learners who are multilingual.

The era of colonialism and the shift of human labour and migrants has drastically altered the linguistic map of the world in the last two centuries. Nations which have been colonized are likely to have policies favouring the continued use of the colonial language to the detriment of local and indigenous languages. In her assessment of African languages in Burkina Faso, Mali and Niger, Alidou believes it crucial that differences in current language policies and the pedagogical use of languages in education be addressed, as existing systems and instructional strategies have meant a continued plague of illiteracy and non-education (Alidou 2003: 103). Roy-Campbell writes of the steadfast position that French, English and Portuguese, remnants of the colonial legacy, still hold as dominant languages of instruction in many multilingual African countries (2003: 83). There is a continuing belief in these nations that children cannot be proficient in more than one language and that this necessitates a choice between an African or European language as language of education. The European language 'wins' because of the perception that it is 'neutral' in a nation where there are many African languages, which makes choices between African languages in education complex.

In the Pacific, the advent of Methodist and Catholic missionaries, sealers, sailors, colonists and immigrant labour, specifically through blackbirding (from other Pacific Islands) and indenture (from India) have shaped the linguistic history of the islands. English (British and American) and French continue to play pivotal roles in education in Pacific Island states. Language in education policies which were formulated during colonial times remain in the Pacific and change has been slow and non-prioritized. A *laissez-faire* policy has been the comfortable option in an environment of multiple languages and political differences. One effect of having *ad hoc* or outdated language policies in education has been the devaluing of the local languages and in the Solomon Islands, Papua New Guinea and Vanuatu, English-based pidgins and creoles have effectively displaced the local pre-colonial languages in critical domains. In Australia, Hawaii, Tahiti and New Zealand language attrition of the local languages has led to massive language loss. Even relatively strong language communities in the Pacific such as Samoan and Tongan are experiencing language shift especially in education where code-switching with English is widespread (Crowley 1998). In the Cook Islands and in New Zealand, the Māori languages of the *tangata whenua* (people of the land) have been so severely eroded that current efforts to revive them are having only limited success despite massive government efforts (Benton 1996; Chrisp 1998; Lameta 1997).

This chapter describes the relationships between the languages used in education in the context of the island nation, Fiji, situated in the South Pacific, where there is a clear dichotomy between education policy and practice in language learning and use. An essential part of language planning is data gathering on current language proficiencies and use in primary schools, knowledge of when, where and for what purposes learners use their known languages in the classroom and their own, the school's and community's attitudes towards the use of these languages in education (Corson 1999). Language planning cannot be effective without a thorough knowledge of these aspects of language use.

Background to Fiji's language situation

Fiji, in the last 20 years, has faced a series of destabilizing events, dictated by politics and driven by race relations. Four *coups* (three military and one led by a civilian) have taken their toll and had a profound effect on the education system of the country. They have particularly affected the position of the Indo-Fijians[1] – who are the descendents of indentured labourers recruited in the late nineteenth century by the British. Almost half the 60,965 *girmitya*[2] chose to stay in Fiji after *girmit* (their period of indenture) (Gillion 1962; Siegel 1987). In the 1996 census Indo-Fijians formed 44 per cent of Fiji's population of 775,077, in relation to the indigenous Fijian population of 51 per cent. In 2006, population projections showed a trend for a falling Indo-Fijian population, placing estimates at 37 per cent Indo-Fijian and 55 per cent Fijian (Fiji Bureau of Statistics 1996; 2006). To 2006 the exodus of Indo-Fijians from Fiji was set to continue, with the minority who remained in Fiji becoming increasingly marginalized (Field 2006). A December 2006 'popular' military coup, however, is perceived as one which may halt this process, the current commander in favour of a multi-ethnic cabinet and a fair, equitable and corruption-free distribution of resources (Keenan 2007: 44, 45).

Language teaching and policy in Fiji

Much of Fiji's policies in education have been influenced by a 100-year colonial heritage followed by sluggish growth and change following four *coups* in its recent history. Fiji has a multiracial, multilingual population. English is the official language and is used as the lingua franca regularly in almost all domains, especially in the capital city of Suva. The majority Fijian population uses Fijian and the Indo-Fijian population, Fiji Hindi for intragroup communication, although here, too, among educated young people in the city English is a popular choice. As this chapter shows, the Fiji situation is not straightforward as individual ability in known languages varies considerably. Language and variety choice among the Indo-Fijian population, who were the main subjects in this study, depends on the purpose of communication, the identity and role of interlocutors, topic choice, the context or situation and the domain of use.

Fiji schools are either mono-ethnic (mainly Indo–Fijian or Fijian) or multiracial. School ethnic profile is determined by the area the school services and the school committee which runs it. Religious committee schools in particular tend to be mono-ethnic as a majority of Fijians are Methodist and Indo-Fijians, Hindu or Muslim. The study that this chapter describes was conducted in four Indo-Fijian and four multiracial schools in Fiji in 1999.

Languages in Indo-Fijian education in Fiji

Indo-Fijians know Fiji Hindi as their mother tongue, English as the lingua franca for use with other ethnic groups and as the official language, learn Hindustani/Shudh Hindi/Urdu (SH) at school and pick up Fijian from their neighbours and friends. Educational policy identifies SH as the 'vernacular' to be used for teaching Indo-Fijian children in the first three years of primary school. The situation with SH is complicated. Hindustani is the name used for the combination of Shudh Hindi and Urdu which is the spoken form of both these languages. The differences exist in the writing script, with Urdu using a Perso-Arabic script and Hindi the *Khariboli*. Religious affiliations to both languages, Hindus with Shudh Hindi and Muslims with Urdu, means that schools with Indo-Fijian children profess to teach one or the other.

The language children are most proficient in, Fiji Hindi (FH), developed as a result of plantation language contact during indenture (1887–1916) and is rarely used for educative purposes. Although a majority of *girmitya* were from North India and spoke similar Hindi dialects, later arrivals were users of the Dravidian languages which were unintelligible to North Indians. Subsequent input from Fijian, English, and other plantation dialects and languages have given FH a unique identity. In 1929, W. J. Hands, an English missionary and linguist who had worked in India, called FH a virtually unrecognizable form of Hindustani (Siegel 1987: 201). It has been termed a creole (Pillai 1975) and a koine (Siegel 1987). More recently I have argued for its identity as a language in its own right as it fulfils criteria for classification as one: it has become informally standardized and although has no writing script and low academic and formal status, it is spoken everyday as mother tongue to more than a third of Fiji's population (Shameem 1994, 1995). It represents a common badge of identity among Indo-Fijians in Fiji and abroad, although with their declining population in Fiji and documented rapid language shift among young Indo-Fijians abroad, writers and researchers are increasingly predicting language shift and eventual death (Barz and Siegel 1988; Field 2006; Shameem 1995). The continued viability of FH as a well-used vernacular also needs to be seen against the fate of three of the other six Overseas Hindis which developed under similar circumstances of indenture in other parts of the world. South African, Trinidad and Guyanan Bhojpuri are virtually extinct and are unlikely to survive into the next generation. Sarnami, Mauritian Bhojpuri and Fiji Hindi survive, but are spoken by smaller numbers in each generation with increasing other-language influence (Barz and Siegel 1988).

Indo-Fijians become literate in English at school. While Standard English is taught and used for formal purposes, for informal and interpersonal communication among peers of all ethnic groups the variety increasingly preferred is Fiji English. Fiji English is characterized by its many lexical and phonological borrowings from the other languages of Fiji (Shameem 2005; Tent and Mugler 1996). Although it has low status in education, teachers often comment on its influence in their students' oral and written classwork.

Indo-Fijians may also have varying levels of proficiency in another minority language (Punjabi, Gujarati, Tamil, Telugu) although recent research evidence suggests that this may be limited to close-knit community groups, home use or amongst older speakers (Mugler and Mamtora 2004). Around 16 per cent of the Indo-Fijian population is Muslim (Fiji Bureau of Statistics 2006) and therefore may also learn Classical Arabic for reciting the Qurān and for formal prayer, and Urdu rather than SH for vernacular literacy. The majority Hindu population has some receptive access to Sanskrit during religious ceremonies, may have learnt SH receptively through the media and India-import Hindi movies, and acquired SH oracy and literacy at school.

In Fiji a transitional language in education policy means that children are expected to receive instruction through the medium of their vernacular with a gradual transition to the use of English from Class 3 (aged 8). The language generally identified as this vernacular is SH. As the current and earlier studies show, Indo-Fijian children have lower proficiency in SH than in English or FH, their mother tongue (Mugler and Tent 1998; Shameem 1995; 2002a; Siegel 1992).

It is perhaps because of the difficulties involved with using a language in which the learners are neither competent nor comfortable (SH) or one which is used only in informal contexts and has no writing script (FH) that English has become the *de facto* language of instruction from school entry. Reality shows that English language use for instruction begins in Class 1 (aged 5/6) although all the known languages are used for various other purposes. This is regardless of the urban or rural, or mono-ethnic (Indo-Fijian) or multiracial background of the school (Shameem 2002b).

Children's language use in education is influenced by their parents and home language use and the attitudes of their teachers and their peers. While the language of instruction might be English in all schools, one needs to look at the ways and for what other purposes children use their other languages. Language choice in the classroom is likely to vary with number and roles of interlocutors, or change in subject matter such as English, Maths or SH. Fiji's blanket language policy in education, which stipulates the use of one language (English) over others for learning or a vernacular for initial instruction, does not reflect the reality of classroom language proficiency and use among multilinguals in this context.

Implications for language planning in education

The use of languages among multilinguals, although determined by the nature of situation, topic, interlocutor, status and role differences, is complex. An *ad hoc* language policy is inadequate to address the issue of language use in classrooms. In Fiji's multi-ethnic classrooms, language use is immediately centred on the use of English to accommodate racial diversity. In mono-ethnic Indo-Fijian schools English language acquisition and use are seen as essential tools in education. There is a limited role for FH, mainly to facilitate English acquisition and for peer interaction.

The issue of language use in formal contexts can be fraught with tension. In Fiji, for example, Indo-Fijian advocates of SH and language purists either deny the existence of FH or condemn its use in religion or education (see, for example, *The Fiji Times*, 6, 13, 26 July, 1, 2, 5, 7 August 2002; *Daily Post*, 16 July 2002). Such negative attitudes to communicative language varieties are not uncommon. Assaf writes that attitudes to modern standard Arabic and Palestinian City Arabic among his Palestinian respondents were influenced by the formality or informality of the situation or context (2001: 46). For Indo-Fijians, while FH use may be ridiculed in formal and literacy contexts, as a tool for spoken communication among Indo-Fijians its role is strong (Mugler and Tent 1998; Mangubhai and Mugler 2006). Students choose to study either SH, Urdu or Fijian as their 'vernacular' in subject classes and schools make their own decisions about how they organize and run vernacular classes. In their recent publication Mangubhai and Mugler write of the importance of research into vernacular language classes to document what occurs in them or the extent to which the centrally set aims of the programme are being fulfilled (2006:61).

In such a complex linguistic situation it is important that educational planning takes into consideration the languages spoken by the new school intake, the ways in which these are used in the community and attitudes to them. This is especially so in communities where a lower status, but best known language is under-utilized in education.

Social interaction in multilingual classrooms

In analysing patterns of language use and language choice in the multilingual classroom, it is necessary to look at teacher and student interactions individually and in whole group and class situations, in pair work between peers who may or may not share the same languages, and in group work with mono- and multi-ethnic peers. In Fiji, few government resources have gone into the development and sustenance of a viable language policy for multilingual education. Research indicates the presence of a blanket unwritten policy for a majority of primary schools, for English language acquisition as quickly as possible, with the mother tongues of the children used to facilitate this. English is therefore both the target language and the medium of instruction, which places quite a burden on the young child entering school at the age of 5 or 6. Gibbons points out that in such classrooms children are not only learning a new dominant language, but are regularly expected to learn *in* and *through* it as well (1998: 99).

At Class 1 level when the FH speaking Indo-Fijian child enters the school system, they are immediately required to use English, and often SH as well, in formal classroom situations for specific academic purposes. They are therefore not just learning two new languages as subjects of study; they are using these languages to understand content, to construct new curriculum knowledge, and to develop new ways of thinking and talking about their personal learning. In Fiji, known languages fulfil communicative and contextual needs in the environment (a situation of primary multilingualism) rather than formally and only in the classroom (secondary multilingualism). This means that the context itself supports a certain amount of stability in the use of languages amongst interlocutors.

Language planning which takes into account rural and urban differences, the multilingual make-up of the school and the languages known by the Class 1 teacher and students is possible in a relatively stable situation like Fiji's. While language preference may indicate a shift in use from FH to English in urban settings and among young professional Indo-Fijians, the role of FH as informal language of communication and language of identity is indisputable. Careful planning for its use as a classroom resource and to facilitate learning will not only benefit the 5-year-old school entrant but will also support a language which may be under threat.

Classroom language use

This chapter looks at the nature of classroom language use among Indo-Fijian children in Fiji at Class 1 level (aged 5/6) when they have just started school. At the time of the fieldwork for this study, they had been at school for six months. While educational policy continues to be one of transitional use of the vernacular, it is unclear whether FH or SH is treated as this vernacular.

Fishman (1972) makes the important observation that amongst bilinguals, language choice is governed by a number of critical factors such as situation, topic, purpose of communication, interlocutor, domain. This is also true for multilinguals for whom language choice involves more than two languages. Multilingual Indo-Fijian children have complex language choices to make, and these, although largely subconscious, are ruled by social and educational conventions. An understanding of these choices and the nature of language proficiency that children bring to school helps us get a clearer picture of how they might influence classroom interaction amongst peers, in group and pair work, in communication with members of another ethnicity, in whole-class situations and with the teacher.

Eight Class 1 classrooms participated in this study of the languages of classroom interaction. Four of these were situated in the capital city of Suva; the other four were either rural or situated near smaller townships on the main island of Viti Levu. Four of the schools were multiracial; the others had mainly Indo-Fijian children.

The classrooms were observed and the classroom language behaviour of students and teachers noted in a broad observation schedule (see Shameem 2000). Two randomly selected students and the teacher in each of the eight classrooms under study were also chosen as case study subjects. These 24 participants were fitted with a Dictaphone for three subject classes: English, Maths and SH or Urdu. In addition the whole class was videoed using a wide-angled lens and strategically placed microphones for group work when case study students were involved. Videos were viewed retrospectively to compare notes of simultaneous observations with recorded data.

Research questions

The data described in this study answer the following research questions:

1. What are the proficiencies in their known languages (Fiji Hindi, English, Shudh Hindi/Urdu) amongst Class 1(age 5/6) Indo-Fijian students entering their first year of schooling?
2. Which languages are used for learning and communication :
   a. Across three subject areas (English, Maths and Shudh Hindi or Urdu)?
   b. With different interlocutors (teacher–student, student–student, students in group work, with Indo-Fijians and non-Indo-Fijians)?

3. Is there a difference between policy and practice in language teaching and use among the participating Class 1 classrooms?

Results

In this study we looked at language use in eight classrooms and closely investigated the patterns and choices of 16 Indo-Fijian children and their teachers in them. To understand some of these choices, however, we need to look first at the range of proficiencies in their known languages that children bring to school.

Language proficiency

To assess the language proficiencies of students aged 5/6, a self-reported functional proficiency scale was used, enabling participants to identify their aural and oral proficiencies in FH, English, SH and Fijian on an ascending scale of linguistic and communicative difficulty (see Figure 13.1). The scale included functions that Indo-Fijians would realistically be expected to perform using their known languages.

The validity for the self-report scales used for FH in this study was established by comparing the results of self-reports with FH performance test results among Indo-Fijian teenage new immigrants in Wellington, New Zealand (Shameem 1995; 1998). The functions included in the performance test included those listed on the self-report scales. During this earlier study, the results of the performance tests strongly correlated with the self-report data, thereby demonstrating the validity of the self-report scale (Shameem 1998). A subsequent study with Māori language users in New Zealand also shows the high degree of validity of similar self-assessment instruments with 80 per cent to 88 per cent of 51 respondents accurately assessing their proficiency in aural and oral Māori (Te Puni Kōkiri 2001).

As Figure 13.2 demonstrates, Class 1 students felt FH was their strongest language. While all reported their aural FH at Level 6, none rated themselves at Level 7 the highest possible level of the aural scale where they felt able to identify non-primary colours and numbers greater than ten. Indo-Fijians tend to use English for these functions. On the oral scale (max = 6) their FH skills were clearly still at a developmental stage (mean = 4.88, sd = 1.2) which is to be expected of the productive capacity of children in their mother tongue at this age (Lightbown and Spada 2006).

Self-report proficiency also showed that after six months of tuition in English and SH, students felt English to be their stronger language. The 16 students had a mean aural proficiency in English of 5.06, (sd 1.06, max = 7), and in oral English of 4.06, (sd 1.2, max = 6). SH proficiencies were lower than this and although not as apparent in aural skills (mean = 4.56, sd = 1.12, max = 7), in oral SH, competence was clearly limited (mean = 1.75, sd = 1.04, max = 6).

Structured interview: Students

Language proficiency

LISTENING

1. To start with, which of these things do you understand in these languages?

	Shudh Hindi/Urdu	English
1. I can understand someone when they greet me or say thank you		
2. I can understand simple questions about my name, family, address		
3. I can understand the teacher when he /she speaks in these languages to me		
4. I can comfortably understand any school broadcast or children's programmes on air.		
5. I can comfortably understand the head-teacher or other formal speakers at school assemblies, prize-giving etc.		
6. I can understand everything including numbers over ten, days of the week, months of the year and non-primary colours (other than black, red, white)		

2. Now which of the following things can you understand in these languages?

	Fiji Hindi	Fijian
1. I can understand someone when they greet me or say thank you		
2. I can understand simple questions about my name, family, address		
3. I can understand when someone speaks slowly to me		
4. I can understand when people talk at normal speed to me		
5. I can understand most conversations in this language		
6. I can comfortably understand all conversations in this language, even between old people from a different province		
7. I can understand all numbers, days of the week and non-primary colours (other than black, red, white)		

Figure 13.1 Proficiency scale: multilingual ability of young Indo-Fijians

SPEAKING

3. Which of these things can you do in these languages?

	Shudh Hindi/ Urdu	English
1. I can greet people and say thank you		
2. I can give basic information about myself and my family		
3. I can describe my school, my home, this area, Fiji		
4. I can easily say what I want to in a conversation		
5. I can question my teacher and the school head-teacher and answer their questions		
6. I can give a formal, impromptu (off the cuff) speech.		

4. Now which of these things can you do in these two languages?

	Fiji Hindi	Fijian
1. I can greet someone and say thank you		
2. I can give basic information about myself and my family		
3. I can describe my school, my home, this area, Fiji		
4. I am easily able to participate in a conversation with a group of friends		
5. I can easily speak to other people including old people from a different province		
6. I know all the days of the week, numbers over ten and non-primary colours (other than black, red, white)		

Figure 13.1 (Continued)

Figure 13.2 shows that although Indo-Fijian Class 1 students have their greatest abilities in FH, they are also able to learn their other classroom languages quite quickly. FH is clearly their greatest resource for accessing content in their school subjects and in learning English and SH, their other languages, in their first year of school. Whether FH was being utilized as such a resource in the surveyed schools was determined by the interactional data gathered in the classrooms participating in this study.

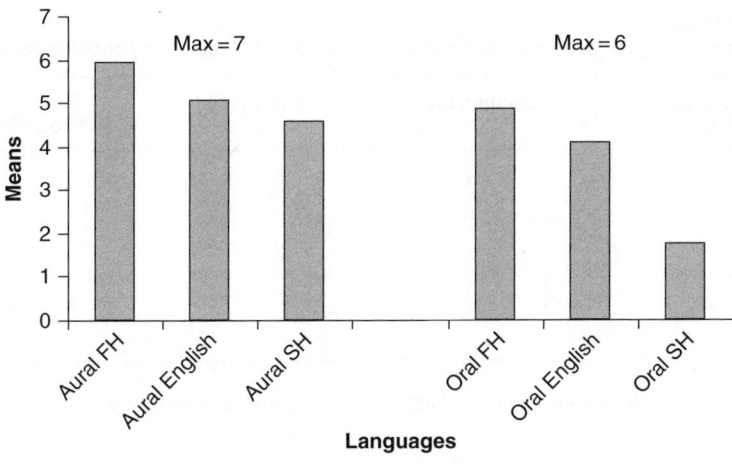

N = 16 students

Figure 13.2 Class 1 self-report language proficiency

Medium of instruction

To be inclusive of school subjects and language lessons, data was gathered from English and Maths and SH/Urdu lessons. Teachers reported the language they used for instruction in these lessons in their pre-class interviews. These reports were then verified through classroom observation using the schedule in Figure 13.3. Simultaneous and delayed observational data and speech transcriptions were used to identify languages of instruction in the participating classrooms. Using multiple sources of data increases the reliability of the results and validates the research instruments used.

Two of the eight participating teachers were non Indo-Fijian and therefore used English as the medium of instruction in their multiracial classrooms. Of the other six teachers, all were using mainly English; two were using English in combination with FH in English classes and three in Maths classes. Only one teacher was using the full range of languages known by her students and this was in a Maths class. Figure 13.4 illustrates the reported and observed instructional medium that teachers were using in the eight participating classrooms.

As Figure 13.4 demonstrates, a much greater use of English was observed than was reported by the teachers, especially in English language and Maths lessons. For example, while three teachers had reported using English and three a combination of English and FH as language of instruction in their English lessons, observation showed that in fact six of the eight teachers were using only English while the other two used both. In Maths classes three

| Teacher |

Language used predominantly (in 5-minute intervals over 1.5 hours = 18 observation points).

Language choice	English class	Maths class	Shudh Hindi Urdu class
English FH SH FH-E SH-E FH-SH Other (specify)			

Figure 13.3 Observation chart for languages of classroom instruction

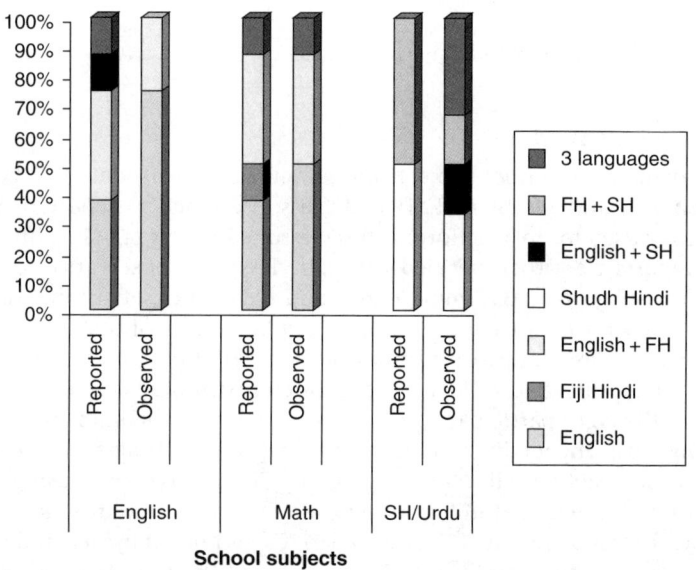

Figure 13.4 Medium of instruction in English, Maths and SH/Urdu classes

teachers reported using English only, three FH and English, one FH, and one all languages as need arose. Observations generally verified these reports except the teacher who had reported using FH was using both FH and English. Even in SH lessons three teachers were using some English in combination with SH or FH, something none of the teachers had reported. The medium also differed according to the subject that was being studied at the time (SH, English, Maths). For instance, English was used as the medium of instruction in the English lessons far more than it was used in Maths (next highest use) or SH/Urdu lessons.

The greatest amount of FH use on the other hand occurred in SH or Urdu language classes where it was usually used alongside English and SH to ensure understanding, to check comprehension or to issue commands (also see Shameem 2002b for classroom functions of languages). Four teachers were using some FH in their SH lessons and in their Maths classes. More teachers were using FH in their Maths lessons than in English, two teachers were using some FH in their English class. No teacher was using FH exclusively in any of the observed lessons.

SH was being dealt with as a school subject from Class 1, rather than as a vernacular for use as the medium of instruction. Use of SH was limited to SH and Urdu lessons and observation showed a somewhat artificial transition from English as language of instruction in school subjects to the use of SH/Urdu in 'vernacular' classes. In these vernacular classes teachers often modelled desired responses in SH before and after eliciting student speech so that parroting and copying were common features of student responses in these lessons. Only one class teacher was using SH for extended discourse in combination with English and FH in his Maths class. The most multilingual use of known languages was during the SH and Urdu lessons. All known languages were being used by four of the six teachers who were observed in these lessons. The other two used SH mainly.

Classroom interaction

The classroom interaction patterns of 16 Class 1 case study students and their teachers were recorded and language choices charted using the schedule in Figure 13.5. The schedule allowed for identification of languages used (including incidents of code-switching) with various interlocutors in the classroom. Notes were also taken on whether each language was used for restricted or extended discourse. Interlocutors were verified by retrospective viewing of video data.

Figure 13.6 describes language choices of the students over the research period of three days per school. In reporting this data I take a general look at language use across all three subject classes: English, Maths and SH/Urdu. All the respondents showed the ability to use at least two languages and in the schools which were teaching SH or Urdu, three. There was no evidence that any student participant had monolingual receptive or productive competence only in FH.

Student language choices showed that in asking teachers a question or initiating discourse with their teacher, eight of the students used English only, while the other eight used both English and FH. In class, the two students who used extended FH discourse during lessons did so to answer their teacher's question in the SH lesson, while in their Maths and English classes they used English. In Maths lessons two students were using both SH and English, six FH and English and eight, English only when responding to

Languages spoken to interlocutors by

TEACHER Languages spoken:	FH	E	SH	C-S	RD	ED
with individual students in groups with class						

STUDENT Languages spoken:	FH	E	SH	C-S	RD	ED

In face-to-face teacher communication
In response to teacher question in whole class
With classmates in group-work:
    Indo-Fijian
    Non-Indo-Fijian
In face-to face communication with classmate:
    Indo-Fijian
    Non-Indo-Fijian						

C-S = code-switching
RD = restricted discourse (words, clause, sentence)
ED = extended discourse (longer stretches of speech)

Figure 13.5 Observation schedule: patterns of classroom language use with various interlocutors

their teacher. Children who used combinations of Hindi languages and English all had Indo-Fijian teachers. Evidence of bi- and trilingual language use was greatest in SH/Urdu lessons, although two students used only SH to answer their teacher's question in the SH class. Chorus and model answers were in English in all English and Maths classes and in SH in the SH and Urdu classrooms.

As Figure 13.6 shows students preferred to use FH in their formal and informal communication with their peers. All 16 students, for example, used FH in face-to-face communication with Indo-Fijian peers and although four children showed some evidence of code-switching between FH and English, this was at lexical level and categorized as restricted rather than extended English discourse. In group work, however, even when the group comprised only Indo-Fijian peers, four students were using both English and FH. When the group included a non-Indo-Fijian child, students were generally using English, although four students continued to use FH as well. One student had a bilingual Fijian deskmate with whom she chatted happily in both English and FH.

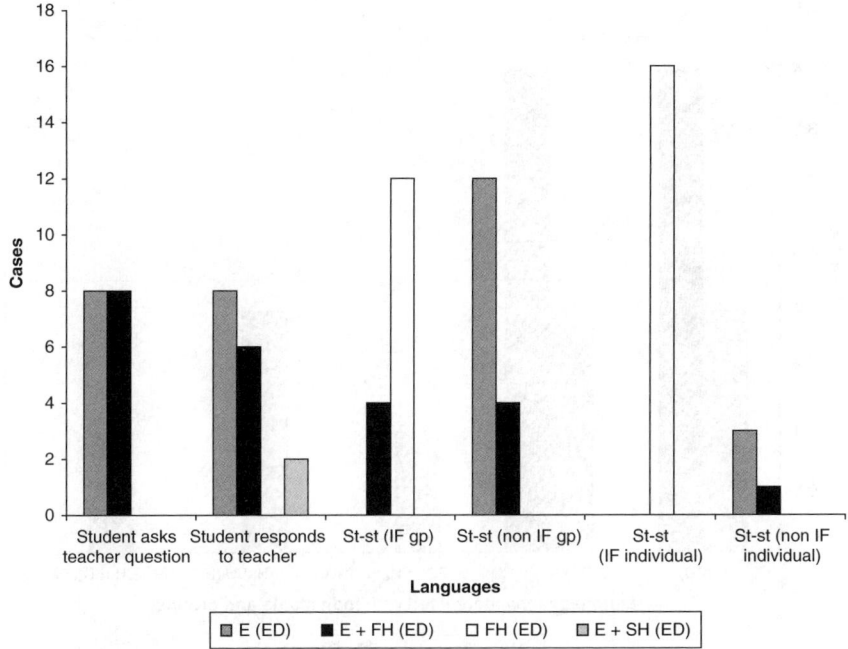

Figure 13.6 Student language choice for classroom interaction in Class 1

Teachers were using a range of languages to interact with their students and language choice depended on the ethnicity of the teacher, the function of discourse and student need (see Figure 13.7).

Data showed that Class 1 teachers are pragmatic and were quite fluent at selecting the appropriate language and register to suit the situation as it arose in the classroom. Student modelling, copying and reformulation of teacher speech occurred frequently in all eight classrooms. These responses were in English in English and Maths lessons and in SH in SH and Urdu lessons. There was evidence, however, that although English was favoured by the teachers in their response to group queries and work, there was some minimal use of FH among four of the eight teachers. With individual students, teachers were selecting from a wider range of known languages in order to explain, illustrate, give examples and ensure comprehension. Figure 13.7 demonstrates that while the language choice of the two non-Indo-Fijian teachers was invariably English the other six were selecting English, FH and SH in restricted and extended discourse and in various combinations in response to individual needs.

One non-Indo-Fijian teacher in a multiracial out-of-city school was able to counter her own non-FH ability by careful grouping of her English competent Indo-Fijian students as resources for explaining English concepts and words to

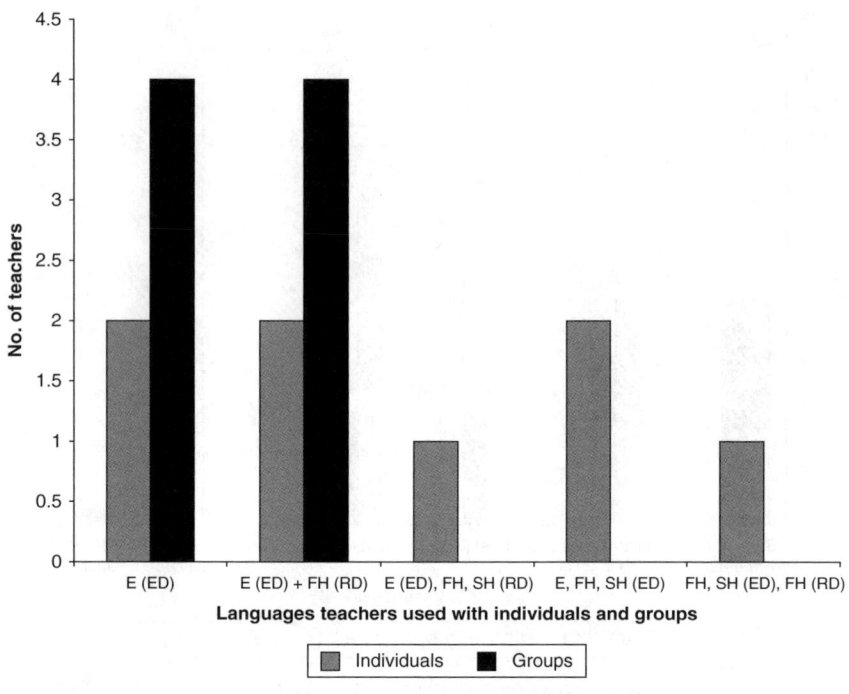

Figure 13.7 Class 1 teacher languages of classroom interaction

less competent Indo-Fijian peers. Recorded data from six of the students in Maths classes showed teachers accepting and responding to their FH use in helping them understand a mathematical problem. Two of them were providing students with spontaneous English translations for their FH utterances or were helping them to reformulate FH utterances into English. There was no evidence that any language was being denigrated or banned in any of the classrooms observed. This included the use of Fiji English among some of the students.

Conclusions

Observations and transcripted classroom talk showed all the languages in the Indo-Fijian speech repertoire being used among various classroom interlocutors at Class 1 level. Despite the emphasis on and push for classroom use of 'standard' English and Hindi in Fiji, in the classrooms which were studied, other languages were also communication tools when needed. There is no clear guideline, however, as to when, where and how a multilingual approach to learning may be more useful or appropriate, and languages were selected by teachers and students on the basis of contextual and individual needs.

This research shows the difference between policy and practice in language use at this level in Class 1. Teachers seemed to operate on the premise that the aim of the educational system is for students to use English for learning and that in order to facilitate this; English should be used as the main classroom medium sooner rather than later in the school system. Hence, while policy continues to espouse the transition to use of English as medium of instruction and classroom learning tool from Class 3 (aged 8), practice clearly indicates that this transition in fact occurs with the blessing of the teacher, parents and other participants at a much earlier stage.

Issues arising from this research

Any education or language policy that deals with language choice for learning in multilingual contexts needs to take into account current practice and use. Disregarding classroom use of languages at the level of lesson delivery will not make for a sound educational system in which languages are important resources and valuable tools for learning. Among Class 1 children the long-term consequences of advantaging children who are choosing English to communicate with their teacher and in group work with their peers will mean that English will continue to play the dominant role. Research evidence from this study does indicate, however, that the mother tongue FH, at least in the short term, will continue to hold its role in student–student communication among individuals both for social and learning purposes. The consistent use of FH in the classroom among peers at this level indicates that it is being used to facilitate learning at the group and individual level and even when code-switching occurs, the predominant language of peer interaction is FH.

In order to cater for the multilingual learner it is important to have as far as possible, high quality and contextualized materials, relevant and appropriate textbooks and trained language teachers for teaching young multilingual learners (see Shameem 2007b for more specific teacher education needs). While authentic written resources may be more easily constructed or sourced in the standard languages English, Fijian, SH and Urdu, oral and verbal resources in the other languages spoken in the classroom (FH, Fijian dialects, Fiji English) would need collection, collation and conscious use by the teacher. In Fiji, as the head-teachers in the study said, it was not uncommon to recruit 'licensed' teachers, who are fluent bilinguals but not trained teachers. Since the classroom use of language is such an important part of curriculum delivery, it is important that the teaching and use of each language be at the right level, authentic, interactive, up-to-date and enable students to function effectively in the multilingual environment existing in and out of their classrooms.

The Fiji book flood programmes of the 1980s (Elley and Mangubhai 1983) show the success and therefore special importance of teaching language through high-interest materials and content in the Fiji context. It has only been in the last two decades that language teaching in Fiji primary schools has moved beyond an audio-lingual approach, teacher-centred lessons and the use of structured readers to more communicative classrooms. In all the classrooms in this study, the reading of big books, which were clearly well loved stories, were hailed with delight by the students. However, only in two of the participating schools in this research was there a library which had books appropriate for students at Class 1 level.

With English having such a major role in Class 1 in Fiji it is important, especially in rural schools, to reduce the disadvantages of children learning subjects such as Maths through the medium of a foreign language. As Moag (1982) pointed out 25 years ago and which holds true today, English language use in rural and peri-urban areas in Fiji is considerably less than in the two cities of Suva and Lautoka. A greater use of FH for teaching content in these schools may be appropriate.·

Language planning and language policy, especially in education, need to reflect real practice. The evidence of multilingual language use was more apparent in SH/Urdu and Maths than in English lessons. Code-switching in both restricted and extended discourse was recorded in all classrooms studied even when interlocutors did not share a common mother tongue. In addition, there was a clear difference between the languages used for formal and instructional purposes (English) and language use in informal contexts and among Indo-Fijian peers (FH). In language planning for education, such features of multilingual classrooms would need to be incorporated and accommodated.

Language teaching approaches in Fiji classrooms reflect possible teacher responses to complex linguistic situations. Teachers have taken an approach in which English is the language used for formal instruction, but other languages have implicitly recognized roles for learning and interaction. Since the strongest language Indo-Fijian children enter school with is FH, perhaps a clearer role differentiation where certain subjects could be taught using a greater mother tongue input may help teachers with the choices they are currently making by instinct in these classrooms.

This research indicates that features of classroom multilingualism need to be taken into account in selecting and using languages for learning. For instance, in Fiji issues of encouraging fluency and accuracy ability as needed in known languages are important considerations, as are the distinctions between language learning for communication and study (English), language learning for literacy (English and SH or Urdu), language use for study, understanding content, processing information and peer interaction (FH), and syllabus design for communicative language and culture studies (FH and Fijian). Mercer and Wegerik (1999: 95) write that a widely accepted aim of research with young learners is the induction of children into ways of using language to seek, share and construct knowledge. Such an aim does not require children to choose one language over another to carry out classroom tasks effectively and collaboratively.

The overt encouragement of a multilingual use of known languages with the emphasis on task achievement could enhance the quality of interaction and support the achievement of conceptual learning goals in group and pair work in multilingual classrooms. Gibbons (1998) for instance, suggests that in ESOL classrooms teacher instruction and teacher-led discussion ought to come *after* children have had the opportunity to develop some understanding of key concepts in small-group work. This allows them a greater opportunity to use all their linguistic resources prior to the teacher introducing new unfamiliar vocabulary, new registers or new ways of making and constructing meaning around learning goals.

One must acknowledge the difficulties of language planning and policy writing in multilingual nations. In Fiji, as in other ex-colonies, policy has been formulated in a top-down process with 'experts' (overseas and local) determining language of instruction and subjects of study, language of material production and textbook writing, and supporting and promoting the use of the colonial language in primary school classrooms. These policies are not necessarily reflective of the actual use of languages in these classrooms. Meanwhile these nations struggle with post-independence political, racial and tribal tensions so that little progress can be made to address some of the urgent policy issues around language choice and use in education. This research showed that rather than wait for policy makers to tell them what to do, teachers are taking a pragmatic, functional approach to language use in their classrooms.

Taking into consideration current language choices and use in classroom interaction means that educational and language planning may go some way towards bridging the divide that seems to exist between the stated language in education policy and classroom practice for children who are only just beginning their school life.

Notes

1. (i) Affirmative action policies post-independence have seen a disproportionate number of special scholarships and places in post-secondary institutions reserved for Fijian students. Funding of enterprises through Fiji's Development Bank also specifically favours Fijian proposals and projects. In 2006, the Fiji Human Rights Commission found the Fiji Social Justice Act 2001, under which affirmative action programmes were put in place, to be unconstitutional.
   (ii) Moreover, 84 per cent of Fiji's land area is inalienable native land and leasehold. Leases are not being renewed for Indo-Fijian farmers who for over a century have been the mainstay of Fiji's sugar industry. Urban drift, unemployment and emigration are direct consequences of this.
2. *Girmitya* (FH) – Indentured labourers in Fiji. *Girmit*, the period of indenture and the hardships it entailed; taken from the word 'agreement'.

14
Untutored Acquisition in Content Classrooms*

Juliet Langman and Robert Bayley
University of Texas at San Antonio and University of California, Davis

Introduction

In the United States, the 1990s witnessed levels of immigration that had not been seen since the early years of the twentieth century, and high levels of immigration have continued in the first years of the twenty-first century. As a result of continuing immigration, as well as a high birth rate among immigrant populations, the United States has become increasingly diverse linguistically. The increase in the Spanish-speaking population was particularly striking. According to the US Bureau of the Census, the number of persons aged 5 and older who claimed to speak Spanish at home grew from 17,862,477 in 1990 to 28,101,052 in 2000, an increase of more than 57 per cent (US Bureau of the Census 2003). The growth of the Spanish-speaking population has continued unabated in the twenty-first century.

The increase in the immigrant population has impacted heavily on schools, which are often unprepared to meet the needs of non-English speaking children who arrive at all the different stages of their school careers. Some immigrant students, although certainly by no means all, enter US schools at the age of 5 or 6 and benefit from well-structured bilingual education or English as a Second Language (ESL) programmes. Students whose first experience in US schools is at the secondary level, however, are likely to have quite a different experience from those who begin their schooling in their new country. In many cases, students receive little or no formal instruction in ESL and subject-matter instruction in their native language is rare indeed.

In this chapter, part of a larger study of second language acquisition and content learning in a middle school (grade 6–8) science class in south Texas, we examine the untutored acquisition of English by 'Manuel Jimenez',[1] a recent immigrant from Mexico. His experience in an English-medium middle school is typical of the experiences of many non-English speaking immigrant students in south Texas and elsewhere in the United States. On arrival, he was placed in English-medium grade level classes under the assumption that he would acquire English without the benefit of formal instruction.

Our focus in this chapter is primarily on Manuel's English production, with particular attention to vocabulary development. The decision to examine production as a measure of his overall language proficiency was motivated by several factors. First, the teacher in the classroom where the study was conducted spoke no more than a few words of Spanish. Thus, Manuel had to produce English if his understanding of the concepts taught was to be recognized by the teacher. Second, throughout the year, most of Manuel's interactions were with bilinguals who, when speaking with Manuel, normally spoke Spanish. Hence, little evidence of his comprehension of English, as opposed to comprehension based on clarifications and explanations in Spanish, was present. In spite of our primary focus on production throughout, we do discuss in the second half of the chapter evidence of his ability and desire to comprehend the overall activities in class through analysis of his participation in interaction.

The study was conducted in a seventh grade science classroom in Madera Middle School, in a traditional *barrio* where the school and community population consists of bilingual as well as monolingual English and Spanish speakers. We chose this setting as representative of the best possible context for language learning offered within the district. Drawing on literature on content-based sheltered instruction (Echevarria, Vogt and Short 2004), many school districts in south Texas and indeed across the country are embracing concepts of sheltered instruction and applying them to all classrooms with English learners (see Langman 2003). In particular, this school and classroom embraced a cooperative ethos, and employed numerous hands-on experimental activities and intensive pair and group work. The teacher was a seasoned professional in science teaching and had participated eagerly in sheltered content ESL in-service training in order to better serve the needs of recent immigrants. This training, which totalled 15 hours of instruction, focused on ways of adapting language and content materials for language learners. The student body included many bilinguals who could potentially serve as language brokers. The classroom also offered some Spanish written resources, mostly dictionaries. While such a context is clearly not optimal for beginners, these conditions do represent what many adolescent learners experience as they enter US schools. Our goal in this chapter is to examine a content area classroom, in this case, science, from the perspective of the language learning opportunities it offers recent adolescent immigrants such as Manuel Jimenez, through the lens of his production of English.

Drawing on a sociocultural framework, our analysis of Manuel's English production seen through the lens of the various contexts created in the classroom, shows that while he actively sought opportunities to practice language, he made very little progress in acquiring the academic language necessary to understand the subject matter. Moreover, he acquired relatively little social language in this context, although, as expected, his acquisition of social language outstripped his acquisition of academic vocabulary.

We suggest that one reason for his lack of progress is that, in the absence of expert help, Manuel did not have the opportunity to acquire the linguistic resources necessary to structure the environment to meet his learning needs. That is, although many of the requisites for language development were in place, Little Manuel lacked the guidance and sustained interactional contexts necessary to orchestrate his learning.

Language learning opportunities

The sociocultural view of learning focuses on learning through collaboration and interaction. Two metaphors tied to this tradition are the metaphor of participation and that of cognitive apprenticeship (Lave and Wenger 1991; Rogoff 1990, 2003; Wenger 1998). This view of learning treats the social process of interaction as cognition and takes particular social conditions as the unit of analysis (Resnick 1991). Through the process of cognitive apprenticeship in particular communities, essentially a process of recurrent participation (O'Connor and Michaels 1996), novices interact with experts as well as peers to negotiate meanings and solve problems, including the problem of language learning. Novices thus are actively involved in their learning and attempt to structure their environment by cueing experts on the nature of the relevant inputs for that learning. This is a task they are capable of accomplishing, because in the case of language learning 'they bring structured knowledge to the flow of speech' (Gelman, Massey and Macmanus 1991: 228).

As learning occurs through recurrent participation, a focus on the conditions for learning provided by diverse contexts will allow us to examine differential success on the part of learners developing language. Within this framework, little research has focused on failures to acquire language in the case of eager learners. O'Connor, however, in her work on the development of mathematical knowledge, outlines three key issues tied to discourse that are pertinent to language learning:

> if we consider a discourse practice as constituting the underpinnings of a developing mathematical [and other academic] behaviour, then access to that practice, or beliefs about it, or culturally conventional restrictions on its use will have consequences for the student's progress in mathematical thinking and communication – consequences that determine which students feel entitled and inclined to engage in discourse practices in ... classrooms.
>
> (1998: 33)

This chapter examines how language learning opportunities sought by a beginning language learner fail to provide him with the necessary input with which to structure his own learning, through an examination of access to that practice, beliefs about learning and culturally conventional restrictions on English language use in the classroom in question.

Setting

Garner School District is one of several school districts in the greater San Ramón metropolitan area. The district, one of the poorest and smallest urban districts in Texas, is located in the city's oldest Hispanic neighbourhood, or *barrio*. The enrolment is overwhelmingly Latino and includes many students from long-established Texas families as well as a smaller number of recent immigrants. Approximately 25 per cent of students in the district are designated as LEP[2] and receive bilingual or ESL instruction. In the elementary schools, about 30 per cent of the students are enrolled in bilingual classrooms. By middle school, all students, including new immigrants, are enrolled in all-English classrooms.

In 2001–02, 628 sixth through eighth grade students were enrolled at Madera Middle School. Of these, 191 were designated as LEP, 52 of whom were new immigrants from Mexico. The classroom selected for our research was a seventh grade science classroom, whose teacher was the science coordinator in the school. Ms Jackson, an English monolingual, had been teaching for nine years, and was generally considered one of the best science teachers in the district. At the beginning of the school year, the class consisted of 22 students. By the end of the year, with numerous students coming and going, 16 of the original 22 students remained. Throughout the year, all but one of the students in the class was Latino, and all but one of those students was of Mexican origin. In addition, although the actual students changed throughout the year, the class remained divided roughly equally into recent immigrants, who had been in the United States from one week to three years, bilinguals with all or most of their elementary schooling in bilingual classrooms, and essentially monolingual English speakers. Although all but two of the monolingual English speakers had at least passive knowledge of Spanish, these students claimed to know no Spanish and were never heard to use Spanish in the classroom.

Examining language learning

During the fall semester, all classes were recorded on both video and audiotape, with the exception of days on which students were taking examinations. Thereafter, visits occurred monthly, and were supplemented with interviews with students. On most days, students worked in no more than five groups, of which we recorded three, one on video and two on audio, using wireless microphones. Two members of the research team were present at all class sessions and took elaborate field notes as well. All recordings were transcribed orthographically and entered into CHILDES for analysis (MacWhinney 1991). The data for this chapter consist of audio and video tapes of six class periods between August and April.

We evaluated language proficiency initially through three measures: (1) English language vocabulary used, including both everyday conversational vocabulary and school-related vocabulary, particularly vocabulary relevant to the science content being taught; (2) question formation; and (3) negation. The first of these measures is clearly related to students' ability to understand the content presented in a grade-level science class. Both question formation and negation have been extensively studied since the earliest days of SLA research and provide useful indications of students' syntactic development (see, e.g., Adams 1978; Cazden, Cancino, Rosansky and Schumann 1975; Schumann 1978; Wode 1976). These measures serve as a counterpoint to the analysis of learning contexts.

For the purposes of evaluating language learning opportunities we analysed each class period from three perspectives: the task the students were involved in (e.g., listening to a lecture, setting up a lab, conducting a lab, writing up results), the types of talk occurring (declarative, procedural, regulatory and social) and the participant frameworks students participated in (e.g., teacher with the group as a whole, teacher with one or a small group of students, and student to student interactions). Within these contexts, we examined interactions in both Spanish and English.

The case of Little Manuel

Manuel Jiménez moved from a border city in Mexico, where he attended six years of primary school, to San Ramón during the summer of 2001. Mexican school records showed that he had been quite a successful student before moving to the United States. However, he had never studied English before being placed in all-English seventh grade classes at Madera Middle School. Neither his lack of English nor his small stature, however, interfered with Little Manuel's, as he was often called in class to distinguish him from a second Manuel, social success. At a school dance held in the middle of the semester, it quickly became apparent that he was the star of the evening and had his pick of young girls to dance with. In fact, one of the teachers, a 15-year veteran of the school, observed that no one had ever danced like Manuel and that 'they are all copying him!'. By the end of the school year, in spite of poor scores on a standardized measure of English proficiency, the Language Assessment Scale (LAS II), and content knowledge, Texas Assessment of Knowledge and Skills (TAKS), Little Manuel was voted by the school staff 'the most improved seventh grader'.

Little Manuel presents an excellent opportunity to test questions of how relatively untutored language learning proceeds. As briefly outlined above, he was a central member of the community of practice formed in the classroom, he was eager to learn, always arriving with a pencil and his notebook, and generally orienting himself to the teacher, the board, and his fellow students in attempts to understand and learn, while also maintaining a vigorous social banter. Indeed, in an interview, Little Manuel expounded on his enthusiasm about learning English and listed all of the opportunities he had for using

English: on rare occasions when his father was home, in the grocery store, and with his one monolingual English friend at school. Notably, he did not talk about using or learning English in school. When pressed, he explained, in Spanish, that his language arts teacher was his English teacher, and in that class he read Spanish translations of English narratives and wrote summaries in Spanish. In spite of being highly motivated and placed with the best teaching team, Little Manuel exhibited almost no improvement in his oral or written production in English over the course of the year, and experienced few if any opportunities to use English in a supportive environment. On a standardized measure, the LAS II administered at the beginning and end of the year, Manuel remained a beginner with a score of Level 1 (out of 5 levels); his raw score was actually lower at the end of the school year than at the beginning.

English language development

During the first half of the school year, Little Manuel exhibited little use of English questions, other than an occasional one-word form such as 'What?' Most of his questions were in Spanish, usually directed to other students in his group. During the second half of the school year, he began to use formulaic questions. Thus, on 1 March, he asked Dominic, an English monolingual, 'What are you doing Dominic?' Moreover, as shown in Extract 1, recorded in April, Little Manuel sometimes uses declarative word order when asking questions (002) as well as question inversion (006).

Extract 1

TEA: = Teacher
LM: = Little Manuel

001	TEA:	and then find one half of that, ok?
002 →	LM:	Miss, miss, this is right?
003	TEA:	sí, three point five times =
004	LM:	oh.
005	TEA:	= and then find one half of that, ok?
006 →	LJE:	Miss, Miss, Miss, Miss, is this right?
007	TEA:	sí.

(04.05.2002)

The picture with negation is similar. During the first half of the school year, most of Little Manuel's negative statements are in Spanish, although he does use some formulaic expressions, such as 'I don't know'. By the second half of the year, we find some use of English negation, including 'don't', which we take to be an unanalysed form (cf. Schumann 1978). Little Manuel also occasionally used non-formulaic expressions of negation, as on 1 March

Table 14.1 Little Manuel's English language vocabulary

Date	30.08.2001	18.09.2001	15.10.2001	27.11.2001	1.3.2002	5.4.2002
Type/token	54/142	26/90	55/121	42/69	91/307	99/335
Social	30	20	49	40	86	82
Academic	24	6	6	2	5	17

when he tells his monolingual partner, 'I don't got the answers'. Note that few of these examples come from extended interactions in English, since, as we will see, Little Manuel is most often grouped with other Spanish speakers.

The third admittedly rough measure of language production, use of vocabulary, is shown in Table 14.1. The totals count individual lexical items and inflected forms where such forms exist separately. The table shows both types and tokens, as well as a breakdown of vocabulary (by type) as social or academic. Academic vocabulary was determined through an examination of the topic of the day and the teacher's use of language. Thus, even though a number of the lexical items classified as 'academic vocabulary' in Table 14.1 are common English words (e.g., 'beach', 'brain', 'rocks'), they are classified as academic vocabulary because they are essential to understanding the lesson of the day.

As Table 14.1 shows, there is a steady increase of social vocabulary throughout the year. In contrast, and indeed as predicted by research on language acquisition (e.g., Cummins 1984), Little Manuel's use of academic vocabulary, with two exceptions, is and remains low throughout the year. Table 14.2 lists the academic vocabulary for each day, together with the topic for the day's lesson.

Table 14.2 Little Manuel's academic vocabulary

Date	Class topic	N	Academic vocabulary
30.8.01	Weight and measurement	24	gram(s), time(s), point [decimal], button, pennies, NUMBERS [12], COLOURS [5]
18.9.01	Levers	6	fifteen, load, point, rocks, ruler, zero
15.10.01	Inertia and momentum	6	bottles, inertia, penny, pennies, speed, velocity
27.11.01	Soil – characteristics	2	rocks, water
1.3.02	Plants – characteristics	5	beach, leave, spreading, stick, water
5.4.02	Brain	17	back, base, body, brain, central nervous system, circle, connect, control centre, cow, diameter, system, control, centre, central

The greater use of academic vocabulary on 30 August is likely accounted for by the nature of the vocabulary, primarily numbers and colours related to measuring and sorting tasks. The relatively high number of academic terms used in April is tied directly to a scaffolded conversation on calf brains with one of the authors during that class period (see Extract 7).

Language learning opportunities

The setting in which Ms Jackson and the students worked was structured to encourage interaction. Students sat in a science lab at high tables in groups of four, facing one another on two sides of each table. A total of six lab tables in two rows made up the available seating. In addition, the class met twice a week for 90 minutes, giving students ample time to engage in hands-on activities. Ms Jackson also employed a collaborative, problem-solving approach most days, so that after a general orientation to the lesson in a lecture format, small groups of students worked together, generally in pairs or foursomes to carry out lab procedures and write up reports, with Ms Jackson circulating from table to table to check on progress and give individual assistance.

Although school policy dictated an alphabetical seating chart, Ms Jackson chose to move her students into groups that she felt would be beneficial in three ways: language support for recent immigrants, academic support and behavioural control. Over the course of the year, Little Manuel was moved five times. In each case, the seating assignment was designed so that he might first receive and later provide language and academic support of different types. While other students were also moved during the year, Little Manuel was moved more often than any other student.

Table 14.3 outlines the different participant frameworks Little Manuel found himself in, as he was moved from lab table to lab table. After three weeks at the back of the room with three other recent immigrants, Little Manuel and Juan, who arrived over the summer, were moved to one of the middle tables (and Big Manuel and Pedro to the other middle table).

Table 14.3 Little Manuel's participant frameworks

Dates	Time 1 26.8– 10.9.2001	Time 2 10.9– 9.10.2001	Time 3 11.10– 14.11.2001	Time 4 16.11– 02.2002	Time 5 March–May
Group Members/ Language*	Big Manuel S Pedro S Juan S	Juan S	Nellie B Marilyn B Tamara B	Big Manuel S Alfonso S Robert E	Dominic E Isaac E

* S- Spanish dominant, E – English monolingual, B – bilingual Spanish English

Although Little Manuel and Juan were then seated with Belinda and Stephanie at this table, there was little interaction between the boys and the girls, and they never worked together on activities. After one month, Juan left school, so Little Manuel was moved with three bilingual academically oriented girls at the front table (see Langman, Hansen-Thomas and Bayley 2005 for a discussion of bilingual negotiations). Again, after one month, Little Manuel was sent as translator and support to sit with Alfonso, a new arrival from Mexico, even though bilingual Big Manuel was already there. At this time, Little Manuel's English use decreased (see Table 14.1, 27.11.2001) as did his academic focus. He essentially spent his time orienting Alfonso, in Spanish, to 'doing school in the US'. After two and a half months with Alfonso, Ms Jackson moved Little Manuel to the front right table with two monolingual English speakers, for the express purpose of improving his English, and indeed, as Table 14.1 shows, there is a substantial increase in his use of English social language.

Four characteristic and recurrent contexts provided Little Manuel with differential access to English language practice. We present Little Manuel's orientation to learning English; that is, the cues he gives and takes for English language development during: (a) whole class teacher-led discussions; (b) one-on-one (or small group) interactions with the teacher; (c) his interactions with bilingual peers; and (d) with monolingual English peers.

Orientation to school – teacher-led discussions

Throughout the school year, Little Manuel's general orientation is to pay attention and do well in school. Hence, during teacher lecture and demonstration time, he actively tracks Ms Jackson's movements around the room, which requires him to swivel around on his lab stool as she moves around the room. So, for example, in Extract 2 the teacher is concluding a discussion on levers and has distributed materials for a lab on levers. In Extract 2, she is pointing out the placement of the zero on the ruler they will use to measure force. She is standing about 15 feet from Little Manuel, at the back of the room, holding up a ruler. Each pair of students also has a ruler to examine at their table. During this interaction, Little Manuel watches the teacher, and asks for the ruler from his partner (006 and 010) in order to examine it more closely. Then he begins to play with the ruler and play with his words.

Extract 2

TEA: = Teacher
PED: = Pedro
BM: = Big Manuel
LM: = Little Manuel
NEL: = Nellie
FRE: = Freddy
ROB: = Robert

001	TEA:	hey this is strange, look how I numbered it (1) zero's in the middle.
002	BM:	eh, Miss!
003	TEA:	did you notice this?
004	BM:	yes.
005	TEA:	no.
006	LM:	pásamelo, pásamelo.
		Pass me that, pass me that
007	TEA:	look at it.
008 →	TEA:	look at the ruler.
009 →	LM:	°°look at the ruler.°°
010	LM:	no, me falta xx xx.
		I lack
011	BM:	what (1) oh.
012	TEA:	look at the ruler.
013	PED:	look at the ruler.
014 →	TEA:	zero's in the middle.
015	NEL:	okay.
016	TEA:	I guess, don't we start at zeros?
017	NEL:	yeah, I already have, xx.
018	TEA:	I hold it here look what happens to the ruler (1) if I hold it here look what happens to the ruler.
...		
019 →	LM:	°°ha, ha, baw, baw, sí ese, es en el cerdo.°°
		yes that one, it's in the pig
020 →	LM:	°° es en el [s]ero.°°
		it's at the zero
021	LM:	hoh, look at me.
022 →	LM:	°°ha ha en el [sirdo],°° en el [z]ero miss.
		at the /sirdo/, at the zero
023	TEA:	you're sharing together.
024 →	LM:	en el [z]ero.

(18.09.2001)

In addition to his orientation to the teacher, Extract 2 shows an example of Little Manuel's frequent repetition of key English words and phrases. He repeats 'look at the ruler' (009). In addition, he combines repetition with word-play in his focus on the teacher's main point (001, 014, 016), namely that the zero is in the middle of the ruler. Little Manuel observes this and then voices, initially quietly (019, 020, 022), and then more loudly as he addresses his finding to the teacher (022, 024). At the same time, he is playing with the pronunciation of 'zero' using the English [z] and then the Spanish [s] for this cognate, as well as two related sound patterns 'cerdo' (019) meaning 'pig' and a nonsense word 'sirdo' (022).

Little Manuel maintains this pattern of repetition throughout the school year with approximately the same frequency. He repeats Ms Jackson's words, and also occasionally those of other students. As Ms Jackson uses key vocabulary regularly during whole-class discussions, this repetition strategy gives Little Manuel some practice with a small subset of the relevant vocabulary. But note that such repetitions are generally not embedded in extended, focused stretches of talk. Nor does he repeat all the key words. So, for example, on 18 September, Ms Jackson employs a range of academic vocabulary, including lever (11), load (20), effort (17), work (54), graph (18), hinge (9), measure (11), Newtons (4), numbers (41), pull (31), push (15), rocks (43), ruler (11), scale (41), spring (8), zero (17). Little Manuel, however, as shown in Table 14.2, uses only four of these terms (loads, rock, ruler and zero).

Teacher interacting one-on-one

After whole-class discussions, Ms Jackson generally circulates around the tables to offer individual support. This context theoretically allows the teacher to reinforce the language and content of the lesson in focused interactions. However, rather than scaffolding and repeating the key terms in lesson, we see that the teacher's pattern of talk changes. That is, as the lesson becomes more contextualized the language becomes less contextualized as seen in Extract 3, which occurs shortly after the demonstration interaction presented in Extract 2. Ms Jackson has been circulating among the students to give individual help. Little Manuel and Juan have balanced their scales, step one in the procedure, after quite some discussion, and begun experimenting with moving the load to different positions, as per the instructions they have understood. They run into difficulties, however, as they are unsure what exactly to measure. They try to get Ms Jackson's attention, calling out 'Miss!' with increasing volume and stridency 13 times. Little Manuel has also raised his hand and called out 'Que levanté la mano!' ('I raised my hand') several times. Through this behaviour it is clear that Little Manuel is well aware of the classroom conventions on how to get the teacher's attention, namely through speech, and without leaving their seats. When Ms Jackson eventually comes over, Little Manuel says, '*Ya lo dejamos parejo*' ('We already have it balanced'), to which Ms Jackson responds with the repetition of English 'Look, you made it balance'. This response is, however, not likely a confirmation of his comment, but rather an independent observation, which becomes clear in Extract 3 where she has the students examine the point of balance.

Extract 3

TEA: = Teacher
Juan: = Juan
LM = Little Manuel

001	TEA:	it's (1) hold on, okay, *mira* [look] (2) let's look. ((as Tea crouches to readjust the scale))
002	LM:	uhhuh.
003	TEA:	Juan come here. ((gestures for him to crouch beside her))
004	TEA:	come here.
005	TEA:	okay, look, *mira* [look], the white numbers, *blanca* [white] (1) the numbers?
006	LM:	uhhuh.
007	TEA:	okay, now (1) how much, *qué mucho* [what much], for it to be (2) can you read that number? ((TEA is looking at ruler closely))
008	LM:	hmm. ((sitting on stool looking in direction of ruler))
009	TEA:	no, I mean look, down here. ((points to spot on ruler))
010	LM:	no.
011	TEA:	two point (1) *dos y* (1). ((LM begins to lean in to look))
012	LM:	*dos* three?
013	TEA:	yeah.
014	TEA:	okay, what if I move it (2) no, come here, you've got to look over here.
015	TEA:	*órale*. listen
016	LM:	[laughs] ((laughing at TEA's use of a Spanish idiom))
017	TEA:	look, see, do you see that?
018	LM:	huh.
019	TEA:	see the number?
020	LM:	whoa, whoa, whoa [laughs]. ((as TEA starts to fall over as leaning too far forward as she points))
021	TEA:	I'm xx [laughs].
022	TEA:	uhuh, I fall down. (1) yijo [sound of surprise].
023	LM:	[laughs] five Miss?
024	TEA:	five?
025	TEA:	very good. (1) try it in different positions, okay?

(18.09.2001)

In Extract 3, Ms Jackson reduces the interaction to a procedure of reading numbers, rather than an experiment for measuring effort, through the simplification of the task and the accompanying English. Ms Jackson uses simplification, almost to the point of telegraphic speech, together with repetitions of simple terms, such as white/*blanca* (005), look/*mira* (001, 005), two point/*dos y* (011) as well as how much/*qué mucho* (007) which is an example of her lack of proficiency in Spanish (*¿cuánto?* is the word she needs). Her final comment (025) to 'try it in different positions, okay?' is uttered over her shoulder as she walks away, exactly at the point when her sustained interaction might lead to some language practice tied to an academic task for Little Manuel. Extract 3 is an example of how discourse was often orchestrated in such a way that little Manuel and other language learners could complete experimental procedures without necessarily tying them to scientific principles the experiments were designed to illustrate. Little Manuel's productive English here, although it fulfils the requirements, consists of minimal responses and one- and two-word utterances (023, 024). Moreover, as is clear from Extract 2, Little Manuel has understood in broad strokes the focus of the lesson, but is not supported to demonstrate that understanding or to expand upon it. This we argue is an example of a language learning opportunity lost.

Interactions with bilingual peers

As we have seen from Table 14.3, Little Manuel spends one month (Time 3) with bilinguals who might provide him with access to English as well as the content. However, while Little Manuel is actively engaged in the procedural aspects of tasks, he rarely needs to use English. He generally uses Spanish to get confirmation or information on what he should be doing, as for example in Extract 4 where he is checking on the task related to a math problem.

Extract 4

NEL: = Nellie
LM: = Little Manuel

001	LM:	ay ¿aquí qué tenemos que hacer? ¿copiar aquello?
		what do we have to do here? copy that?
002	Nel:	no en este pero en otro.
		not on this but in the other
003	LM:	ah. bueno, ¿en esta qué tenemos que hacer?
		ok, in this what do we have do to?
004	NEL:	no más dibújalo asi y luego lo dibujas así.
		just draw it like this and then you draw like this
005	LM:	¿cúal?
		which?
006	Nel:	dibújalo asi y luego lo dibujas así.
		draw it like this and then you draw like this

(15.10.2001)

When English does enter in, it sometimes takes Little Manuel by surprise as in Extract 5 when Tamara asks him for a pen, to which he first answers 'no!' (002) and then apparently realizes the meaning and corrects himself calling for her attention to hand her a pen (003). Immediately thereafter, the teacher gives an instruction (004) and Little Manuel seeks confirmation from the group to which Marilyn answers in an odd way, with a type of foreigner talk, that this is an individual rather than a group assignment (006).

Extract 5

TAM: = Tamara
LM: = Little Manuel
TEA: = Teacher
MAR: = Marilyn

001	TAM:	do you have a pen?
002	LM:	no!

...

003	LM:	oh, pen, yes, Tamara! Tamara!
004	TEA:	um, in your interactive notebook we're going to page, twenty-three.
005	LM:	eh, vamos a hacer estos? *are we going to do these?*
006	MAR:	uh, I write, no, I write, you too.
007	LM:	yeah?

(15.10.2001)

As with Little Manuel's use of English with the teacher, we see that little sustained English interaction, tied to science or social tasks, is taking place with bilingual peers.

Monolingual English peers

In March, Little Manuel was grouped with two of the non-Spanish-speaking students, Dominic and Richard. Extract 6 shows interaction with Dominic, recorded while the teacher was leading a whole-class discussion about the properties of plants. This extract shows that he has developed some ability to interact in English and he even exhibits self-correction in one instance. However, Little Manuel's transcript on this day contains no examples of use of the academic vocabulary relevant to the class. His focus, which Dominic shares, is on social interaction.

Extract 6

TEA: = Teacher
STU: = Unidentified Student
LM: = Little Manuel
DOM: = Dominic

001	TEA:	what do they do with that sunlight?
002	STU:	they eat it.
003	LM:	Dominic you is my best friend right.
004	DOM:	hmm.
005	LM:	you is you's are my best friend.

006 DOM: hmm.I think xx
007 TEA: sun and water make what from the plant?
008 LM: callate Dominic.
            shut up

(1.3.2002)

Conclusions

This case study has tracked the language use and language development of an adolescent recent immigrant to the United States. What this study shows is that in the case of eager learners, the school context in which he and many other adolescent immigrants find themselves is not conducive to the development of English. We have presented evidence of how Little Manuel orients to school tasks throughout the year, seeks support from his peers and teacher to get information on what he is to do, and as much as possible uses repetition to practise English words. However, as we also have shown, the contexts in which he has the opportunity to practise sustained English while focusing on tasks are largely absent. In other words, the contexts in this classroom do not provide him with sufficient access to develop his English language abilities. Returning to O'Connor (1998), we argue that this limited access to practise, derives from the myths about language learning held by the teacher and students, as well as the cultural conventions in the classroom. With respect to myths, we refer particularly to three that the teacher's practices and later her words confirm: first that students will learn English naturally and easily, because they are hearing it all day long. Second, that language learners, when grouped with bilinguals do receive, through language brokering, a complete translation of science content as well as procedure and thus will be able to transfer that knowledge to English. Third, that simplified speech on the part of the teacher is the best approach to providing language input to learners. Indeed, Ms Jackson, who serves as the primary model of English for Little Manuel, often reduces her own language to formulaic simplified expressions, and the use of junk Spanish, in order to develop rapport and promote understanding – the polar opposite of the type of input that would support language learning. These myths about the language classroom tie in with the cultural conventions of the classroom and work in opposition to the school's objectives as well as Little Manuel's own goals – namely to develop English through content-area instruction. Rather, conventions in the school and community support bilingual language use, and in particular the use of Spanish by the bilingual students for the purposes of socializing and creating community in the classroom. Second, although the students are aware of the cultural conventions that suggest they should help the recent immigrants – in fact, this is often overtly stated by the teacher as well as the principal – the exact nature of such help is not made clear. Help, when offered, is thus given in Spanish as well as by passing papers for students to copy, rather than through the medium of focused task-related English.

In this context, then, we see that Little Manuel has few opportunities to practise English, remains largely untutored and advances very little. The contrast to this general picture is presented in Extract 7, when Little Manuel works with a tutor to write his observations about a calf brain he has examined. Extract 7 begins with Little Manuel reading out loud from a worksheet. As the tutor (the first author) joins him, they look at the worksheet together and take turns pointing at the relevant information on the page.

Extract 7
LM: = Little Manuel
JUL: = Juliet

001 LM: what is the function of the xx nervous system xx?
002 LM: xxx. The diameter.
003 JUL: what is the function, what does it do?
004 LM: this
005 JUL: it is the control centre.
006 LM: oh, (2) control?
007 JUL: um huh.
008 LM: centre.
009 JUL: centre.
010 JUL: all right, here you said what the parts are.
011 LM: oh yeah.
012 JUL: but this is what is the function (2) what is the peripheral (1) what is its function, so it consists of the nervous system, uh huh, that's good for this part, now what is the function?
013 LM: um, (3) the same?
014 JUL: no, it's gonna say down here, (2) the function to connect it to the rest of the body.
015 LM: oh, thank you, Miss.
016 LM: connect (2) it to the rest (3) rest of the body.

Here, through scaffolding, Little Manuel produces a sustained, albeit repetitious stretch of academic discourse.

For Rogoff, 'human development is a process of people's changing participation in sociocultural activities in their communities' (2003: 52). In this chapter, we have shown how the community of this particular classroom, and many other middle school classrooms with large numbers of bilinguals speaking the same two languages, create disproportionately few contexts for sociocultural activities that allow for sustained and focused use of English by recent immigrants. This chapter thus adds another dimension to consider in the complex question of how best to support the learning trajectories of an increasingly diverse student population.

Notes

* We gratefully acknowledge the support of the Spencer Foundation.
1. Little Manuel and all other names of people and places are pseudonyms.
2. The term LEP (Limited English Proficient) has come under criticism for classifying students by what they lack rather than what they can do. However, in the United States, school districts continue to use the term as an official designation.

15
Learning Styles in Multicultural Classrooms

Tony Young and Itesh Sachdev
Newcastle University and the School of Oriental and African Studies University of London

Introduction: learning style in current pedagogy

The construct of learning style is at the very centre of current pedagogical thought, with over 300 studies using 'learning style' in lists of keywords in the period 2000–06 (Thompson Scientific 2006). Learning style indexes and inventories represent attempts to construct tools for getting to grips with learners' sensory characteristics and their psychosocial and cognitive involvement in their studies (De Vita 2001). Much of the pedagogical literature describing teacher–learner interaction in recent years has put increased emphasis on learner autonomy, learner independence and on the role of teacher as facilitator. An understanding of learning styles is seen as an important element in attempts to centre learning around the learner, moving away from a largely methodological focus. Taxonomies of learning styles also frequently serve an important role in curricular innovation, guiding innovation into areas where it is most likely to be compatible with learners' style preferences.

Research into learning style is prominent in a wide variety of educational fields. These include Information and Communication Technology education (see, for example, Carswell et al. 2000; Federico 2000; Gilbert and Han 1999; Lewis and Orton 2000; Mehlenbacher et al. 2000; Palmquist and Kim 2000; Smith and Woody 2000). It is also important across a diversity of higher and tertiary educational disciplines from nursing, medicine and veterinary science (see, for example, Colucciello 1999; Linares 1999; Stickle et al. 1999) to general teacher education (Hatvia and Birenbaum 2000). It is also a prevalent concept in language learning pedagogy research (e.g., Carson and Longhini 2002; Chi 2001; Dreyer 1998; Ehrman and Oxford 1990; Gallin 1999; Rossi Le 1995).

Over the past 30 years in the field of language pedagogy the movement away from methodology to learner-centredness has been particularly marked in 'Western' contexts such as the United States, Canada, Europe, Australia and New Zealand. Oxford (1998), for example, sees over this period a dramatic movement away from an emphasis on teacher–learner social interaction based on the teacher – specifically, what a teacher does in following particular guidelines – to the current focus on the *learner* – specifically who the learner is and what he/she wants, needs and thinks. One result of this movement is a change in the role of the teacher from the fount of all wisdom and director of classroom activity, to a facilitator of learning and guide towards greater autonomy for the language learner. Self-access and self-directed learning are now key features of language learning curricula (e.g., Hedge 2000). It has been argued that central to the role of teacher-as-facilitator is an awareness of learners' approaches to learning (e.g., Tudor 1996).

Learning styles theory has been a major underpinning for approaches to learner centredness since the mid-1980s, although the notion has been seen as problematic in some respects. Ely and Pease-Alvarez (1996) recognize the complexity of dealing with the notions of learning styles and strategies in general, observing that learner-centredness involves building up a complex picture of the student as both a product of his or her past and as an individual with future potentialities: knowing a learning style entails knowledge of the learner at the very deepest level. Teachers need to find out as much as possible about how their students have been socialized and educated, and then, it is suggested, build upon the student's current style preferences. Such knowledge may involve an engagement with their culturally informed learning style.

Notions of culture are complex, and particularly controversial when applied to language learning (see, for example, Atkinson 1999). Within the critical linguistic tradition, some researchers have identified an approach to culture in English as a Foreign Language (EFL) teaching and learning which characterizes culture as essence rather than as a social construction (e.g., Holliday 1999; Kubota 2001, Spack 1997; Zamel 1997). It is argued that such a tendency has the effect of stereotyping individuals as cultural types, and of essentializing culture; that is, ascribing an individual's behaviour largely or entirely to that individual's cultural origin. Despite this critique, it is nevertheless widely perceived that although it is a problematic notion, culture plays a strong, possibly dominant, role in determining how an individual will prefer to learn (e.g., Hofstede 1986; Shiraev and Levy 2004). Numerous studies have claimed to show that particular cultural and national groups share features of preferred learning style which are often different from those preferred by a dominant ethnic or linguistic majority (for a summary of cases see Oxford and Anderson 1995). Attempts to understand and acknowledge differences of culturally derived learning styles are the key to an understanding of the affective, cognitive and executive factors and processes which inform social interaction in multicultural classrooms. Such attempts are particularly important in the case of EFL teaching and learning. English, the 'World' or 'Global' language' (e.g., Crystal 2003) is the main means of intercultural communication in a world where intercultural contact is increasing (Graddol 2006).

Definitions of learning style

The language pedagogy literature offers many definitions and taxonomies of learning style. Aspects often overlap, and terminology has been characterized as confused and confusing: Galloway and Labarca joke that 'readers reviewing the literature on learning styles will benefit from a high tolerance of ambiguity' (1991:113). De Vita sees in the literature 'an extremely rich but fragmented theoretical landscape' (2001: 166). However, even within this apparently confused theoretical background, it is possible to discern some commonalities. For example, Keefe's (1979: 4) definition of learning style, drawn from the field of general educational psychology, is the one most frequently cited by second language theoreticians (see, for example, De Vita 2001; Dreyer 1998; Eliason 1995; Ellis 1994; Nelson 1995). Here learning style is defined as:

> the characteristic cognitive, affective and psychological behaviours that serve as relatively stable indicators of how learners perceive, interact with and respond to the learning environment.... Learning style is a consistent way of functioning that reflects underlying causes of behaviour.
>
> (Keefe 1979: 4)

Ehrman and Oxford refine Keefe's 'characteristic' and 'relatively stable' into the *'preferred or habitual* patterns of mental functioning and dealing with new information' (1990: 311). Scarcella sees learning styles as 'cognitive and interactional patterns which affect the ways students perceive, remember and think' (1990:114).

The general conclusion of researchers who accept the broad validity of the construct of learner styles is that the instruments used to test and measure it have as their central purpose the building up of self-knowledge in the learner (e.g., Oxford and Anderson 1995; Tudor 1996). Whatever the frequently stated (and usually freely acknowledged) theoretical vagueness of the construct of learning style, the learner can, it is argued, ultimately take or leave any attempt to taxonomize his or her style. Even if they opt for the latter, they will, in the very act of self-reflection, have helped to develop autonomy.

Tudor (1996), in examining learner centredness in language education, states that the notion of learning style is a very powerful one. He notes also that it is *practically orientated*, based less on a relational or causative analysis of the way in which an individual's psychosocial, cognitive or sensory characteristics produce a given set of behaviours, than on the analysis and grouping of *observed behavioural preferences*. The main goal of research, in his view, is to help teachers get to grips with their students' learning behaviours around a finite number of poles of difference, and thereby to be better able to respond to learners' subjective needs in an informed manner.

The study

Background

One of the largest providers of EFL services in Europe was in the process of curricular overhaul. This process involved consultation with both teachers and learners. One aspect of this consultation was to investigate whether an assessment of students' learning styles should take place as part of the testing process for new arrivals. This study therefore addressed the question of whether, despite its theoretical vagueness, the construct of learning style is seen by teachers of multicultural classes as a useful tool in informing their interactions with their students, that is, whether it has the practical pedagogical utility that Tudor (1996) and other theoreticians ascribe to it. In a multicultural classroom setting, are individual learning styles discernible, and if discernible, useful, to teachers and to learners? Beyond individual styles, could 'cultural' style preferences be found among different national groups of teachers and learners? Previous research (e.g., Dreyer 1998; De Vita 2001) has suggested both that such 'cultural' styles exist, and that there was a pressing need to address them in multicultural learning environments. No research previous to this study, however, has investigated the attitudes or beliefs of learners and teachers of multicultural classes toward the notion of cultural learning styles.

The settings for the study were four schools in the United Kingdom belonging to the EFL organization. Teachers working for the organization in the United Kingdom were almost all British, but learners came from more than 50 different countries in Europe, South and Central America, South East and East Asia and Africa. The vast majority of learners had come to the United Kingdom specifically to improve their English language skills, and undertook EFL courses of between four and eight weeks. Three main research questions were addressed in the investigation:

1. Are specific learning style preferences characteristic of groups, particularly cultural groups?
2. What were experienced teachers' perceptions of different groups of learners' preferred learning styles?
3. What was the utility of a learning style instrument in the teaching and learning of EFL, as perceived by teachers and learners?

Methodology and participants

The investigation consisted of two stages. In the first stage, all teachers and high level learners in the schools at the time of the study were asked to complete Oxford's (1995) Style Analysis Survey (SAS). The SAS had previously been employed in a number of studies investigating learning styles in adult second language learning (e.g., Carson and Longhini 2002; Chi 2001; Dreyer 1998; Gallin 1999). The full version of the SAS was chosen for this study after consultation with teachers and learners. It was preferred to other instruments as it had previously been employed as a style measuring instrument in multi-cultural settings, and had been validated on both native- and non-native English speaking populations (Oxford 1995). Previous research had also shown it to have high reliability, and control and concurrent validity (e.g., Dreyer 1998). In addition, it was a self-contained instrument, suitable for a learner-autonomous approach, offering the participant the opportunity to self-score, then giving descriptors of styles based on these scores, and ending with tips for applying these styles most successfully.

Table 15.1 details the SAS as a learning styles measuring instrument. Each polarity had ten related items, each of which were scored on 4-point Likert scales (from 0 – 3), giving each polarity a maximum score of 30. Example items for each dimension and learning style aspect in the SAS are given below.

Physiological

- VI: I remember something better if I write it down.
  I take lots of notes.
- AU: I remember things better if I discuss them out loud.
  I need oral directions for tasks.
- HO: I avoid sitting at a desk if I don't have to.
  Manipulating objects helps me to remember.

Social and affective

- EX: I prefer to work or study with others.
  I like to be in groups of people.
- IN: I prefer to work or study alone.
  I prefer individual hobbies and sports.

Cognitive and executive (1)

- IV: I can think of many different solutions to a problem.
  It feels fine if a teacher or boss changes the plan.
- CS: I prefer realism instead of new, untested ideas.
  I prefer to avoid too many options.

Cognitive

- GL: I ignore details that do not seem relevant.
  I can summarize information rather easily.
- AN: I prefer detailed answers instead of short answers.
  I prefer looking for differences rather than similarities.

Cognitive and executive (2)

- CO: I reach decisions quickly.
  I make lists of things I need to do.
- OP: I like to let things happen, not plan them.
  Lists of tasks make me feel tired or upset.

Table 15.1 Oxford's *Style Analysis Survey* (Reid 1995: 208–15)

Dimensions	Learning Style Aspect	Polarities	Summary of Oxford's (1995) descriptor
Physiological	Sensory characteristics and preferences of the learner	Visual (VI)	Generally prefer to read and receive visual input
		Auditory (AU)	Generally comfortable with oral instructions and aural input
		Hands-on (HO)	Preferring movement, action, touch, a.k.a. haptic, tactile, kinesthetic
Social and affective	Preferred level of involvement of others in the learning process	Extrovert (EX)	Preferring the involvement of others in learning
		Introvert (IN)	Preferring to work alone while learning
Cognitive and executive (1)	How a learner prefers to handle possibilities and degrees of certainty/uncertainty	Intuitive (IV)	Intuitive, non-linear, random-access mode, a.k.a intuitive-random.
		Concrete Sequential (CS)	Prefers sequential, linear, concrete input and mental organization
Cognitive	How a learner deals with ideas	Global (GL)	a.k.a. relational, field dependent, right-brain dominant. Tends to go from 'the big picture' to detail.
		Analytic (AN)	a.k.a. field independent, left-brain dominant. Detail orientated, moving from detail to the whole
Cognitive and executive (2)	How a learner approaches tasks	Closure orientated (CO)	a.k.a. 'judging', seeks early decisions or judgments, disliking uncertainty
		Open (OP)	a.k.a. 'perceiving' , i.e., perceiving a great deal of input and postponing decision or judgment, tolerant of ambiguity of uncertainty

There were 2 groups of participants for this stage of the study. First, qualified and experienced teachers of EFL (47 participants, of the 50 who had been invited to participate). Over 80 per cent of participating teachers had at least ten years' EFL teaching experience, with 100 per cent having at least five years. All of the teacher participants were British, all were English first language speakers, and all were qualified to at least the *Cambridge Diploma in Teaching English Language to Adults* (DELTA) level. Mean age among the British teacher participants was 32.

The second group of participants were 87 adult EFL learners undertaking courses of study in the schools; 90 learners of the requisite level had been invited to participate. These learners were all undertaking EFL learning programmes at the time of the study. Among the learner participants, 39 were Brazilian, 19 Argentinean, 18 were European (either Swiss, German, Danish, Greek, Polish or Italian), and 11 were students of other non-Latin American or European nationality (Japan, South Korea, Peoples Republic of China (PRC), United Arab Emirates (UAE) and Saudi Arabia). All learner participants were of at least Council of Europe Level C2, or 'lower advanced', as the instrument was only available in an English language form. All had considerable previous experience of EFL study. Mean age among the learner participants was 26. Fees for the course undertaken by the learners at the four schools in this investigation were high, in the order of £1500 for a 4-week course in the United Kingdom, and all were from the higher socioeconomic groups in their countries.

The procedure for teachers in the first stage of the investigation was as follows. Teachers completed a pack consisting of a consent form and a Personal Information sheet, which included details of gender, age and years of EFL teaching experience. The next part of the pack consisted of the SAS; the fourth element detailed opinions about the utility of the SAS: specifically, 'how useful would the SAS be to you as a teaching aid'. Finally, teachers were asked to predict the learning style profile that would result from different national groups that they taught – Brazilians and Japanese were specified. Teachers were asked to indicate which polarity students of these nationalities were, in general, likely to prefer: it was specified that teachers could indicate more than one polarity for each aspect if they felt this was appropriate. Teacher-attributed learning styles amongst Brazilians was chosen as this was the largest single national group in the schools at this time, and all teacher participants had had recent experience of working with Brazilians. Japanese attributed learning style was chosen for purposes of comparison: all teachers participating in the research had previously taught Japanese EFL learners.

Procedure for learner participants in this stage of the investigation differed slightly. The learners completed a similar instrument to the teachers in terms of consent form, personal information, the SAS and perceptions of the utility of the SAS to them as learners, but they were not asked for predictions of Brazilian or Japanese learning style preferences.

The second stage of the investigation consisted of two focus group interviews, one with teachers and one with learners. All participants in the focus groups had previously taken part in the first stage. Each focus group consisted of eight participants, four male and four female. The teacher group had all taught EFL for at least ten years in at least two different countries, and all were British. The learner group had participants from Brazil (2), Argentina, Switzerland, Japan, South Korea, Saudi Arabia and the PRC. Participants in each focus group interview were asked the same questions relating to the utility of the SAS and to the notion of learning style in general in their teaching or learning of EFL. Mean ages for both groups of participants were broadly similar to those of the participants in the first stage of the investigation.

Findings

Findings from the survey are described first, these are then related to findings from the focus groups.

The survey: group style preference profiles

The responses to the items on the SAS of members of the two largest national participant groups were analysed and compared. These were British teachers and Brazilian learners. There were insufficient Japanese learner participants ($N = 2$) for analysis. Findings from the British teacher participants are shown in Figure 15.1, and findings for analysis of each aspect and polarity detailed in turn below. Findings from the Brazilian learner participants are shown in Figure 15.2 and detailed below that. Findings relating to the two groups are then compared with each other and with those attributed to Japanese learners by the British teachers.

1. *Physiological: Sensory characteristics.* A test of between subjects effects (one-way ANOVA) revealed that British participants were **more visual** (m = 15.7) **than auditory** (m = 12.7) or **hands-on** (m = 12.3), df = 43, p < 0.001.
2. *Social and affective: preferred level of involvement of others in learning.* Paired sample t-tests revealed that British participants were **more extrovert** (m = 15.9) **than introvert** (m = 12.3), t = 2.89, df = 43, p < 0.006.
3. *Cognitive and executive (1)*: **handling possibilities**. British participants were more **intuitive** (m = 16.6) than **concrete sequential** (m = 12.6) when handling possibilities, t = 4.61, df = 43, p < 0.001.
4. *Cognitive: dealing with ideas.* British participants were **more closure-orientated** (m = 17.9) **than open** (m = 13.5) in their approach to tasks, t = 4.11, df = 43, p < 0.001.
5. *Cognitive and executive (2): approaching tasks.* British participants were more **global** (m = 17.1) than **analytic** (m = 11.9) when dealing with ideas, t = 5.59, df = 43, p < 0.001.

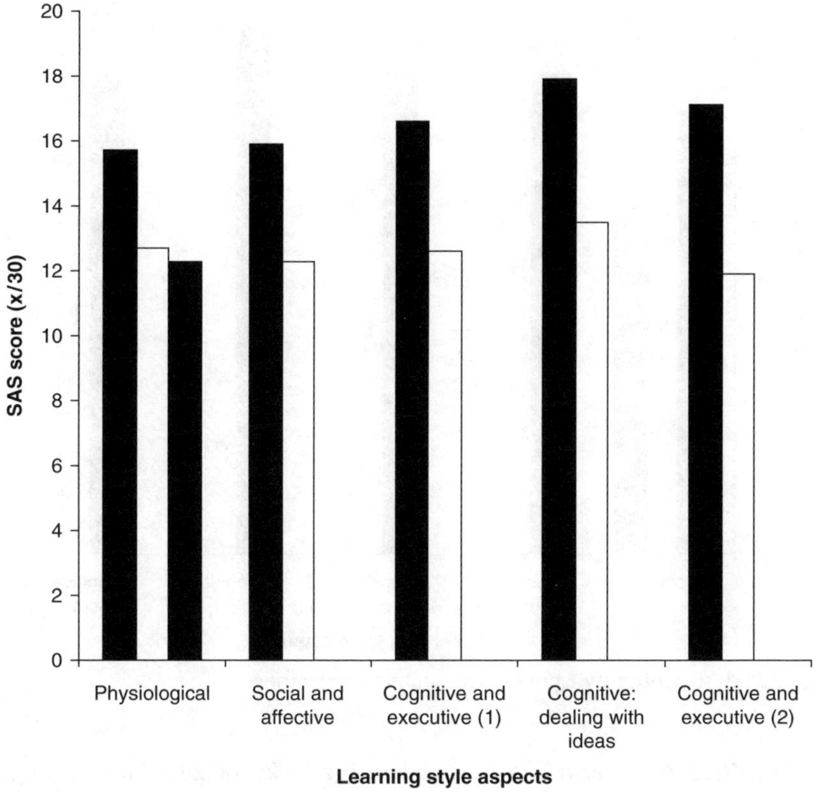

Figure 15.1 Learning style preferences of British teachers

1. *Physiological: Sensory characteristics.* A test of between subject effects (one-way ANOVA) revealed that Brazilian learners were more **visual** (m = 16.3) than **hands-on** (m = 14.0) or **auditory** (m = 12.9) in their preferred physical learning style (df = 38, p < 0.001).
2. *Social and affective: preferred level of involvement of others in learning.* Paired sample t-tests revealed that Brazilian learners were more **extrovert** (m = 17.7) than **introvert** (m = 12.2) when dealing with others, t = 3.45, df = 38, p < 0.001.
3. *Cognitive and executive (1):* **handling possibilities.** Brazilian learners were more **intuitive** (m = 17.9) than **concrete-sequential** (m = 13.8) when handling possibilities, t = 4.01, df = 38, p < 0.001.
4. *Cognitive: dealing with ideas.* Brazilian learners were more **closure-orientated** (m = 19.4) than **open** (m = 13.0) in their approach to tasks, t = 5.28, df = 38, p < 0.001.

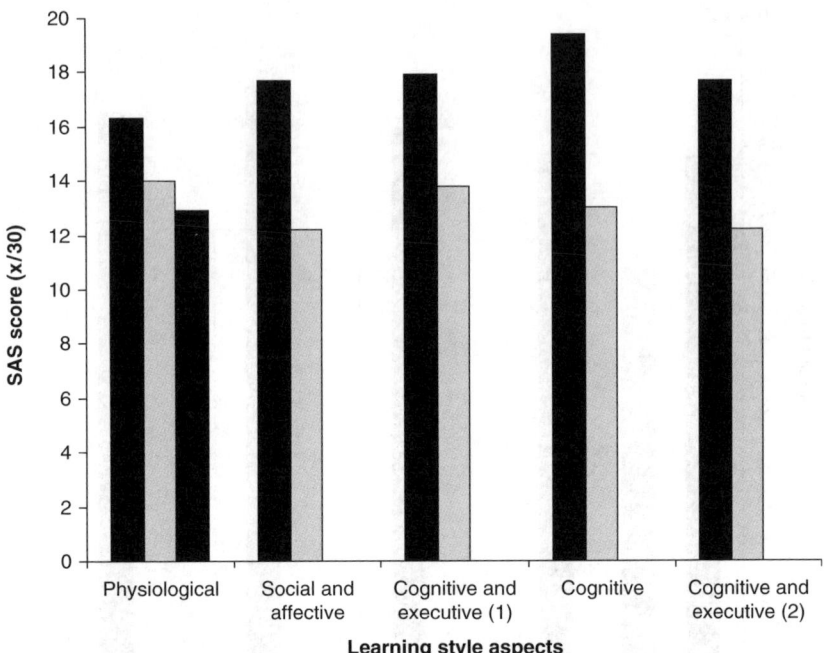

Figure 15.2 Learning style preferences of Brazilian learners

5. **Cognitive and executive (2): approaching tasks.** Brazilian learners were more **global** (m = 17.7) than **analytic** (m = 12.2) in dealing with ideas t = 4.41. df = 38, p < 0.001.

Thus analysis revealed that the groups of British teacher and of Brazilian learner participants expressed the same polarity preferences in all of the aspects of learning style examined by the SAS. It is interesting to note that nationality was the only grouping variable to show a commonality of preferred learning style. Analysis revealed no significant relationship between other grouping variables and preferred learning style – age group and gender were also analysed and it was found that no age group among the participants shared a style profile to a significant degree, and that neither male nor female participants shared a common group profile.

British teachers' attributions of group learning styles

Teachers' attributions of preferred learning styles of Brazilian and Japanese learners were analysed, and these were compared with Brazilian learning style preferences as revealed by the SAS. Findings are detailed in Table 15.2.

Table 15.2 A comparison of teachers' attributions with actual learning style preferences

Dimension and aspect of style	Teachers' predictions (% of all valid teacher responses)		Actual Brazilian preference on the SAS	Confirmation of prediction?
Physiological: Sensory characteristics	VI AU HO	26 42 32	VI	No
Social and affective: Level of involvement of others in learning	EX IN	79 21	EX	Yes
Cognitive and executive (1): Handling possibility and uncertainty	IV CS	81 29	IV	Yes
Cognitive: Dealing with ideas	GL AN	83 17	GL	Yes
Cognitive and executive (2): Approaching tasks	OP CO	70 30	CO	No

Thus analysis revealed that in two of the five aspects under investigation teachers' predictions were different from those actually expressed by a significant majority of Brazilian learners. Interestingly, attributions for Japanese learners made by the British teacher participants were different, but consistent and strong. Teachers felt that Japanese learners would prefer visual (62 per cent of teachers attributed this as preference for Japanese learners), introverted (89 per cent), concrete-sequential (72 per cent), analytical (78 per cent) and closure-orientated (72 per cent).

The utility of the SAS to teachers and learners

Table 15.3 compares teacher and learner opinions. Analysis revealed a bimodal distribution among the teachers. While 41 per cent of them responded positively, an equal number responded negatively. Learners generally were much more positively disposed towards the proposition that the instrument was useful: 75 per cent responded positively and only 13 per cent negatively.

246 *Multilingual and Multicultural Classrooms*

Table 15.3 Perceived utility of the SAS (% of valid responses)

Degree of perceived utility	Very useful	Useful	So-so	Not very useful	Not at all useful
Teachers	11	30	18	28	13
Learners	31	44	12	13	0

Focus groups

All teachers reported that they did perceive styles, or aspects of style, among learners of different cultural backgrounds. Numerous examples were given, including a perception that East Asian learners exhibited an analytic approach to dealing with ideas, and a concrete-sequential approach to possibility and uncertainty. Teachers also reported even more strongly, however, that they saw this as stereotyping people, and that many exceptions to such types existed. Teachers were unanimously of the opinion that learners should be approached as individuals and that any attempt, no matter how principled and apparently scientific, to group people by cultural type was undesirable in a learner-centred environment of the type they worked in.

Opinion was divided fairly equally among learner participants about cultural style preferences. Half of the participants felt that these existed, and that therefore it would be useful to taxonomize them. The other half felt that a cultural group was unlikely to exhibit a single set of preferred characteristics of the type defined and measured by the SAS. The learner participants who felt cultural profiles *did* exist felt able to identify aspects of the learning styles of out-group members, but had more difficulty in identifying in-group preferences in all cases.

The teacher focus group was asked if they would like to use the SAS as a resource for their work. Opinions were equally divided, with half of the eight participants saying they would like to use the SAS as a tool, and the other half saying they would not. This finding therefore closely mirrored the perceived utility of the instrument reported among teachers in the first stage of the investigation. Those teachers who stated that they would use the SAS gave the following reasons:

1. They perceived it to give an accurate picture of their own (and therefore learners') styles. Perceived instrument accuracy and its utility were closely linked in these teachers' minds.
2. They felt it would be a useful instrument at the beginning of a course. By making learners aware of their learning style preferences, teachers would be able to relate specific course content to these preferences.
3. It would give them and the learners a common vocabulary with which to discuss learning in a meaningful way and thus aid learner centring during

a course. Such a vocabulary would extend the ability of teachers to investigate, with learners, learning preferences, and to be able to relate preferred styles to learning strategies in order to facilitate language acquisition.

Those who stated they wouldn't use the SAS gave the following broad reasons:

1. A minority said that they distrusted the validity of the survey
2. Even if the validity of the survey was not questioned, these teachers felt unsure what to do with the results. What, for example, if they were presented with a plethora of different styles within one group of learners they were teaching?

The learner focus group was much more uniformly positive about the utility of the SAS. None questioned its validity, all were happy that the profile it produced of them as learners was accurate. All felt that it would be a useful tool in sharing their preferences with other learners and with teachers, thus aiding class integration. All felt it would have been useful as part of an induction process on the EFL course they were undertaking, and that it had helped them to reflect deeply on themselves as learners.

Discussion

A number of implications arose from the findings of the study, and these, along with possible directions for future research, are detailed first. A summary of what this study tells us about learning styles in the multicultural EFL classroom and beyond is then given as a conclusion.

The first main implication relates to cultural group profiling. Here there emerged a strong awareness among teachers of the social undesirability of stereotyping out-groups members as cultural types in any terms, even in the psychosocial, sensory and cognitive terms employed by the SAS. On the focus group evidence this was even the case among teachers who said that they would find the SAS useful. Critical perspectives on culture, cultural essentialism and cultural stereotyping in English language teaching (e.g., Holliday 1999; Kubota 2001; Spack 1997; Zamel 1997) thus gain some support from these findings. Teachers were aware (acutely aware, in many cases) of the dangers of basing approaches to social interaction on perceptions of group characteristics. On the evidence of this investigation, strong and consistent perceptions of outgroup members do, however, exist among experienced teachers of multicultural EFL classes. These seem to be erroneous as regards Brazilian learners' physiological, and cognitive and executive, dimensions of style. There may therefore be a case for confronting perceptions during teacher training. The nature of the relationship between teacher beliefs about, and their interactions with, culturally different learners is also clearly worthy of further investigation.

A second set of implications relates to the possible validity and reliability of the SAS. Two cultural groups, Brazilian students and British teachers were found to have very similar learning style profiles. A number of implications are possible from this. The findings of this study may be a product of the instrument – further testing of the validity of the SAS in different cultural contexts may be needed. An alternative possibility is that the two groups may not be actually different in their preferred sensory, psychosocial and profile and cognitive processing. Educational background, ethnicity and social class, common to both the groups investigated here, may be stronger determinants of style than 'national culture'. Previous studies which have shown a difference of style between groups have tended to investigate groups defined in terms of ethnicity and from the lower ends of the socioeconomic spectrum (e.g., Dreyer's 1998 investigation of Setswana/Sesotho-speaking South Africans, Nelson's 1995 study of Hawaiian Americans, and Harshbarger and colleagues' 1986 study of Hispanic-Americans). Further investigation of commonalities of style between the higher socioeconomic groups in different societies may be warranted. Some have suggested (e.g., Atkinson 1999) that in a globalizing world 'cultural' differences among such groups may be less significant than other factors which they may have in common. The findings here among British and Brazilian 'world villagers' may give some indications that learning style is among these commonalities.

A third set of implications arising from this investigation relate to learners and to learner-centredness. This investigation gave strong indications that learners exposed to the notion of learning style were positively disposed towards it, and felt it to be a valuable tool in getting to know themselves, and others, as learners. This would imply strongly that there is a place for attempts to index individual learning styles in learner-centred language curricula, and that profiles arising may be useful tools for both learners and for teachers who are prepared to use them.

A fourth and final set of implications relates to teachers. The EFL teachers in this study were generally more ambivalent about learning styles than the learners were. Some did see learning styles as a potentially valuable tool in effective learner-centredness as a general approach to social interaction, but others questioned the validity of the construct, and the utility of an instrument measuring it. Some also seemed afraid of the implications of operating with a multicultural class which may have a multiplicity of preferred learning styles. Further investigation is clearly warranted, but there are indications from the findings here that many teachers are still thinking in terms of a methodological approach to EFL pedagogy, where the diversity of preferred approaches to learning among language learners is not a social reality to be addressed, but a problem to be ignored, avoided or even denied.

Turning finally to what the study tells us about learning styles in broader terms. Conceptually, the construct remains problematic – no clear evidence emerged here that enhanced its validity. Despite this, those theoreticians who advocate its practical utility did receive, for the first time, some strong empirical support. Most learners, and many teachers, were of the view that knowledge of learning styles was a valuable tool for making teacher–learner interactions more effectively focused on successful learning.

* * *

As a final observation it is interesting to note what the EFL organization which commissioned this study decided to do in the light of its findings. Learners are now offered the opportunity to self-test their learning style at the beginning of courses using the SAS. Teachers are made aware of who has self-tested in this way, and are encouraged to discuss the individual style profile of the learner, and its implications for the learning process. No 'cultural' group profiles are referred to in such interactions between teachers and learners. While teachers have been given guidance as to how to deal with individual aspects and polarities of style, their approach to culture and intercultural communication is not guided by any reference to learning styles. Under the organization's new curricular framework it is, however, guided by reference to a broadly intercultural approach (e.g., Byram 1997). While recognizing the likely influence of upbringing and previous educational experience on individuals, this approach aims to avoid cultural essentialization by encouraging individuals to relativize their own perspectives and behaviours and those of the people whose behaviours and perspectives may be different.

16
Language Learning and Teaching as Discursive Practice

Richard F. Young
University of Wisconsin-Madison

The contributors to this book discuss how language is used in educational contexts both in and out of classrooms, and they describe how language learners do social actions, reflect on their own identities and mediate their own learning. In this concluding chapter, I take the opportunity to reflect on the theoretical positions that the other contributors to this book espouse, respond to some of their narratives, and attempt to recast their diverse approaches to language learning and teaching as a coherent approach to language and social action, which I call Discursive Practice. I argue that integrating diverse approaches into a coherent framework provides greater insights into language learning and teaching, and I begin by examining the relationship between language and context and argue that it is mutually reflexive. In this vein, I continue by expanding the notion of context to include self-identities of participants in social interaction. Such a broader view of context nudges linguistic phenomena from centre stage, and I complain that by a historical focus on language we have ignored important non-verbal semiotic systems that make significant contributions to the social dynamic of interaction.

All the above will, I hope, clear the ground for a presentation of Discursive Practice, which I offer as an extension of Practice Theory to talk-in-interaction. With its emphasis on socially constructed knowledge, discursive practice is an approach in which language learning is viewed not as the changing cognition of individual learners, but as their changing participation in discursive practices: what is learned is not the language but the practice. I then go on to frame some of the interactions presented in various chapters as discursive practices, and show what a discursive practice approach seeks to explain, what practices are examined, and what a consideration of talk-in-interaction as discursive practice reveals about the relationship between talk and context.

Language and context

A central focus of the contributions to this book is language and the relationship between language and context, and authors in the three sections of the book interpret context in appreciably different ways. To some authors, a context for a particular use of language is what is said before and what is said after; for other authors context extends beyond the sequence of speech to the social and political environment of schools; for others context includes a sense of belonging and shared history that we might call 'culture'; and to yet other authors, context is a very personal and conscious sense of the self and an awareness of individual agency in managing learning.

It is perhaps not surprising that scholars should differ in their interpretations of the relationship between language and context because the concept – and the relationship – are difficult to define. In their introduction to a collection of essays on context written by anthropologists and sociolinguists, C. Goodwin and Duranti review eight different traditions in the analysis of social context, but they note that in all traditions: 'The notion of context ... involves a fundamental juxtaposition of two entities: (1) a focal event; and (2) a field of action within which that event is embedded' (1992: 3). According to their disciplinary training, individual scholars choose to focus on one aspect of the relationship or the other: Linguists prefer to describe in detail the focal event, while sociologists of education tend to write more about the social and political context, and social psychologists interpret the field of action as cognitive structures and beliefs. The differences of emphasis are important but by their very difference they reify a dichotomy between focus and field of action, which I argue is chimerical.

One of the principal fault lines in the argument over context can be found in the conversation analysis (CA) literature. In the tradition of ethnomethodology, from which CA draws its theoretical stance and many of its practical procedures, the characteristics of social participants such as age, gender and social class, and the names of activities such as interview, seminar and service transaction are not considered in advance of analysis of social interaction. As Pomerantz and Fehr remark, in CA context is used in two senses. In the first sense:

> Conduct is produced and understood as responsive to the immediate, local contingencies of interaction. What an interactant contributes is shaped by what was just said or done and is understood in relation to the prior.
> (1997: 69)

And in another sense, context is brought into being by the actions of interactants. As Pomerantz and Fehr continue:

> Rather than treating the identities of the participants, the place, the occasion, etc., as givens, conversation analysts and ethnomethodologists recognize that there are multiple ways to identify parties, the occasion, etc. and that the identifications must be shown to be relevant to the participants.
> (1997: 69)

In the ethnomethodological tradition, then, the distinction made is not between language and a context which is beyond the immediate interaction; it is rather between people's conduct in interaction and the immediate sequential context (what was just said). This tradition in the study of context is seen in chapters that form the first part of this book (Gardner 2007; Kasper and Kim 2007; Markee 2007; Pekarek Doehler and Ziegler 2007; Seedhouse 2007). To the extent that interactants invoke other aspects of context, then those aspects influence the interpretation of their conduct, but if it is not invoked then the analyst must ignore it.

The ethnomethodological approach to context has been criticized by some scholars who have been working within the CA tradition because it appears that so much of an analyst's interpretation of what happens in interaction depends on the analyst and the participants sharing a common cultural (i.e., contextual) background. Cicourel (1992), for example, pointed out that such an extreme empiricist approach can be problematic because it obscures information that was available to the researcher during collection and analysis of data, and he distinguished between 'narrow' and 'broad' senses of context – the broad sense incorporating extra-situational information. Cicourel illustrated his argument in his own work on interactions between physicians, patients and technicians in a teaching hospital (Cicourel 1983, 1992), and especially by his work on construction of expertise in the same community (Cicourel 1995, 2000). In his work on the construction of expertise in medical settings, Cicourel found that in order to understand interaction it was necessary to go far beyond the sequential context, to explore fully the background of participants. Cicourel described part of that process as follows.

> I tried to understand aspects of the process of acquiring expertise by spending months observing and recording in a particular medical service. I then asked a few attendings to listen to recordings of their residents in order to pinpoint aspects of the experts' views about the novice's use of language and reasoning during the medical interview and physical examination. I was present during the novice's interview and during the account given to the attending after the novice's encounter with the patient. I also observed the attending if he or she accompanied the resident back to the patient ...
>
> I also tried to understand the acquisition of expertise by attending the microbiology/infectious disease classes required of medical students to learn something about relevant concepts and about the laboratory exercises students were assigned. I also spent several months observing and recording the deliberations of attendings, residents, and occasional medical students during microbiology rounds each morning at University Hospital.
>
> (2000: 69)

The kind of data that Cicourel described goes far beyond the situational context of a particular interaction, but is essential in order to understand how participants make inferences about expertise from their talk. It also goes far beyond the methods of conversation analysis. Cicourel criticized these approaches, saying that because they deal with interactions and participants with which the researchers and their readers are familiar, they make use of implicit knowledge without acknowledging it, and that as soon as researchers move outside a cultural context with which they are familiar, it is necessary to do the kind of ethnographic work that Cicourel described in order to understand participants' conduct in interaction.

Another view of context, which goes beyond the sequential environment of an utterance is Hymes's notion of *setting*, which he defined as 'the time and place of a speech act and, in general, to the physical circumstances' (1974b: 55). Although this definition seems to be a straightforward description of time and place, what counts in the interpretation of setting is not a physical description of the time and place of interaction, but their meanings for the participants and, in order to investigate setting, we have to go beyond adjacent space and contemporary time. In particular, we need to consider features of context that do not belong in the same time period as the focal event, especially those that happened before the focal event. Bourdieu argued that participants are not completely free to act or to talk in any way in a particular social situation. Although participants are certainly not automata that respond in pre-programmed ways in social situations, they are nonetheless constrained in their actions and in their talk by their own history, laid down in their formative years by the cultural environment of the home. Participants' predispositions to act and to talk in certain ways in particular situations, Bourdieu (1977a) called *habitus*. Habitus refers to participants' socially acquired predispositions, tendencies, propensities or inclinations, which are shown in mental phenomena such as opinions and outlooks, linguistic phenomena such as ways of talking, and physical phenomena such as deportment and posture, as well as ways of walking, sitting and dressing.

A good example of what Bourdieu meant by habitus is a speaker's accent. Although it is possible for people to change accents during their lifetime, most features of pronunciation that we recognize as an accent are formed in childhood and adolescence, and they reflect the geographical and social background of a speaker. A third major influence on a person's accent is ethnicity. White Americans tend to speak differently from African Americans, and both groups tend to speak differently from Latinos. For example, many white Americans pronounce two consonants in final consonant clusters such as 'lift' but many African Americans produce a single consonant, 'lif'. Another example of habitus is language alternation: both purposeful and spontaneous use of two or more spoken languages. Bilingual Latinos, for example, often rapidly alternate between their two languages and play on the differences between the Spanish and English pronunciation of words, as in the poem 'Bésame Mucho' by hybrid poet and performance artist Guillermo Gómez-Peña (1996):[1]

kiss me, kiss me my chola
como si fuera esta noche the last migra raid
kiss me, kiss moi mi chuca
que tengo miedo perderte somewhere in L.A.

watcha' que maybe mañana yo estaré en la pinta
longing for your ass (digo eyes)
y que quizá me deporten de nuevo a Tijuana
por ser ilegal

Where individuals grew up and the people from the social class and race that they hang out with all influence how participants speak in a particular conversation. These features of personal history allow other people to categorize you as belonging to a larger group of people who share your geographical, class and ethnic background; in Bourdieu's terms, accent and language choice are habitus, and habitus is something which does not generally reach conscious awareness and, unless it does, it limits the ways in which we can act and talk. In other words, habitus is temporal context; it is an index of personal history that every speaker brings to spoken interaction and that every writer brings to literacy practices.

Such an index of history that speakers bring to interaction can be seen as both creating their self-identities in the minds of others at the same time as permitting speakers to strategically manage their own identity. A bilingual's choice of which language to use in a specific situation or the ability of a bidialectal person to choose one dialect over another can be seen as both a product of social expectations, as resistance to those expectations, or as a playful exploration of self-identity. As Gómez-Peña demonstrates in 'Bésame Mucho', a bilingual can simply play with two language codes and even two pronunciations for effect: 'longing for your ass (digo eyes)'.

The temporal aspect of Hymes's setting thus goes far beyond the immediate time of production. The spatial aspect of setting, in particular participants' understanding of place, is also an important resource in understanding context. In many communities, it is common to find different spaces where members of the community expect different activities to occur: a temple or church is a spatial context for religious activities, a schoolroom is a context for education, a law court provides a context for legal proceedings, a theatre is where entertainment occurs, and long-distance travel happens on a highway. These spaces serve as a means of reproducing certain activities and often create roles that participants play: A judge normally sits at a higher physical level than other participants in a court of law, and most classrooms have spaces that are designed for a teacher and different spaces that are intended for students. Thus the built environment is a way in which social relations of power are reproduced. The notion of place, however, does not determine these relations in a mechanistic way, and spatial setting is not necessarily static but can be reframed when it is used for different activities.

The discussion of context thus far has considered context as immediate and sequential, context as background, context as personal history, and the contextual interpretations of physical space. These examples take the definition of context far beyond the static view of context that is one interpretation of C. Goodwin and Duranti's (1992) 'field of action', within which an event is embedded. Through these examples, I have tried to show how context not only influences talk, but context can itself be created by communicative events. Although conventional notions of context separate language as the object of focal attention from the non-linguistic frame in which it transpires, Ochs (1979) described a view of context in which the context of language is language itself. In this view, talk-in-interaction both makes reference to context outside the talk itself and at the same time provides context for other talk in the same interaction. The most apparent way in which language serves as context for itself is through the operation of *genre*, a kind of communicative style that Bauman defined as 'a constellation of systemically related, co-occurrent formal features and structures that serves as a conventionalized orienting framework for the production and reception of discourse' (2000: 84). The recognition by participants that an interaction is within a specific genre helps participants to interpret language within the interaction, while, in another genre, participants may interpret differently the same language.

In the discussion so far, I have shown how a single utterance can be interpreted by speakers on the basis of the interactional and linguistic context, but the notion of language as context applies not only to a larger discourse providing the contextual frame for a single utterance. The nature of language as its own concept is wider than that. Goffman's (1974) notion of *frame* captures this idea as both a social and cognitive concept by revealing that a participant in an interaction constructs the interaction within a certain cognitive frame. In other words, one participant can frame an interaction as a story, as a joke, as an interview and, if all participants share the frame, they interpret communication within that interaction according to the expectations that the frame provides. How do other participants interpret an interaction as within a certain frame? What are the cues that participants use in interpreting a frame? Detailed answers to these questions have been provided by Gumperz (1982, 1992, 2000) with his theory of Conversational Inference. According to Gumperz (1992), participants interpret any situated utterance within the context of an interactive exchange, and their perception of the interaction is influenced by contextualization cues. Contextualization cues are linguistic features of an interaction and include intonation, stress, paralinguistic signs such as speech tempo, pausing, hesitation, conversational synchrony, choice of a particular code such as language alternation by bilinguals or choice of dialect or speech style, and the choice of words or formulaic expressions. According to Gumperz, these cues are 'speakers' and listeners' use of verbal and non-verbal signs to relate what is said at any one time and in any one place to knowledge acquired through past experience' (1992: 230). An example of this process of inference is a conversation between two students sitting in a coffee shop gossiping about their landlords.

1 A: But she's a FLAKE.
2 B: ((fast tempo)) Ya know we should probably watch it.
3   They're [probably sitt'n there.
4 A: [I know
5 B: It's just nice going to cafes now and I feel like
6   I don't have [to avoid anybody
7 A: [THIS is the LIFE.

(Gumperz 2000: 132)

Gumperz points out that the way the two speakers' turns overlap in lines 3 and 4, and again in lines 6 and 7 shows that A is in perfect agreement both with the propositional content of B's previous utterances and also shares with B the background knowledge that allows both A and B to make the same inference. Gumperz explains this as follows: 'Only if we assume that *B*'s phrase about not having "to avoid anybody" indirectly indexes or evokes a normative principle – "do not gossip about people when there is a chance they can hear you" – does her reply make sense. When *A* replies with an overlapping "I know", we conclude that the two are engaged in shared inferencing' (2000: 132).

When participants in an interaction do not share common background knowledge, then the inferences that they make from utterances may be quite different. The process of inferencing is based on knowledge that a participant has accumulated over a lifetime, and different inferences may lead to misunderstanding in interactions between participants from different cultures as Gumperz, Jupp and Roberts (1979) and Bremer and colleagues (1996) have shown. And as Ross (1998) has shown in the context of assessment, different interpretations of the frame of a language proficiency interview by an interviewer and candidate from two different cultures may lead to a low assessment of the candidate's ability to speak a second language.

Language thus serves as a context for itself in interaction, and this means that participants' interpretation of what is happening in an interaction is influenced by the linguistic features of genres that participants have previously experienced and by contextualization cues that they use to construct an interpretive frame for the interaction. In this understanding of language as both the focal event *and* the context of that event, we have moved even further away from C. Goodwin and Duranti's conceptual separation of the two. A further investigation into how self-identities are constructed through interaction provides a further challenge to the placing of language at centre stage.

Language and identity

Several chapters in the present book consider the concept of identity, especially the self-identities of learners and the identities of teachers. Block (2007c) tells the story of Carlos, a Colombian immigrant to Britain who appears to invoke different self-identities when interacting in English with professionals in positions of power and when he is talking with workmates. Driagina and Pavlenko (2007) reflect on the differences between the reduced range of affective identity terms used in Russian by American learners in comparison with Russian native speakers. Hua (2007) analyses the differences between construction of identity in application letters for an academic position written by British native speakers of English and Chinese students writing in English. Miller (2007) describes the challenges that non-native speakers of English face in constructing an identity as a teacher of English as a second language in Australian schools. Identity in these chapters is a way of interpreting what learners and teachers say and write and is at the same time a way of creating self-identities. In this respect, identity is another facet of the context of interaction and is in some ways parallel to the features of context that we have described so far. As Harré (2001) has argued, self-identity is a threefold concept: a context of perception, a context of reflection and a context of social interaction.

I argue here that what the contributors invoke by the term 'identity' is no different to the notion of context that we have discussed so far. Just as C. Goodwin and Duranti's theory of the relationship between language and context has promoted the view of language as the focal event in a field of action called 'context', so the authors in Part 2 of this book have centred their attention on the relationship between language and identity. The connections that they have drawn between language and identity parallel the connections that I have shown between language and context: Just as context is seen as sequential in interaction, so identity can be viewed as a means of interpreting utterances; just as the temporal dimension of context is deep, so some aspects of identity are fixed; just as space creates context, so identities vary according to the physical environment; and just as Gumperz shows that language can create a context for interpretation, so some aspects of identity can change through talk-in-interaction. A description and explanation of these different aspects of identity are presented by Tracy (2002).

In presenting her theory of four aspects of self-identity, Tracy reflects on what are apparently contradictory uses of the concept: in one sense, self-identity is described by stable and fixed aspects of selfhood, the kind of things that you check off on census forms; and in another sense self-identity is an accomplishment, not a thing, it is fragmentary and in flux, and people change identities to suit the needs of the moment. In order to incorporate these different senses of identity, Tracy distinguishes among four kinds: master identity, interactional identity, personal identity and relational identity. Master identities are relatively stable and unchanging, such as gender, ethnicity, age, national and regional origins; interactional identities refer to roles that people take on in a communicative context with specific other people; personal identities[2] are expected to be relatively stable and unique and reference ways in which people talk and behave toward others: as hot-headed, honest, forthright, reasonable, overbearing, a gossip, a brown-nose and so on; relational identities refer to the kind of relationship that a person enacts with a particular conversational partner in a specific situation, these identities are negotiated from moment to moment and are highly variable. Each of these identities is a context for constructing and interpreting talk-in-interaction and literacy practices.

We have seen in the discussion of *habitus* how **master identities** influence the production of talk and how interlocutors altercast speakers on the basis of the language that they hear; it is the interplay between speakers' production and interlocutors' altercasting of identity that allows us to play with master identities by shifting language styles and by alternating language codes. **Interactional identities** are inherently variable because of the diversity of roles that individuals play in a community: The same person can be a teacher, a student, a colleague, a mother, a partner in interactions with different people and in different physical surroundings. Interactional identities create expectations of language forms, of topics of conversation and of ways of speaking that differ according to the identity role. Teachers' conversations with students in a classroom often take the form of the well-known three-part sequence of initiation by teacher, response by student, and evaluation or feedback by teacher. The same kind of interaction can be found in conversations between parents and young children in their homes (Seedhouse 2004), but is rarely found in conversations between colleagues in the teachers' staff room.

Personal identities are frequently contested because the identity altercast by an interlocutor may not be the personal identity that the speaker wishes to project, but personal identities also provide a context for interpreting language. If a meeting is arranged with several persons, some regarded as punctual and some regarded as habitually late for meetings, linguistic assessments may be produced if the punctual individuals arrive late or if the people who are habitually late arrive on time. The contents of a personal story told to a person regarded as a gossip may differ from the contents of the same personal story told to a person regarded as someone who can keep a secret. And finally, **relational identities** provide a context for interpreting the dynamics of interaction. Relational identities must be negotiated from one moment to the next and they are highly variable. Within a single conversation, relational identities may change and provide a context for interpreting the talk, an example of which is provided by Gumperz:

> The graduate student has been sent to interview a black housewife in a low income, inner city neighborhood. The contact has been made over the phone by someone in the office. The student arrives, rings the bell, and is met by the husband, who opens the door, smiles, and steps towards him:
> *Husband*: So y're gonna check out ma ol lady, hah?
> *Interviewer*: Ah, no. I only came to get some information. They called from the office.
> (Husband, dropping his smile, disappears without a word and calls his wife.) The student reports that the interview that followed was stiff and quite unsatisfactory. Being black himself, he knew that he had 'blown it' by failing to recognize the significance of the husband's speech style.
> (1982: 133)

How did the student know that he had blown it? At the beginning of the conversation between the husband and the student, the husband uses African American Vernacular English to address the student, attempting to create solidarity with a brother. The student, by replying in Standard English, rejects the identity altercast by the husband and instead claims the more distant identity of researcher. All this happens in the space of two turns in the conversation, but it has resonances in the later conversation, which the student found to be 'quite unsatisfactory'.

Understood in the framework proposed by Tracy (2002), then, self-identity is a context, a field of action, in which we choose to focus on language used by a person and by others to reference that person. As I have illustrated, and has been further shown in the chapters by Block (2007c), Driagina and Pavlenko (2007), Hua (2007) and Miller (2007), self-identity is both indexed by language and provides a context within which language use can be interpreted.

Language and other semiotic systems

So far I have been concerned to establish the different ways in which context can be understood, and I have tried to show that the nexus between language and context is stronger than the image relayed by C. Goodwin and Duranti as 'a fundamental juxtaposition of two entities: (1) a focal event; and (2) a field of action within which that event is embedded' (1992: 3). The question also arises, however, of the nature of the focal event. Up to this point we have considered language as occupying that spotlight alone, but the primacy of language in the discussion should not be considered definitive; rather, our focus on language is a consequence of the amount of research which has been done on the relationship of language to context. As recognized by semioticians, language is the human semiotic system *par excellence* and because of its centrality in social life and the permanence of written language, it has received a great amount of attention to the detriment of other 'non-verbal' semiotic systems including bodily gesture, facial expression, clothing, spatial positioning, ritual practices and expressive systems such as the visual arts. However, as was elaborated by Goffman (1979) in his essay on 'footing', a communicative social event is much more than the production and reception of speech: the relative positioning of participants with respect to each other and to the built environment, their gaze and their facial expression must all be considered in an understanding of the social organization of participants, which Goffman referred to as 'participation framework'. The importance of these dimensions of interaction have been demonstrated by M. H. Goodwin (1990) in her study of interaction among adolescent African-American children by C. Goodwin (1981) in his study of family interaction, and illustrated by Hanks (1996b) in his analysis of communicative practice. In addition to the evidence that these scholars and others have demonstrated of the importance of non-verbal semiotic systems in the analysis of interaction, much recent work by Kendon (1980, 1990) and McNeill (1992, 2000) has described in great detail the function of gesture in communicative interaction.

Discursive practice

The role of language as only one of several semiotic systems in communicative interaction, and the importance of context and of identity in constructing and reflecting the meaning of social interaction, indicates that an exclusive focus on language is to ignore crucial dimensions of interaction. A broader concept is needed, one which includes both the focal event and the field of action, both the participants in social interaction as agents and as identities, and both verbal and non-verbal semiotic systems. In the field of anthropology, scholars have also struggled with the problem of explaining the mutual interactions between human activity and social systems. What anthropologists have been concerned to understand is both how social systems such as gender, class and culture influence everyday human activity, but also how humans are able to affect social structures through their actions. Clearly, the anthropological question is an exploration of wider issues than simply the relationship between language and context of situation, but the development of modern Practice Theory in anthropology by Bourdieu (1977a), Sahlins (1981), and as reviewed by Ortner (1984) has given rise to an examination of talk-in-interaction by linguists referred to as *discursive practice*.

Practice is anything that people do, and one of the most accessible definitions of discursive practice is given by Tracy, who describes discursive practices as 'talk activities that people do'. She continues:

> A discursive practice may refer to a small piece of talk (person-referencing practices) or it may focus on a large one (narratives); it may focus on single

features that may be named and pointed to (speech acts) or it may reference sets of features (dialect, stance). Discursive practices may focus on something done by an individual (directness style) or they may refer to actions that require more than one party (interaction structures).

(Tracy 2002: 21)

Such activities have been called interactive practices (Hall 1995a, 1995b) communicative practices (Hanks 1996b), and I follow Tracy and refer to them here as *discursive practices*. The discursive practice approach to language-in-interaction is grounded in a view of social realities as discursively constructed, of meanings as negotiated through interaction, of the context-bound nature of discourse, and of discourse as social action.

Some of the origins of this view may be seen in the work of the London School of Linguistics, in particular the work of J. R. Firth and his students and, first, in the writings of Malinowski. Malinowski (1923) recognized that in all societies, language is indistinguishable from action and that the function of language usually studied by linguists – the communication of referential information – is less central than social action. Firth elaborated the idea of language as action by describing the ways in which linguistic action relates to the social context in which it is performed, which Firth (1957) referred to as context of situation. One of the earliest descriptions of a discursive practice was Mitchell's (1957) study of the practice of buying and selling in a North African market. More recently, linguistic anthropologists such as Ochs, Gonzalez and Jacoby (1996) and Hanks (1996a) have developed further the theory of language as action in context by describing discursive practices as diverse as lab meetings among research physicists and exorcism performed by a Maya shaman.

Shifting focus from an analysis of learning and teaching as linguistic interaction to a recognition of the multifaceted discursive practices that constitute these activities also requires us to consider learning and teaching in a new light, and the title of this book, *Language Learning and Teaching as Social Interaction*, encourages us to do just that. In several chapters in the third part of the book, authors reflect on issues in learning and teaching that are wider than language. Conteh (2007b) examines a multilingual classroom in Britain and addresses the wider sociopolitical issues that have influenced discursive practices in mainstream primary classrooms in England, and examines the role that the children's habitus (learned in their home communities) has in their learning activities. Shameem (2007a) describes the disconnect between national ideology as realized by language and education policies in Fiji and the actual practices she finds in multilingual classrooms. And Langman and Bayley (2007) argue that learning should be understood as participation in discursive practices, which they summarize in a quote from Rogoff (2003: 52): 'Human development is a process of people's changing participation in sociocultural activities in their communities.' However, as they point out, full participation in classroom practices by a bilingual child does not necessarily mean that the linguistic code used is English.

Learning as changing participation

The view of learning as changing participation is radically different from theories of second language acquisition that frame language learning as a cognitive process residing in the mind-brain of an individual learner (Long and Doughty 2003). The view that is invoked by Langman and Bayley, and which I wish to argue for here is, instead, of second language acquisition as a situated, co-constructed process, distributed among participants. This is a learning theory that takes social and ecological interaction as its starting point and develops detailed analyses of patterns of interaction in context. In this perspective, language learning is manifested as participants' progress along trajectories of changing engagement in discursive practices, changes which lead from peripheral to fuller participation and growth of self-identity. The controversies in the field of education between a cognitive view of learning and an appreciation of learning as changing participation were debated a decade ago in *Educational Researcher*. At the conclusion of that debate, Sfard (1998) described these two different ways of conceptualizing learning as the 'acquisition metaphor' and the 'participation metaphor.' In Sfard's review, she noted a long tradition in the study of learning in which the process has been analysed as development of basic units of knowledge, which are gradually accumulated, refined and combined in order to become rich cognitive structures. As she says, 'The language of "knowledge acquisition" and "concept development" makes us think of the human mind as a container to be filled with certain materials and about the learner as becoming an owner of these materials' (Sfard 1998: 5).

In contrast, Sfard notes that in recent publications in the field of education, talk about states of knowledge has been replaced with discussions of knowing, an action has replaced a state, and

> The ongoing learning activities are never considered separately from the context in which they take place. The context, in its turn, is rich and multifarious, and its importance is pronounced by talk about situatedness, cultural embeddedness, and social mediation.
>
> (Sfard 1998: 6)

The participation metaphor that Sfard invokes views 'the learner as a person interested in participating in certain kinds of activities rather than in accumulating private possessions' (1998: 6). Among several theories of learning that have envisioned the learning task as one in which all participants in an interaction change the nature of their participation, Situated Learning or Legitimate Peripheral Participation (Lave 1993; Lave and Wenger 1991) is perhaps the most familiar. In Situated Learning theory, learning does not only involve the individual acquiring propositional knowledge; more significantly, it involves all participants in a discursive practice changing their patterns of social co-participation. A relevant model for situated learning is apprenticeship, a situation in which apprentices and their masters change through acting as co-learners. In situated learning the skilful learner acquires the ability to play various roles in participation frameworks, the ability to anticipate what can occur in certain discursive practices, a pre-reflective grasp of complex situations, the ability to time actions relative to changing circumstances, and the ability to improvise. Hanks, who has made significant contributions to the theory of discursive practice, has argued that situated learning is an appropriate learning theory to understand how novices acquire expertise in a new practice (Hanks 1991).

One study of second language learning that has been inspired by Situated Learning theory is Young and Miller's (2004) longitudinal study of revision talk in weekly writing conferences between a student of English as a second language and his writing teacher. In this study, the practice of 'revision talk' was defined as a sequence of actions that resulted in a revised essay. Before each writing conference, the student had written a draft of an essay on a topic assigned by the teacher and during revision talk the teacher and student identified problem areas in the student's writing, talked about ways to improve the writing and revised the essay. Although the sequence of actions remained relatively constant in each instance of the practice, the participation framework of the practice changed over the four-week period of observation. The participation of both teacher and student changed, and changed in a way that showed mutual co-construction of their roles. In the initial conference, the teacher laid out the sequence of eight actions that constitute revision talk, performed seven of the eight actions herself, and directed the student to perform the final action of revising the essay. Observation of the conference four weeks later, however, showed the student now performing many of the acts that were initially performed by the teacher: He identified problem in his writing, he explained the need for revision, he suggested candidate revisions, and he revised his essay without being directed to do so by the teacher. It is not simply that the quantity of student's talk increased through the series of four conferences; instead, the student showed that he had mastered the practice by performing all acts except those that uniquely construct the role of teacher.

In addition to their analysis of the language of the interaction, Young and Miller described certain gestural and positional features of the interaction that defined certain actions. For example, the opening of revision talk was indexed by both the student and teacher leaning forward slightly and directing their gaze down to the paper positioned on the desk between them.

Toward the end of revision talk, the teacher directed the student to write a revision which they had agreed on, and this action was accompanied by movement of the student's paper from a common space shared by teacher and student to a place on the table closer to the student so that he could begin to write. Participants' talk at this moment in the interaction was coordinated with gesture and positioning. The teacher nudged the student's paper toward the student, and requested that he rewrite his main idea sentence. The slight shifting of the paper toward the student seemed to anticipate the teacher's verbal request. She followed the request with another slight nudge of the paper toward the student and then immediately produced a directive for him to rewrite the sentence. This coordination of gesture and talk (use of verbal and non-verbal semiotic systems) was also apparent in the change of participation that indexed learning. The student's non-verbal participation in the writing conference held in the fourth week of observation demonstrated fuller participation. During this interaction, the teacher produced no verbal or non-verbal prompts directing the student to write a revision, but after the student uttered a candidate revision he immediately pulled his paper toward himself and began writing the revision.

The view of learning as changing participation which is illustrated by Young and Miller demonstrates that participation in both linguistic and non-linguistic semiotic systems changes over time. Similar close analyses of the role that gaze, bodily positioning, and the built environment play in talk-in-interaction have been provided by Markee (2000, 2004, 2007) and have confirmed the role that these non-verbal systems play. The change in participation that I have argued is an index of learning in interaction is based on the identification of activities that occur at different moments in development; that is, a discursive practice needs to be defined independently of any specific instance of the practice. In other studies of practices such as testimony at Bible study sessions (Yanagisawa 2000) and pharmacist–patient consultations (Nguyen 2003, 2006), the identification of a practice has been by means of identifying discursive components of the practice, including patterns of turn-taking, topical structure, participation framework, sequential organization, register and resources for meaning-making (He and Young 1998; Young 1999; Young and Miller 2004). When recurring activities are configured in similar ways, with a similar discursive 'architecture', it is possible to identify different activities as instances of the same practice. In the participation metaphor for learning, then, the fundamental unit of analysis is neither language nor the positioning of participants; rather, it is a discursive practice. The practice is what is learned, not the language.

Discursive practice as used by Tracy (2002) and in the studies reviewed above differs from the way the term 'practice' is used by linguistic anthropologists in discussions of practice theory (Bourdieu 1977b; Ortner 1984). Although practice is literally anything people do, for most linguistic anthropologists 'the most significant forms of practice are those with intentional or unintentional political implications' (Ortner 1984, p. 149). From the discussion of the wider social context of talk with which this essay began, and a review of many of the chapters on multilingual and multicultural classrooms in Part 3 of this book, the importance of the political implications becomes clear, but it is an emphasis which is absent from linguists' discussions of discursive practice (including my own earlier work). Practice is the construction and reflection of social realities through actions which invoke identity, ideology, belief and power. A discursive practice approach to talk-in-interaction thus seeks to examine both how the language, gesture and positioning of specific interactions are determined by the social context of interaction and how that context – conceived broadly enough to include the political implications of the practice and the identities of the participants – is constructed by their verbal and non-verbal actions.

How is an approach to language learning and teaching as discursive practice parallel to or divergent from the theoretical stances taken by authors of the chapters in this book? The way to approach this question is by examining the contributions to the three sections of this book separately and to ask three questions: What does a discursive practice approach seek to explain? What is the practice being examined? And what does a consideration of talk-in-interaction as discursive practice reveal about the relationship between talk and context?

Discursive practice and conversation analysis

In the conversation analysis literature, as Kasper and Kim (2007) indicate, repair of problems that participants perceive in talk-in-interaction has received much attention, and a large amount of research attests to the organization of repair, sequential positions of repair, types of repair and the preference for self-repair. Instances of repair can be identified in conversations on the basis of these features, but because of the diversity of contexts in which repair occurs, repair itself cannot be considered a discursive practice. As Seedhouse points out, 'there is no single, monolithic organization of repair in the L2 classroom. There is a reflexive relationship between the pedagogical focus and the organization of repair; as the pedagogical focus changes, so does the organization of repair' (2004: 142). Seedhouse identified three different pedagogical contexts for L2 classrooms: form-and-accuracy, meaning-and-fluency, and task-oriented contexts. In each of these contexts, repair functions differently. Seedhouse notes that in a form-and-accuracy context, 'any learner contribution which does not correspond exactly to the precise string of linguistic forms required by the teacher may be treated as trouble by the teacher and may be treated as repairable' (2004: 149). In form-and-accuracy contexts, however, 'overt correction is undertaken only when there is an error which impedes communication. The teacher may adopt a policy of not repairing learner utterances even when they are of a minimalized reduced nature and full of linguistic errors' (Seedhouse 2004: 153). And in task-oriented contexts, trouble is defined as 'anything which hinders the learner's completion of the task, and repair is focused on removing any such hindrances' (Seedhouse 2004: 153).

In Seedhouse's functional treatment of repair, the context in which repair occurs is an essential part of the description of repair, unlike a generic treatment of repair in language classrooms which attempts to seek parallels between L2 classroom repair and repair in mundane conversational interaction described by Schegloff, Jefferson and Sachs (1977) and others. In particular, the form-and-accuracy context is one in which the generic sequential action of repair may not be the way in which the social context of the action is made relevant. As Macbeth puts it, 'Though correction may be a kind of repair in natural conversation, in classrooms these actions share a different category relationship: Correction in classrooms is an identifying task and achievement of classroom teaching' (2004: 705). The position espoused by Seedhouse and Macbeth is that classroom correction is a discursive practice that both creates and reflects the social context of the classroom and the reciprocal identities of teacher and students.

Discursive practice and identity

Earlier in this essay, I reported Tracy's (2002) discussion of the nature of identity and her description of master, personal, interactional and relational identity. Master identity is created by accent, choice of language, dialect or speech style, as well as ways of bodily deportment and, as Bourdieu argued, such habitus predisposes participants to talk and act in certain ways and for their interlocutors to altercast them in the master identity that they give off. Interactional identity is often related to the physical space and positioning of participants in a built environment. Personal identity provides a context for interpreting the use of certain forms of talk and for the absence of some others. And relational identities are created on the fly by means of the process of conversational inference described by Gumperz. The close relationship between language use and the construction and realization of these different identities is well illustrated by Block's analysis of the conversations in London between a Colombian migrant, Carlos Sanchez, and his workmates, his lawyer, and with Block himself. Thanks to Block's presentation of the conversations in a social context that includes the personal history of Carlos, and a description of his social role *vis-à-vis* the other participants in the conversations, we are able to see the integration of talk with social context that is the hallmark of discursive practice.

In the interaction involving Carlos and his workmates Bob and Dan, Carlos's talk differs greatly from his conversation with a lawyer, and also from his conversations with Block. While in the first two conversations Carlos uses English, the self-identities that he creates are different. While Dan attempts to create what seems to be the relational identity of British male working class, indexed by his complaint about his cold, his complaint about the poor performance of the football club he supports, and his frequent use of the intensifier 'fucking', Carlos provides only brief response tokens in support of Dan's long turns-at-talk. In this conversation, then, Carlos has not availed himself of the opportunity to express a solidary relational identity with Dan, and Block interprets Carlos's actions as a strategic denial of the opportunity to avail himself of the relational identity available to him. The second conversation in English that Block reports is Carlos's phone conversation with a lawyer, during which he appears to command a vocabulary and phrasing that index a relational identity of professional and a personal identity as a capable individual. Block describes Carlos's master identity in detail: in Colombia, he was a university professor of philosophy and was active in leftist political movements; because of his opposition to the government in his home country and for personal reasons he migrated to England, where he works in low-level manual service jobs. Carlos's construction of self-identity in London is strategic: he prefers not to interact with fellow Colombians because he finds their practices of playing football on Sundays, salsa dancing and festivals to be rituals in which he cannot create his personal and relational identity as an intellectual. The language used in these practices is Spanish but, as his conversation with Dan and Bob showed, Carlos also prefers to avoid the same topics of conversation in English. In his interaction in English with the lawyer and with Block in Spanish, however, he is able to create the more desirable relational identity of fellow intellectual or fellow professional. He does so by much longer turns at talk in English and by coherent narratives in Spanish in which he recounts that in his interactions with his British workmates, 'Yo estoy allí pero ... ((encogiéndose de hombros.))'.[3] It is noteworthy that Carlos's strategic creation of identity does not seem to depend on the language that he uses for, in Block's description, he is equally adept in English and in Spanish in creating an identity of intellectual and professional and in rejecting the identity of migrant worker.

Equally interesting, is the way that Carlos frames his agency in Block's descriptions. That is, Carlos's actions are certainly influenced by larger social and political structures, but at the same time he attempts to create social conditions that express resistance to the identity of migrant worker. In Practice Theory, the role of human agency in affecting the social context in which people interact is the key to how social change comes about.

Discursive practice and 'the system'

In the third section of this book, several authors describe learning and teaching in public (i.e., state) schools and the relationship that they see between what goes on in classrooms and public policy. In this section I wish to consider how Practice Theory frames a relationship between activity and organized social situations and political institutions, which I refer to (albeit with a certain negative connotation) as 'the system'. In her chapter on bilingualism in mainstream primary classrooms in England, Conteh

(2007b) tells the story of British government policy on bilingualism in schools by recounting the developing position expressed in position papers and policy directives published over the past 30 years, all of which recognize that children whose home language is not English are both an asset to the school and the community, and at the same time recognize the need to provide special services such as bilingual teaching assistants to help children transition to monolingual English schooling. One of the systemic obstacles to achieving the status of a child's home language as an 'asset' in education that Conteh mentions is that the majority of teachers in primary schools are not bilingual, and although the number of bilingual teachers is increasing, they may not know the languages of all their pupils in a multilingual community. Language alternation by a bilingual may, as we have seen, influence and be influenced by the social context in at least three ways: choice of language may reflect social expectations, it may index resistance to those expectations, or it may be a playful exploration of self-identity. If the overt government policy is to view bilingualism as an asset, then a teacher who does not share the language of her pupils is, in effect, expressing resistance to that policy because of the way that she is able to control the language used in her classroom and thus to construct 'legitimate knowledge' (Apple 1993) as expressed in the majority language and implicitly sanction knowledge expressed in another language. In her chapter, Conteh shows us a rather different situation of a bilingual teacher who regularly alternates between the majority language (English) and the community language (Punjabi). She notes that such alternation altercasts an identity of her Punjabi pupils as sharing access to legitimate knowledge, but also demonstrates to her monolingual English-speaking students that knowledge expressed in the community language is legitimate.

While the implications of the classroom conversation that Conteh describes can be seen as supporting official bilingual policy in England, Shameem's chapter (2007a) shows the disconnect between the official language education policy in Fiji and the language used in multilingual primary school classrooms. In multilingual Fiji, the community language of Fijians of Indian origin is Fiji Hindi, a common language that evolved over the years from the dialects of Hindi spoken by indentured labourers brought to the Fiji islands by the British in the nineteenth century. Fiji Hindi has diverged significantly from the varieties of Hindi and Urdu spoken on the Indian subcontinent. The colonial government of Fiji established a different variety of Hindi, known as Shudh (or 'pure') Hindi as the standard because this variety enjoyed the status of official language in India. It was a variety that was already codified and was incorporated as a language of education in Fiji. The diglossic situation of Fiji Hindi and Shudh Hindi is complicated by the colonial language, English, which is the official language. Shameem (2007a) reports that the official language policy is to use Shudh Hindi for teaching Indo-Fijian children in the first three years of primary school before transitioning to English in the later years of schooling, although the community language is Fiji Hindi, which differs from the standard. Shameem's research shows that, in their responses to questionnaires, primary school teachers reported much greater use of Shudh Hindi than was the case when she observed actual language use. She reports that 'while three [first grade] teachers had reported using English and three a combination of English and F[iji] H[indi] as language of instruction in their English lessons, observation showed that in fact six of the eight teachers were using only English while the other two used both' (2007a: 209). The divergence between reported and actual language use has two important implications when viewed from the perspective of discursive practice. First, although 'the system' may constrain language choice by these teachers to some degree, the constraint is much more effective on their consciousness, that is, the way that they mediate their own language choice. The system provides a ready-made internalization for these teachers of their own practice, a practice which actually diverges from their mediation of it. Second, the systematic encouragement of the use of the High variety of Hindi over the Low variety in education appears to do little to maintain either variety as a community asset and, in fact, encourages maintenance of the colonial language – English. The Fijian situation thus appears parallel to many postcolonial situations, where the use of English is encouraged at the expense of indigenous languages (Phillipson 1992).

From the perspective of discursive practice, these two studies demonstrate certain interesting relationships between talk-in-interaction and 'the system'. It is evident that the system shapes, guides and to some extent dictates behaviour, but the effect that the system has is more evident and more insidious in the ways that individual actors make sense of their practice, in fact by mystifying them about the nature of their own behaviour. The Fijian primary school teachers believe that they are practising a language policy that is more in line with the official ideology than in fact they are doing. As Bourdieu has argued, the social conditions and official ideology of which actors are aware do not result in automatic reproduction of systemic values by people through discursive practice. In fact, actors' resistance to the expectations of the system may lead to change within the system itself. In the case of the mainstream English primary schools, the use of the community language by teachers does not simply recognize bilingualism in minority communities as an asset that the official policy (rather patronizingly drafted by speakers of the dominant language) encourages, but demonstrates to the children who speak the dominant language that they can at times be excluded from interactions and denied access to teacher-legitimated knowledge as a consequence of their normally privileged position as monolingual speakers of the dominant language.

Concluding remarks

In the preceding pages I have tried to describe the discursive practice approach to talk-in-interaction, and to show some of the insights that it can provide for language learning and teaching. Beginning with a critical analysis of the dichotomous view of language and context, I proposed that the two are a unity that should not be divided and that our focus on language to the exclusion of context is an inheritance from the disciplinary history of linguistics and related social sciences. The methodological strength and the enthusiastic labour of so many in the language sciences have also distracted us from work on other semiotic systems that are just now beginning to be investigated, work which is confirming the reflexive relationship between language, gesture and context. Illustrations of the mutual reflexivity of action (both verbal and non-verbal) and context are found most pertinently when we examine how self-identities are constructed through language, how they are reflected in talk-in-interaction, and how our self-identities are altercast by other participants in interaction. Discursive practice is an approach to talk-in-interaction which brings with it important insights into the social meaning of practices and, in particular, implies that learning involves changes of the participation framework in successive instances of the same practice. Participation in discursive practice is not limited, however, to the observable behaviours of participants but constitutes action on a broader political stage, having an effect on the relations of power and equity among participants but also contributing to reproduction of, or resistance to, dominant ideologies within the community at large.

In his chapter in this collection, Block recounts that his intention in his 2003 book was to make a case for 'a move towards SLA research which engages with the fuzzy and unclear social, cultural, historical, political and economic aspects in and around second language learning'. Through the present discussion of a discursive practice approach, I hope to have made some of those aspects less fuzzy.

Notes

1. Kiss me, kiss me my darling / As if tonight were the last INS raid. / Kiss me, kiss me my honey / Cos I'm afraid of losing you somewhere in LA. // Who knows maybe tomorrow I'll be in jail / Longing for your ass (I mean eyes) / And maybe they'll deport me back to Tijuana / Cos I'm an illegal alien.
2. Personal identity in Tracy's sense differs from the concept of personal identity found in discussions of philosophy and in psychological approaches to identity, in which personal identity has the sense of something in an individual body that persists through time (e.g., Rorty 1976).
3. I'm there, but ((shrugging his shoulders)).

Bibliography

Adam, R. S. 1984. Social factors in second language learning, with special reference to the Fiji Islands. PhD dissertation. University of London, 1959. Cited in P. A. Geraghty, Language policy in Fiji and Rotuma, *Duivosavosa: Fiji languages, their use and their future, Fiji Museum Bulletin*, 8: 32–73.

Adams, M. 1978. Methodology for examining second language acquisition. In E. Hatch (ed.), *Second Language Acquisition: A book of readings*. Rowley, MA: Newbury House, pp. 278–96.

Alidou, H. 2003. Language policies and language education in Francophone Africa: A critique and a call to action. In S. Makoni, G. Smitherman, A. F. Ball and A. K. Spears (eds), *Black Linguistics*. London: Routledge, pp. 103–16.

Apple, M. 1996 Series editor's introduction. In P. Carspecken, *Critical Ethnography in Educational Research*. NewYork: Routledge, pp. ix–xii.

Apple, M. W. 1993. *Official Knowledge: Democratic education in a conservative age*. New York: Routledge.

Assaf, A.S. 2001. Palestinian students attitudes towards Modern Standard Arabic and Palestinian City Arabic, *RELC Journal*, 32(2): 45–62.

Aston, G. 1986. Trouble-shooting in interaction with learners: The more the merrier? *Applied Linguistics*, 7: 128–43.

Atkinson, D. 1999. TESOL and culture. *TESOL Quarterly*, 33(4): 625–54.

Austin, J. 1962. *How to do things with words: The William James lectures delivered in Harvard University in 1955*. Cambridge, MA: Harvard University Press.

Baker, C. 1996. *Foundations of Bilingualism and Bilingual Education*. Clevedon: Multilingual Matters.

Bange, P. 1992. A propos de la communication et de l'apprentissage de L2. *Acquisition et Interaction en Langue Etrangère – AILE*, 1: 53–85.

Bardovi-Harlig, K. and Z. Dörnyei. 1998. Do language learners recognize pragmatic violations? Pragmatic vs. grammatical awareness in instructed L2 learning. *TESOL Quarterly*, 32: 233–62.

Barron, A. 2003. *Acquisition in Interlanguage Pragmatics*. Amsterdam: Benjamins.

Barwell, R. 2004. *Teaching Learners of English as an Additional Language: A review of official language*. Watford: National Association for Language Development in the Curriculum NALDIC.

Barz R. K. and J. Siegel (eds). 1988. *Language Transplanted: The development of overseas Hindi*. Wiesbaden: Otto Harrassowitz.

Bauman, R. 2000. Genre. *Journal of Linguistic Anthropology*, 9(1–2), 84–7.

Bayley, R., H. Hansen-Thomas and J. Langman. 2005. Language brokering in a middle school science class. In J. Cohen, K. McAlister, K. Rolstad and J. MacSwan, (eds), *ISB4: Proceedings of the 4th International Symposium on Bilingualism*. Somerville, MA: Cascadilla Press, pp. 223–32.

Beach, W. A. 1993. Transitional regularities for 'casual' 'Okay' usages. *Journal of Pragmatics*, 19: 325–52.

Benton, R. A. 1996. The Māori language in New Zealand education and society. In F. Mugler and J. Lynch (eds), *Pacific Languages in Education*. Suva: Institute of Pacific Studies and Vanuatu: Department of Literature and Language, Pacific Languages Unit, pp. 209–27.

Bermúdez Torres, A. 2003. *Navigation Guide to Refugee Populations in the UK: Colombians*. London: ICAR (Information Centre about Asylum and Refugees in the UK.
Bhatia, V. 1993. *Analysing Genre: Language use in professional settings*. New York: Longman.
Bizzell, P. 1982a. College composition: Initiation into the academic discourse community. *Curriculum Inquiry*, 12(2): 191–207.
Bizzell, P. 1982b. Cognition, convention and certainty: What we need to know about writing. *PRE/TEXT*, 3(3): 213–41.
Blackledge, A. 2004. Constructions of identity in political discourse in multilingual Britain. In A. Pavlenko and A. Blackledge (eds), *Negotiation of Identities in Multilingual Contexts*. Clevedon: Multilingual Matters, pp. 68–92.
Blecher, D. 2001. Does second language writing theory have gender? In T. Silva and P.K. Matsuda (eds), *On Second Language Writing*. Mahwah, NJ: Lawrence Erlbaum, pp. 59–71.
Block, D. 2003. *The Social Turn in Second Language Acquisition*. Edinburgh: Edinburgh University Press.
Block, D. 2006. *Multilingual Identities in a Global City: London stories*. London: Palgrave.
Block, D. 2007a. *Second Language Identities*. London: Continuum.
Block, D. 2007b. The increasing presence of Spanish-speaking Latinos in London: An emergent community? *Journal of Language, Identity and Education*.
Block, D. 2007c. Socialising second language acquisition. In Z. Hua, P. Seedhouse, L. Wei and V. Cook (eds), *Language Learning and Teaching as Social Interaction*. Basingstoke: Palgrave Macmillan.
Bond, M. H., and T.-S. Cheung. 1983. College students' spontaneous self concept: The effect of culture among respondents in Hong Kong, Japan, and the United States. *Journal of Cross-Cultural Psychology*, 14: 153–71.
Bourdieu, P. 1977a. *Outline of a Theory of Practice*. Cambridge: Cambridge University Press.
Bourdieu, P. 1977b. The economics of linguistic exchanges. *Social Science Information*, 16(6): 645–68.
Bourdieu, P. 1984. *Distinction: A Social Critique of the Judgement of Taste*. London: Routledge.
Bourdieu, P. 1991. *Language and Symbolic Power*. Oxford: Polity Press.
Bourne, J. 2001. Doing what comes naturally: How the discourses and routines of teachers' practice constrain opportunities for bilingual support in UK primary schools. *Language and Education*, 15(4): 250–68.
Braine, G. (ed.) 1999. *Non-Native Educators in English Language Teaching*. Mahwah, NJ: Erlbaum.
Bremer, K., C. Roberts, M.-T. Vasseur, M. Simonet and P. Broeder. 1996. *Achieving Understanding: Discourse in intercultural encounters*. London: Longman.
British Council. 1985. *Teaching and learning in focus: Edited lessons* (4 Vols). London: British Council.
Brouwer, C. E. and J. Wagner 2004. Developmental issues in second language conversation. *Journal of Applied Linguistics*, 1(1): 29–47.
Brouwer, C. E., G. Rasmussen and J. Wagner. 2004. Embedded corrections in second language talk. In R. Gardner and J. Wagner (eds) *Second Language Conversations*. London, New York: Continuum, pp. 75–92.
Brumfit, C. 1984. *Communicative Methodology in Language Teaching*. Cambridge: Cambridge University Press.

Brumfit, C. and K. Johnson (eds). 1979. *The Communicative Approach to Language Teaching*. Oxford: Oxford University Press.
Burton, J. 2005. The importance of teachers' writing on TESOL. *TESL-EJ Teaching English as a Second or Foreign Language*. Retrieved 27 May 2006, from: http://tesl-ej.org/ej34/a2.pdf.
Byram, M. 1997. *Teaching and Assessing Intercultural Communicative Competence*. Clevedon: Multilingual Matters.
Camilleri, A. 1994. Talking bilingually, writing monolingually. Paper presented at the Sociolinguistics Symposium, Lancaster University, March 1994.
Carroll, D. 2004. Restarts in novice turn beginnings: Disfluencies or interactional achievements? In R. Gardner and J. Wagner (eds), *Second Language Conversations*. London: Continuum.
Carson, J. G. 1992. Becoming biliterate: First language influences, *Journal of Second Language Writing*, 1(1): 37-60.
Carson J. G. and A. Longhini. 2002. Focusing on learning styles and strategies: A diary study in an immersion setting. *Language Learning*, 52(2): 401-38.
Carswell, L., P. Thomas, M. Petre, B. Price and M. Richards. 2000. Distance learning via the internet: the student experience. *British Journal of Educational Technology*, 31(1): 29-46.
Cato, A. C. 1984. An investigation into Methodist mission education in Fiji. MA thesis, University of London, 1939. Cited in P. A. Geraghty, Language policy in Fiji and Rotuma, *Duivosavosa: Fiji languages, their use and their future, Fiji Museum Bulletin*, 8: 32-73.
Cazden, C., H. Cancino, E. Rosansky and J. Schumann. 1975. *Second Language Acquisition Sequences in Children, Adolescents, and Adults. Final Report*. Washington, DC: National Institute of Education.
Central Advisory Council for England. 1967. *Children and their Primary Schools (The Plowden Report)*. London: HMSO.
Chi, J. C. 2001. The relationship between learning style preferences and listening strategy use for advanced ESL learners. Unpublished Master's thesis, Department of English as a Second Language, University of Minnesota.
Chrisp, S. 1998. Government services and the revitalisation of the Māori language; Policies and practices. *Te Reo*, 41: 106-15.
Cicourel, A.V. 1973. *Cognitive sociology*. London: Macmillan.
Cicourel, A. V. 1983. Hearing is not believing: Language and the structure of belief in medical communication. In S. Fisher and A. D. Todd (eds), *The Social Organization of Doctor-Patient Communication*. Washington, DC: Center for Applied Linguistics, pp. 221-39.
Cicourel, A. V. 1992. The interpenetration of communicative contexts: Examples from medical encounters. In A. Duranti and C. Goodwin (eds), *Rethinking Context: Language as an interactive phenomenon*. New York: Cambridge University Press, pp. 293-310.
Cicourel, A. V. 1995. Medical speech events as resources for inferring differences in expert-novice diagnostic reasoning. In U. M. Quasthoff (ed.), *Aspects of Oral Communication*. Berlin, New York: W. de Gruyter, pp. 364-87.
Cicourel, A. V. 2000. Expert. *Journal of Linguistic Anthropology*, 9(1-2), 72-5.
Cole, M. 1985. The zone of proximal development: Where culture and cognition create each other. In J. V. Wertsch (ed.), *Culture, Communication and Cognition: Vygotskyan perspectives*. New York: Cambridge University Press.
Cole, M. 1996. *Cultural Psychology: A once and future discipline*. Cambridge, MA: Berknap Press.
Colucciello, M. L. 1999. Relationships between critical thinking dispositions and learning styles. *Journal of Professional Nursing*, 15(5): 294-301.

Connor, U. 1996. *Contrastive Rhetoric: Cross-cultural aspects of second language writing.* Cambridge: Cambridge University Press.
Conteh, J. 2003. *Succeeding in Diversity: Culture, language and learning in primary classrooms.* Stoke-on-Trent: Trentham Books.
Conteh, J. 2006. Widening the inclusion agenda: Policy, practice and language diversity in the primary curriculum. In R. Webb (ed.), *Changing Teaching and Learning in the Primary School.* Buckingham: Open University Press.
Conteh, J. 2007a. Opening doors to success in multilingual classrooms: Bilingualism, codeswitching and the professional identities of 'ethnic minority' primary teachers. *Language and Education,* 21(3) (forthcoming).
Conteh, J. 2007b. Bilingualism in mainstream primary classrooms. In Z. Hua, P. Seedhouse, L. Wei and V. Cook (eds), *Language Learning and Teaching as Social Interaction.* Basingstoke: Palgrave Macmillan.
Cook, V. (ed.) 2002a. *Portraits of the L2 User.* Clevedon: Multilingual Matters.
Cook, V. 2002b. Background to the L2 User. In V. Cook (ed.), *Portraits of the L2 User,* Clevedon: Multilingual Matters, pp. 1–28.
Cordero-Guzmán, H. R., R. C. Smith and R. Grosfoguel (eds). 2001. *Migration, Transnationalization, and Race in a Changing New York.* Philadelphia: Temple University Press.
Corson, D. 1999. *Language Policy in Schools: A resource for teachers and administrators.* Mahwah, NJ: Lawrence Erlbaum.
Coughlan, P. and P. A. Duff. 1994. Same task, different activities: Analysis of a SLA task from an activity theory perspective. In J. Lantolf and G. Appel (eds), *Vygotskian Approaches to Second Language Research.* Norwood, NJ: Ablex, pp. 173–94.
Coupland, J. (ed.). 2000. *Small Talk.* London: Longman.
Coupland, N., J. M. Wiemann and H. Giles. 1991. Talk as 'problem' and communication as 'miscommunication': An integrative analysis. In N. Coupland, H. Giles and J. M. Wiemann (eds), *'Miscommunication' and Problematic Talk.* London: Sage, pp. 1–17.
Cousins, S. 1989. Culture and selfhood in Japan and the U.S. *Journal of Personality and Social Psychology,* 56: 124–31.
Creese, A. 2005. *Teacher Collaboration and Talk in Multilingual Classrooms.* Clevedon: Multilingual Matters.
Crookes, G. and R. W. Schmidt. 1991. Motivation: Reopening the research agenda. *Language Learning,* 41: 469–512.
Crowley, T. 1998. How many languages will survive in the Pacific? *Te Reo,* 41: 116–25.
Crystal, D. 1997. *The Cambridge Encyclopedia of Language,* 2nd edn. Cambridge: Cambridge University Press.
Crystal, D. 2003. *English as a Global Language,* 2nd edn. Cambridge: Cambridge University Press.
Cummins, J. 1984. *Bilingualism and Special Education: Issues in assessment and pedagogy.* Clevedon: Multilingual Matters.
Cummins, J. 2001. *Negotiating Identities: Education for empowerment in a diverse society,* 2nd edn. Ontario, CA: California Association for Bilingual Education.
Cummins, J. A. 2005. Proposal for action: Strategies for recognizing heritage language competence as a learning resource within the mainstream classroom. *The Modern Language Journal,* 89(4): 585–92.
Daily Post. 2002. Letters to the editor. 16 July 2002.
Davidson, J. 1984. Subsequent versions of invitations, offers, requests, and proposals dealing with potential or actual rejection. In J. Atkinson and J. Heritage (eds), *Structures of Social Action.* Cambridge: Cambridge University Press, pp. 102–28.

Davies, A. 2003. *The Native Speaker: Myth and reality*, 2nd edn. Clevedon: Multilingual Matters.
De Vita, G. 2001. Learning styles, culture and inclusive instruction in the multicultural classroom: A business and management perspective. *Innovations in Education and Teaching International*, 38(2): 165– 74.
Dempsey, R. and J.C. Lema. 1998. *La comunidad colombiana en Londres*. Peterborough, UK: Open Channels.
Department for Education and Skills (DfES). 2002. *Languages for All: Languages for Life*. Accessed 20 June 2006 at: http://www.standards.dfes.gov.uk/primary/publications/languages/framework/introduction/languages_strategy/ (consulted).
Department for Education and Skills (DfES). 2006. *The Key Stage 2 Framework for Languages*. Accessed 20 June 2006 at: http://www.standards.dfes.gov.uk/primary/features/languages/
Department of Education and Science (DES). 1975. *A Language for Life* (*The Bullock Report*). London: HMSO.
Department of Education and Science (DES.) 1985. *Education for All – The Report of the Committee of Inquiry into the Education of Children from Ethnic Minority Groups* (*The Swann Report*). London: HMSO.
Dewaele, J. -M. 2004a. Blistering barnacles! What language do multilinguals swear in?! *Estudios de Sociolingüística*, 5(1): 83–106.
Dewaele, J. -M. 2004b. The emotional force of swearwords and taboo words in the speech of multilinguals. *Journal of Multilingual and Multicultural Development*, 25(2/3): 204–22.
Dewaele, J. -M. 2004c. The acquisition of sociolinguistic competence in French as a foreign language: An overview. *Journal of French Language Studies*, 14: 301–19.
Dewaele, J. -M. 2004d. Perceived language dominance and language preference for emotional speech: The implications for attrition research. In M. S. Schmid, B. Köpke, M. Kejser and L. Weilemar (eds), *First Language Attrition: Interdisciplinary perspectives on methodological issues*. Amsterdam, Philadelphia: John Benjamins, pp. 81–104.
Dewaele, J. -M. 2005a. The effect of type of acquisition context on perception and self-reported use of swearwords in the L2, L3, L4 and L5. In A. Housen and M. Pierrard (eds), *Investigations in Instructed Second Language Acquisition*. Berlin: Mouton De Gruyter, pp. 531–59.
Dewaele, J. -M. 2005b. Investigating the psychological and the emotional dimensions in instructed language learning: Obstacles and possibilities, *The Modern Language Journal*, 89 (3): 367–380.
Dewaele, J. -M. 2006. Expressing anger in multiple languages, in A. Pavlenko (ed.), *Bilingual Minds: Emotional experience, expression, and representation*, Clevedon: Multilingual Matters, pp. 118–151.
Dewaele, J. -M. 2007. Diachronic and/or synchronic variation? The acquisition of sociolinguistic competence in L2 French. In D. Ayoun (ed.), *Handbook of French Applied Linguistics*. Amsterdam: Benjamins, pp. 208–36.
Dewaele, J. -M. Forthcoming. Interindividual variation in self-perceived oral proficiency of English L2 users. In E. Alcón Soler and M. P. Safont Jordà (eds), *The Intercultural Speaker: Using and acquiring English in the foreign language classroom*. Berlin: Springer Verlag.
Dewaele, J. -M. and A. Pavlenko. 2001. Web questionnaire. *Bilingualism and Emotions*. University of London .
Dewaele, J. -M., D. Petrides and A. Furnham. 2006. The effect of trait emotional intelligence and sociobiographical variables on communicative anxiety among adult polyglots. Unpublished manuscript, University of London.

Dörnyei, Z. 2003. Attitudes, orientations and motivation in language learning: Advances in theory, research and applications. *Language Learning*, 53: 3–32.
Dörnyei, Z. 2005. *The Psychology of the Language Learner*. Mahwah, NJ, Lawrence Erlbaum Associates.
Doughty, C. and M. Long (eds). 2003. *The Handbook of Second Language Acquisition*. Oxford: Blackwell.
Doughty, C. and J. Williams, J. (eds). 1998. *Focus on Form in Classroom Second Language Acquisition*. Cambridge: Cambridge University Press.
Drew, P. 1984. Speakers' rereportings in invitation sequences. In J. Atkinson and J. Heritage (eds), *Structures of Social Action*. Cambridge, Cambridge University Press, pp. 129–51.
Drew, P. 1997. 'Open' class repair initiators in response to sequential sources of troubles in conversation. *Journal of Pragmatics*, 28, 69–101.
Drew, P. and J. Heritage. 1992. Analyzing talk at work: An introduction. In P. Drew and J. Heritage (eds), *Talk at Work: Interaction in institutional settings*. Cambridge: Cambridge University Press, pp. 3–65.
Dreyer, C. 1998. Teacher-student style wars in South Africa: The silent battle. *System*, 26: 115–26.
Driagina, V., and A. Pavlenko. 2007. Identity repertoires in narratives of advanced American learners of Russian. In Z. Hua, P. Seedhouse, L. Wei and V. Cook (eds), *Language Learning and Teaching as Social Interaction*. Basingstoke: Palgrave Macmillan.
Dunn, W., and J. Lantolf. 1998. Vygotsky's zone of proximal development and Krashen's i + 1: Incommensurable constructs; incommensurable theories. *Language Learning*, 48, 411–42.
Duranti, A., and C. Goodwin (eds). 1992. *Rethinking Context: Language as an interactive phenomenon*. New York: Cambridge University Press.
Echevarria, J., M. Vogt and D. Short. 2004. *Making Content Comprehensible for English Learners: The SIOP model*, 2nd edn. Boston, MA: Pearson.
Edwards D. and N. Mercer. 1987. *Common Knowledge: The development of understanding in the classroom*. London: Methuen.
Egbert, M. 2004. Other-initiated repair and membership categorization – some conversational events that trigger linguistic and regional membership categorization. *Journal of Pragmatics*, 36: 1467–98.
Egbert, M., L. Niebecker and S. Rezzara. 2004. Inside first and second language speakers' trouble in understanding. In R. Gardner and J. Wagner (eds), *Second Language Conversations*. London: Continuum, pp. 178–200.
Ehrman M. E. and R. L. Oxford. 1990. Adult language learning styles and strategies in an intensive training setting. *Modern Language Journal*, 74(3): 311–27.
Eliason, P. 1995. Difficulties with cross-cultural learning-styles assessment. In J. M. Reid (ed.), *Learning Styles in the ESL/EFL Classroom*. Boston, MA: Heinle and Heinle, pp. 18–33.
Elley W. B. and F. Mangubhai. 1983. The impact of reading on second language learning, *Reading Research Quarterly*, 19: 53–67.
Ellis, N. 1999. Cognitive approaches to SLA. *Annual Review of Applied Linguistics*, 19: 22–42.
Ellis, R. 1994. *The Study of Second Language Acquisition*. Oxford: Oxford University Press.
Ellis, R. 2003. *Task-Based Language Learning and Teaching*. Oxford: Oxford University Press.
Ellis, R. 2007. *The Study of Second Language Acquisition*, 2nd edn. Oxford: Oxford University Press.
Ellis, R. and G. Barkhuizen. 2005. *Analysing Learner Language*. Oxford: Oxford University Press.

Ellis, R., H. Basturkmen and S. Loewen. 2001. Learner uptake in communicative ESL lessons. *Language Learning*, 51: 281–318.
Ellis, R., S. Loewen and H. Basturkmen. 2006. Disentangling focus on form: A response to Sheen and O'Neill. *Applied Linguistics*, 27(1): 135–41.
Ely, C. and Pease-Alvarez L. 1996. Learning styles and strategies in ESOL, *TESOL Journal*, 1(5).
Federico, P. A. 2000. Learning styles and student attitudes towards various aspects of network-based instruction. *Computers in Human Behaviour*, 16(4): 359–79.
Field, M. 2006. Fiji: The Indian factor, why more and more are leaving the islands? *Islands Business*. Accessed 16 June 2006 at: http://www.islandsbusiness.com/archives/islands_business/index_dynamic/
Fiji Bureau of Statistics. 1996. *Fiji Census of Population and Housing*. Suva: Parliamentary Paper 43.
Fiji Bureau of Statistics. 2006. Accessed 6 April 2006 at: http://www.statsfiji.gov.fj/
Fiji Human Rights Commission. 2006. *Report on Government's Affirmative Action Programmes: 2020 plan for indigenous Fijians and Rotumans and the blueprint*. Suva: Fiji Human Rights Commission.
Fiji Times. 2002. Letters to the editor. 6, 13 and 26 July, 1, 2, 5 and 7 August 2002.
Firth, A. 1996. The discursive accomplishment of 'normality': On 'lingua franca' English and Conversation Analysis. *Journal of Pragmatics*, 26: 237–59.
Firth, A. and J. Wagner 1997. On discourse, communication, and (some) fundamental concepts in SLA research. *The Modern Language Journal*, 81(3): 285–300.
Firth, A. and J. Wagner. 1998. SLA property: No trespassing!. *Modern Language Journal*, 82(1): 91–4.
Firth, J. R. 1957. *Papers in Linguistics: 1934–1951*. London: Oxford University Press.
Fishman, J. A. 1972. The relationship between micro- and macro-linguistics in the study of who speaks what language to whom and when. In J. B. Pride and J. Holmes (eds), *Sociolinguistics*. London: Penguin Books, pp. 15–32.
Fitzpatrick, F. 1987. *The Open Door: The Bradford bilingual project*. Clevedon Multilingual Matters.
Flower, L. S., and J. R. Hayes. 1981. A cognitive process theory of writing. *College Composition and Communication*, 32: 365–87.
Ford, C. and S. Thompson. 1996. Interactional units in conversation: Syntactic, intonational, and pragmatic resources for the management of turns. In E. Ochs, E. Schegloff and S. Thompson (eds), *Interaction and Grammar*. Cambridge: Cambridge University Press, pp. 134–84.
Fouron, G. E. and N. Glick Schiller. 2001. The generation of identity: Redefining the second generation within a transnational social field. In H. R. Cordero-Guzmán, R. C. Smith and R. Grosfoguel (eds), *Migration, Transnationalization, and Race in a Changing New York*. Philadelphia: Temple University Press, pp. 58–86.
Fraenkal, J. 2003. Minority rights in Fiji and the Solomon Islands. Suva: Commission on Human Rights, Working group on minorities, Ninth session, 12–16 May, 2003.
Frawley, W. 1997. *Vygotsky and Cognitive Science: Language and the unification of the social and computational mind*. Cambridge, MA: Harvard University Press.
Gajo, L. 2001. *Immersion, bilinguisme et interaction en classe*. Paris: Didier Editions.
Gallin, R. 1999. Language learning styles and their effect on the reading comprehension stategies of ESL students. Unpublished Double Plan B Paper. Department of English as a Second Language, University of Minnesota.
Galloway, V. and Labarca, A. 1991. From student to learner: Style process and strategy. In D. W. Birckbichler (ed.), *New Perspectives and New Directions in Foreign Language Education*. Lincolnwood, IL. National Textbook Co., pp. 111– 58.

Gardner, R. 2004. On delaying the answer: Question sequences extended after the question. In R. Gardner and J. Wagner (eds), *Second Language Conversations*. London: Continuum, pp. 246–66.
Gardner, R. 2007. 'Broken starts': Bricolage in turn starts in L2 talk. In Z. Hua, P. Seedhouse, L. Wei and V. Cook (eds), *Language Learning and Teaching as Social Interaction*. Basingstoke: Palgrave Macmillan.
Gardner, R. and J. Wagner 2004. *Second Language Conversations*. London, Continuum.
Garfinkel, H. 1967. *Studies in Ethnomethodology*. Englewood Cliffs, NJ: Prentice Hall.
Gass, S. 1988. Integrating research areas: A framework for second language studies. *Applied Linguistics*, 9(2): 198–217.
Gass, S. 1997. *Input, Interaction, and the Second Language Learner*. Mahwah, NJ: Erlbaum.
Gass, S. 1998. Apples and oranges: Or why apples are not oranges and don't need to be. A response to Firth and Wagner. *Modern Language Journal*, 82(1): 83–90.
Gass, S. M. 2003. Input and interaction. In C. J. Doughty and M. H. Long (eds), *Handbook of Second Language Acquisition*. Oxford: Blackwell, pp. 224–55.
Gass, S. and L. Selinker. 2001. *Second Language Acquisition: An introductory course*, 2nd edn. Mahwah, NJ: Lawrence Erlbaum.
Gee, J. P. 1996. *Social Linguistics and Literacies: Ideologies in discourses*, 2nd edn. London: Taylor & Francis.
Gelman, R., C. Massey and M. Macmanus. 1991. Characterizing supporting environments for cognitive development: Lessons from children in a museum. In L. Resnick, J. Levine and S. Teasley (eds), *Perspectives on Socially Shared Cognition*. Washington, DC: American Psychological Association, pp. 226–56.
Gibbons, P. 1998. Classroom talk and the learning of new registers in a second language, *Language and Education*, 12(2): 99–118.
Giddens, A. 1991. *Modernity and Self-Identity: Self and society in the late modern age*. Cambridge: Polity Press.
Gilbert J. E. and C. Y. Han. 1999. Adapting instruction in search of a 'significant difference'. *Journal of Network and Computer Applications*, 22(3): 149–60.
Gillion, K. L. 1962. *Fiji's Indian Migrants: A history of the end of indenture in 1920*. Melbourne: Oxford University Press.
Goffman, E. 1974. *Frame Analysis*. New York: Harper & Row.
Goffman, E. 1979. Footing. *Semiotica*, 25(1), 1–29.
Golato, A. 2002. German compliment responses. *Journal of Pragmatics*, 34: 547–71.
Golato, A. 2003. Studying compliment responses: A comparison of DCTs and recordings of naturally occurring talk. *Applied Linguistics*, 24(1): 90–121.
Golato, A. 2005. *Compliments and Compliment Responses: Grammatical structure and sequential organization*. Amsterdam, Philadelphia, John Benjamins.
Goldstein, T. 1996. *Two Languages at Work: Bilingual life on the production floor*. New York: Mouton de Gruyter.
Gómez-Peña, G. 1996. *The New World Border: Prophecies, poems & loqueras for the end of the century*. San Francisco: City Lights.
Goodwin, C. 1981. Notes on the organization of engagement. *Conversational Organization*. New York: Academic Press, ch 3.
Goodwin, C. 2000. Action and embodiment within situated human interaction. *Journal of Pragmatics*, 32: 1489–522.
Goodwin, C., and A. Duranti. 1992. Rethinking context: An introduction. In A. Duranti and C. Goodwin (eds), *Rethinking Context: Language as an interactive phenomenon*. New York: Cambridge University Press, pp. 1–42.

Goodwin, M. H. 1990. *He-said-she-said: Talk as social organization among Black children.* Bloomington, IN: Indiana University Press.
Goodwin, M. and C. Goodwin. 1986. Gesture and coparticipation in the activity of searching for a word. *Semiotica*, 62(1–2): 51–75.
Graddol, D. 2006. *English Next.* London: British Council.
Grice, P. 1975. Logic and conversation. In P. Cole and J. Morgan (eds), *Syntax and Semantics, Vol. 3: Speech Acts.* New York: Academic Press, pp. 41–58 .
Grosjean, F. 1998. Studying bilinguals: Methodological and conceptual issues. *Bilingualism: Language and Cognition*, 1: 131–49.
Gumperz, J. J. 1982. *Discourse Strategies.* Cambridge: Cambridge University Press.
Gumperz, J. J. 1992. Contextualization and understanding. In A. Duranti and C. Goodwin (eds), *Rethinking Context: Language as an interactive phenomenon.* New York: Cambridge University Press, pp. 230–52.
Gumperz, J. J. 2000. Inference. *Journal of Linguistic Anthropology*, 9(1–2), 131–3.
Gumperz, J. J., T. C. Jupp and C. Roberts. 1979. *Crosstalk: A study of cross-cultural communication* [Film]. London: BBC Enterprises.
Hall, J. K. 1993. The role of oral practices in the accomplishment of our everyday lives: The sociocultural dimension of interaction with implications for the learning of another language. *Applied Linguistics*, 14(2): 145–66.
Hall, J. K. 1995a. (Re)creating our worlds with words: A sociohistorical perspective of face-to-face interaction. *Applied Linguistics*, 16(2): 206–32.
Hall, J. K. 1995b. 'Aw, man, where you goin'': Classroom interaction and the development of L2 interactional competence. *Issues in Applied Linguistics*, 6(2): 37–62.
Hall, J. K. 1997. A consideration of SLA as a theory of practice: A response to Firth and Wagner. *The Modern Language Journal*, 81: 301–6.
Hall, J. K. 1999. A prosaics of interaction: The development of interactional competence in another language. In E. Hinkel (ed.), *Culture in Second Language Teaching and Learning.* New York: Cambridge University Press, pp. 137–51.
Hall, J. K. 2004. Language learning as an interactional event. *The Modern Language Journal*, 88(4): 607–11.
Hall, J. K. and L. S. Verplaetse (eds). 2000. *Second and Foreign Language Learning through Classroom Interaction.* Mahwah, NJ: Lawrence Erlbaum Associates.
Hall, S. 1996. Introduction: Who needs identity? In S. Hall and P. du Gay (eds), *Questions of Cultural Identity.* London: Sage Publications, pp. 1–17.
Hands, W. J. 1987. *Polynesia.* Westminster: Society for the Propagation of the Gospel in Foreign Parts, 1929. Cited in J. Siegel, *Language Contact in a Plantation Environment: A sociolinguistic history of Fiji.* Cambridge: Cambridge University Press.
Hanks, W. F. 1991. Foreword by William F. Hanks. In J. Lave and E. Wenger (eds), *Situated Learning: Legitimate peripheral participation.* New York: Cambridge University Press, pp. 13–24.
Hanks, W. F. 1996a. Exorcism and the description of participant roles. In M. Silverstein and G. Urban (eds), *Natural Histories of Discourse.* Chicago: University of Chicago Press, pp. 160–200.
Hanks, W. F. 1996b. *Language and Communicative Practices.* Boulder, CO: Westview.
Harré, R. 2001. Metaphysics and narrative: Singularities and multiplicities of self. In J. Brockmeier and D. A. Carbaugh (eds), *Narrative and Identity: Studies in autobiography, self and culture.* Amsterdam and Philadelphia: Benjamins, pp. 59–74.
Harris, C. L., J. B. Gleason and A. Ayçiçegi. 2006. Why is a first language more emotional? Psychophysiological evidence from bilingual speakers. In A. Pavlenko (ed.),

Bilingual Minds: Emotional experience, expression, and representation. Clevedon: Multilingual Matters, pp. 257–83.

Harshbarger, B. T. Ross, S. Tafoya and J. Via. 1986. *Dealing with Multiple Learning Styles in the ESL Classroom*. Boston, MA: Heinle and Heinle.

Harvey, D. 1989. *The Condition of Postmodernity*. Oxford: Blackwell.

Hatch, E. M. (ed.) 1978a. *Second Language Acquisition: A book of readings*. Rowley, MA: Newbury House.

Hatch, E. M. 1978b. Discourse analysis and second language acquisition. *Second Language Acquisition: A book of readings*. Rowley, MA, Newbury House, pp. 402–35.

Hatvia N. and M. Birenbaum. 2000. Who prefers what? Disciplinary differences in learners' preferred approaches to teaching and learning styles. *Research in Higher Education*, 41(2).

Hauser, E. 2005. Coding 'corrective recasts': The maintenance of meaning and more fundamental problems. *Applied Linguistics*, 26: 293–316.

Have, P. ten 1999. *Doing Conversation Analysis: A practical guide*. London: Sage.

Hawkins, M. 2004. *Language Learning and Teacher Education: A sociocultural approach*. Clevedon: Multilingual Matters.

Hayashi, M. 1999. Where grammar and interaction meet: A study of co-participant completion in Japanese conversation. *Human Studies*, 22: 475–99.

He, A. W. and R. Young 1998. Language proficiency interviews: A discourse approach. In R. Young and A. W. He, *Talking and Testing: Discourse approaches to the assessment of of oral proficiency*. Phildelphia: John Benjamins, pp. 1–24.

Heath, S. B. 1983. *Ways with Words: Language, life and work in communities and classrooms*. New York: Cambridge University Press.

Hedge, T. 2000. *Teaching and Learning in the Language Classroom*. Oxford: Oxford University Press.

Heritage, J. 1984. A change-of-state token and aspects of its sequential placement. In J. M. Atkinson and J. Heritage (eds), *Structures of Social Action*. Cambridge: Cambridge University Press, pp. 299–345.

Heritage, J. 1995. Conversation analysis: Methodological aspects. In U.M. Quasthoff (ed.), *Aspects of Oral Communication*. Berlin, New York: Walter de Gruyter, pp. 391–418.

Heritage, J. 1998. Oh-prefaced responses to inquiry. *Language in Society*, 27: 291–334.

Higgins, C. 2003. Ownership of English in the Outer Circle: An alternative to the NS-NNS dichotomy. *TESOL Quarterly*, 37(4): 615–44.

Hinds, J. 1987. Reader versus writer responsibility: A new typology. In U. Connor and R. B. Kaplan (eds), *Writing across Languages: Analysis of L2 text*. Reading, MA: Addison-Wesley, pp. 141–52.

Hinkel, E. 2002. *Second Language Writers' Text: Linguistic and rhetorical features*. Mahwah, NJ: Lawrence Erlbaum.

Hofstede, G. 1986. Cultural differences in teaching and learning. *International Journal of Intercultural Relations*, 10: 301–20.

Hofstede, G. 1997. *Cultures and Organizations: Software of the mind: Intercultural Cooperation and its importance for survival*. New York: McGraw Hill.

Holliday, A. 1999. Small Cultures. *Applied Linguistics*, 20(2): 237–64.

Holmes, J. 2000. Doing collegiality and keeping control at work: Small talk in government departments. In J. Coupland (ed.), *Small Talk*. London: Longman, pp. 32–61.

Hosoda, Y. 2000. Other-repair in Japanese conversations between nonnative and native speakers. *Issues in Applied Linguistics*, 11(1): 39–65.

Hosoda, Y. 2006. Repair and relevance of differential language expertise in second language conversations. *Applied Linguistics*, 27: 25–50.
House, J., G. Kasper and S. Ross. 2003. Misunderstanding talk. In J. House, G. Kasper and S. Ross (eds), *Misunderstanding in Social Life*: Discourse approaches to problematic talk. Harlow: Longman/Pearson Education, pp. 1–21.
Hundeide, K. 1985. The tacit background of childre's judgments. In J. Wertsch (ed.), *Culture, Communication and Cognition: Vygotskian perspectives*. Cambridge, Cambridge University Press.
Huston, N. 1999. *Nord perdu*. Arles: Actes Sud.
Hua, Z. 2007. Presentation of 'self' in application letters. In Z. Hua, P. Seedhouse, L. Wei and V. Cook (eds), *Language Learning and Teaching as Social Interaction*. Basingstoke: Palgrave Macmillan.
Hutchby, I. and R. Wooffitt. 1998. *Conversation Analysis*. Cambridge: Polity Press.
Hyland, K. 2003. Genre-based pedagogies: A social response to process. *Journal of Second Language Writing*, 12(1): 17–29.
Hymes, D. 1972. *Towards Communicative Competence*. Philadelphia: University of Pennsylvania Press.
Hymes, D. 1974a. *Foundations in Sociolinguistics: An ethnographic approach*. Philadelphia: University of Pennsylvania Press.
Hymes, D. 1974b. Ways of speaking. In R. Bauman and J. Sherzer (eds), *Explorations in the Ethnography of Speaking*. New York: Cambridge University Press, pp. 433–51.
Iles, Z. 1996. Collaborative repair in EFL classroom talk. *York Papers in Linguistics*, 17: 23–51.
Jacoby, S. and T. MacNamara 1999. Locating competence. *English for Specific Purposes*, 18(3): 213–41.
Jefferson, G. 1983. Two explorations of the organization of overlapping talk in conversation: Notes on some orderliness in overlap onset. *Tilburg Papers in Language and Literature*, No. 28. Tilburg, NL: Tilburg University.
Jefferson, G. 1984a. Transcription notation. In J. M. Atkinson and J. Heritage (eds), *Structures of Social Action*. Cambridge: Cambridge University Press, pp. ix–xvi.
Jefferson, G. 1984b. On stepwise transition from talk about a trouble to inappropriately next-positioned matters. In J. M. Atkinson and J. Heritage (eds), *Structures of Social Action*. Cambridge, Cambridge University Press, pp. 191–222.
Jefferson, G. 1987. On exposed and embedded correction in conversation. In G. Button and J. R. E. Lee (eds), *Talk and Social Organisation*. Clevedon: Multilingual Matters, pp. 86–100.
Jefferson, G. 1989. Preliminary notes on a possible metric which provides for a 'standard maximum' silence of approximately one second in conversation. In D. Roger and P. Bull. (eds), *Conversation: An interdisciplinary perspective*. Clevedon: Multilingual Matters, pp. 166–96.
Jeon, E. H. and T. Kaya. 2006. Effects of L2 instruction on interlanguage pragmatic development. In J. M. Norris and L. Ortega (eds), *Synthesizing Research on Language Learning and Teaching*. Amsterdam, Philadelphia: Benjamins, pp. 165–211.
Johnson, K. 1995. *Understanding Communication in Second Language Classrooms*. Cambridge: Cambridge University Press.
Johnson, K. 2006. The sociocultural turn and its challenges for second language teacher education. *TESOL Quarterly*, 40: 235–57.
Jung, K. 2004. L2 vocabulary development through conversation: A conversation analysis. *Second Language Studies*, 23(1): 27–55.
Kagan, O. and F. Miller. 1996. *V puti: Russian grammar in context*. Upper Saddle River, NJ: Prentice Hall.

Kanagy, R. 1999. Interactional routines as a mechanism for L2 acquisition and socialization in an immersion context. *Journal of Pragmatics*, 31: 1467–92.
Kaplan, R. B. 1966. Cultural though patterns in intercultural education. *Language Learning*, 16: 1–20.
Kaplan, R. B. 1988. Contrastive rhetoric and second language learning: Notes toward a theory of contrastive rhetoric In A. C. Purves (ed.), *Writing across Language and Cultures*. Newbury Park, CA: Sage, pp. 275–304.
Kasper, G. 1997. 'A' stands for acquisition: A response to Firth and Wagner. *The Modern Language Journal*, 81: 307–12.
Kasper, G. 2004. Participant orientations in conversation-for-learning. *Modern Language Journal*, 88, 4: 551–67.
Kasper, G. 2005. Beyond repair: Conversation analysis as an approach to SLA. *Association Internationale de Linguistique Appliquée*. Madison, Wisconsin.
Kasper, G. 2006a. Discussant's remarks. Panel on Learning Talk. *ICCA*. Helsinki, Finland.
Kasper, G. 2006b. When once is not enough: Politeness of multiple requests in oral proficiency interviews. *Multilingua*, 25: 323–49.
Kasper, G., and Y. Kim. 2007. Handling sequentially inapposite responses. In Z. Hua, P. Seedhouse, L. Wei and V. Cook (eds), *Language Learning and Teaching as Social Interaction*. Basingstoke: Palgrave Macmillan.
Kasper, G. and K. Rose. 2001. Pragmatics in language teaching. In K. Rose and G. Kasper (eds), *Pragmatics in Language Teaching*. Cambridge: Cambridge University Press, pp. 1–10.
Kasper, G. and K. R. Rose. 2002. Pragmatic development in a second language. *Language Learning*, 52, supplement 1: 1–352.
Kasper, G., and Ross, S. In press. Multiple questions in language proficiency interviews.
Keefe, J. W. 1979. Learning style: An overview. In J. W. Keefe, (ed.), *Student Learning Styles: Diagnosing and prescribing programs*. Reston, VA: National Association of Secondary School Principals, pp. 1–17.
Keenan, E. 2007. Now the good new, *Time*, 5 February: 44–5
Kendon, A. 1980. Gesticulation and speech: Two aspects of the process of utterance. In M. R. Key (ed.), *The Relationship of Verbal and Nonverbal Communication*. The Hague: Mouton, pp. 207–27.
Kendon, A. 1990. *Conducting Interaction: Patterns of behavior in focused encounters*. Cambridge, New York: Cambridge University Press.
Kidwell, M. 2000. Common ground in cross-cultural communication: Sequential and institutional contexts in front desk service encounters. *Issues in Applied Linguistics*, 11 (1): 17–37.
Kinginger, C. 2004. Bilingualism and emotion in the autobiographical works of Nancy Huston. *Journal of Multilingual and Multicultural Development*, 25(2/3): 159–78.
Kinginger, C. and J. A. Belz. 2005. Socio-cultural perspectives on pragmatic development in foreign language learning: Microgenetic case studies from telecollaboration and residence abroad. *Intercultural Pragmatics*, 2(4): 369–421.
Kinginger, C. and K. Farrell Whitworth. 2004. Assessing development of meta-pragmatic awareness in study abroad. *Frontiers: The Interdisciplinary Journal of Study Abroad*, 10: 19–42.
Koshik, I. 2002. Designedly incomplete utterances: A pedagogical practice for eliciting knowledge displays in error correction sequences. *Research on Language and Social Interaction*, 35(3): 277–309.
Krapels, A. R. 1990. An overview of second language writing process research. In B. Kroll (ed.), *Second Language Writing: Research insights for the classroom*. Cambridge: Cambridge University Press, pp. 37–57.

Krashen, S. 1981. *Second Language Acquisition and Second Language Learning*. Oxford: Pergamon.
Krashen, S. 1985. *The Input Hypothesis: Issues and implications*. London: Longman.
Kress, G., C. Jewitt, J. Ogborn and C. Tsatsarelis (eds). 2001. *Multimodal Teaching and Learning: The rhetorics of the science classroom*. London, New York: Continuum.
Kubota, R. 2001. Discursive constructions of the images of U.S. classrooms. *TESOL Quarterly*, 35(1): 24–35.
Kubota, R. 2003. New approaches to gender, class, and race in second language writing. *Journal of Second Language Writing*, 12(1): 31–47.
Kubota, R. 2004. Critical multiculturalism and second language education. In B. Norton and K. Toohey (eds), *Critical Pedagogies and Language Learning*. Cambridge: Cambridge University Press, pp. 30–52.
Kurhila, S. 2001. Correction in talk between native and non-native speaker. *Journal of Pragmatics*, 33: 1083–110.
Kurhila, S. 2004. Clients or language learners – being a second language speaker. In R. Gardner and J. Wagner (eds), *Second Language Conversations*. London, New York: Continuum, pp. 58–74.
Kurhila, S. 2005. Different orientations to grammatical correctness. In K. Richards and P. Seedhouse (eds), *Applying Conversation Analysis*. Basingstoke: Palgrave Macmillan, pp. 143–58.
Lameta, E. 1997. *Cook Islands Languages Policy 1997, a report*. Rarotonga: Cook Islands Ministry of Education.
Langman, J. 2003. The effects of ESL endorsed instructors: Reducing middle school students to incidental language learners. *Prospect*, 18: 14–26.
Langman, J., H. Hansen-Thomas and R. Bayley. 2005. Bilingual negotiations in the science classroom. In J. Cohen, K. McAlister, K. Rolstad and J. MacSwan (eds), *ISB4: Proceedings of the 4th International Symposium on Bilinguals*. Somerville, MA: Cascadilla Press, pp. 1287–96.
Langman, J., and R. Bayley. 2007. Untutored acquisition in content classrooms. In Z. Hua, P. Seedhouse, L. Wei and V. Cook (eds), *Language Learning and Teaching as Social Interaction*. Basingstoke: Palgrave Macmillan.
Lantolf, J. and A. Pavlenko. 1995. Sociocultural theory and second language acquisition. *Annual Review of Applied Linguistics*, 15: 108–24.
Lantolf, J. and S. Thorne. 2006. *Sociocultural Theory and the Genesis of Second Language Development*. Oxford: Oxford University Press.
Lantolf, J. P. (ed.). 2000. *Sociocultural Theory and Second Language Learning*. Oxford: Oxford University Press.
Lave, J. 1993. The practice of learning. In S. Chaiklin and J. Lave (eds), *Understanding Practice: Perspectives on activity and context*. New York: Cambridge University Press, pp. 3–32.
Lave, J. and E. Wenger. 1991. *Situated Learning: Legitimate peripheral participation*. Cambridge: Cambridge University Press.
Lazaraton, A. 2002. *A Qualitative Approach to the Validation of Oral Language Tests*. Cambridge, Cambridge University Local Examinations Syndicate.
Leech, G. 1983. *Principles of Pragmatics*. London: Longman.
Lerner, G. H. 1994. Responsive list construction: A conversational resource for accomplishing multifaceted social action. *Journal of of Language and Social Psychology*, 20: 441–58.
Lerner, G. 1996. On the 'semi-permeable' character of grammatical units in conversation: Conditional entry into the turn space of another speaker. In E. Ochs, E. Scheggloff and S. Thompson (eds), *Interaction and Grammar*. Cambridge: Cambridge University Press.

Lerner, G. 1999. The collaborative construction of delicate formulations: Negotiating the authorship/ownership of unkind words: Paper delivered at the 85th Annual Meeting of the National Communication Association, Chicago, Ilinois.
Leung, C., R. Harris, and B. Rampton. 1997. The idealised native speaker, reified ethnicities, and classroom realities. *TESOL Quarterly*, 31(3): 543–60.
Levontina, I. Milyi, dorogoi, lubimyi ... [Sweet, dear, beloved ...]. 2005. In Levontina, I. and A. Shmelyov (eds), *Kluchevye Idei Russkoi Yazykovoi Kartiny Mira* [The Key Ideas in the Russian Linguistic World View]. Moscow: Yazyki Slavyanskoi Kul'tury, pp. 238–58.
Lewis N. J. and P. Orton. 2000. The five attributes of innovative e-learning. *Training and Development*, 54(6): 47–56.
Liddicoat, A. and C. Crozet. 2001. Acquiring French interactional norms through instruction. In K. Rose and G. Kasper (eds), *Pragmatics in Language Teaching*. Cambridge: Cambridge University Press, pp. 125–44.
Lightbown, P. 1998. The importance of timing in focus on form. In C. Doughty and J. Williams (eds) 1998. *Focus on Form in Classroom Second Language Acquisition*. Cambridge: Cambridge University Press, pp. 177–96.
Lightbown, P. and N. Spada. 2006. *How Languages are Learned*, 3rd edn. Oxford: Oxford University Press.
Linares, A. Z. 1999. Learning styles of students and faculty in selected health care professions. *Journal of Nursing Education*, 38(9): 407–14.
Linell, P., J. Hofvendahl and C. Lindholm. 2003. Multi-unit questions in institutional interactions: Sequential organization and communicative functions. *Text*, 23: 539–71.
Lippi-Green, R. 1997. *English With an Accent: Language, ideology and discrimination in the United States*. London: Routledge.
Loewen, S. 2002. The occurrence and effectiveness of incidental focus on form in meaning-focussed ESL lessons. Unpublished doctoral thesis, University of Auckland, New Zealand.
Long, M. H. 1981. Input, interaction and second-language acquisition. In H. Winitz (ed.), *Native Language and Foreign Language Acquisition. Annals of the New York Academy of Sciences*, 379: 259–78.
Long, M. H. 1991. Focus on form: A design feature in language teaching methodology, In D. de Bot, R. Ginsberg and C. Kramsch (eds), *Foreign Language Research in Cross-Cultural Perspective*. Amsterdam: John Benjamins, pp. 179–92.
Long, M. H. 1996. The role of linguistic environment in second language acquisition. In W. Ritchie and T. Bhatia (eds), *Handbook of Second Language Acquisition*. London: Academic Press, pp. 413–68.
Long, M. H. 1997. Construct validity in SLA research: A response to Firth and Wagner. *The Modern Language Journal*, 81: 318–23.
Long, M. H., and C. J. Doughty. 2003. SLA and cognitive science. In C. J. Doughty and M. H. Long (eds), *The Handbook of Second Language Acquisition*. Malden, MA, and Oxford: Blackwell, pp. 866–70.
Long, M., S. Inagaki and L. Ortega. 1998. The role of implicit negative feedback in SLA: Models and recasts in Japanese and Spanish. *The Modern Language Journal*, 82(3): 357–71.
Luke, A. 1998. Critical discourse analysis. In L. Saha (ed.), *International Encyclopedia of the Sociology of Education*. New York: Elsevier Science, pp. 50–7.
Lyster, R. 1994. The effect of functional-analytic teaching on aspects of French immersion students sociolinguistic competence. *Applied Linguistics*, 15: 263–87.

Macbeth, D. 2004. The relevance of repair for classroom correction. *Language in Society*, 33(5), 703–36.
MacIntyre, P. D. and R. C. Gardner. 1994. The subtle effects of language anxiety on cognitive processing in the second language. *Language Learning*, 44: 283–305.
MacWhinney, B. 1991. *The CHILDES Project*. Hillsdale, NJ: Lawrence Erlbaum.
Malinowski, B. 1923. The problem of meaning in primitive languages. In C. K. Ogden, I. A. Richards, B. Malinowski, F. G. Crookshank and J. P. Postgate (eds), *The Meaning of Meaning: A study of the influence of language upon thought and of the science of symbolism*. London: Kegan, Paul, Trench, Trubner, pp. 296–336.
Mangubhai, F. and F. Mugler. 2006. The language situation in Fiji. In R. B. Baldauf Jr and R. B. Kaplan (eds), *Language Planning and Policy in the Pacific, Vol. 1: Fiji, The Philippines and Vanuatu*. Clevedon: Multilingual Matters, pp. 7–22.
Mann, C. W. 1935. *Education in Fiji*. Melbourne: Melbourne University Press.
Markee, N. 2000. *Conversation Analysis*. Mahwah, NJ: Lawrence Erlbaum Associates.
Markee, N. 2001. Reopening the research agenda: Respecifying motivation as a locally-occasioned phenomenon. *American Association of Apllied Linguistics*. St. Louis, Michigan.
Markee, N. 2004. Zones of interactional transition in ESL Classes. *Modern Language Journal*, 88(4): 585–96.
Markee, N. 2005. The organization of off-task talk in second language classrooms. In K. Richards and P. Seedhouse (eds), *Applying Conversation Analysis*. Basingstoke, Palgrave MacMillan, pp. 197–213.
Markee, N. In press. Issues in the emerging research agenda of conversation analysis-for-second-language acquisition. University of Illinois at Urbana-Champaign.
Markee, N. In press. Toward a learning behavior tracking methodology for CA-for-SLA. University of Illinois at Urbana-Champaign.
Markee, N. 2007. Invitation talk. In Z. Hua, P. Seedhouse, L. Wei and V. Cook (eds), *Language Learning and Teaching as Social Interaction*. Basingstoke: Palgrave Macmillan.
Markee, N. and G. Kasper 2004. Classroom talks: An introduction. *The Modern Language Journal*, 88(4): 491–500.
Markus, H. R. and S. Kitayama. 1991. Culture and the self: Implications for cognition, emotion, and motivation. *Psychological Review*, 98(2): 224–53.
Martin, C. and A. Zaitsev. 2001. *Russian Stage Two*. Dubuque, IA: Kendall/Hunt.
Martin-Jones, M. and M. Saxena. 1995. Supporting or containing bilingualism? policies, power assymetries and pedagogic practices in mainstream primary schools. In J. Tollefson (ed.), *Power and Inequality in Language Education*. Cambridge: Cambridge University Press.
Martin-Jones, M. and M. Saxena. 1996. Turn-taking, power asymmetries, and the positioning of bilingual participants in classroom discourse. *Linguistics and Education*, 8: 105–23.
Martin-Jones, M. and M. Saxena. 2003. Bilingual resources and 'funds of knowledge' for teaching and learning in multi-ethnic classrooms in Britain. *International Journal of Bilingual Education and Bilingualism*, 6(3–4): 267–81.
Mathers, J. 1990. *An Investigation into Feedback in an L2 Classroom*. Unpublished masters dissertation, Canterbury Christ Church College, UK.
Matsuda, A. and P. Matsuda. 2001. Autonomy and collaboration in teacher education: Journal sharing among native and nonnative English speaking teachers. *The CATESOL Journal*, 13(1): 109–21.
Maum, R. 2002. Nonnative-English-speaking teachers in the English teaching profession. CAL Digest. Accessed 20 January 2006 at: http://www.cal.org/resources/digest/0209maum.html

McCroskey, J. C. and L. L. McCroskey. 1988. Self-report as an approach to measuring communication competence, *Communication Research Reports*, 5: 106–13.
Mcilwaine, C. 2005. *Coping Practices among Colombian Migrants in London*. London: Queen Mary, University of London.
McKay, S. 2003. Toward an appropriate EIL pedagogy: Re-examining common ELT assumptions. *International Journal of Applied Linguistics*, 13(1): 1–22.
McLemore, C. 1991. *The Pragmatic Interpretation of English Intonation: Sorority speech*. Unpublished PhD dissertation, University of Texas at Austin.
McNeill, D. 1992. *Hand and Mind: What gestures reveal about thought*. Chicago: University of Chicago Press.
McNeill, D. (ed.). 2000. *Language and Gesture*. Cambridge, New York: Cambridge University Press.
Mehan, H. 1979. *Learning Lessons: Social organization in the classroom*. Cambridge, MA, and London: Harvard University Press.
Mehlenbacher, B., C. R. Miller, D. Covington and J. S. Larsen. 2000. Active and interactive learning online: A comparison of web-based and conventional writing classes. *IEEE Transactions on Professional Communication*, 43(2): 166–84.
Mercer, N. 1995. *The Guided Construction of Knowledge: Talk amongst teachers and learners*. Clevedon: Multilingual Matters.
Mercer, N. 2001. Language for teaching a language. In C. Candlin and N. Mercer (eds), *English Language Teaching in its Social Context*. Buckingham, Sydney: Open University/Routledge/Macquarie University, pp. 243–57.
Mercer N. and R. Wegerif. 1999. Children's talk and the development of reasoning in the classroom. *British Educational Research Journal*, 25(1): 95–111.
Miller, C. R. 1984. Genre as social action, *Quarterly Journal of Speech*, 70(2): 151–67. Reprinted in A. Freedman and P. Medway (eds), *Genre and the New Rhetoric*. London: Taylor & Francis, 1994, pp. 23–42.
Miller, J. 2003. *Audible Difference: ESL and social identity*. Clevedon: Multilingual Matters.
Miller, J. 2004. Social languages and schooling: The uptake of sociocultural perspectives in school. In M. Hawkins (ed.), *Social and Cultural Approaches to Language Learning and Teaching, and Teacher Education*. Clevedon: Multilingual Matters.
Miller, J. 2007. Identity construction in teacher education. In Z. Hua, P. Seedhouse, L. Wei and V. Cook (eds), *Language Learning and Teaching as Social Interaction*. Basingstoke: Palgrave Macmillan.
Miller, J. (in press). Reconciling the roles: Reflections of an academic practitioner in TESOL. In A. Burns and J. Burton (eds), *Language Teacher Research in Australia*. TESOL.
Miller, J. and B. Glassner. 1997. The 'inside' and 'outside': Finding realities in interviews. In D. Silverman (ed.), *Qualitative Research: Theory, method and practice*. London: Sage Publications, pp. 99–112.
Mitchell, R. and F. Myles. 2004. *Second Language Learning Theories*, 2nd edn. London: Edward Arnold.
Mitchell, T. F. 1957. The language of buying and selling in Cyrenaica. *Hespéris*, 44: 31–71.
Mittag, K.C. 1999. Measuring the Jungian personality types of Hispanic high school students. *Assessment*, 6(3): 293–300.
Moag, R.F. 1982. English as a foreign, second, native and basal language: A new taxonomy of English using societies. In J. B. Pride (ed.), *New Englishes*. Rowley, MA: Newbury House, pp. 21–39.
Modern Language Journal. 2004. 88(4).

Moll, L., L. C. Amanti, C. Neff, and N. Gonzalez. 1992. Funds of knowledge for teaching: Using a qualitative approach to connect homes and classrooms. *Theory into Practice*, 31(2): 132–41.
Mondada, L. 1999. L'accomplissement de l'"étrangéité" dans et par l'interaction: procédures de catégorisation des locuteurs. *Langages*, 134: 20–34.
Mondada, L. and Pekarek Doehler, S. 2000. Interaction sociale et cognition située: quels modèles pour la recherche sur l'acquisition des langues? In *Acquisition et Interaction en Langue Etrangère – AILE*, 12: 147–74. (http://aile.revues.org/document947.html)
Mondada, L. and Pekarek Doehler, S. 2004. Second language acquisition as situated practice. *The Modern Language Journal*, 88(4): 501–18.
Mori, J. 2002. Task design, plan, and development of talk-in-interaction: An analysis of small group activity in a Japanese language classroom. *Applied Linguistics*, 23(3): 323–47.
Mori, J. 2004a. Negotiating sequential boundaries and learning opportunities: A case from a Japanese language classroom. *Modern Language Journal*, 88(4): 551–67.
Mori, J. 2004b. Pursuit of understanding: Rethinking 'negotiation of meaning' in view of projected action. In R. Gardner and J. Wagner (eds), *Second Language Conversations*. London: Continuum, pp. 157–77.
Mori, J., and M. Hayashi. 2006. The achievement of intersubjectivity through embodied completions: A study of interactions between first and second language speakers. *Applied Linguistics*, 27: 195–219.
Morris, G., M. Vyatytnev. and L. Vokhmina. 1993. *Russian Face to Face: A communicative program in contemporary Russian*. Lincolnwood, IL: National Textbook Company.
Mugler F. and J. Mamtora. 2004. The Gujarati language in Fiji. *Te Reo*, 17: 29–61.
Mugler F. and J. Tent. 1998. Some aspects of language use and attitudes in Fiji. In J. Tent and F. Mugler (eds), *SICOL: Proceedings of the Second International Conference on Oceanic Linguistics, Language Contact, Pacific Linguistics* 1, C-141, pp. 109–34.
Mugler, F. 1996. 'Vernacular' language teaching in Fiji. In F. Mugler and J. Lynch (eds), *Pacific Languages in Education*. Suva: Institute of Pacific Studies and Vanuatu: Department of Literature and Language, Pacific Languages Unit, pp. 273–87.
National Curriculum Council (NCC). 1991. *Linguistic Diversity and the National Curriculum*, circular number 11. York: National Curriculum Council.
National Curriculum online. 2006. *Geography at Key Stage 2*. Accessed 23 June 2006 at: http://www.nc.uk.net/webdav/harmonise?Page/@id=6001andSession/@id= D_kIBYIRMXCqlIeS0uop2dandPOS[@stateId_eq_main]/@id=3487andPOS [@stateId_eq_ note]/@id=3529.
Nelson, G. 1995. Cultural differences in learning styles. In J.M. Reid (ed.), *Learning Styles in the ESL/EFL Classroom*. Boston, MA: Heinle and Heinle, pp. 3–18.
Nguyen, H. T. 2003. The development of communication skills in the practice of patient consultation among pharmacy students. Unpublished PhD dissertation, University of Wisconsin-Madison.
Nguyen, H. T. 2006. Constructing 'expertness': A novice pharmacist's development of interactional competence in patient consultations. *Communication and Medication*, 3 (2): 147–60.
Niezgoda, K. and C. Röver. 2001. Pragmatics and grammatical awareness: A function of the learning environment? In K. Rose and G. Kasper (eds), *Pragmatics in Language Teaching*. Cambridge: Cambridge University Press, pp. 63–79.
Nisbett, R. E. 2003. *The Geography of Thought*. London: Nicholas Brealey Publishing.
Norton, B. 2000. *Identity and Language Learning*. London: Longman.

Norton, B. 2001. Non-participation, imagined communities and the language classroom. In M. Breen (ed.), *Learner Contributions to Language Learning*. London: Longman, pp. 25–43.
Norton, B. (2006). Identity as sociocultural construct in second language education. In K. Cadman and K. O'Regan (eds). Special issue of *TESOL in Context*: 22–33.
Norton, B. and K. Toohey (eds). 2004. *Critical Pedagogies and Language Learning*. Cambridge: Cambridge University Press.
Nystand, M. 1989. A social-interactive model of writing. *Written Communication*, 6(1): 66–85.
Ochs, E. 1979. Introduction: What child language can contribute to pragmatics. In E. Ochs and B. B. Schieffelin (eds), *Developmental Pragmatics*. New York: Academic Press, pp. 1–17.
Ochs, E., P. Gonzalez and S. Jacoby. 1996. 'When I come down I'm in the domain state': Grammar and graphic representation in the interpretive activity of physicists. In E. Ochs, E. A. Schegloff and S. A. Thompson (eds), *Interaction and Grammar*. New York: Cambridge University Press, pp. 328–69.
O'Connor, M. 1998. Language socialization in the mathematics classroom: Discourse practices and mathematical thinking. In M. Lampert and M. Blunk (eds), *Talking Mathematics in School: Studies of teaching and learning*. Cambridge: Cambridge University Press, pp. 17–55.
O'Connor, M., and S. Michaels. 1996. Shifting participant frameworks: Orchestrating thinking practices in group discussion. In D. Hicks (ed.), *Discourse, Learning and Schooling*. Cambridge: Cambridge University Press, pp. 63–100.
Odell, L. and D. Goswami. 1985. *Writing in Non-Academic Settings*. New York: Guilford Press.
Ohta, A. 2001. *Second Language Acquisition Processes in the Classroom: Learning Japanese*. Mahwah, NJ: Lawrence Erlbaum.
Ohta, A. 2005. Interlanguage pragmatics in the zone of proximal development, *System*, 33: 503–17.
Oller, J. W. jr. 2005. Common ground between form and content: The pragmatic solution to the bootstrapping problem. *Modern Language Journal*, 89(1): 92–114.
Ortner, S. B. 1984. Theory in anthropology since the sixties. *Comparative Studies in Society and History*, 126(1): 126–66.
Osborne, A. B. 1996. Practice into theory into practice: Culturally relevant pedagogy for students we have marginalised and normalised, *Anthropology and Education Quarterly*, 27(3): 285–314.
Ouseley, H. 2001. *Community Pride, not Prejudice: Making diversity work in Bradford*. Bradford: Bradford Vision.
Oxford, R. L. 1995. The style analysis survey. In J. M. Reid (ed.), *Learning Styles In the ESL/EFL Classroom*. Boston, MA: Heinle and Heinle, pp. 208–15.
Oxford, R. L. 1998. Language teachers: New roles, new perspectives, *System*, 26: 1–2.
Oxford R. L. and N. J. Anderson. 1995. A crosscultural view of learning styles. *Language Teaching*, 28: 201–15.
Palmquist R. A. and K. S. Kim. 2000. Cognitive style and on-line database search experience as predictors of web search performance. *Journal of the American Society for Information Science*, 51(6): 558–66.
Park, Y. -Y. 1997. A cross-linguistic study of the use of contrastive connectives in English, Korean, and Japanese conversations. Unpublished doctoral dissertation, University of California at Los Angeles.
Pavlenko, A. 1998. Second language learning by adults: Testimonies of bilingual writers. *Issues in Applied Linguistics*, 9(1): 3–19.

Pavlenko, A. 2001. 'In the world of the tradition I was unimagined': Negotiation of identities in cross-cultural autobiographies. *The International Journal of Bilingualism*, 5 (3): 317–44.
Pavlenko, A. 2002. Poststructuralist approaches to the study of social factors in second language learning and use. In V. Cook (ed.), *Portraits of the L2 User*. Clevedon: Multilingual Matters, pp. 277–302.
Pavlenko, A. 2004a. 'The making of an American': Negotiation of identities at the turn of the 20th century. In A. Pavlenko and A. Blackledge (eds), *Negotiation of Identities in Multilingual Contexts*. Clevedon: Multilingual Matters, pp. 34–67.
Pavlenko, A. 2004b. 'Stop doing that, la Komu Skazala!': Language choice and emotion in parent-child communication, *Journal of Multilingual and Multicultural Development*, 25(2/3): 179–203.
Pavlenko, A. 2005. *Emotions and Multilingualism*. Cambridge: Cambridge University Press.
Pavlenko, A. 2006a. Bilingual selves. In A. Pavlenko (ed.), *Bilingual Minds: Emotional experience, expression, and representation*. Clevedon: Multilingual Matters, pp. 1–33.
Pavlenko, A. 2006b. *Emotion and Multilingualism*. Cambridge: Cambridge University Press.
Pavlenko, A. and A. Blackledge (eds). 2003. *Negotiation of Identities in Multilingual Contexts*. Clevedon: Multilingual Matters.
Pavlenko, A. and V. Driagina. 2007. Russian Emotion Vocabulary in American Learners' Narratives, *Modern Languages Journal*, 2.
Pekarek-Doehler, S. 2002. Mediation revisited: the socio-interactional organization of mediation in learning environments. *Mind, Culture and Activity*, 9(1): 22–42.
Pekarek Doehler, S. 2005. De la nature située des compétences en langue. In J.-P. Bronckart et al. (eds), *Repenser l'enseignement des langues. Comment identifier et exploiter les competences*. Paris: Septentrion, pp. 41–68.
Pekarek Doehler, S. and G. Ziegler. 2007. Sequential organization in immersion classrooms. In Z. Hua, P. Seedhouse, L. Wei and V. Cook (eds), *Language Learning and Teaching as Social Interaction*. Basingstoke: Palgrave Macmillan.
Pennycook, A. 2004. Critical moments in a TESOL praxicum. In B. Norton and K. Toohey (eds), *Critical Pedagogies and Language Learning*. Cambridge: Cambridge University Press, pp. 327–46.
Perlmutter, H. V. 1991. On the rocky road to the first global civilization. *Human Relations*, 44(9): 897–920.
Phillipson, R. 1992. *Linguistic Imperialism*. Oxford: Oxford University Press.
Pickworth G. E. and W. J. Schoeman. 2000. The psychometric properties of the learning style inventory and the learning style questionnaire: Two normative measures of learning styles. *South African Journal of Psychology*, 30(2): 44–52.
Pillai, R. C. 1975. Fiji Hindi as a creole language. Unpublished MA thesis, Linguistics Department, Southern Illinois University.
Pomerantz, A. 1984. Agreeing and disagreeing with assessments: Some features of preferred/dispreferred turn shapes. In J. Atkinson and J. Heritage (eds), *Structures of Social Action*. Cambridge, Cambridge University Press, pp. 57–101.
Pomerantz, A., and Fehr, B. J. 1997. Conversation analysis: An approach to the study of social action as sense making practices. In T. A. van Dijk (ed.), *Discourse Studies: A multidisciplinary introduction*. Vol. 2: *Discourse as social interaction*. Thousand Oaks, CA: Sage, pp. 64–91.
Prior, P. 1995. Redefining the task: An ethnographic examination of writing and response in six graduate seminars. In D. Belcher and G. Braine (eds), *Academic Writing in a Second Language: Essays on research and pedagogy*. Norwood, NJ: Ablex, pp. 47–82.

Rampton, B. 1997. Retuning in applied linguistics. *International Journal of Applied Linguistics*, 7(1): 3–25.
Reid J. M. (1995). The learning style preferences of ESL students, *TESOL Quarterly*, 21(1): 87–111.
Resnick, L. 1991. Shared cognition: Thinking as social practice. In L. Resnick, J. Levine and S. Teasley (eds), *Perspectives on Socially Shared Cognition*. Washington, DC: American Psychological Association, pp. 1–22.
Roberts, C. 2001. Language acquisition or language socialization in and through discourse. In C. Candlin and N. Mercer (eds), *English Language Teaching in its Social Context*. London: Routledge, pp. 108–21.
Rogoff, B. 1990. *Apprenticeship in Thinking: Cognitive development in social context*. New York: Oxford University Press.
Rogoff, B. 2003. *The Cultural Nature of Human Development*. Oxford: Oxford University Press.
Rorty, A. (ed.). 1976. *The Identities of Persons*. Berkeley: University of California Press.
Rosengrant, S. and E. Lifschitz. 1996. *Focus on Russian: Interactive approach to communication*. New York: John Wiley.
Ross, S. 1998. Divergent frame interpretations in language proficiency interview interaction. In R. Young and A. W. He (eds), *Talking and Testing: Discourse approaches to the assessment of oral proficiency*. Amsterdam, Philadelphia: John Benjamins, pp. 333–53.
Rossi Le, L. 1995. Learning styles and strategies in adult ESL students. In J. M. Reid (ed.), *Learning Styles in the ESL/EFL Classroom*. Boston, MA: Heinle and Heinle.
Roy-Campbell, Z. M. 2003. Promoting African languages as conveyers of knowledge in educational institutions. In S. Makoni, G. Smitherman, A. F. Ball and A. K. Spears (eds), *Black Linguistics*. London: Routledge, pp. 83–102.
Sacks, H. 1984. Notes on methodology. In J. M. Atkinson and J. Heritage (eds), *Structures of Social Action: Studies in conversation analysis*. Cambridge: Cambridge University Press, pp. 2–17.
Sacks, H. 1992. *Lectures in Conversation*, ed. G. Jefferson (2 volumes). Oxford: Blackwell.
Sacks, H., and E. A. Schegloff. 1979. Two preferences in the organization of reference to persons in conversation and their interaction. In G. Psathas (ed.), *Everyday Language: Studies in ethnomethodology*. New York: Irvington, pp. 15–21.
Sacks, H., E. Schegloff and G. Jefferson. 1974. A simplest systematics for the organisation of turn-taking in conversation. *Language*, 50: 696–735.
Sahlins, M. D. 1981. *Historical Metaphors and Mythical Realities: Structure in the early history of the Sandwich Islands kingdom*. Ann Arbor: University of Michigan Press.
Santoro, N. and A. Allard. 2005. (Re)Examining Identities: Working with diversity in the preservice teaching experience. *Teaching and Teacher Education*, 21: 863–73.
Sapir, E. 1921. *Language: The introduction to the study of speech*. New York: Harcourt, Brace & World.
Scarcella, R. 1990. *Teaching Minority Children in the Multicultural Classroom*. Englewood Cliffs, NJ: Prentice Hall.
Schegloff, E. A. 1968. Sequencing in conversational openings. *American Anthropologist*, 70: 1075–95.
Schegloff, E. A. 1979. The relevance of repair to syntax-for-conversation. In T. Givón (ed), *Syntax and Semantics, Volume 12: Discourse and Syntax*. New York: Academic Press, 261–86.
Schegloff, E. A. 1980. Preliminaries to preliminaries: 'Can I ask you a question?' *Sociological Inquiry*, 50: 104–52.

Schegloff, E. A. 1987. Recycled turn-beginnings: A precise repair mechanism in conversation's turn-taking organisation. In G. Button and J. R. E. Lee (eds), *Talk and Social Organisation*. Clevedon: Multilingual Matters, pp. 70–85.

Schegloff, E. A. 1989. Reflections on language development, and the interactional character of talk. In M. H. Borstein and J. S. Bruner (eds), *Interaction in Human Development*. New York, Lawrence Erlbaum Associates, pp. 139–53.

Schegloff, E. A. 1991. Conversation analysis and socially shared cognition. In L. Resnick, J. Levine, and S. Teasley (eds), *Perspectives on Socially Shared Cognition*. Washington, DC: American Psychological Association pp. 150–71.

Schegloff, E. A. 1992a. In another context. In A. Duranti and C. Goodwin (eds), *Rethinking Context: Language as an interactive phenomenon*. Cambridge: Cambridge University Press, pp. 191–228.

Schegloff, E. A. 1992b. Repair after next turn: The last structurally provided defense of intersubjectivity in conversation. *American Journal of Sociology*, 97: 1295–345.

Schegloff, E. A. 1996a. Confirming allusions: Toward an empirical account of action. *American Journal of Sociology*, 102(1): 161–216.

Schegloff, E. A 1996b. Turn organization: One intersection of grammar and interaction. In E. Ochs, E. Schegloff and S. Thompson (eds), *Interaction and Grammar*. Cambridge: Cambridge University Press.

Schegloff, E. A. 2000. When 'others' initiate repair. *Applied Linguistics*, 21(2): 205–43.

Schegloff, E. A. and H. Sacks. 1973. Opening up closings. *Semiotica*, 8: 289–327.

Schegloff, E. A., G. Jefferson and H. Sacks. 1977. The preference for self-correction in the organization of repair in conversation. *Language*, 53: 361–82.

Schegloff, E., E. Ochs and S. Thompson. 1996. Introduction. In E. Ochs, E. Schegloff and S. Thompson (eds), *Interaction and Grammar*. Cambridge: Cambridge University Press.

Schiffrin, D. 1987. *Discourse Markers*. New York: Cambridge University Press.

Schumann, J. 1978. *The Pidginization Process: A model for second language acquisition*. Rowley, MA: Newbury House.

Searle, J. 1969. *Speech Acts*. Cambridge: Cambridge University Press.

Seedhouse, P. 1997a. Combining form and meaning. *ELT Journal*, 51: 336–44.

Seedhouse, P. 1997b. The case of the missing 'no': The relationship between pedagogy and interaction. *Language Learning*, 47: 547–83.

Seedhouse, P. 2004. *The Interactional Architecture of the Language Classroom: A conversation analysis perspective*. Malden, MA: Blackwell.

Seedhouse, P. 2005. Conversation analysis and language learning. *Language Teaching*, 38(4): 165–87.

Seedhouse, P. 2007. Interaction and constructs. In Z. Hua, P. Seedhouse, L. Wei and V. Cook (eds), *Language Learning and Teaching as Social Interaction*. Basingstoke: Palgrave Macmillan.

Sfard, A. 1998. On two metaphors for learning and on the dangers of choosing just one. *Educational Researcher*, 27(2): 4–13.

Shameem, N. 1994. The Wellington Indo-Fijians: Language shift among teenage new immigrants, *Journal of Multilingual and Multicultural Development*, 15(4): 399–418.

Shameem, N. 1995. *Hamai log ke boli*. Language shift in an immigrant community: The Wellington Indo-Fijians. Unpublished PhD thesis, Victoria University of Wellington.

Shameem, N. 1998. Validating self-reported language proficiency by testing performance in an immigrant community: The Wellington Indo-Fijians. *Language Testing*, 15(1): 86–108.

Shameem, N. 2000. Methodology in a study of classroom multilingualism: A study of primary school Indo-Fijians in Fiji. *New Zealand Studies in Applied Linguistics*, 6: 67–88.

Shameem, N. 2002a. Multilingual proficiency in Fiji primary schools. *Journal of Multilingual and Multicultural Development*, 23(5): 388–407.
Shameem, N. 2002b. Classroom language use in a multi-lingual community – the Indo-Fijians in Fiji. *Journal of Intercultural Studies*, 23(3): 267–84.
Shameem, N. 2005. Comparing conceptual and lexical items in English and Fiji Hindi: Implications for language learning. *New Zealand Studies in Applied Linguistics*, 11(2): 1–24.
Shameem, N. 2007a. Social interaction in the multilingual classroom. In Z. Hua, P. Seedhouse, L. Wei and V. Cook (eds), *Language learning and teaching as social interaction*. Basingstoke, UK: Palgrave Macmillan.
Shameem, N. 2007b forthcoming. Language education needs for multilingualism in Fiji primary schools. *International Journal of Educational Development*.
Shardakova, M. and A. Pavlenko. 2004. Identity options in Russian textbooks. *Journal of Language, Identity, and Education*, 3(1): 25–46.
Shiraev E. and D. Levy. 2004. *Cross Cultural Psychology: Critical thinking and contemporary applications*. Boston, MA: Allyn & Bacon.
Shmelyov, A. Druzhba. 2005. v russkoi yazykovoi kartine mira [Friendship in Russian linguistic world view]. In I. Levontina and A. Shmelyov (eds), *Kluchevye Idei Russkoi Yazykovoi Kartiny Mira* [The Key Ideas in the Russian Linguistic World View]. Moscow: Yazyki Slavyanskoi Kul'tury, pp. 289–303.
Siegel, J. 1973. A survey of language use in the Indian speech community in Fiji. Field study project for the culture learning institute and practicum project for ESL 730. Honolulu: Unpublished paper.
Siegel, J. 1975. Fiji Hindustani. Working Papers in Linguistics, University of Hawai'i, Department of Linguistics, 7(3): 127–44.
Siegel, J. 1987. *Language Contact in a Plantation Environment. A sociolinguistic history of Fiji*. Cambridge: Cambridge University Press.
Siegel, J. 1992. Indian languages and identity in Fiji. *Journal of Asian Pacific Communication*, 3(1): 115–32.
Silva, T. 1993. Toward an understanding of the distinct nature of L2 writing: The ESL research and its implication, *TESOL Quarterly*, 27: 657–77.
Skeggs, B. 2004. *Class, Self, Culture*. London: Routledge.
Smith S. M. and P. C. Woody. 2000. Interactive effect of multimedia instruction and learning styles. *Teaching of Psychology*, 27(3): 220–23.
Smith, P. J. 2000. Vocational students' learning preferences: The interpretability of ipsative data. *Psychological Reports*, 86(1): 25–39.
Spack, R. 1997. The rhetorical construction of multilingual students. *TESOL Quarterly*, 31(2): 765–74.
Starfield, S. 2004. Word power: Negotiating success in a first-year sociology essay, in L. Ravelli and R. Ellis (eds), *Analysing Academic Writing: Contextualised frameworks*. London: Continuum, pp. 66–83.
Stickle, J. E., J. Lloyd, W. F. Keller and E. Cherney. 1999. Learning styles in veterinary medicine: Relation to progression through the professional curriculum and integration into the profession. *Journal of Veterinary Medical Education*, 26(2).
Swain, M. 1985. Communicative competence: Some roles of comprehensible input and comprehensible output in its development. In S. Gass and C. Madden (eds), *Input in Second Language Acquisition*. Rowley, MA: Newbury House, pp. 235–53.
Swain, M. 1995. Three functions of output in second language learning. In G. Cook and B. Seidlhofer (eds), *Principle and Practice in Applied Linguistics: Studies in honour of H. G. Widdowson*. Oxford: Oxford University Press, pp. 125–44.

Swales, J. M. 1990. *Genre Analysis – English in Academic and Research Settings*. Cambridge: Cambridge University Press.
Taleghani-Nikazm, C. 2002a. A conversation analytical study of telephone conversation openings between native and nonnative speakers. *Journal of Pragmatics*, 34: 1807–32.
Taleghani-Nikazm, C. 2002b. Telephone conversation openings in Persian. In K. K. Luke and T-S. Pavlidou (eds), *Telephone Calls*. Amsterdam, Philadelphia: John Benjamins, pp. 87–109.
Tansley, A. E. and M. Craft. 1984. Mother tongue teaching and support: A schools council enquiry. *Journal of Multilingual and Multicultural Development*, 5: 366–84.
Tarone, E. and M. Swain. 1995. A sociolinguistic perspective on second language use in immersion classrooms. *The Modern Language Journal*, 79: 166–78.
Te Puni Kōkiri. 2001. *A Comparative Evaluation of Four Self-Assessment Instruments of Māori Language Proficiency in a Survey of the Health of the Māori Language*. Wellington: Māori Language Commission.
Tent J. and F. Mugler. 1996. Why a Fiji corpus? In S. Greenbaum (ed.), *Comparing English Worldwide*. Oxford: Clarendon Press, pp. 249–61.
Thomas, J. 1983. Cross-cultural pragmatic failure. *Applied Linguistics*, 4: 91–112.
Thompson, M. A. 2000. *The Global Resume And CV Guide: From the experts in executive research and recruiting*. New York: John Wiley & Sons.
Thomson Scientific. 2006. 'ISI Web of Knowledge'. Accessed 30 May 2006 at: http://www.thomsonisi.com/
Tillit, B. and M. Newton Bruder. 1985. *Speaking Naturally: Communication skills in American English*. New York: Cambridge University Press.
Tracy, K. 2002. *Everyday Talk: Building and reflecting identities*. New York: Guilford.
Triandis, H. C., C. McCusker and C. H. Hui. 1990. Multimethod probes of individualism and collectivism. *Journal of Personality and Social Psychology*, 59(5): 1006–20.
Trompenaars, F. and C. Hampden-Turner. 1998. *Riding the Waves of Culture*. New York: McGraw-Hill.
Tudor, I. 1996. *Learner Centredness as Language Education*. Cambridge: Cambridge University Press.
US Bureau of the Census. 2003. *File QT-P16: Language Spoken at Home: 2000*. Washington, DC: Dept. of Commerce.
Üstünel, E. and Seedhouse, P. 2005. Why that, in that language, right now? Code-switching and pedagogical focus. *International Journal of Applied Linguistics*, 15(3): 302–24.
Van Lier, L. 1988. *The Classroom and the Language Learner*. London: Longman.
van Lier, L. 2000. From input to affordance: Social-interactive learning from an ecological perspective. In J. Lantolf (ed.), *Sociocultural Theory and Second Language Learning*. Oxford: Oxford University Press, pp. 245–60.
Vygotsky, L. 1978. *Mind in Society: The development of higher psychological processes*. Cambridge, MA: Harvard University Press.
Wagner, J. 1996. Foreign language acquisition through interaction – A critical review of research on conversational adjustments. *Journal of Pragmatics*, 26: 215– 36.
Wagner, J. 1998. On doing being a guinea pig – A response to Seedhouse. *Journal of Pragmatics*, 30: 103–13.
Wagner, J. 2004. The classroom and beyond. *The Modern Language Journal*, 88(4): 612–16.
Wagner, J. and A. Firth. 1997. Communication strategies at work. In G. Kasper and E. Kellerman (eds), *Communication Strategies: Psycholinguistic and sociolinguistic perspectives*. London: Longman, pp. 323–44.
Wagner, J. and R. Gardner. 2004. Introduction. In R. Gardner and J. Wagner (eds), *Second Language Conversations*. London: Continuum, pp. 1–17.

Wenger, É. 1998. *Communities of Practice: Learning, meaning, and identity*. Cambridge: Cambridge University Press.
Wierzbicka, A. 1984. Diminutives and depreciatives: Semantic representation for derivational categories. *Quaderni di Semantica*, 5(1): 123–30.
Wierzbicka, A. 1992. *Semantics, Culture, and Cognition: Universal human concepts in culture-specific configurations*. New York: Oxford University Press.
Wierzbicka, A. 1997. *Understanding Cultures through their Key Words: English, Russian, Polish, German, and Japanese*. New York: Oxford University Press.
Wierzbicka, A. 1999. *Emotions across Languages and Cultures: Diversity and universals*. Cambridge: Cambridge University Press.
Wode, H. 1976. Developmental sequences in naturalistic L2 acquisition. *Working Papers in Bilingualism*, 11: 1–31.
Wong, J. 2000. Delayed next turn repair initiation in native/nonnative speaker English conversation. *Applied Linguistics*, 21: 244–67.
Wong, J. 2004. Some preliminary thoughts on delay as an interactional resource. In R. Gardner and J. Wagner (eds), *Second Language Conversations*. London: Continuum.
Wong, J. 2005. Sidestepping grammar. In K. Richards and P. Seedhouse (eds), *Applying Conversation Analysis*. Basingstoke: Palgrave Macmillan, pp. 159–73.
Yanagisawa, M. 2000. How Japanese immigrants can be Christians: Analyzing Christian testimonies by Japanese 'new first generation' in Hawaii. In E. Németh (ed.), *Pragmatics in 2000: Selected Papers from the 7th International Pragmatics Conference*. Antwerp: International Pragmatics Association, Vol. 2, pp. 611–24.
Ye, Veronica Zhengdao. 2003. La Double Vie de Veronica: Reflections on my life as a Chinese migrant in Australia, *Mots Pluriels*, 23. http://www.arts.uwa.edu.au/motspluriels/MP2303vzy.html.
Young, R. 1999. Sociolinguistic approaches to SLA. *Annual Review of Applied Linguistics*, 19: 105–32.
Young, R. 2002. Sociolinguistic approaches to SLA. *Annual Review of Applied Linguistics*, 19: 105–32.
Young, R. and A. W. He (eds). 1998. *Talking and Testing*. Amsterdam, Philadelphia: John Benjamins.
Young, R. and H. Nguyen 2002. Modes of meaning in high school science. *Applied Linguistics*, 23: 348–72.
Young, R. F. and E. R. Miller. 2004. Learning as changing participation: Discourse roles in ESL writing conferences. *Modern Language Journal*, 88(4): 519–35.
Zamel, V. 1997. Towards a model of transculturation. *TESOL Quarterly*, 31(2): 341–52.
Zhu Hua, Li Wei and Y. Qian. 2000. The sequential organisation of gift offering and acceptance in Chinese. *Journal of Pragmatics*, 32: 81–103.
Ziegler, G. 2004. Zur Funktion von Stereotypisierungen in der Unterrichtskommunikation. In C. Altmayer et al. (eds), *Deutsch als Fremdsprache in Wissenschaft und Unterricht*. Frankfurt/Main, Berlin: Lang.
Ziegler, G. and K. Mutz, K. 2003. C'est canard – c'est un vert. Der Artikelgebrauch im frühen gesteuerten Erwerb des Französischen. In W. Klein and R. Franceschini (eds), *Einfache Sprachen. Zeitschrift für Literaturwissesnschaft und Linguistik*, 131: 76–105.

Index

A
Accent 70, 96, 150, 179–80, 254–5, 267
Acquisition 9, 11, 70, 74, 85, 90, 92, 101, 113, 117, 168–70, 172, 176–8, 180–1, 219
Affiliation, social 107, 114, 116, 120, 122–4
African-American students 103
Age 2, 101, 104–5, 107, 110, 116, 120, 122–4, 142, 144, 148, 168–9, 180, 204–6, 241–2
American learners 106, 108–10, 117, 257
Attitudes 1, 2, 96, 133, 135, 141–2, 169, 172, 200, 203–4, 238
Australia 3, 15, 148, 153, 156–7, 164, 200, 235
Awareness 165–6, 190, 192, 196, 236, 252

B
Background 39, 91–2, 96, 99, 100, 148, 152, 165, 200, 237–8, 253, 256
Bilingualism 151, 161, 163, 187–8, 190–1, 196–7, 268–70
Bilinguals 169, 186, 188–9, 191, 205, 219, 221, 226, 230, 232–3, 255, 257, 269
Brazilian learners 243–5, 247
Bricolage 3, 58, 62, 70–1
British students 134, 136, 142–3

C
CA 2, 9–11, 20–2, 251
CA-for-SLA 11, 42, 44, 56
Canada 67–8, 100, 132, 235
Categories 73, 107, 110, 112, 115, 128, 133–8, 140, 147, 150–2
Children 12, 94, 116, 126, 130, 138, 185–96, 199, 202, 204–7, 212, 215–17, 262, 269–70
China 127, 129–30, 132, 137, 142–3, 158, 164
Chinese 126, 137–8, 140, 143, 146, 169
    students 134, 136, 142–4, 149, 152, 258

Class 42, 44–5, 54, 63–4, 67, 73, 77, 79, 80, 148–9, 159–62, 185–6, 192–6, 202–6, 211–16, 221–3
Classroom
    activities 39, 81, 83, 236
    interaction 2, 9, 12, 14–15, 17, 19, 21, 38, 83, 168, 190, 196, 198, 205, 213–14
Classrooms 3, 4, 13–14, 19, 20, 84–6, 156–8, 162, 165–6, 187–91, 196–7, 203–6, 208–9, 213–17, 219–22, 232–3, 266–9
    bilingual 75–6, 221
Code-switching 19–21, 24, 116, 118, 191–4, 196, 200, 211–12, 215–16
Colombians 94–5, 97–9
Communicative
    anxiety 168–9, 171–9, 181
    competence 43, 89, 97, 101, 150
Communities 98–100, 103, 128, 144, 186–9, 192, 194–6, 200, 204, 220, 232–3, 253, 255, 259, 269
Competence, linguistic 62, 154–5
Concepts 4, 12, 14, 43, 57, 90, 99, 126, 128–9, 151, 194, 219, 252–3, 256, 258
Constructs 9, 11, 13, 15, 17, 19, 21, 37, 149–50, 162, 186
Context 5, 13, 93–4, 104, 127–31, 143–4, 157–8, 200–1, 203–4, 219–20, 228, 232–3, 251–63, 266–7, 271
    of acquisition 168–70, 174, 176–7, 180–1
    of situation 261–2
Conversation 3, 15, 23–4, 32, 37–8, 44, 55, 63, 91, 93–4, 97–8, 185–6, 207–8, 259–60, 266–8
    analysis 2, 9, 10, 22, 56, 76, 89, 252, 254, 266
Countries 2, 67–8, 127, 130–1, 141, 143, 153, 156, 188, 192, 200, 218–19, 238, 241–2
Cultures 100, 126–31, 134–6, 143–4, 151, 189–90, 197–8, 236, 247, 249, 252, 257

D

Differences 11, 36, 56, 97, 105, 107, 109, 126–7, 131, 143, 199, 236–7, 248, 252, 258
Discourse 129, 149–50, 152, 154, 158, 165, 187, 190, 213, 220, 229, 256, 262
Discursive practice 5, 251, 261–8, 270–71

E

Education 4, 40, 109, 112, 131, 149, 187, 199–204, 215–17, 252, 255, 263, 269–70
EFL 4, 236, 240–2, 247
Embedded corrections 12–13, 23, 38–40, 74, 80–2
English
 language 92, 100, 203, 216, 220
 speakers 94, 134, 155, 161, 164, 190, 221, 226
ESL 42, 56, 148–9, 152–3, 218
Etic 9–11, 21
Expertise 160, 253–4, 264

F

Fiji English 202, 214–15
Fiji Hindi 201, 205, 207–8, 268–9
Fluency 14–15, 17, 63–4, 68, 153–6, 167, 216

G

Gaze 59–61, 74, 260, 263–4
Gender 90, 107, 116, 120, 122–4, 128, 133, 149, 168, 180, 241, 244, 252, 259, 261
Genres 4, 35, 126–9, 131, 144, 154, 156, 256–7
Gestures 36, 44, 47, 56, 229, 261, 265–6, 271
Groups 4, 77–8, 80, 105, 107, 129–30, 136–7, 152–3, 161, 185–6, 204–5, 212, 214–15, 221–3, 248

H

Habitus 253–4, 258, 261
Hawaii 31–2, 36, 200
Hesitancy 62–3, 66–7
Hofstede 130–2, 236

I

Identity 2, 3, 11, 118, 128–9, 144, 148–50, 152, 156–7, 161–3, 196–7, 201–2, 251–2, 258–9, 261, 266–9
 altercast 259–60
 construction 4, 104, 162, 258
 interactional 259, 267
 master 259, 267
 non–native speaker 152
 personal 259, 267–8, 271
 relational 259–60, 267–8
 repertoires 103–4, 107, 109, 111, 113, 115, 117, 119, 123
 social 1, 101
 terms 104–5, 107, 110, 116–18, 120, 123
Immersion classroom 72–3, 75–7, 79, 81, 83–5, 170
Inapposite Responses 22–3, 25, 27, 29, 31, 33, 35, 37, 39, 41
Indo-Fijians 200–3, 205–6, 209, 212–13
Instruction 4, 14, 24, 85, 181, 194, 199, 202–3, 209–11, 219, 228, 230
Interviews 18, 104–6, 116, 159, 166, 221–2, 252–3, 256, 260
Invitation 42–3, 45, 47, 49, 50, 52–3, 55–7

J

Japan 127, 130, 132, 156, 242

K

Kaplan 126
Korean learners 64

L

L2 2, 20, 38, 116, 163, 165, 167, 169–73, 175–7, 179, 181
Language
 acquisition 70, 168, 224, 247
 alternation 253, 256, 268
 choice 19, 20, 168, 180, 203–5, 210–11, 213, 215, 217, 255, 267, 269–70
 classrooms 14, 24, 157, 162, 266
 competence 4, 84–5, 149, 153, 161
 education 150, 188, 237
 learners 62, 91, 219–20, 230, 232, 236, 248, 251

Language – *continued*

learning 1–3, 5, 9–11, 19, 20, 44, 74–5, 85, 126, 149–50, 152, 200, 216, 219–21, 232, 251
 opportunities 5, 219–20, 225
 planning 200, 203–4, 216–17
 policy 199, 204, 215–16, 269
 teaching 1, 19, 39, 89, 201, 206, 215

Languages 1–5, 21–2, 62–3, 70–7, 79–85, 89, 90, 99, 100, 149–55, 160–3, 167–73, 179–81, 185–90, 196, 198–217, 251–71
 target 24, 76, 91, 104, 166, 189, 204

Latinos 98–9, 221, 253

Learner
 autonomy 235
 centredness 236–7

Learner-centredness 235–6, 248

Learners 1–4, 10–21, 23–4, 44, 62–4, 69, 70, 74–6, 85, 103–7, 109–19, 155–6, 165–9, 235–8, 240–1, 245–49

Learning 1, 9–11, 19–22, 70–2, 75–7, 84–5, 155, 169–71, 185–92, 196–7, 203–5, 214–16, 220, 236, 262–5
 styles 5, 90, 136, 142, 235–9, 242–4, 246–9

Lesson 3, 13, 57, 63–5, 73, 76–7, 80–3, 159–61, 192–4, 196, 209, 211, 224–5, 228, 230

Linguistic forms 3, 13–18, 22–3, 25, 35, 62, 74, 79, 80, 82–3, 93, 267

Linguistics 131, 137, 139, 141–2, 146, 262, 271

M

Middle school classrooms 233

Misunderstandings 23–8, 32–3, 38, 114–15, 257

Motivation 2, 13, 43, 90, 118, 133–5, 139–40, 147, 157, 172

Multicultural classes 5, 238, 248

Multicultural Classrooms 235–7, 239, 241, 243, 245, 247, 249, 266

Multilingual
 classrooms 4, 199, 201, 203–5, 209, 211, 213, 215–17, 262
 and Multicultural Classrooms 183, 186, 188, 190, 192, 194, 196, 198, 200, 202, 204, 206, 208, 210, 212

Multilinguals 4, 5, 153, 167, 169, 186, 188–9, 199, 203, 205, 266, 269

N

Names 35–6, 57, 80, 104, 118, 132, 134–7, 145, 147–8, 151–3, 160, 198, 201, 207, 234

National Curriculum 186, 188, 191–2

Nations 189, 199

Native speakers 23, 40, 44, 62, 93, 104–5, 107, 114, 117, 126–7, 129, 148–56, 161–2, 166

Non-native speakers 100, 150, 154–6, 162, 258

NTRI 25–6, 32–3, 35, 39

O

Off-task 3, 42–3, 45, 54–6

Organization, sequential 3, 72, 79, 81, 83, 265

P

Participant frameworks 225

Participants 10, 21–4, 39, 40, 56–8, 74–6, 83–4, 104–5, 131–6, 165–6, 168–74, 177–8, 180–1, 238–42, 251–7, 263–7

Participation 11, 32, 77, 85, 101, 196, 219–20, 262–3, 271

Pauses 34, 37, 60, 65–6, 69, 80–1

Perceptions 4, 115, 117, 143, 152, 156, 164, 167–9, 172–4, 177, 181, 199, 238, 241, 246–7

Personality 116, 133–5, 141–2, 147

Perspectives 10, 12, 14, 21, 30, 117, 128, 137, 149–51, 157–8, 219, 222, 247, 249, 263

Practise 232–3

Pragmatic Development 165, 167, 169, 171, 173, 177, 179, 181

Pragmatics 163, 165–7, 170, 181

Pre-beginnings 59, 60

Preferences 133–5, 139, 142, 147, 240, 245–7, 266

Primary schools 4, 185, 187–8, 191, 200–1, 204, 222, 269

Problems 15–16, 21–3, 25–6, 33, 35, 40, 67–8, 74–5, 116–17, 151–2, 156, 158, 161–2, 166–7, 220

Process 2, 3, 11, 52, 70, 93, 126–7, 144, 149–52, 155, 192, 220, 238, 253, 257, 262–3

Production 58–9, 62, 64, 68, 150, 182, 219, 223, 255–6, 259, 261
Proficiency 67, 164–5, 167–8, 172, 175, 177, 202, 205–6, 229
Proximal development, zone of 64, 68–71
Punjabi 169, 185–6, 191–6, 202, 269

R

Relationship 1, 9, 10, 14, 20–1, 96, 108, 149, 167, 197, 200, 244, 247, 251–2, 258–61, 268
Repair 15–17, 22–7, 29–33, 35, 38–40, 43, 60, 74, 80, 82–3, 266–7
Repetitions 17, 40, 60–3, 189, 195, 227–9
Research 1, 22, 42, 56, 60, 76, 89, 90, 100–1, 129, 137–43, 151, 203–4, 215–17, 220–1, 237–9
Responses 9, 12, 23, 28, 30, 34–5, 37, 39, 40, 50, 157, 160–1, 211–13, 228, 242, 259
Revision 11, 30, 57, 264–5
Russian 104–5, 109–18, 169

S

SC 9, 10, 21
Scaffolding 2, 13–15, 17, 20, 67, 70, 158, 228, 233
Schegloff 10, 21–2, 24–5, 29, 32, 34, 40, 44, 58–62, 65–7, 74, 80, 267
Schools 26–7, 112–13, 145–6, 148, 161–3, 185–7, 189–92, 200–6, 208, 216, 218–19, 221–3, 226, 241, 268–9
Second language 1–5, 11, 42–3, 72, 75, 85–6, 100, 126–9, 144, 148–9, 155, 165, 168–9, 257–8, 264
  acquisition 3, 9, 75, 84, 89–92, 102, 165, 218, 263
  interactions 38, 72–4
  Learner 62
  speakers 57–9, 62–7, 69–72
Self-identities 251, 255, 258, 260, 263, 267–8, 271
Self-repairs 16, 60, 69, 266
Sequence 13–14, 19, 20, 23, 27–8, 32, 35–7, 58, 70, 79, 80, 83, 85, 143, 159, 194, 252
Setting 1, 3, 14, 128, 219, 222, 225, 238, 254–5
Silences 50, 59, 61, 63, 65, 67, 69

Situation 18–19, 63, 80, 127–8, 140, 158, 167, 171, 174, 178, 201, 203–5, 213, 254–5, 261–2
SLA 3, 9, 13, 42, 85, 89–91, 101, 165–6
Social
  context 76, 126, 128, 144, 166, 252, 262, 266–9
  interaction 1, 2, 4, 5, 57, 63, 73, 163, 168, 179–81, 204, 231, 236, 247–8, 251–2, 258, 261–2
Society 2, 9, 96, 138, 144, 160–1, 186–7, 197–8, 248, 262
Sociolinguistics 2, 9, 89, 90, 169
Speakers 2, 3, 15, 22–9, 31–3, 38–41, 57–65, 67–70, 72, 86, 93, 114–15, 154, 169–70, 254–7, 259
Students 80–5, 103–6, 112–14, 116–18, 127–9, 139–42, 152–62, 202–9, 211–16, 220–3, 225–6, 232–3, 236–8, 259–60, 264–5
Swann 187–8

T

Talk-in-interaction 11, 22, 43, 58, 72, 84–5, 251, 256, 258, 261, 265–6, 270–71
Tasks 2, 44, 56–7, 62, 66, 76, 84, 94, 103–4, 106, 118, 127–8, 229–30, 239, 242–5
TCU 29, 35, 40, 59–61, 65
Teacher Education 1, 148–9, 151, 153, 155, 157, 159, 161, 215, 235
Teachers 12–13, 15–20, 80–4, 113–14, 189–98, 202–17, 221–4, 226–8, 230–2, 235–6, 238–41, 244–9, 258–9, 264–7, 269–70
  bilingual 151, 186, 191, 193, 196–8, 268
Teaching 1, 2, 4, 5, 10–11, 44, 113, 144, 149–52, 155–62, 182, 187, 189–92, 197, 215, 251, 262
Theory 90, 145, 149, 152, 256, 258, 262, 264
Third-position repair 24–6, 28, 30, 32–3, 38–40
Topic 13, 24, 27–9, 32, 34, 36–8, 46–7, 55, 64, 68, 75, 80, 117–18, 157, 224
Troubles 22, 25, 45–7, 55–6, 66, 70, 266–7
Turn
  beginnings 59, 61–2, 67, 69
  construction 59, 70
Turn-taking 12, 58–9, 61, 63, 74, 265

U

United Kingdom 5, 95, 112, 131, 188, 192, 195, 238, 241
United States 2, 3, 44, 95, 104, 112, 130, 218, 221–2, 232, 234–5
University 4, 22, 26–7, 44, 72, 94, 96, 98–9, 112, 129, 133, 137–43, 145
Untutored Acquisition in Content Classrooms 218–19, 221, 223, 225, 227, 229, 231, 233
Urdu 185, 201, 203, 205, 207–8, 211, 215–16, 269

V

Vocabulary 63, 67, 73–4, 80–1, 115, 117, 158–9, 167, 178, 195, 222, 224–5, 228, 247, 268
Voice 2, 4, 5, 18, 53, 76, 126, 149, 159–61, 227
Vygotsky 64, 68, 70–1

Z

ZITs 42, 44, 54
ZPD 2, 10, 13–15, 17, 20–1